Beryl Cook

Life and Art

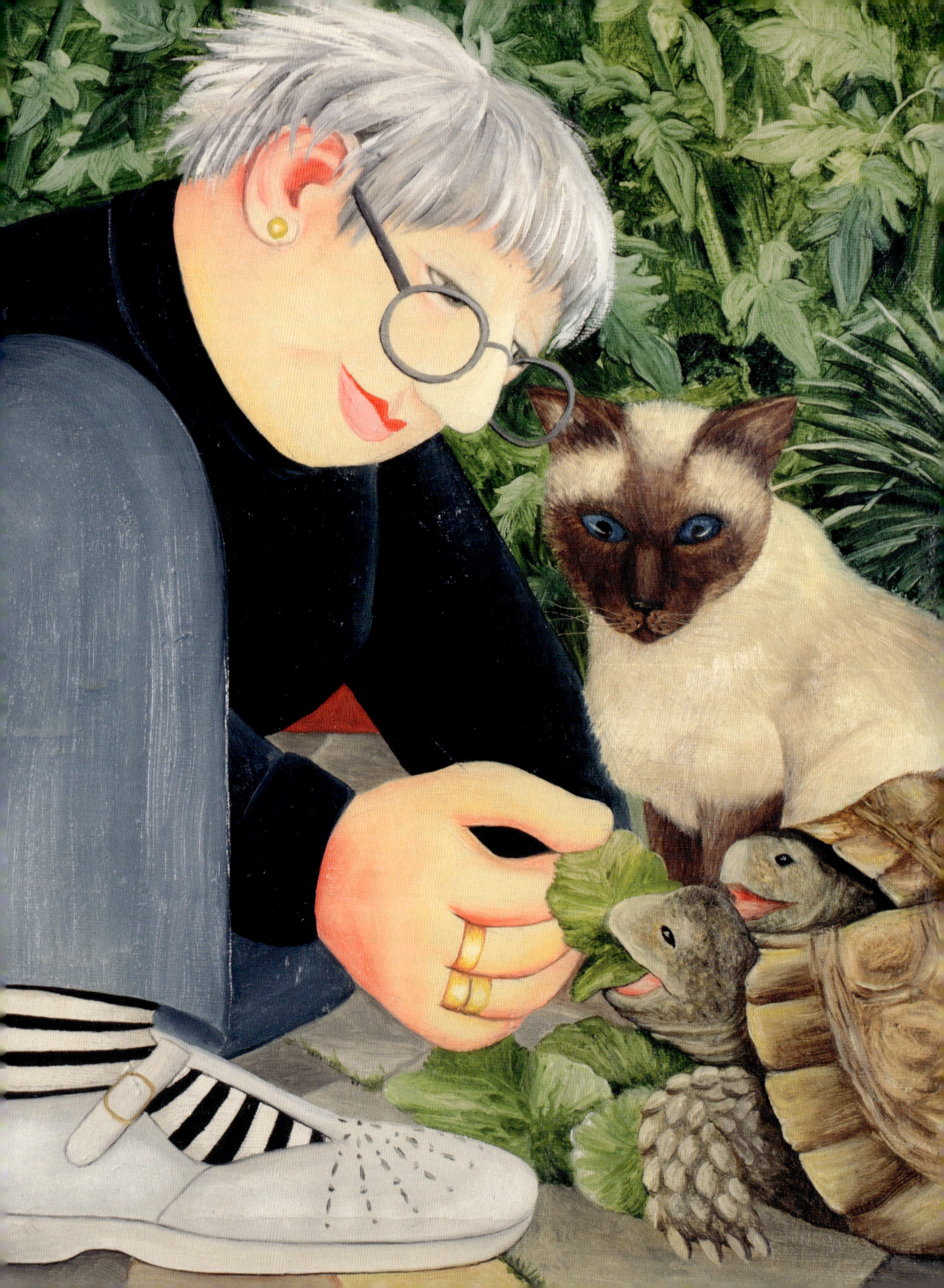

FRANCES
LINCOLN

Hilary
Bracegirdle

Beryl Cook

Life and Art

6
Introduction

8
Author's Note

10
Dramatis Personae

15
The First Forty Years

25
Cornwall & The Start of Art

37
Plymouth Inspires

53
The Seaside Landlady

65
Overnight Success & Lifelong Friendships

77
Managing Success

93
A Flash of Genius – Critical Reaction

99
Media Coverage

109
Life as a Painter

125
Painting Technique

145
Painting to Order

161
Influences & Emulations

177
Plymouth & the World

199
Bristol & Beyond

215
Re-evaluation

232
References

233
Picture Credits
About the Author

234
Acknowledgements

236
Index

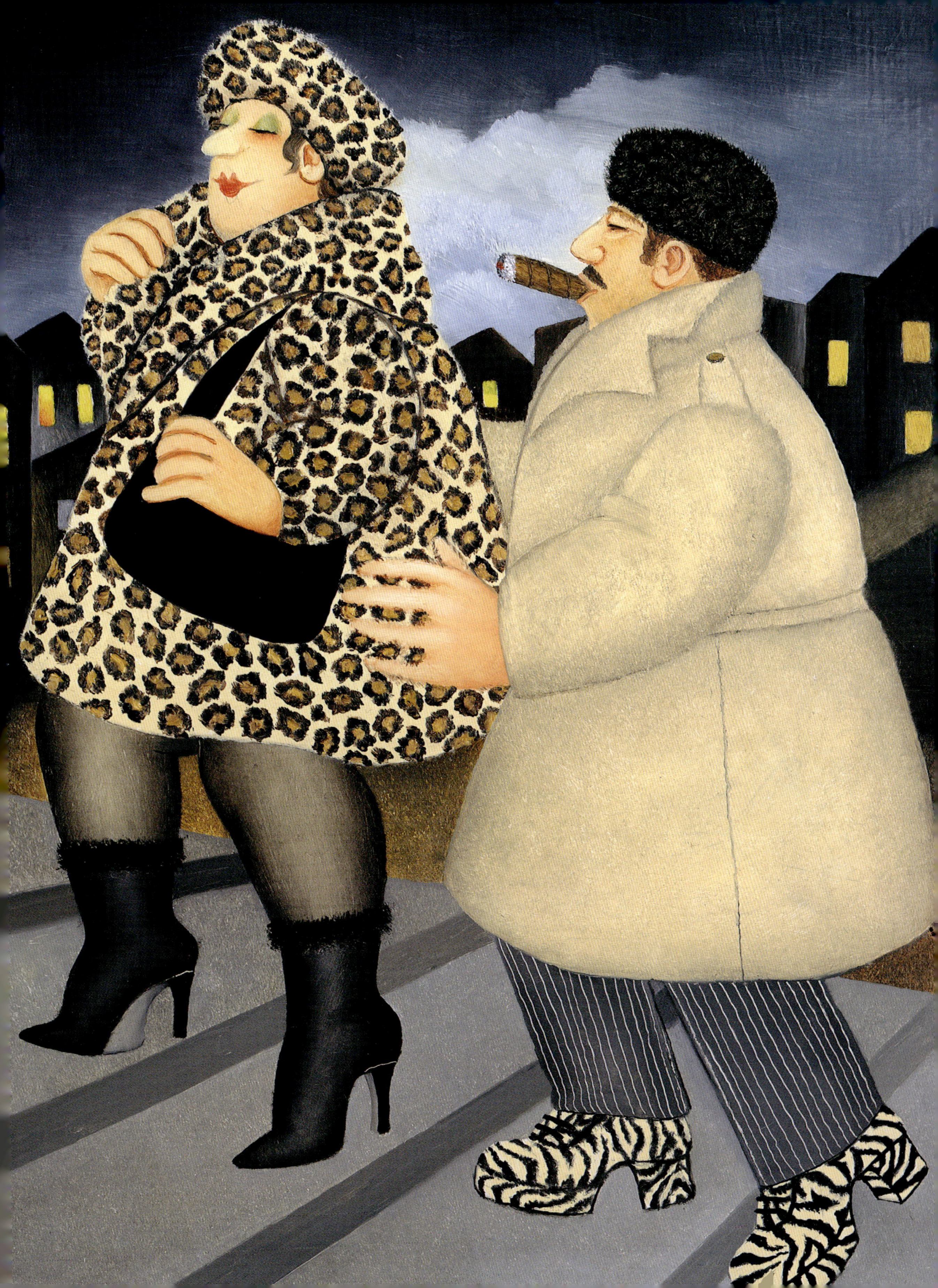

Introduction

Beryl Cook was very careful to maintain a low profile despite her fame and wit. She was a naturally shy person who genuinely believed that she had nothing to say that would interest anyone. She only allowed herself to be interviewed out of a sense of duty to agents, publishers and friends, and was parsimonious with facts and opinions. I faced a huge challenge as her biographer.

However, her family provided me with unfettered access to their huge archive of correspondence, press cuttings, tapes of television interviews, radio transcripts and fan letters. The family and others who knew the real Beryl fleshed out who she really was and what mattered to her. A fuller picture of this extraordinary, shy, modest genius emerged.

I learned how much joy her paintings bring to so many people across the world. I learned more of the people who she painted and the places where she painted them. I travelled into her inner circle of friends, family and pets. Beryl always stated that she had no message, but I found proof she was wrong.

I hope you enjoy finding out things about Beryl that have never been published before and I just hope you are not too easily shocked. Oh, and as a warning, there may be a few bits of art history. After all, it's time her work was reassessed.

Sometimes I wish I was bad, or on drugs. Or that I'd had five husbands and hundreds of lovers. But the truth is that I live an absolutely mundane existence. And all I can offer you is this: a happy marriage, some paintings and a house in Plymouth.

Beryl Cook, quoted in Robert Chalmers, 'Laughing all the way to the canvas', *The Daily Telegraph*, 4 May 1992

My God, Mum, I'm going to have to tell them something after you've gone.

John, Beryl's son, quoted in Judith Bumpus, 'Artist at work: Beryl Cook', *Art and Artists*, September 1982

PAGE 2
Feeding the Tortoises
(c 1983). Beryl has portrayed herself in the clothes and jewellery she typically wore, although she was actually more slender. Tortoises Ted and Tina are watched by Lottie the cat.

PAGE 5
Camel Hair Coat
(2007). A very late work where Beryl has returned to themes that she particularly enjoyed painting – fur and fake fur textures, cigars and footwear

Author's Note

In the course of writing this book, I have drawn on interviews with Beryl's family and friends. I have read published books and essays, thousands of press cuttings and letters, and business papers. As a result, I have uncovered all sorts of previously unknown facts, sometimes surprising even Beryl's family. If I say Beryl did something, or had a particular opinion, I have a primary source to prove it.

However, opinions and even 'facts' vary, especially over a long career. Beryl tended to repeat the same stories in interviews, but towards the end of her life she did reveal a little more. For example, there are several versions of the 'first ever painting' story – I have used a later version that I found to be the most convincing, and provided a quotation to substantiate that choice.

Establishing facts about the paintings and craftworks is equally problematic. Beryl generally painted six days a week, breaking off only for working holidays or business trips to Bristol and London. She produced many gifts for family and close friends that have never passed through a gallery and are thus unrecorded. There is no complete list.

Even the titles of her works changed over time. I decided to use the versions written on the backs of the paintings, where applicable, or as named in Beryl's publications. There are some loan lists and gallery lists in the archive. Otherwise, the family and I have used a description, but we haven't tried to be as witty as Beryl.

Dates of works have been particularly troublesome. Some paintings are mentioned in Beryl's correspondence as having just been finished, so I can give an exact date. If the date can be narrowed down by subject matter, research visit, first appearance in a publication or an exhibition, I have put, for instance, c 1988 or a date range. The wider the date range the more uncertain I am. However, the family and I have used our knowledge of her style, the passing whimsies of blue eyeshadow and platform shoes, or other informed guesswork to be as accurate as possible.

Unless otherwise mentioned, the paintings are in private ownership or their location is now unknown. Names from any private papers, auction records and sales lists from the Portal Gallery are confidential, but in a few instances (before people had to be careful about such things) names were published in newspapers. We know that Yoko Ono, Jackie Collins, Whoopi Goldberg and Chris de Burgh all bought paintings.

All Beryl's paintings and craftworks, wherever they are, are still in copyright. Please contact the Beryl Cook estate via the family website (ourberylcook.com) if you want to reproduce them. Please also get in touch if you know about an undiscovered Beryl Cook painting out there in the wild. One day we may be able to compile a catalogue raisoneé, just as an artist of Beryl Cook's stature deserves.

A final warning. Immersion in Beryl Cook's art can make you see Beryl subjects everywhere. In my case, total immersion has made me into a Beryl Cook subject.

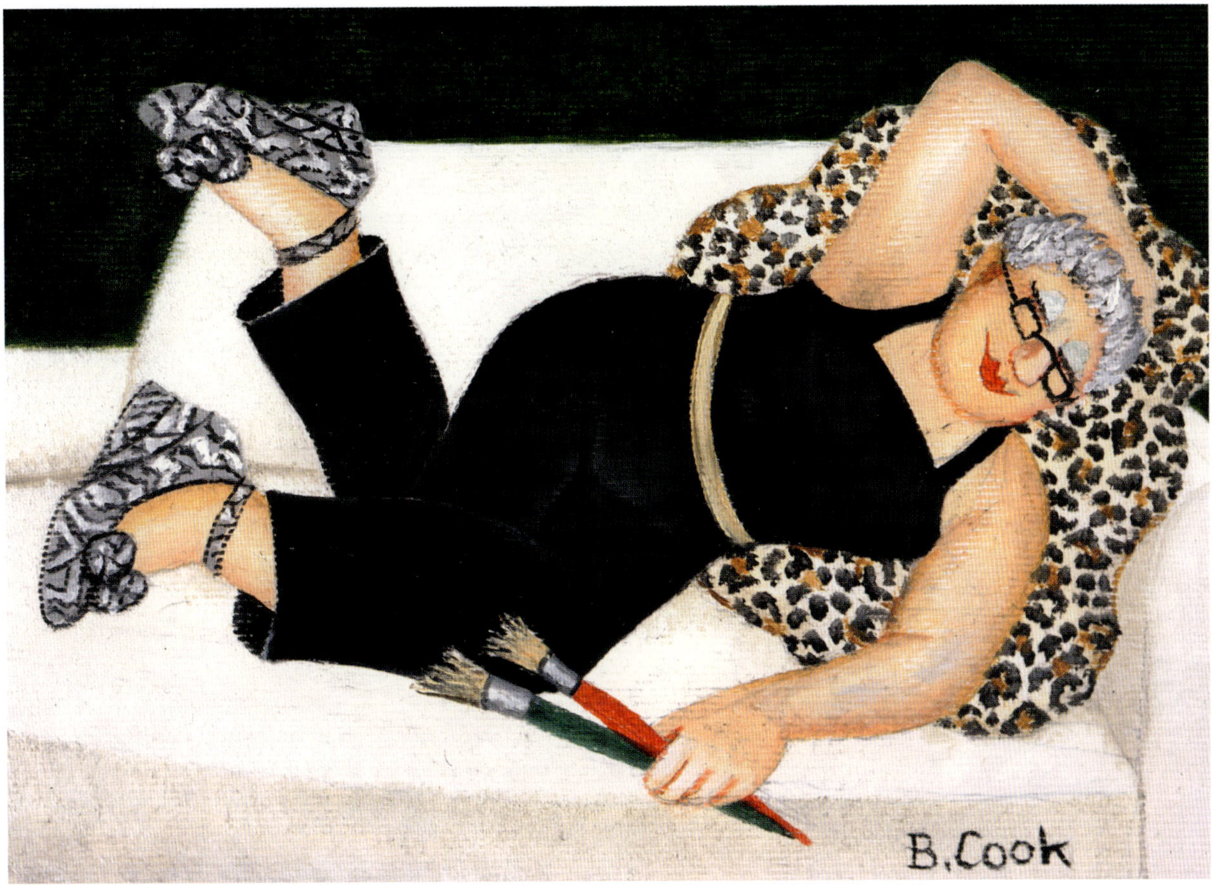

At Ease

(c 1998). A fantasy self-portrait of Beryl painted for Jess Wilder of the Portal Gallery. She is wearing shoes she bought second-hand, which in fact didn't fit her.

Dramatis Personae

Family

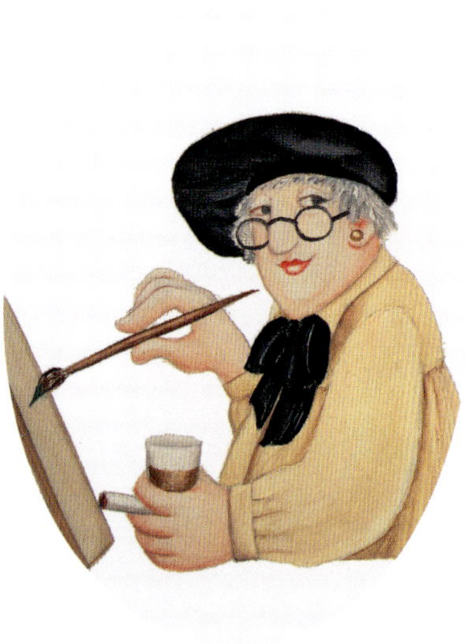

Beryl, *Painter*

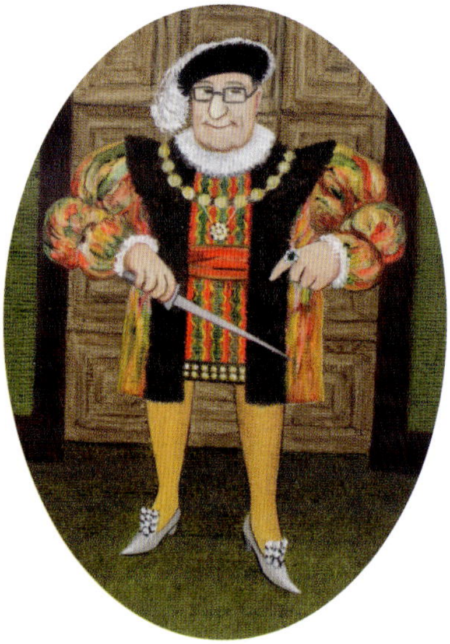

John Senior, *Husband and soulmate, m. 1948*

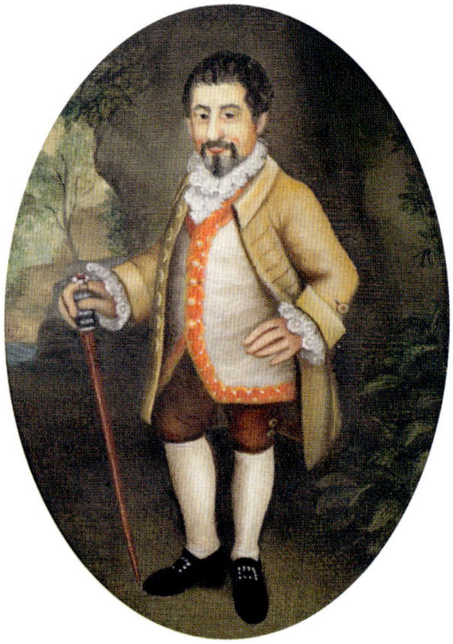

John Junior, *Son, b. 1950*

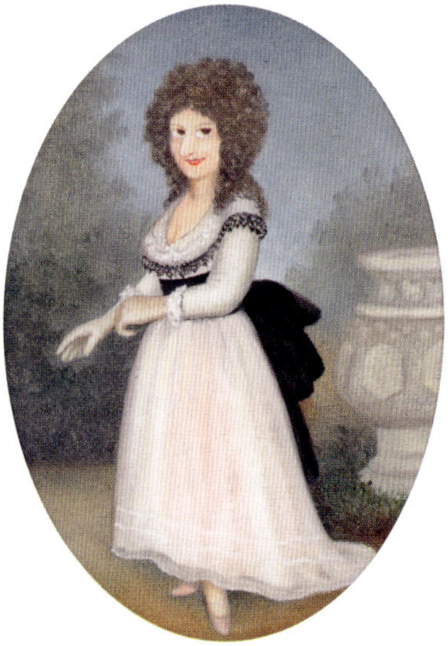

Teresa, *Daughter-in-law*

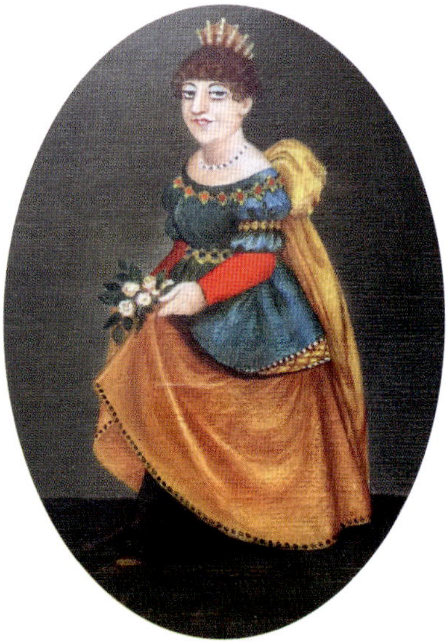

Alexa, *Granddaughter*

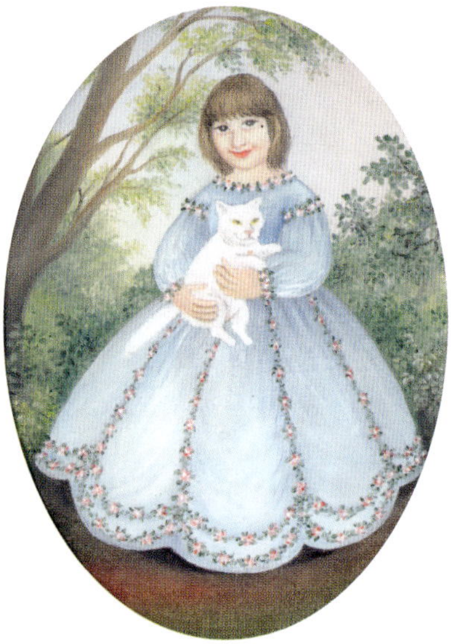

Sophie, *Granddaughter*

Cats

Lottie
Cedric
Percy
Ruby
Felix
Smokey
Ginger

Dogs

Bonzo
Lizzie
Lottie

Tortoises

Hercule and Desiree
(aka Ted and Tina)

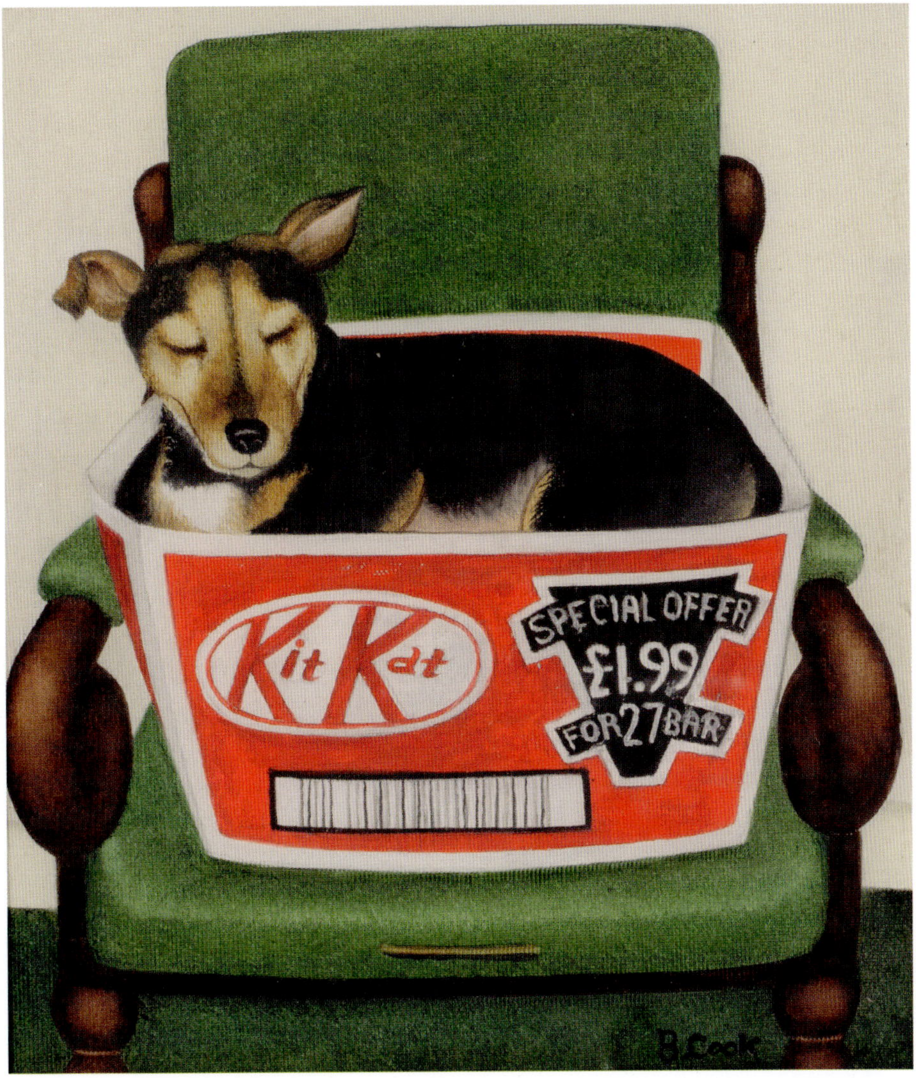

Lizzie

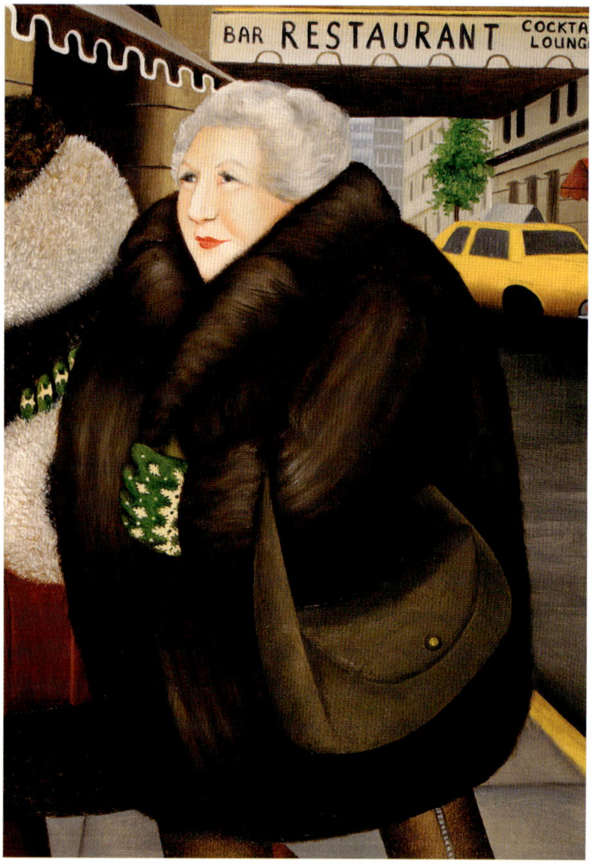

Barbara Key-Seymer

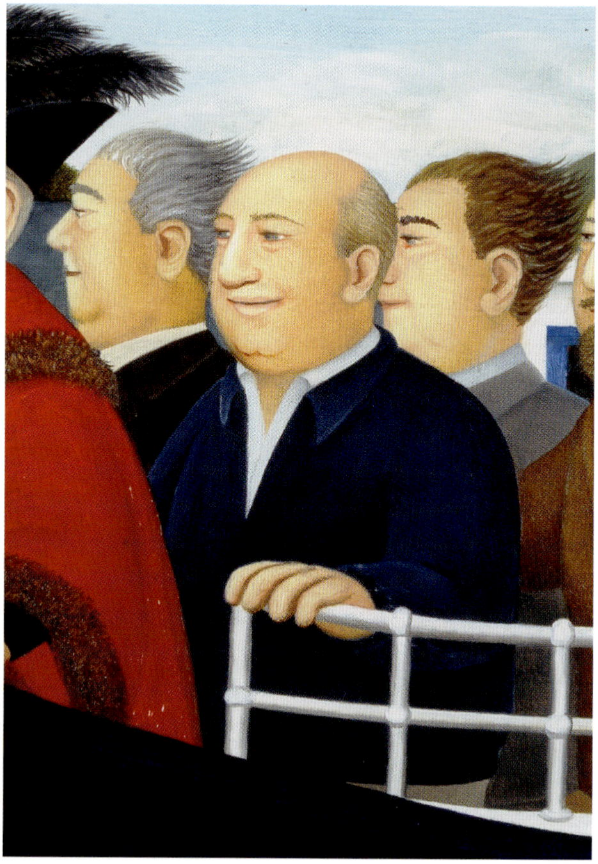

Bernard Samuels

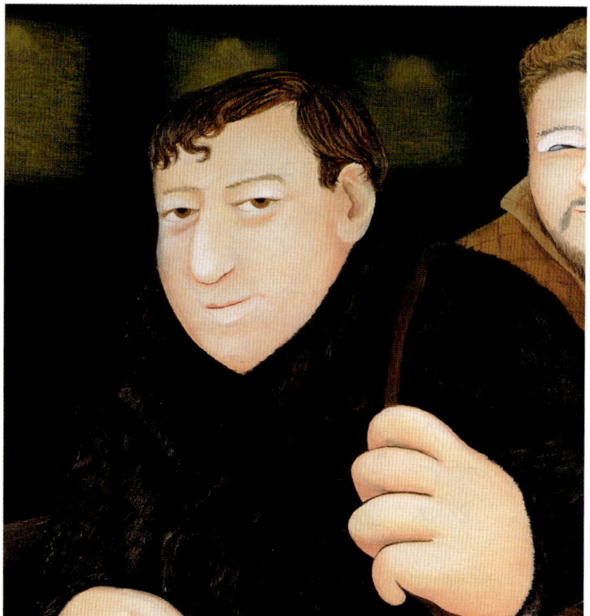

Edward (Ted) Lucie-Smith

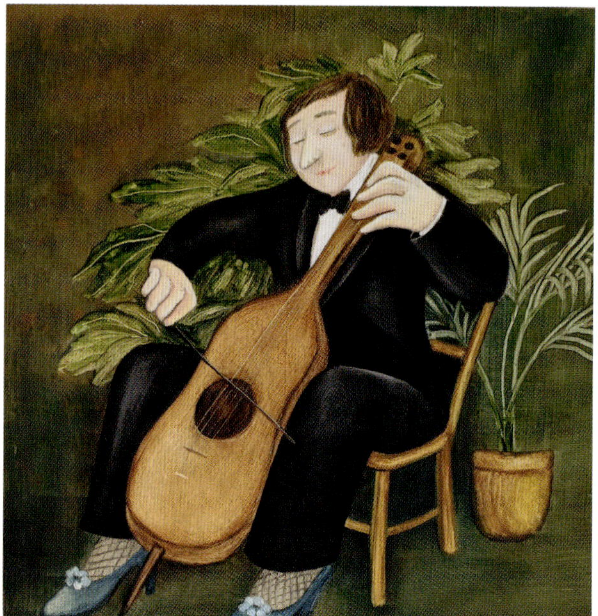

Tony Martin

Friends

Dan Farson (1927–1997),
photographer, journalist, writer and broadcaster

John George,
editor of Art and Artists

Barbara Ker-Seymer (1905–1993),
photographer and Bright Young Thing in 1930s Soho, and her partner Barbara (Bar) Roett (1927–2016), sculptor

Edward (Ted) Lucie-Smith (b. 1933),
writer, poet, art critic, curator and broadcaster, and his dog Bertie

Tony Martin,
antique dealer

Brian Pearce/Ruby Venezuela,
drag artist

Bernard Samuel,
director of Plymouth Arts Centre, and his cat Miro

Faith Stewart-Gordon (1932–2020),
owner of The Russian Tea Room in New York

Joanna Tope (1944–2024),
actress (Emmerdale Farm, The Omega Factor, The Tomorrow People, Z Cars) and guest at the Cook's B&B

Business partners

Eric Lister (1926–1988), Lionel Levy (1927–2016) and Jess Wilder,
the Portal Gallery

Jan Pienkowski (1936–2022),
author, illustrator and designer,
and his civil partner David Walser,
Gallery Five greetings card company

Jock Murray (1909–1993) and Joe Whitlock Blundell,
John Murray publishers

Jim Fardon and John Cleverdon,
Alexander Gallery, publisher of lithograph prints in Bristol

Norman and Barbara Henry,
Flanagan Graphics, publisher of silkscreen prints in the USA

Pat White,
Rogers, Coleridge and White Literary Agents

Walk-on parts

Allen Saddler (1923–2012),
journalist and backstabber

Julian Spalding (b. 1947),
museum director (Gallery of Modern Art Glasgow) and champion of Beryl

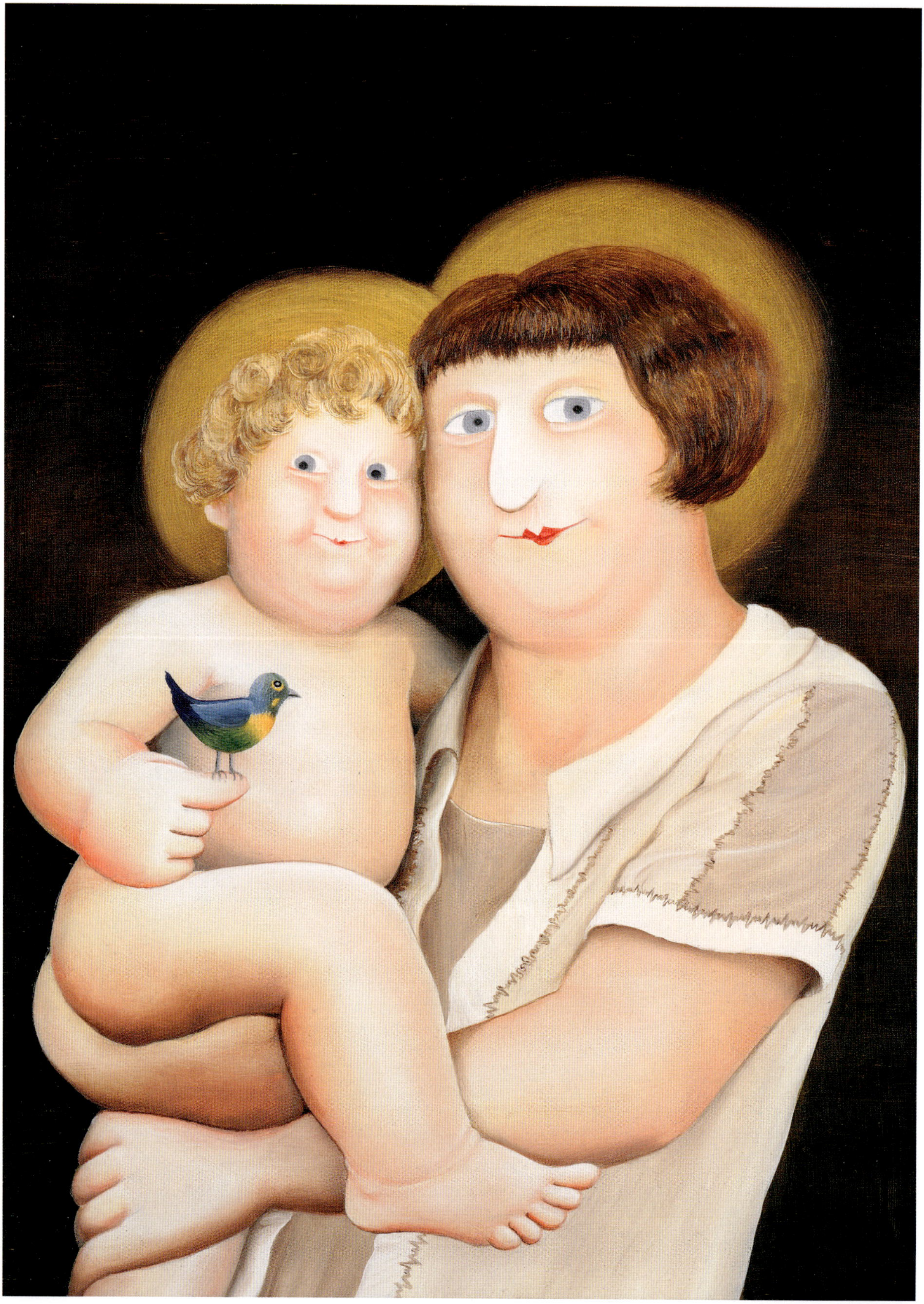

01

The First Forty Years

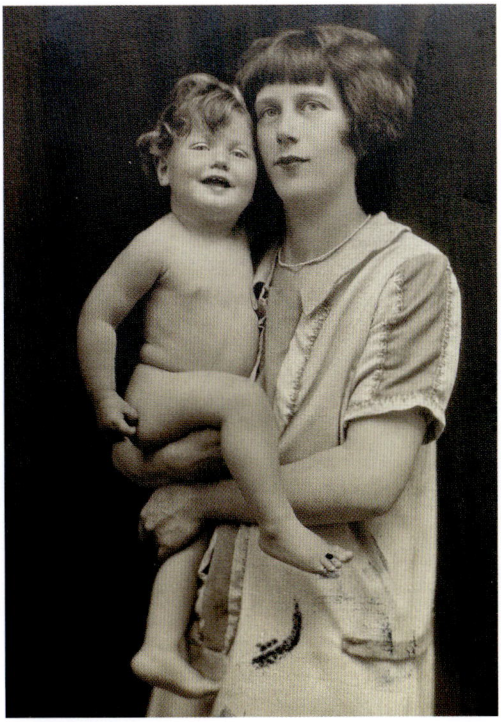

LEFT

Virgin & Child

(c 1980). Beryl was asked to paint a nativity scene by a friend. She based it on the photograph above: her mother, Ella, is firmly clasping Beryl as an enormous baby to her hip (c 1928). Beryl added golden curls, a 'roguish smile' and a little bird. She may have been inspired to do so by a Renaissance painting in the Villa Borghese in Rome.[1]

Beryl Cook was forty before she began to paint seriously, with no prior indications that she would develop into a world-famous artist. This is not an excuse to skip her early life, because she drew on her childhood and later time in Southern Africa as subjects for her paintings, aided by an exceptional visual memory and her characteristic sense of humour.

Beryl Francis Lansley was born in Egham, Surrey, on 10 September 1926, Francis being her mother Ella's maiden name. Her father was Adrian Stephen Barton Lansley from Bournemouth. The couple married in 1920 and settled near Ella's parents. This was the time of the post-First World War recession, and despite having served as an engineer in the Royal Air Force and at an engineering company in Bournemouth, he was unable to find work.[2] The couple separated when Beryl was four. By this time, Beryl had three sisters.

Nevertheless, Beryl's paternal grandfather Stephen Lansley played a large part in her life, providing financial support and a house. Ella and her daughters moved to 108 Wokingham Road, Reading, close to her parents William and Mary Pope, who lived in a village nearby. Beryl recalled, 'My mother brought up four girls on her own; I was the second youngest. We all loathed each other. Each of us wished that we were the only one.' *Sisters Fighting* recalls such an occasion, with Beryl, Cynthia, Freda and Mary fighting for a ball and pulling each other's hair in their garden, while their mother rests serenely in a hammock. As was his habit, the boy next door is probably throwing stones at them with surprising accuracy. Beryl was later to marry him.

Beryl's son John remembers his grandmother Ella very clearly: 'she had a remarkable detachment in life, and nothing seemed to fluster or worry her. Sadly, she died in the sixties and never saw her daughter's artwork.'[3]

A photograph of Beryl and her sisters shows them with Eton crops, which are rather more severe than in the paintings. She remembered, 'I had this hairstyle as a child. In those days this was regarded as rather eccentric of my mother at the school I went to. My grandfather had purchased grey flannel trousers and a walking stick for each of us to go walking with him (four girls) also regarded as rather strange I should think in those days.'[4] Happily, at Kendrick School, Reading, she was able to wear school uniform, as she showed in *Self-portrait in Science Lesson at Kendrick School* which she donated to the school in 2002 in celebration of their 125th anniversary.

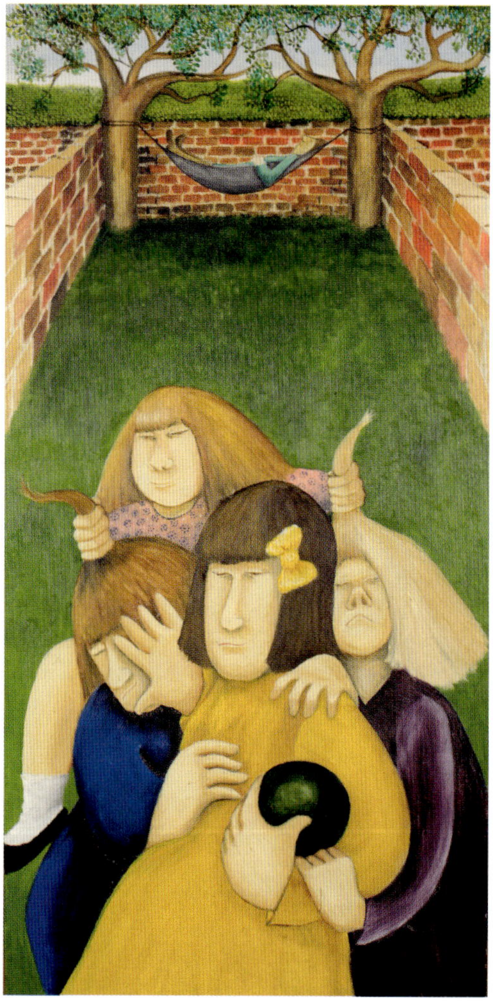

Sisters Fighting
(1973–5). This painting shows the sisters in the back garden of their house in Reading. Their mother is relaxing in a hammock at the bottom ignoring fracas.

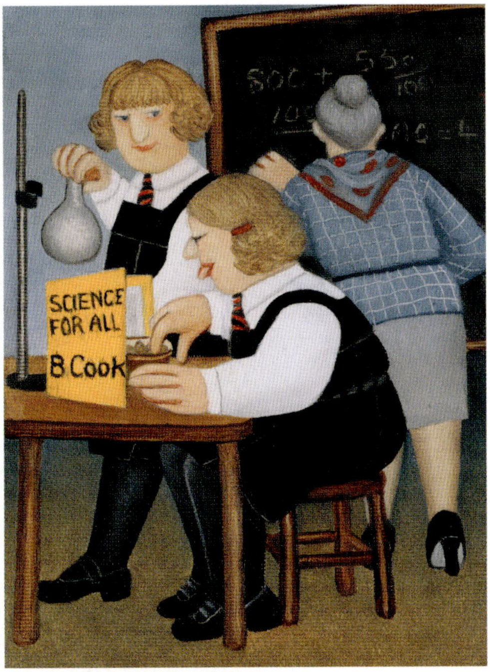

Self-portrait in Science Lesson
at Kendrick School
(c 2002)

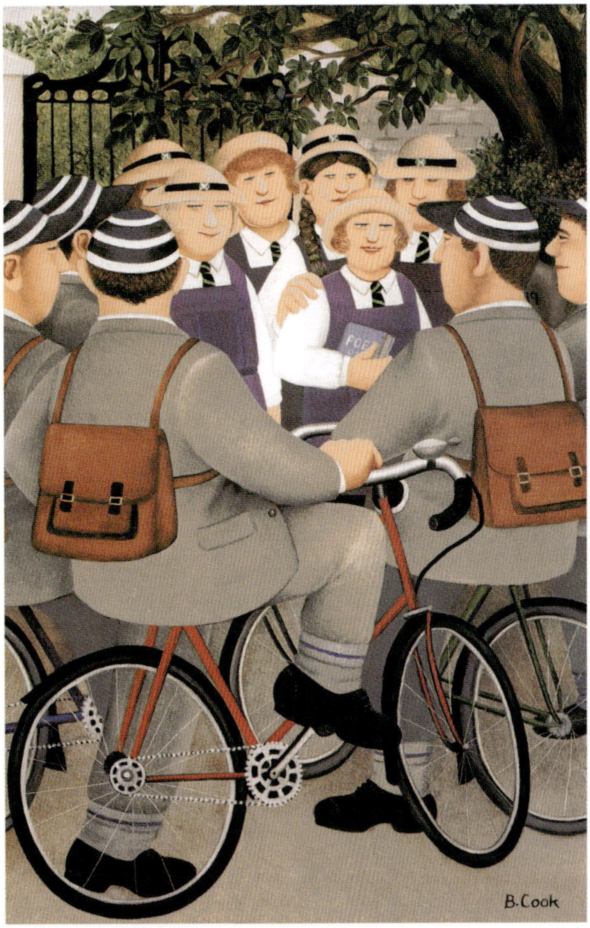

Don't be a lout, Andrew
(c 1998). An illustration commisioned by the Folio Society for *The Prime of Miss Jean Brodie*

She explained that it was an episode from her school days 'when I could go from a cookery to a science lesson, and sit there quietly eating the product of the earlier class under cover of a book. The others were busy with Bunsen burners and such like.'[5]

Beryl also sent a copy of *The Prime of Miss Jean Brodie* which she had illustrated for the Folio Society, because she had based the schoolboys' uniforms on Reading School uniform, which John-next-door attended.

Beryl left school at the age of 14 in 1941, to take a shorthand and typing course. In 1944 she moved with her family to Marylebone, London, where she joined her sister Freda as a showgirl in a touring production of The Gypsy Princess, and later modelled. Much was made of her being a showgirl and modelling when she became famous, but Beryl admitted later in life that 'Well the showgirl was really just because it was wartime and they couldn't find anyone else. My sister was a dancer so they hired me just to saunter about trying to look glamorous. And the modelling was only done for small firms showing to buyers.'[6]

In 1947 Ella bought a property on the River Thames at Hampton for the whole family and converted part of it into a tearoom. The following year, Beryl married John Cook, the boy-next-door of her childhood, now a Merchant Seaman.

Their son John Cook Junior was born in 1950 and has describes his early life vividly:

> My father was still at sea and we were living at Hampton, though I have no clear recollection of it. What I do recall is when my mother worked for a while as a cook and we both lived in at an hotel where she worked as a chef. Then father left the sea and my parents took over running a village pub in Stoke by Nayland, Suffolk. It was a delightful ancient building with a thatched roof and a courtyard of outbuildings out the back, enclosed by an old orchard on one side and fields on the other.
>
> We housed chickens, bantams and geese in the outbuildings, even raising some pigs. But Mother, who was always keen on animals, became very fond of them, and could not bring herself to let them go to slaughter. Soon we had a pair of very large pigs eating what little profits that the pub made. Eventually my father sent her out on a long errand one day, and had the pigs taken away in her absence. Beautiful and 'olde worlde' though the pub was, it was neither profitable nor modernized. Along with few or no customers there was no bathroom and we had to make do with a tin bath in the kitchen.

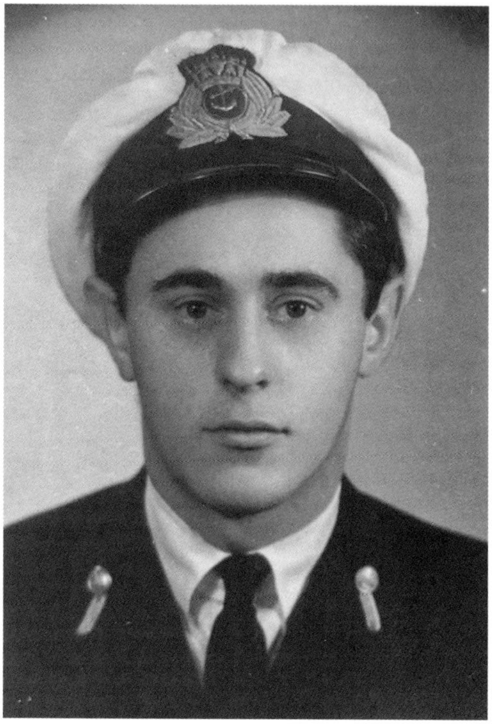

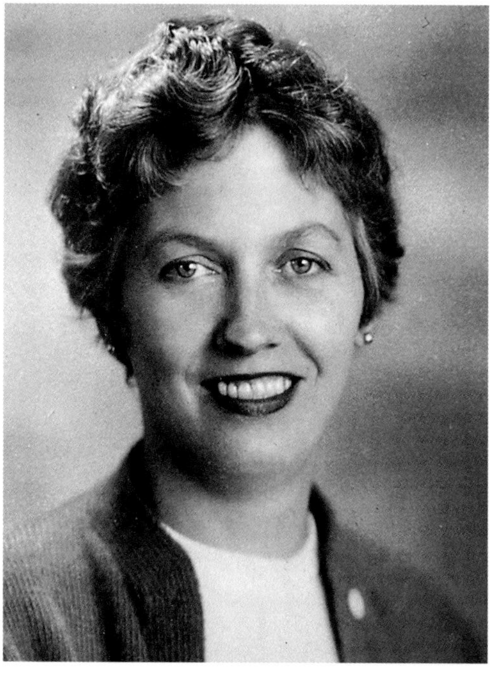

Family photographs of John (1952) and Beryl (1960). Unfortunately, no wedding pictures have survived. Beryl recalled that they fell into the river together from a punt at the start of their honeymoon.[7]

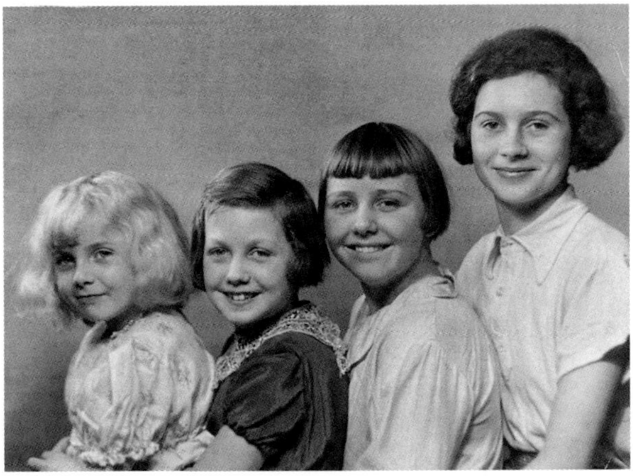

Photograph of Beryl and her sisters. From left to right, Freda, Beryl, Mary and Cynthia (c 1932)

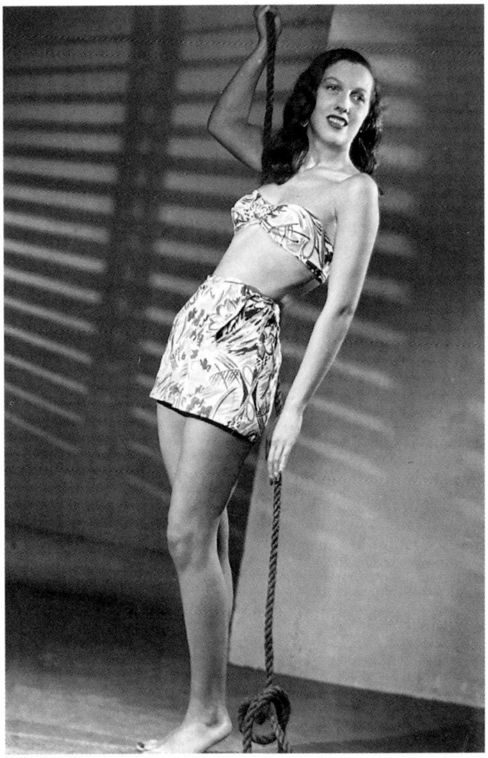

A studio shot of Beryl (c 1945)

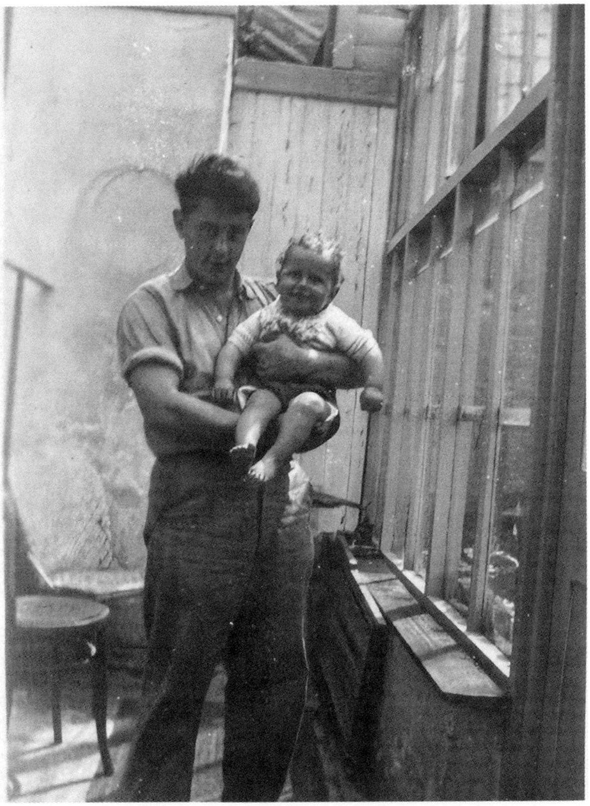

John Senior with John Cook Junior (c 1952)

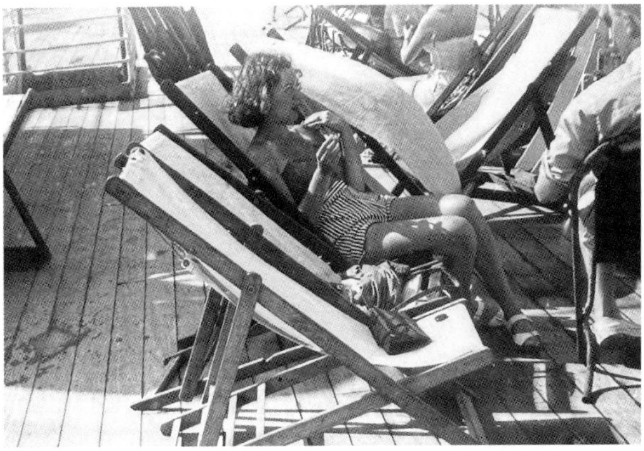

Photograph of Beryl en route to Africa (c 1957)

After a couple of years my parents had had enough, then they received a letter from my mother's sister Mary and her husband who were living in Africa. My aunt and uncle were then living in Salisbury, now known as Harare, in Southern Rhodesia, now known as Zimbabwe. They were enjoying a good life out there and encouraged my parents to join them, saying that there was plenty of opportunity to get on.

In 1956 we joined my aunt and uncle out in Africa. Just travelling there was an adventure in itself. Our house was a single storey building with a corrugated iron roof, which became very hot in the African sun. The front and side were covered in bougainvillea vine, and for the rest of her life this vine remained a favourite with Mother. For many years she kept some growing in her conservatory in England.

As a young boy I had an adventurous and exciting life while we lived in Africa, spending a lot of time hunting and trekking in the bush. For our holidays we sometimes took a fantastic long drive to camp on the beach at Beira in what was then called Portuguese East Africa [now Mozambique]. At other times we visited game reserves and the mountain resort Inyanga [Nyanga], which is in the high grounds near Umtali [Mutare]. This was a place of cold streams and great beauty.

For my parents, it was not such a carefree existence; my father found work as a car salesman while Mother worked as a bookkeeper for a local coach-building business. Mother was never a great enthusiast for rugged outdoor activities, and she found it difficult to adjust to the almost constant company of insects, frogs, lizards and often snakes. Unfortunately at one point she became very ill after catching tick fever.

One event that occurred around 1960 that stays in mind, is the first time I ever saw her with an artist's paint brush in her hand. I was indolent and bored one day and in her efforts to occupy and motivate me, she produced a child's painting set and suggested that we copy a little Indian painting that she'd found. This painting illustrated a young woman with her somewhat pendulous bare breasts hanging over what appeared to be a wall. To this day I can recall telling her of what a good painting I would do, while I doubted her own ability to paint. I shall not forget the crestfallen moment I experienced as we both contemplated the results of our efforts . . . Mine a barely recognizable image, and hers a remarkably good copy of the original painting. We know now that this little picture helped give Mother an impetus and the confidence to take up painting again later on. Echoes of its style can be seen in some of her early works.[8]

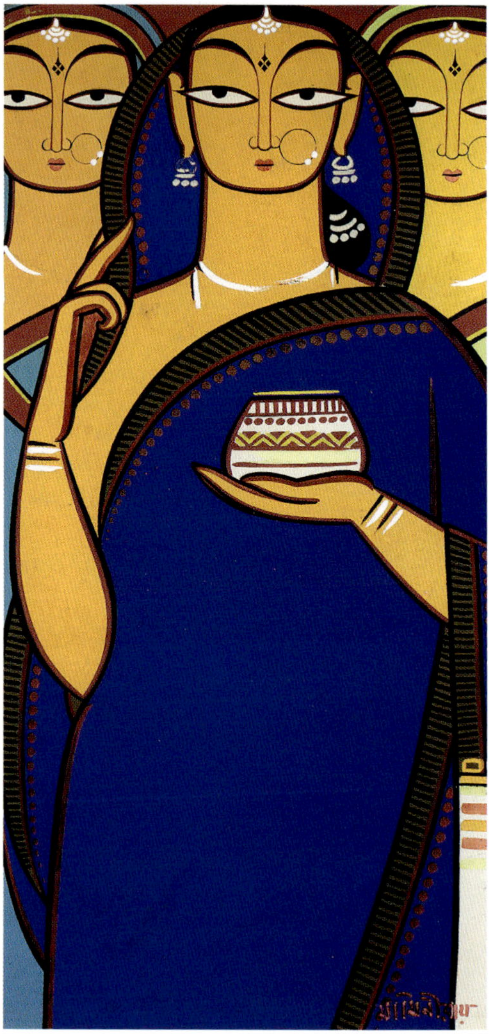

Bride and Two Companions, Jamini Roy, 1936

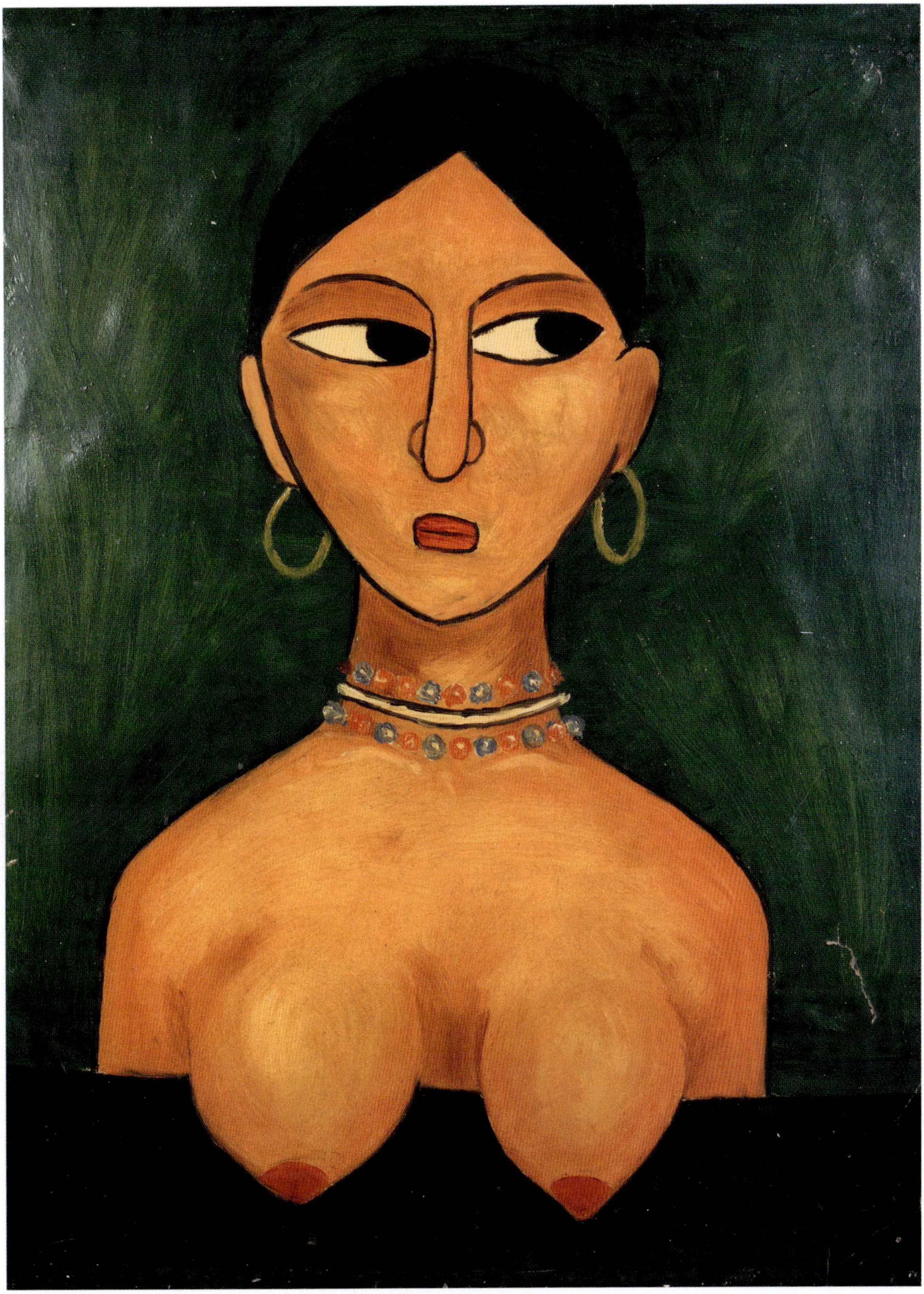

Hangover
(c 1960). Beryl's first painting, named
Hangover by her husband

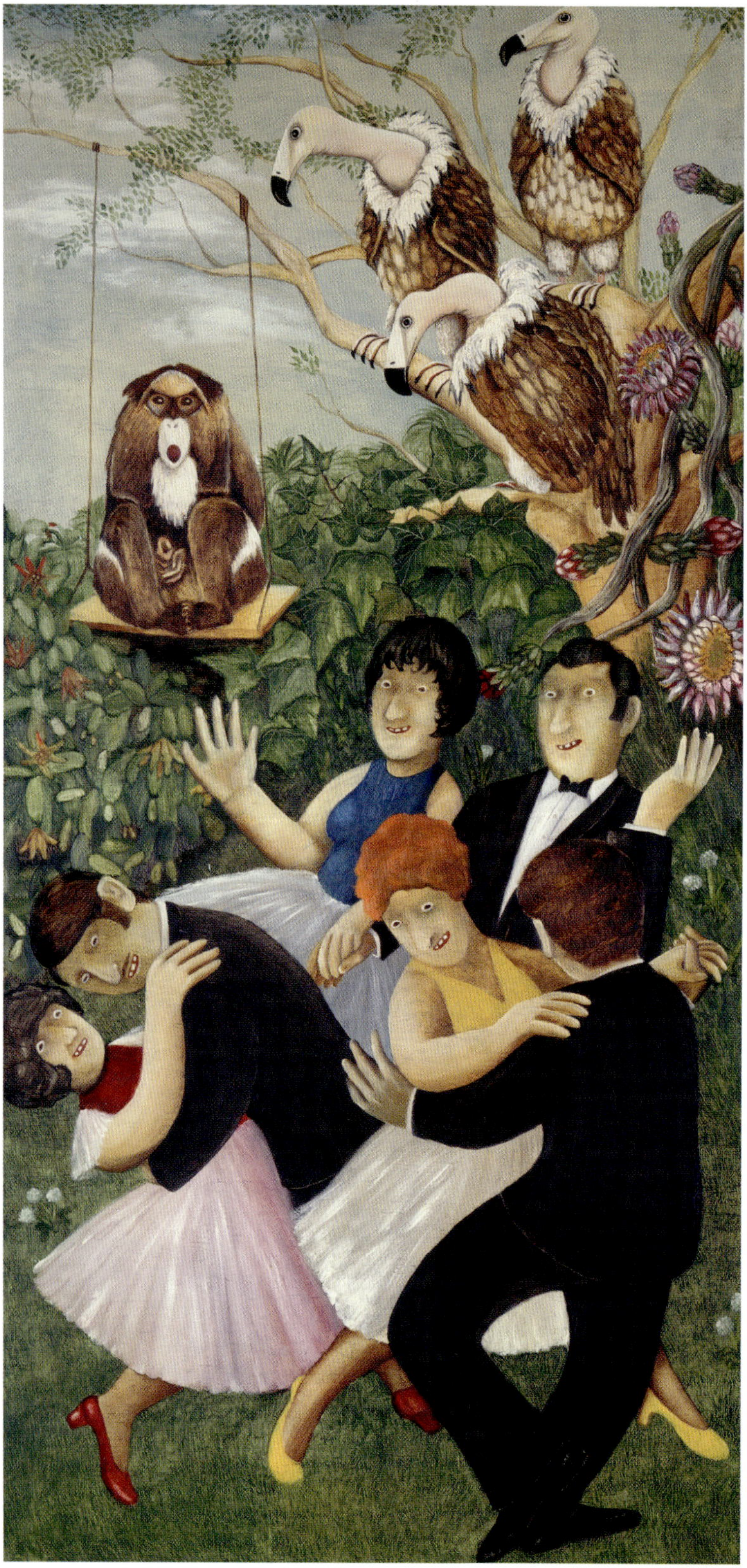

Vultures

(1972). Painting of the white minority in Rhodesia dancing, unaware of the vultures perched above their heads

I have wondered if the print of the Indian painting was of one by Jamini Roy (1887–1972), like the one shown on page 20, or another of the Bengali School. Southern Africa at the time was made up of a mixture of races and ethnic groups, including Indians, and Roy was internationally famous. Beryl did say in a newspaper interview that 'I had a little print of some Indian ladies and I thought: I'll try and paint one of those and just touch up the bust'.[9]

Beryl grew increasingly unhappy in Southern Rhodesia, which was already part of a federation of countries moving towards independence. British expatriates formed a small tight-knit community, typically taking full advantage of the cheap, strong alcohol at a never-ending series of parties. As Peter Farrell-Vinhay recalled:

> For well-off whites who asked no questions, thought as little as possible, ignored the social and economic gaps between them and blacks, and supported the status quo it was a wonderful life, full of barbecues and marital infidelity (you never asked a child what their father did since they tended to burst into tears and run, or ignore you).
>
> For anyone else there was a sense of growing unease and a feeling of being trapped.[10]

Beryl's son John recalls a particular incident. The manager of the coach-building company for whom she worked was unexpectedly absent. She found out that he had been in court, charged with shooting a Black man whom he had caught stealing from his orchard. He was back at work the next day, having paid a very nominal fine.

Eventually, the oppressive sense of colonial entitlement, the heat and the insects took their toll, and when Beryl and John Junior travelled to England for a holiday in 1964, she did not want to return to Africa. John Senior put their affairs in order and six months later joined them in England.

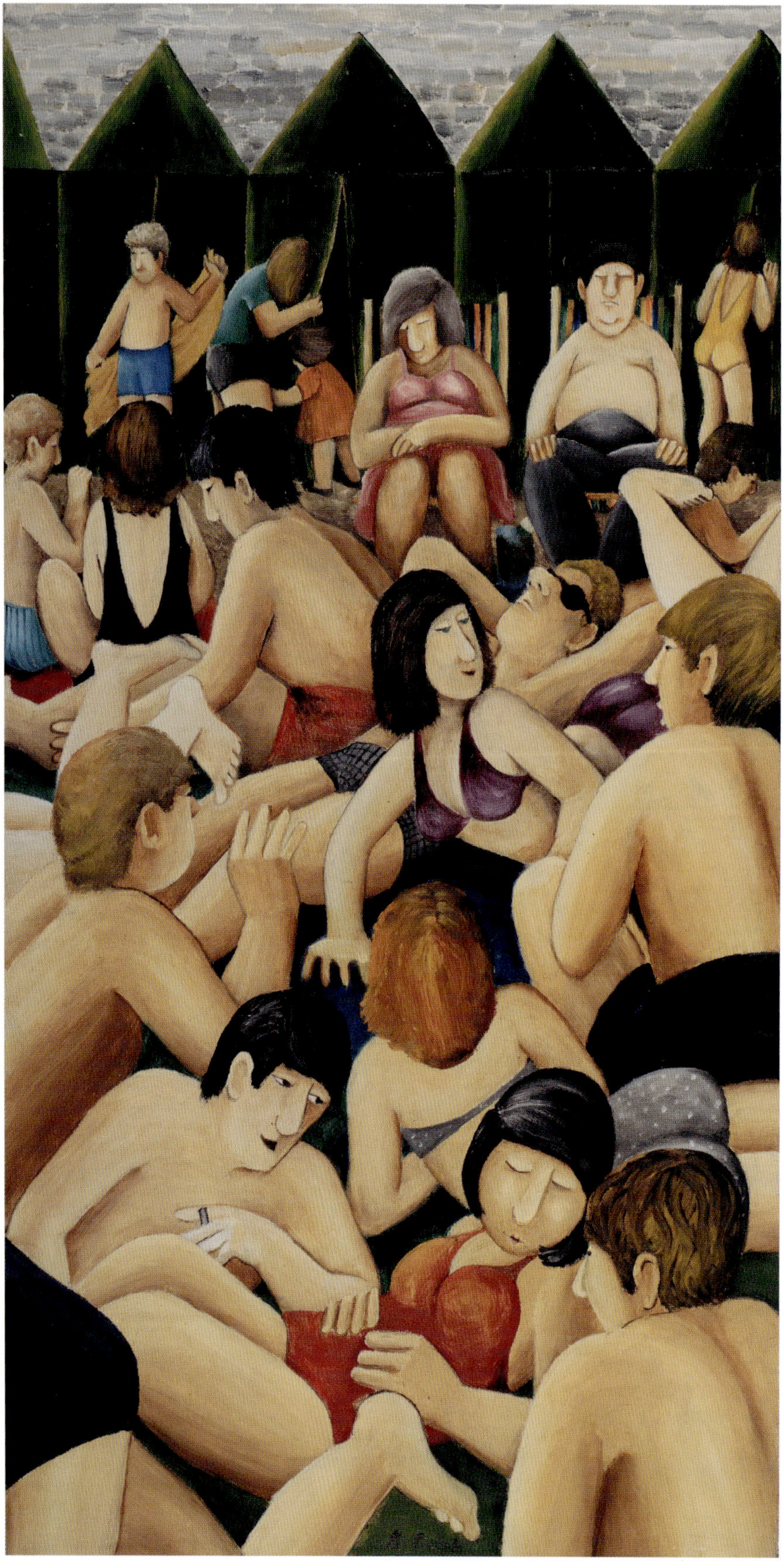

02

1965–1968: Cornwall & The Start of Art

LEFT
Beach at Looe
(c 1969). This painting was purchased by Plymouth City Art Gallery (now The Box) in 1975.

Beryl had always dreamed of living in a seaside cottage, and in 1965 the family settled in Looe in Cornwall. Looe epitomizes the traditional Cornish fishing village. It has crooked streets, several beaches, cliffs, rock pools, a river and a harbour with bobbing boats a-plenty. It even has its own island (privately owned at the time). Its history is astounding – smugglers, secret passageways, pirates, an exploding whale, a scold's cage and ducking stool, and a Guildhall incorporating timbers from a Spanish galleon. Most remarkable perhaps, it is said that Joseph of Arimathea and the boy Jesus spent time on Looe Island.

The 1963 *Looe Official Guide* does a wonderful job of describing the quaintness and charm of Looe, but does not neglect its attraction as a place to live:

> Over the years Looe has grown as a residential district and within the last decade has become extremely popular. Owing to the equable climate and the fact that snow, frost and fog are virtually unknown to Looe, the health-giving properties of its balmy air are being widely appreciated. Thus, the little fishing village of some fifty years ago has developed into a charming residential area, without in any way losing its old-world characteristics.[1]

The combination of a working fishing village with temperate weather and a high sunshine record would have particularly appealed to Beryl. John was able to stay in the motor trade and eventually took over the management of a garage and car sales site in Bodmin, about 20 miles inland.

The family lived in an old fisherman's cottage, tucked moments away from the quayside. It was built with thick walls and small windows, and is at right angles to the harbour, so that it is protected from the gales and storms which the *Official Guide* fails to mention. Still painted white inside as it was when the Cooks lived there, there is a kitchen and sitting room downstairs and two bedrooms and a bathroom upstairs.

Beryl recalled, 'the walls of our house were empty, so I thought I'd paint the odd Stanley Spencer – just like that. Ridiculous, I know, but I love Stanley Spencer. Of course, it soon dawned on me that I had neither Stanley Spencer's skill nor his spirituality, so I developed my own style.'

Beryl knew Stanley Spencer's work well, as he lived in the village of Cookham a few miles away from her childhood home. Spencer (1891–1959) is known for populating his religious paintings with scenes and people from his own village.

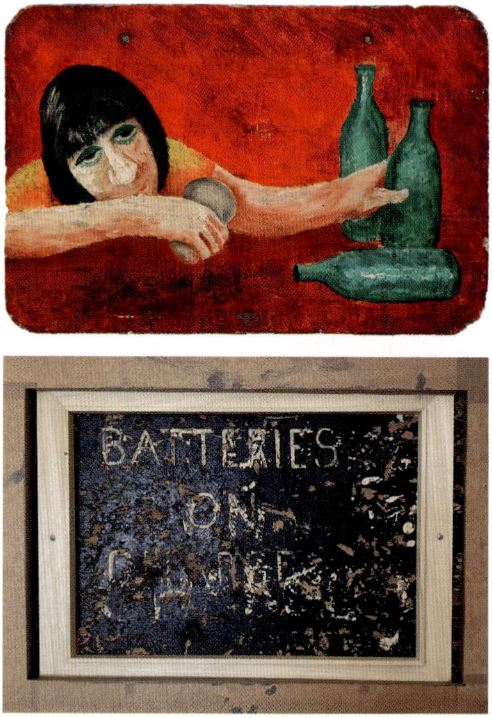

Three Green Bottles
(c 1965), front and back, painted on wood and probably originally hung without a frame

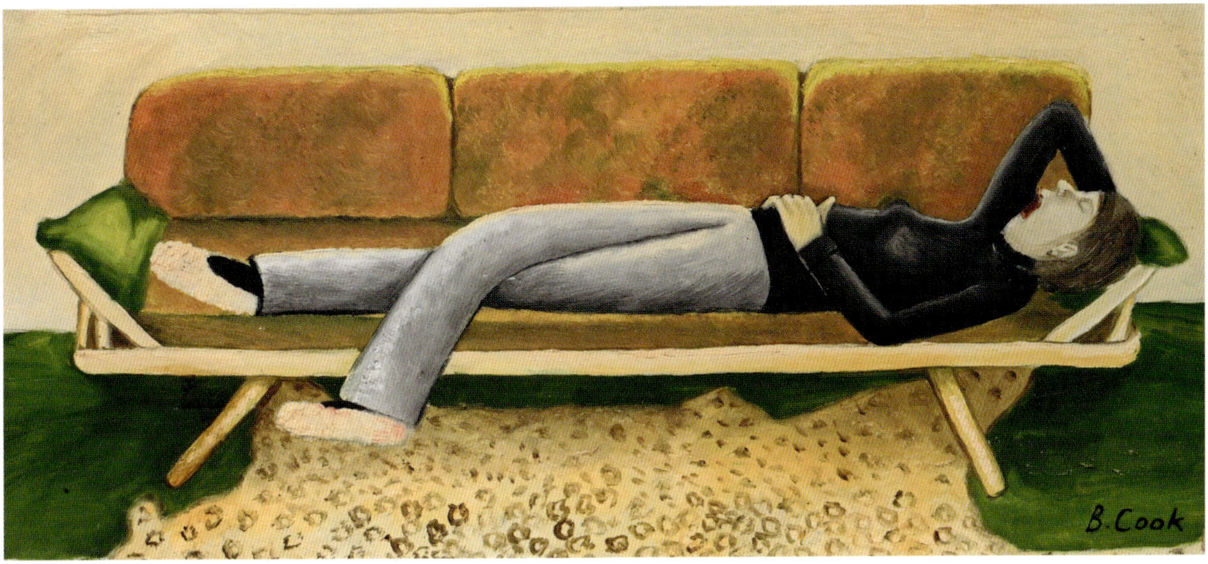

Beryl Asleep
(1965–8). The Cooks furnished their house with Ercol furniture. The leopard skin was brought back from Southern Africa.

Beryl too was influenced by life in her own village. She could so easily have painted the busy harbour, with its gaily painted fishing luggers, crab and lobster boats, yachts and speedboats, and the excitement of unloading the daily catch of turbot, skate, pilchards and conger eels. Instead, John bought her an oil painting set, and she started by repainting *Hangover*, the painting she had done with John Junior in Africa (see page 21). She then continued in the same comical vein.

Beryl's early paintings show signs of what was to become her signature style. To create her paintings, Beryl used whatever wood came to hand. *Three Green Bottles* is a very early painting, on the back of a piece of driftwood. The sea has eroded the surface along the grain of the wood so that the paint needed to be very thickly and deliberately applied, but even so we can still see the signature Beryl Cook style, not least in the humour. The lady is happily drunk, in the very act of reaching out for another bottle, and the colours vibrate. This, and another early work called *Pegleg* (see page 30), have a distinct two-dimensional quality reminiscent of *Hangover*.

Bosom Belles solves the question of three dimensionality with judicious use of egg cartons. It was painted on a fire screen made at school by John Junior and is slightly reminiscent of *Hangover*, but with 1960s European ladies.

However, *Piano and Percussion* (see page 28) is more sophisticated. Beryl has added a sense of depth by making the farthest drumstick more shadowy. The hands and arms have gained some shape and definition. The ladies are poised for a thunderous final chord.

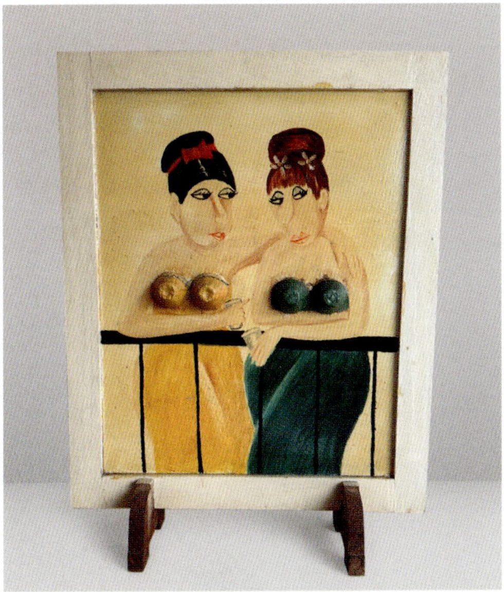

Bosom Belles
(1965–8)

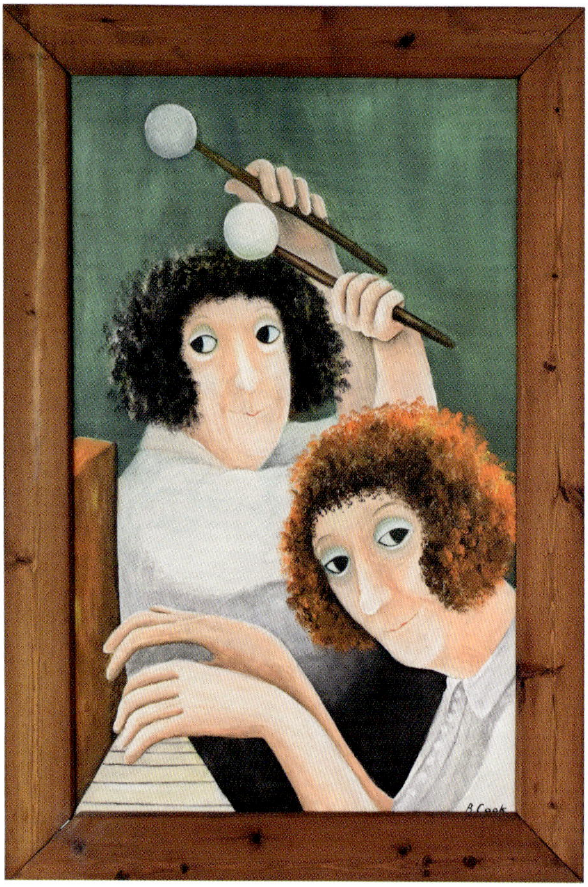

Piano and Percussion
(1965–8)

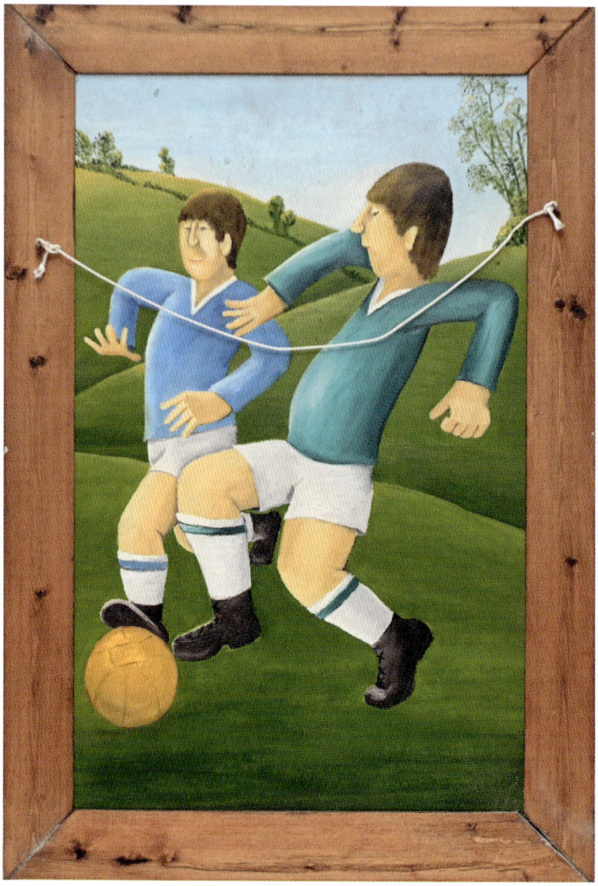

The painting on the reverse of
Piano and Percussion

If Beryl ran out of wood but not inspiration, she would use the back of a painting. On the reverse of *Piano and Percussion* is a painting I call '*Bendy Footballers'*.

In *Juggling with Beer Bottles (see page 31)*, sometimes known as *Bottle Throwers*, movement is given by the twist of the juggler's body, in contrast with the onlookers who are firmly plonked in their seats. They are amused – but not enough to stop snacking. The subject was suggested by a line in *The Likely Lads* television sitcom, a favourite of John and Beryl's. Little did she know that Rodney Bewes, who played Bob, would later own one of her paintings.

Beryl continued to use driftwood boards, a broken-down wardrobe, old boxes and even a breadboard.[2] The shapes and sizes of these boards often seem to have suggested a composition to her, and throughout her painting career, she used panels that suited her ideas rather than being constrained by traditional formats. As the walls of the cottage filled up, she began to use plywood cut to size and primed by John, who also framed her works.

Footballers on Looe Beach (see page 32) shows growing confidence, particularly in the sinuous rhythm of the arms. A similar composition has been used on the bacchanal that runs round the *log box* (see page 32). Yes, the figures are naked, but there is nothing that a teenage John Junior shouldn't see in the sitting room, such as nipples and navels.

Reclining Nude (see page 33) does have nipples, and a wonderful sense of fun. The nude is joyful, and completely happy in her own skin. It owes something to Modigliani.

Beryl's painting quickly gathered momentum, encouraged by local antique shop owner Tony Martin. Tony's friendship was critical to Beryl's development as an artist, and her sense that she was producing something worthwhile. Not only did he rescue some pieces from the skip, but he also created his own collection. As Beryl said, 'he took an interest in my paintings right from the start and was always very encouraging and helpful. It's lovely to have your own family praising your work, but you know very well that they can't judge it artistically. But when someone like Tony, who deals in paintings, approves of what you are doing, it really means something.'[3]

Tony's own collection of Beryl's Cornwall work included many of the paintings shown in this chapter, including *Tonging the Curls* (see page 33), the wonderful painting of a lady titivating her ginger hair.

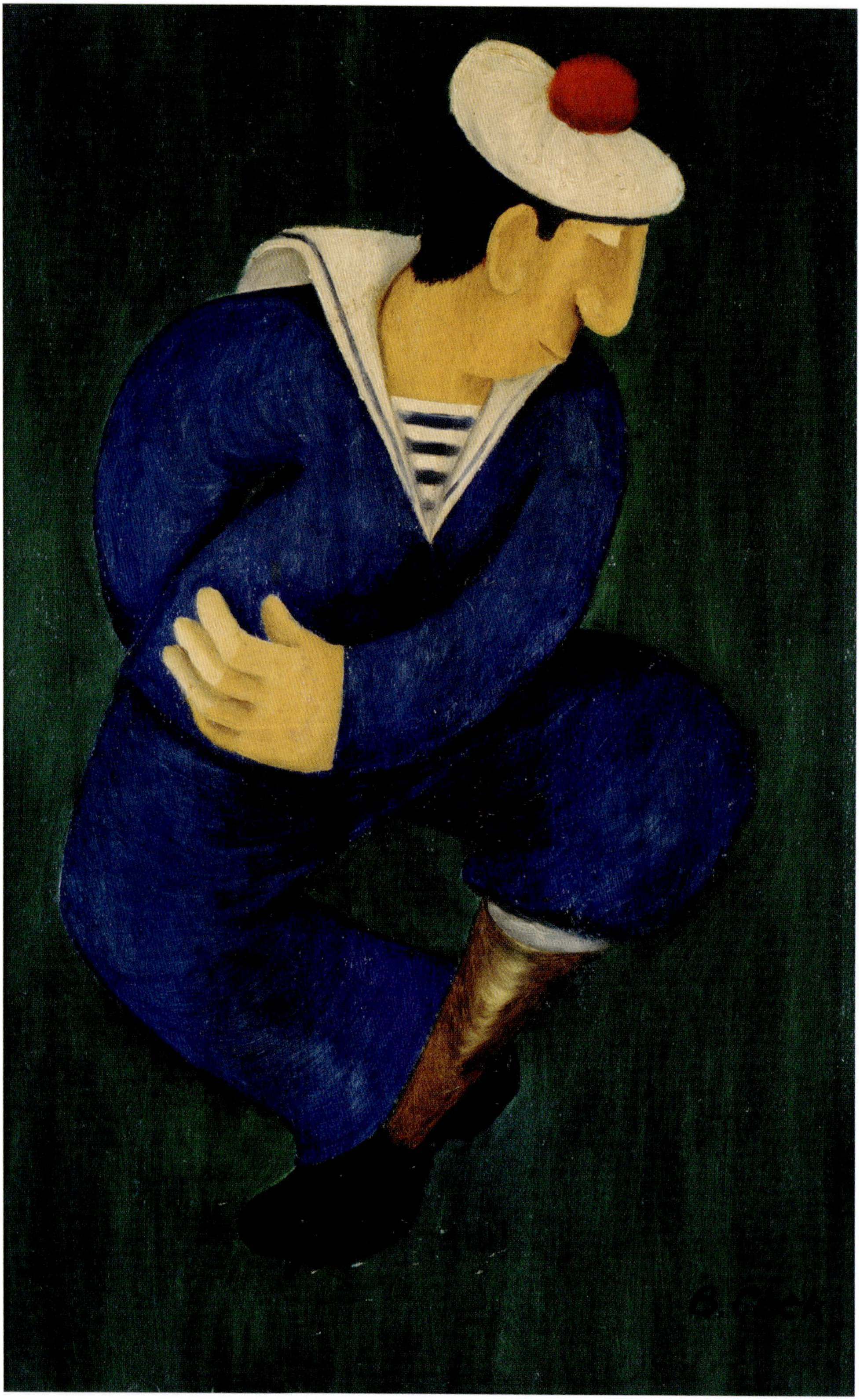

Pegleg
(c 1968). The family recall that this was nailed through the wood straight to the wall.

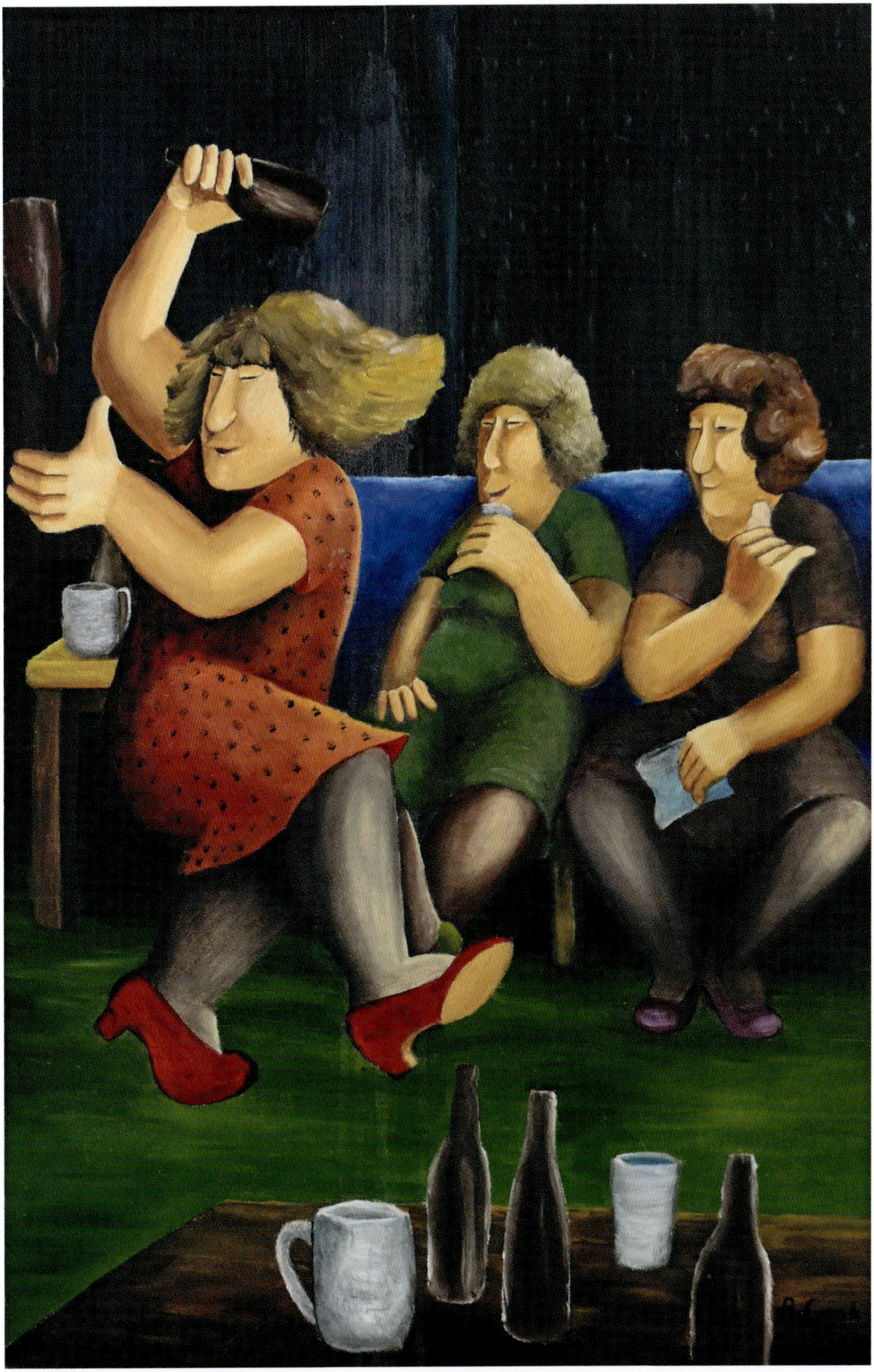

Juggling with Beer Bottles
(1968)

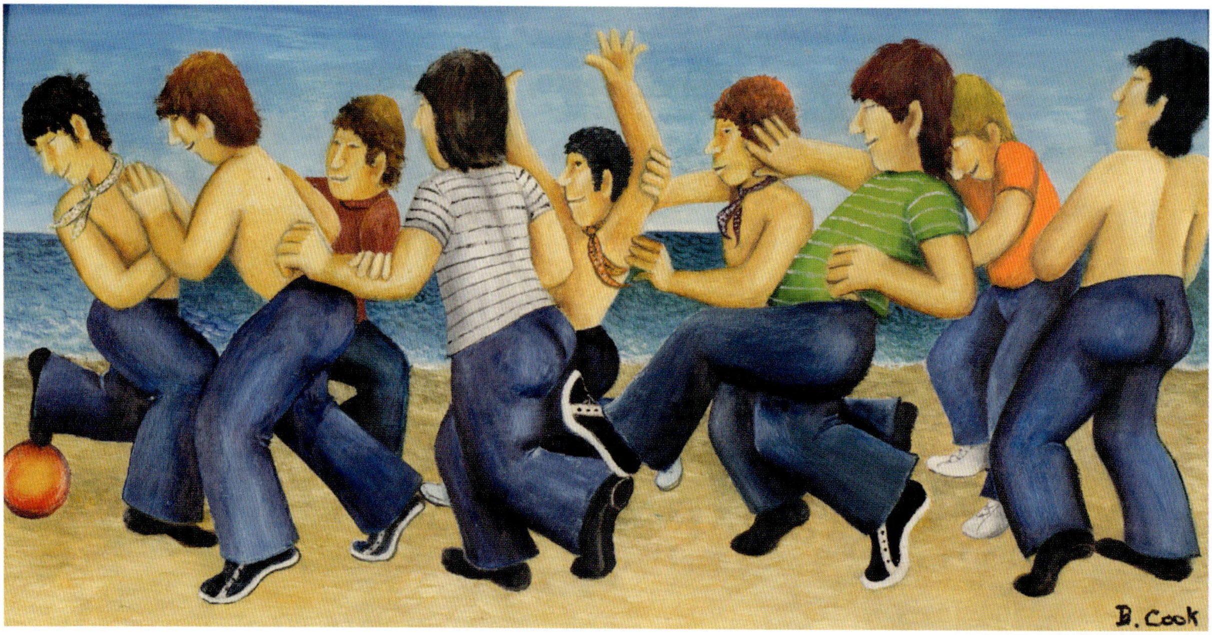

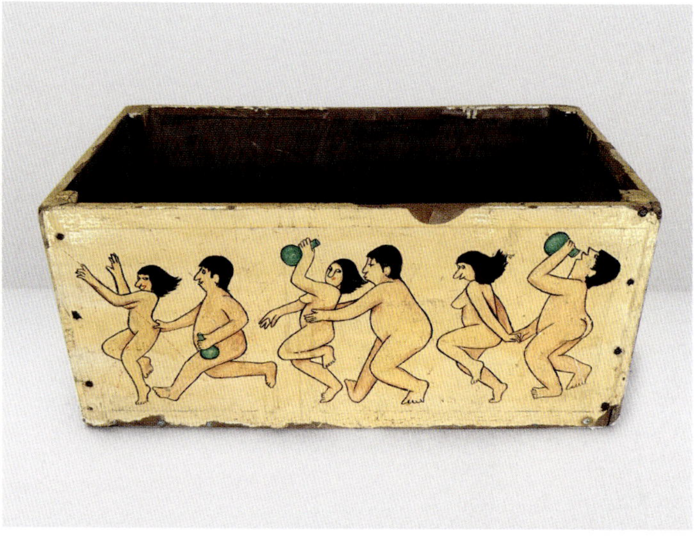

Footballers on Looe Beach
(1966)

Painted log box
(c 1965), also used as a toy box

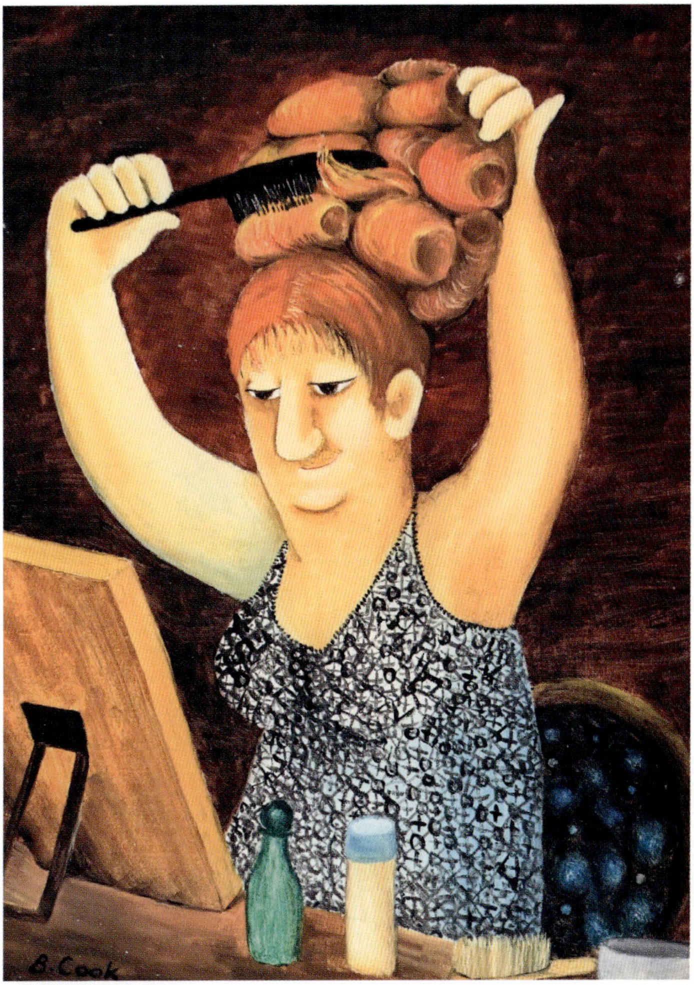

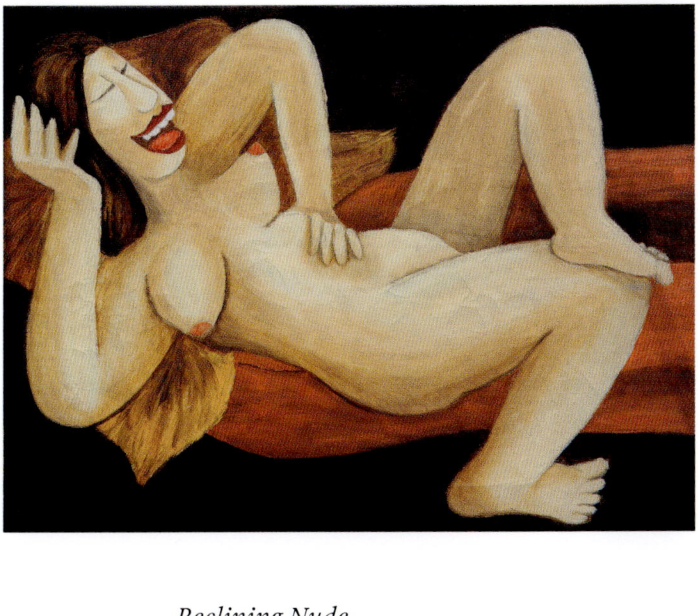

Reclining Nude
(1965–8)

Tonging the Curls
(1968)

Teresa (Beryl's future daughter in law) was a shampooist at about this time, and recalls the style, which was called 'petals'. It was built up over false hairpieces and had to be created weekly, with a mid-week visit to the hairdresser to have it combed and relacquered. One woman with this style had a spider make a nest in it, and hundreds of baby spiders emerged. No wonder hairdressing, and ginger hair, became a repeating subject for Beryl.

Beryl may have enjoyed outlandish hair in principle, but when her son came home with his hair dyed blonde she threatened to make him a ward of court and sent him back to their hairdresser, Denni, to be returned to his normal colour. Part-way through his hair went red, at which point John Junior ducked home to give his mother a further fright.

On another occasion Tony found an architectural painting which they both agreed was somewhat boring. 'Leave it with me,' said Beryl, and added some figures – and the signature Beryl Rembrandt.

Eventually, however, the delights of living in a tourist town began to wane. Looe's population was only about 3,800 but it swelled enormously in the summer; well over half the pages of the 1963 *Looe Official Guide* consist of adverts for hotels, guest houses, furnished flats and caravans. The narrow, crooked streets were so crowded that it was rumoured one resident attached a needle to her shopping basket to help her force her way through.

Beach at Looe (see page 24) shows Beryl's recollection of holiday makers crammed ever closer together as the tide comes in. At the back are the bathing tents. John Junior recalls how he and his friends used to wait until the tents came down at the end of the season, by which time some miracle of the tide had returned all the earrings, rings and coins lost in the course of people changing their clothes.

Out of season, on the other hand, the town felt deserted. Everyone was interested in everyone else's business, there was ongoing political infighting between East and West Looe and it was easy to feel trapped.

Looe was no longer enough for Beryl. In 1968 the Cook family relocated to the saltier delights of Plymouth.

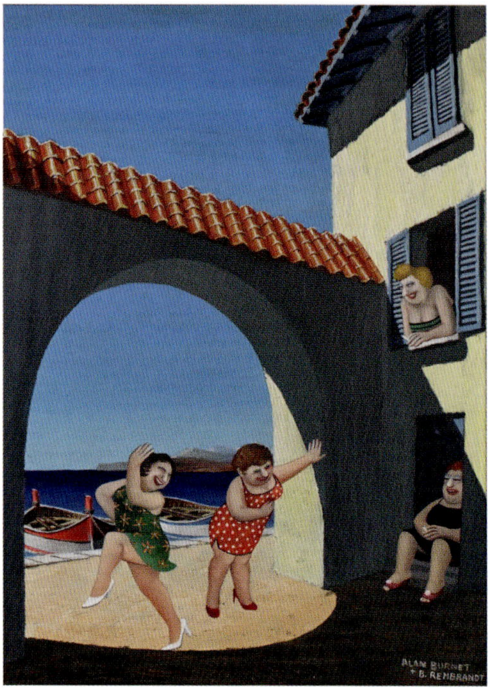

Untitled
(1965–8). Beryl added figures to liven up a dull painting by someone else for her antique-dealer friend Tony.

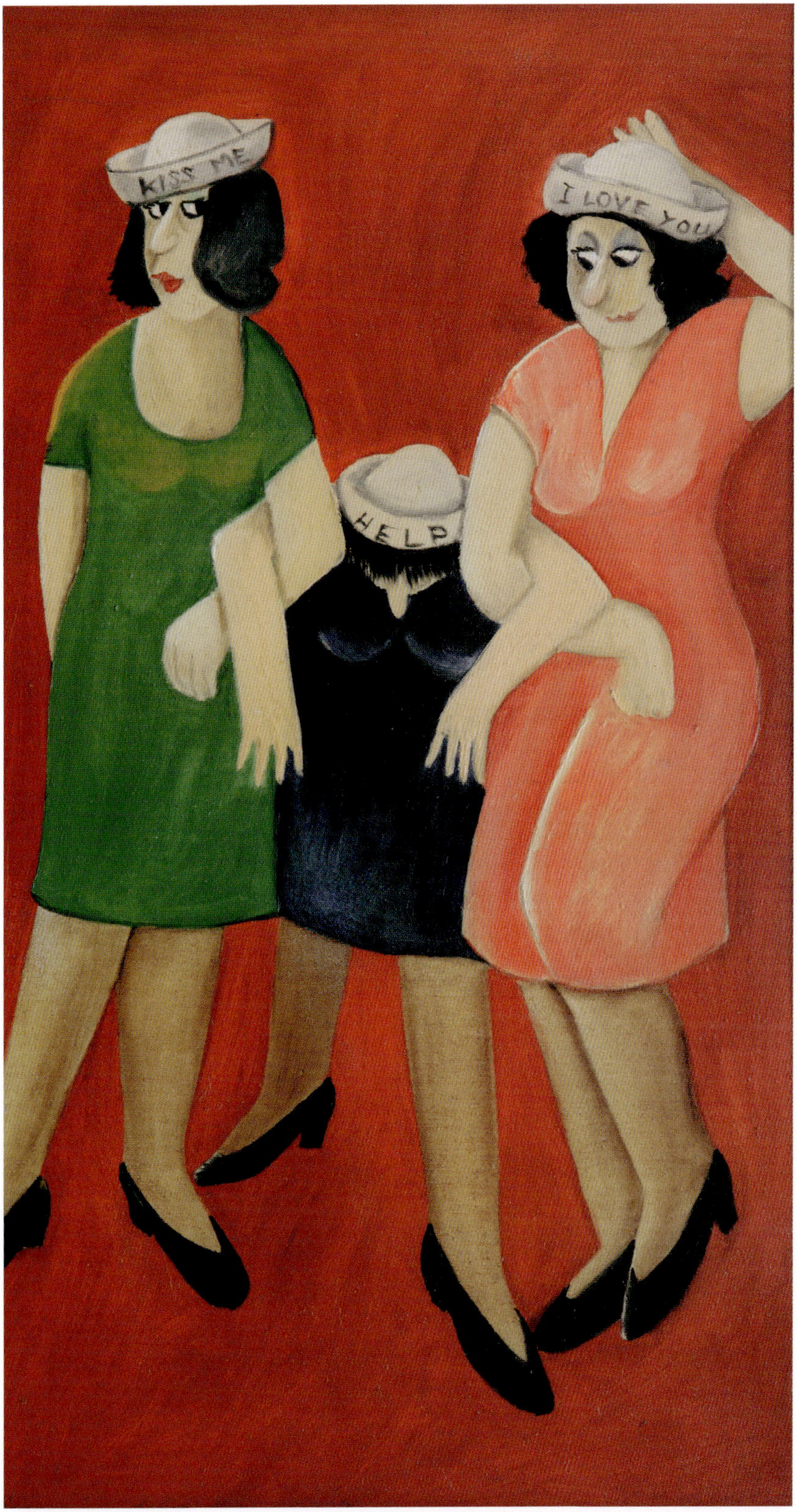

Holiday Trio
(1965–8)

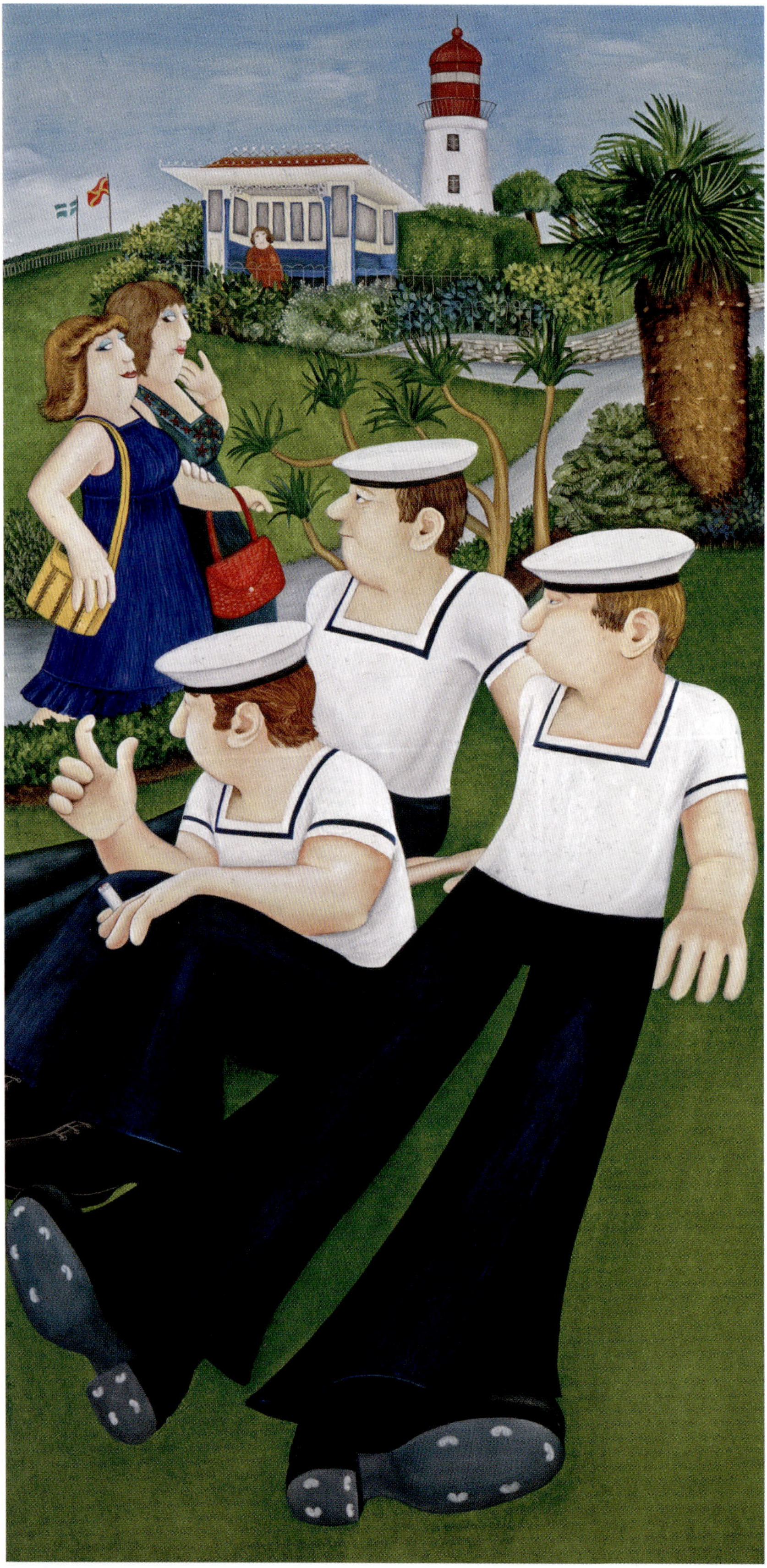

03

1968–1976: Plymouth Inspires

LEFT
Sailors and Virgins
(late 1970s). Beryl was inspired by hearing some sailors calling out to two girls 'Are you virgins?' The girls giggled but didn't reply.

The Cooks purchased Glanville House, a Bed and Breakfast in Plymouth, in 1968. Already a going concern, it is superbly positioned in Athenaeum Street near to the Hoe. John Senior continued to work in the motor trade at Bodmin, while Beryl, later joined by daughter-in-law Teresa, ran the B&B for five months during the summer. The rest of the year was free for holidays and for painting. Plymouth is an unpretentious place, where locals and visitors mix with the Royal Navy, fishermen, artists and dockyard workers, as well as incoming waves of sailors of all nations. There was no need for Beryl to actively seek out ideas, because inspiration was all around, day and night. She found it during her daily walks with the dog on the Hoe, while shopping for supplies for the B&B, and on weekend evenings out at the pubs and clubs.

Turning south from the B&B, the street leads to the grassy expanse of the Hoe, overlooking one of the world's great natural harbours. It is a place for wandering, gathering and playing, nailed to the land above the sea by Smeaton's Tower, a belvedere known as The Wedding Cake, the Sir Francis Drake Statue, and assorted war memorials and flag poles. The top of Smeaton's Tower is part of a quintessential lighthouse relocated from the perilous Eddystone rock, and said to be the first lighthouse to be painted in red stripes. Steps down lead to a 1930s lido, and there are stunning views across to Drake's Island and Mount Edgcumbe park beyond.

Beryl returned to this subject several times. Of course, Plymouth Hoe was the location for Sir Francis Drake's nonchalant game of bowls, played in 1588 whilst waiting for the tide to turn before engaging with the Spanish Armada. There is still a Plymouth Hoe Ladies' bowls club.

Beryl and John took their dog Bonzo for his walk on the Hoe very early every day, and there was always plenty going on and other dogs to meet.

On their return, Beryl would often turn north out of Atheneum Street. This area was so heavily bombed during the Blitz that it made Churchill cry. It was redeveloped after the War into a grid pattern, bisected north–south by a grand boulevard leading to the Hoe. It divides opinion today, but to me it is a fabulous piece of urban planning – at least in principle. In practice, parts of it have not aged well, and in those streets the wind rearranges your features and murders your umbrella. But when Beryl lived there, it was thriving. She was in easy reach of the delights of Dingles Department

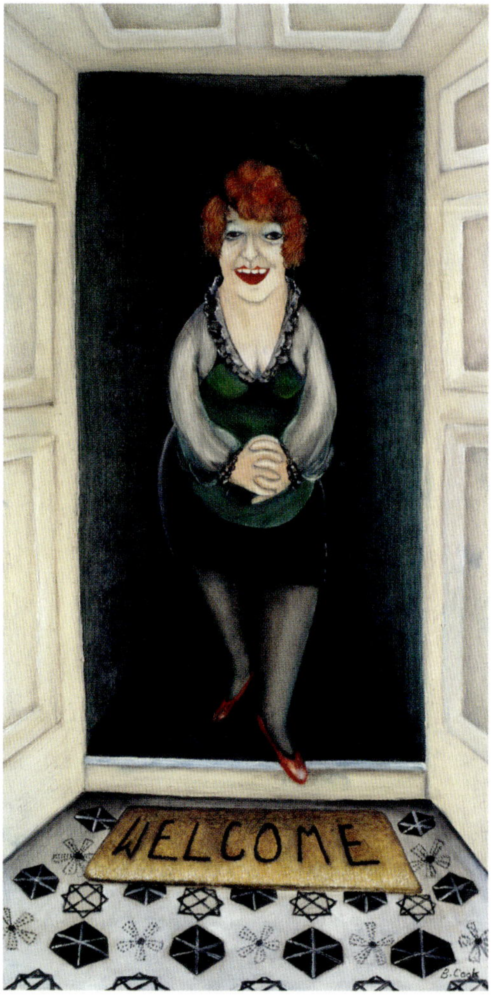

Welcome
(1972). Beryl claimed this was how she felt when she opened the door, but in fact it was partly inspired by a neighbouring B&B landlady.

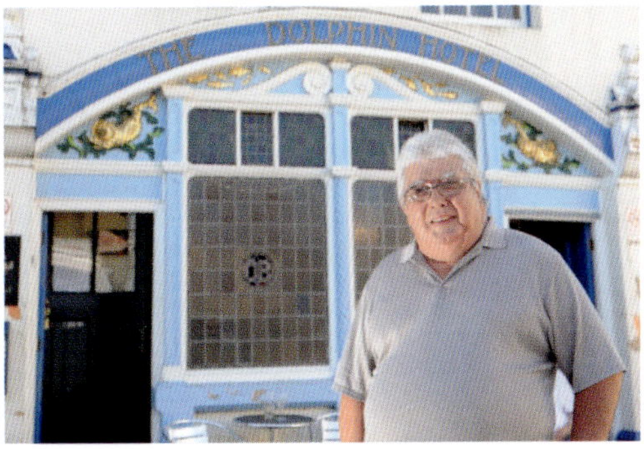

Billy Holmes (1941–2018), landlord of The Dolphin, appeared in several of Beryl's paintings.

Store, Woolworths, the covered Pannier Market and – perhaps the best of all – Littlewoods. This proximity was important when running a busy guest house.

Apart from early morning visits to the Fish market, the Barbican was more of an evening destination. This area is redolent of Plymouth's origins as a port, home of much of the English fleet, and historic point of arrival and departure – the Mayflower Steps are here (the actual site is under the ladies' toilets in a pub), as well as Elizabethan merchants' houses and old warehouses and shops. The Cooks enjoyed an evening drink on Friday and Saturday nights in The Dolphin Hotel or the Queen's Arms, the latter being John's favourite.

The Dolphin Hotel is no longer a hotel but a very traditional, 'dry' pub which does not serve food. Among its claims to fame is that the Tolpuddle Martyrs stayed there in 1838 on their return from Australia to which they had been transported for Trade Unionism. The face of The Dolphin for nearly 40 years was Billy, who took good care to avoid frightening the regulars by doing the place up. Billy had an impressive 54-inch girth (nearly 140cm), possibly because of his nightly habit of sidling across to Platters Seafood Restaurant for fish and chips, next door but two. There is a wonderful film of Beryl and Billy chatting in The Dolphin, in which Beryl chuckles slightly self-consciously. I can't understand a word Billy is saying, but it appears to relate to the time a punter fell off his stool and lay dead on the floor with everyone stepping over him, until the ambulance arrived.

Very near to the B&B was the Lockyer Tavern (now demolished). Like The Dolphin, this inspired several paintings. Beryl wrote, 'There were two bars, one of them gay, with singing and dancing, talent competitions and pantomime in drag, all performed by the locals.'[1]

Drag then was deliberately less polished than *Ru Paul's Drag Race* today. There was no attempt to look realistically female. As Brian Pearce, a lifelong friend of the Cooks and drag artist who appeared under the name Ruby Venezuela, said: 'It amazes me when people think Ruby is a real woman. Middle-aged women come up to me and say: "Do you dress like that in the daytime?" No woman would make herself up like that – with eyebrows half way up her forehead.'[2] There was no lip synching; the entertainment came from the humour and vigour of the performance rather than the quality of the voice. Ruby's repertoire included 'Viva suspenders' to the tune of 'Viva Las Vegas'.

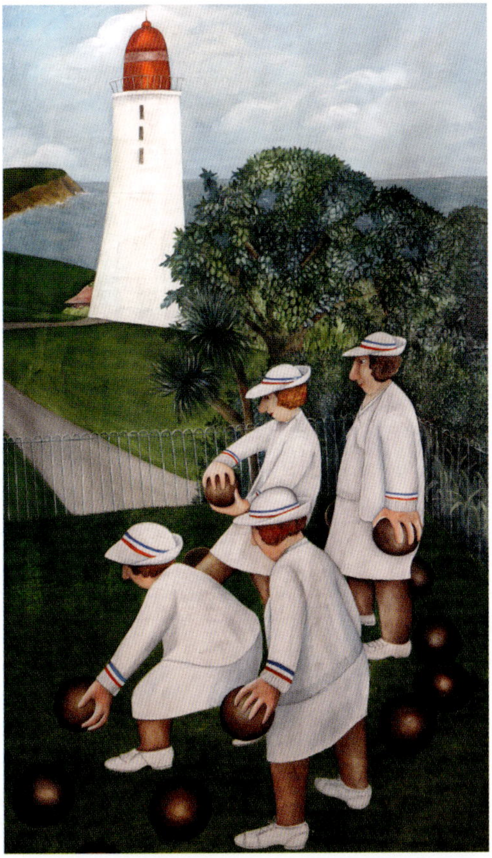

Bowlers of the Hoe
(1973–5). Painted on an old window blind, and purchased by the Plymouth City Museum & Art Gallery (now The Box) in 1975.

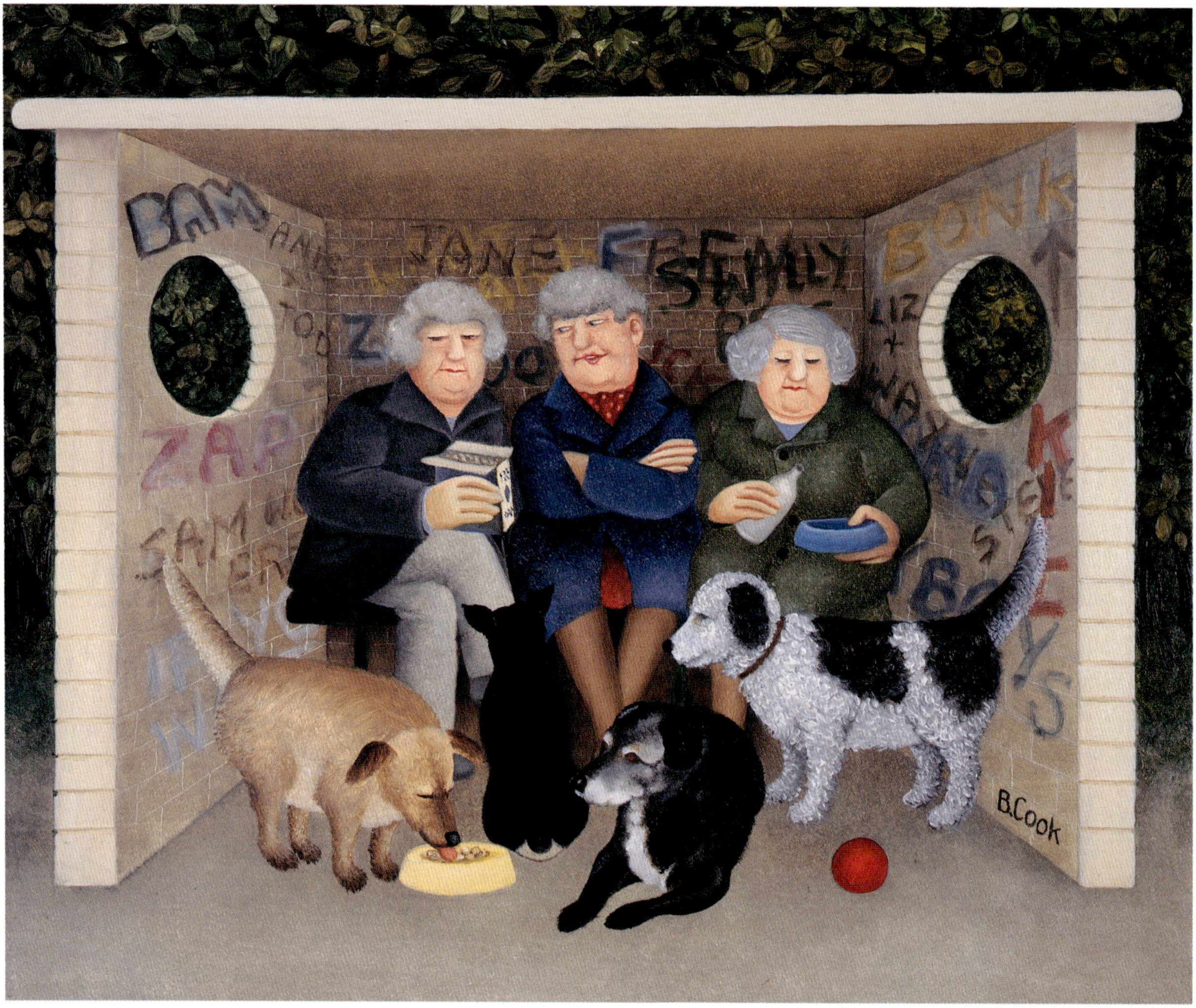

A Short Pause

(late 1970s). The graffiti is all genuine. Beryl didn't want to be seen copying it down, so she memorized it and quickly ran back home to make notes.

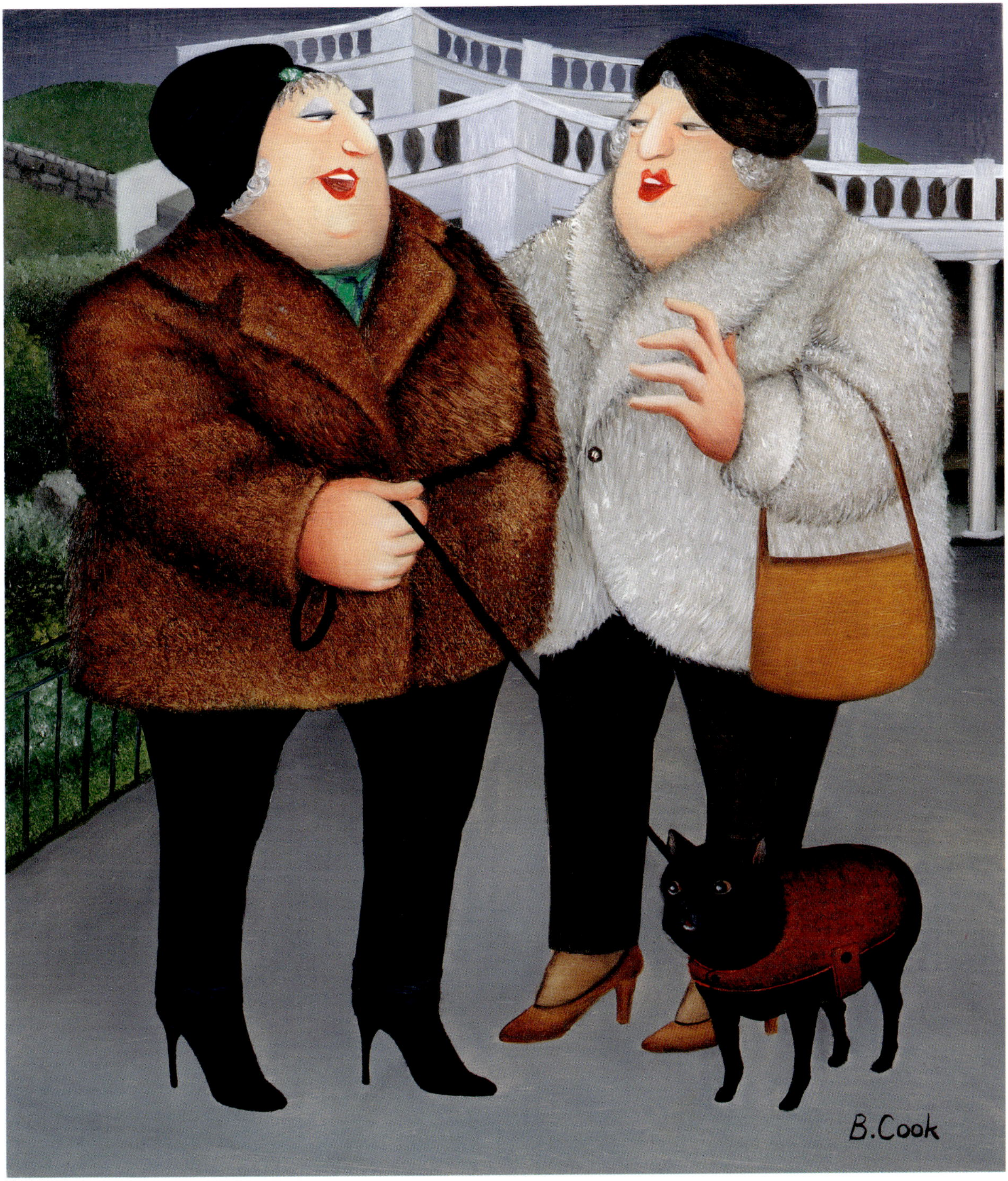

Walkies
(1980), with The Belvedere, known locally as The Wedding Cake, in the background

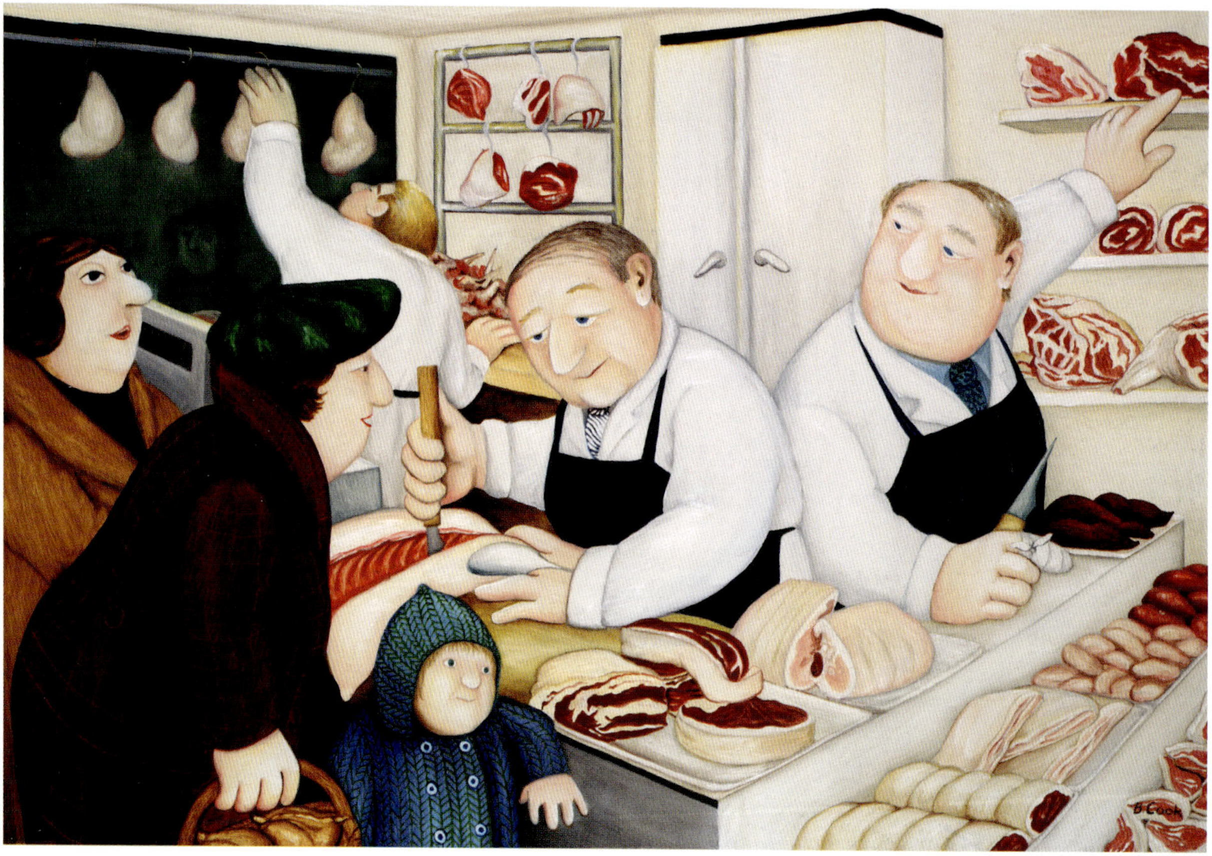

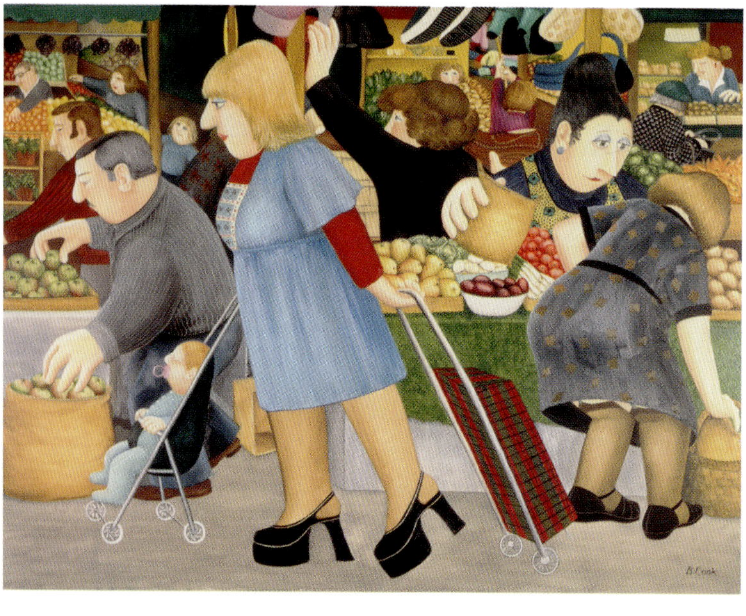

The Pannier Market
(1980s), with its famous fruit stall

The Butchers
(1976), complete with bandaged fingers

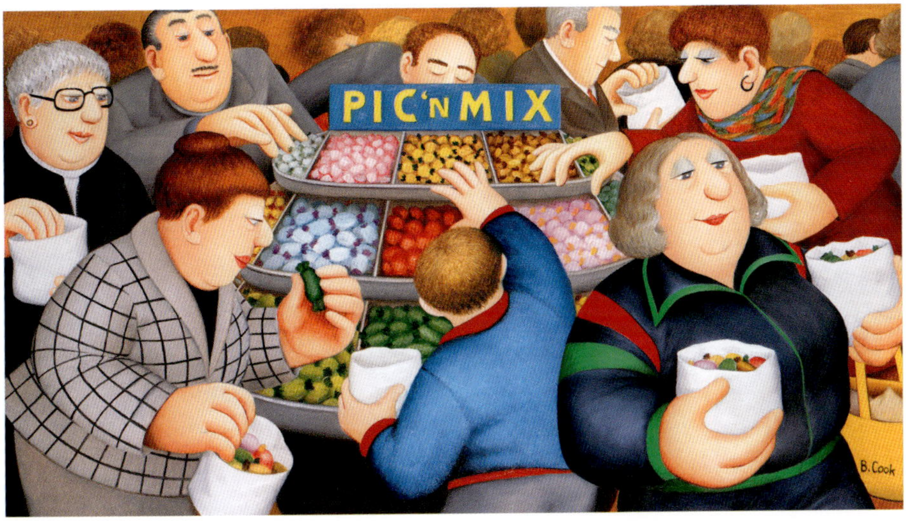

Pick n Mix
(1991). Beryl's memory of one of the highlights of Woolworths. Beryl herself can be seen back left.

Pride Life editor Nigel Robinson said that Ruby/Brian was a kind-hearted person and talented performer: 'I hesitate calling her a drag queen/artiste because she was more than that, more like a bonkers tornado coming in from Kansas, the lovechild of Mrs Shufflewick, Ethel Merman, Mervyn Peake and Beryl Cook, but above all else her very own character, bringing delight to everyone, young and old.'[3]

Another source of fascination for Beryl was Union Street in Plymouth. The Street was built between 1812 and 1820 to unite what had been two separate towns of Plymouth and Devonport. It was a bustling artery joining the docks to the centre of Plymouth until it was decimated by bombs during the Second World War. Nevertheless, it was internationally famous for its nightlife during the 1970s and 1980s, with pubs, nightclubs, take-aways, taxis, police and military police swarming about, particularly at weekends. The 'working girls' would perk up every time a ship arrived and disgorged its matelots, now no longer in uniform due to possible IRA activity.

The girls tended to operate from The Phoenix, a Victorian pub with a red and white frontage, now sadly closed and neglected. They were very much part of the community and Beryl, John and Tony often went there for a drink. In those days pubs had to shut at 10.30 or 11.00 p.m., at which stage the clubs opened their doors. There was a variety to choose from, all open until 2.30 a.m., after which everyone went for fish and chips at the Palace Fish Bar or to a kebab bar.

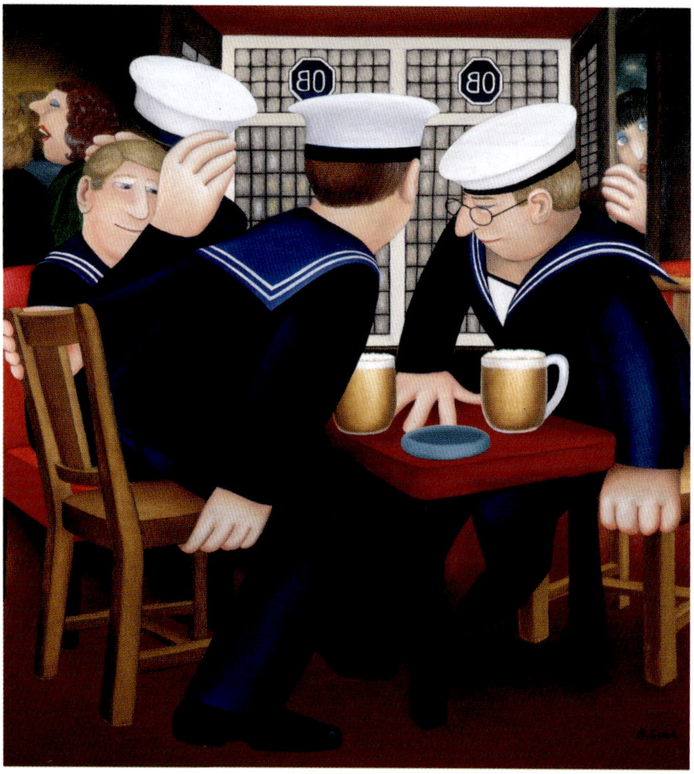

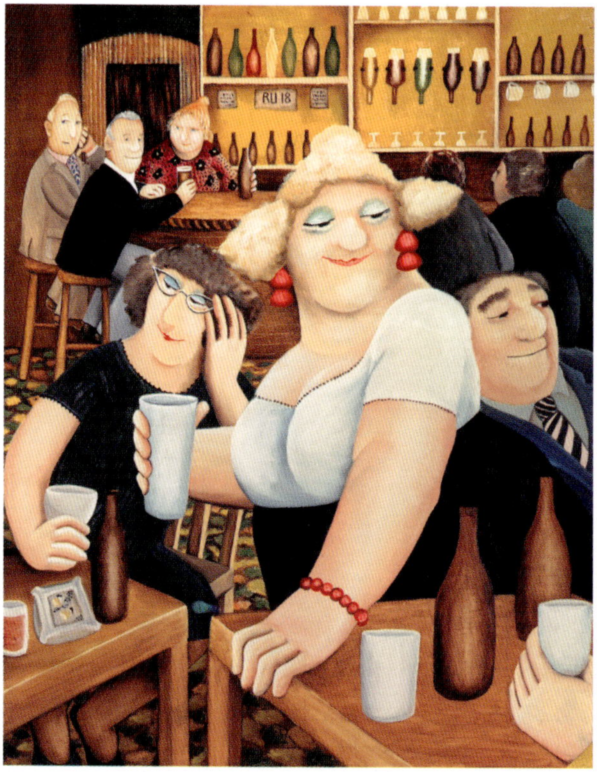

Sailors in The Dolphin
(1980s). The 'OB' on the windows stands for Octagon Brewery.

The Lockyer Tavern
(c 1974). This was Beryl's first painting of the Lockyer, and is of the front bar.

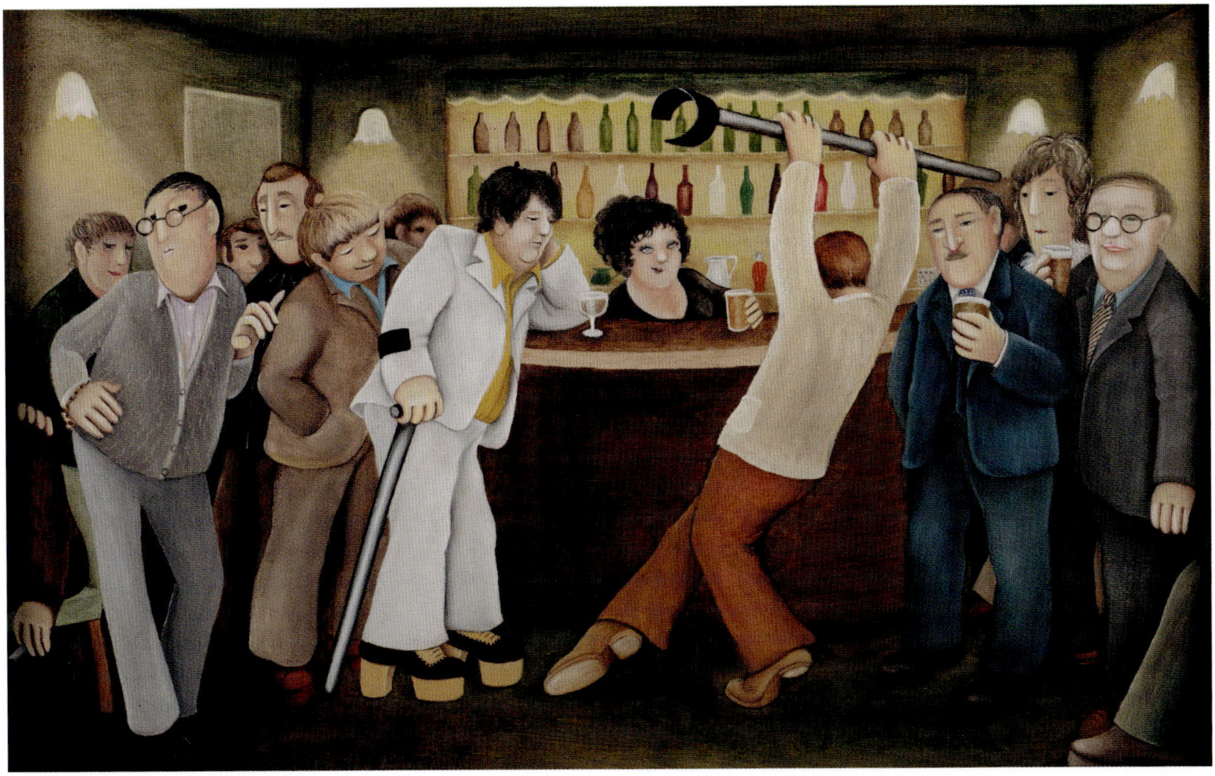

Back Bar of the Lockyer Street Tavern

(1976). Beryl donated this painting to the Plymouth City Museum and Art Gallery (now The Box). It is sometimes known as *Crutch Dancing*. There are brief notes on the back about who is featured, and a card in The Box's collections index which gives the full names. Tommy Jones is dancing. Tom Wilde in the blue suit is the landlord. The barmaid is Shirley, and the man in the white suit is Beryl's neighbour and friend Brian Pearce.

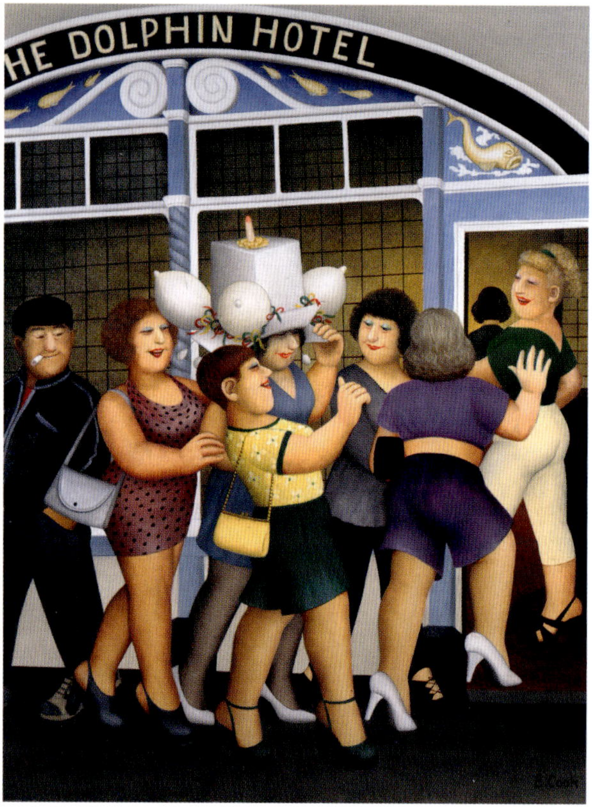

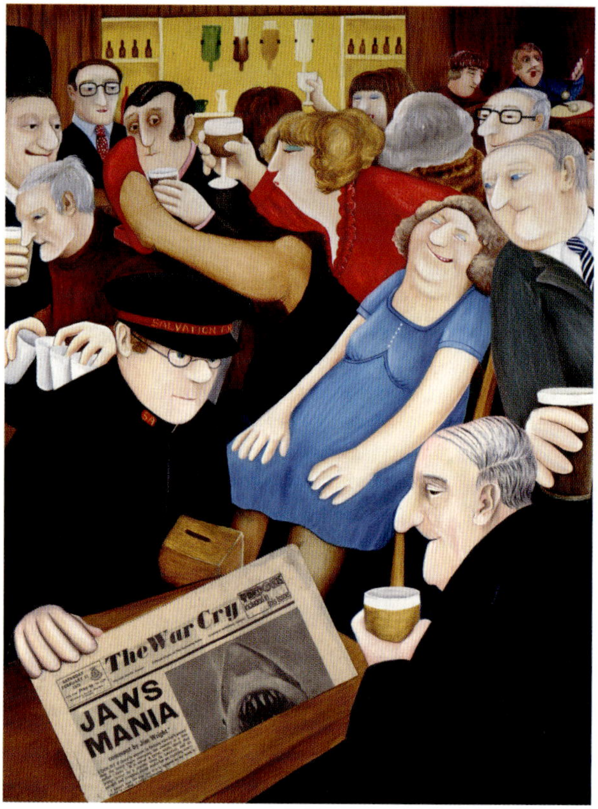

Hen Party 1
(c 1994). One of many paintings of The Dolphin, this time showing Beryl's hairdresser's hen party on a pub crawl. Beryl was especially fascinated by the saucy hat.

Jaws Mania
(c 1975). This painting shows the *The War Cry* being sold in The Dolphin by a member of the Salvation Army in uniform. The drummer at the back is peforming where, today, folk musicians play music at The Dolphin.

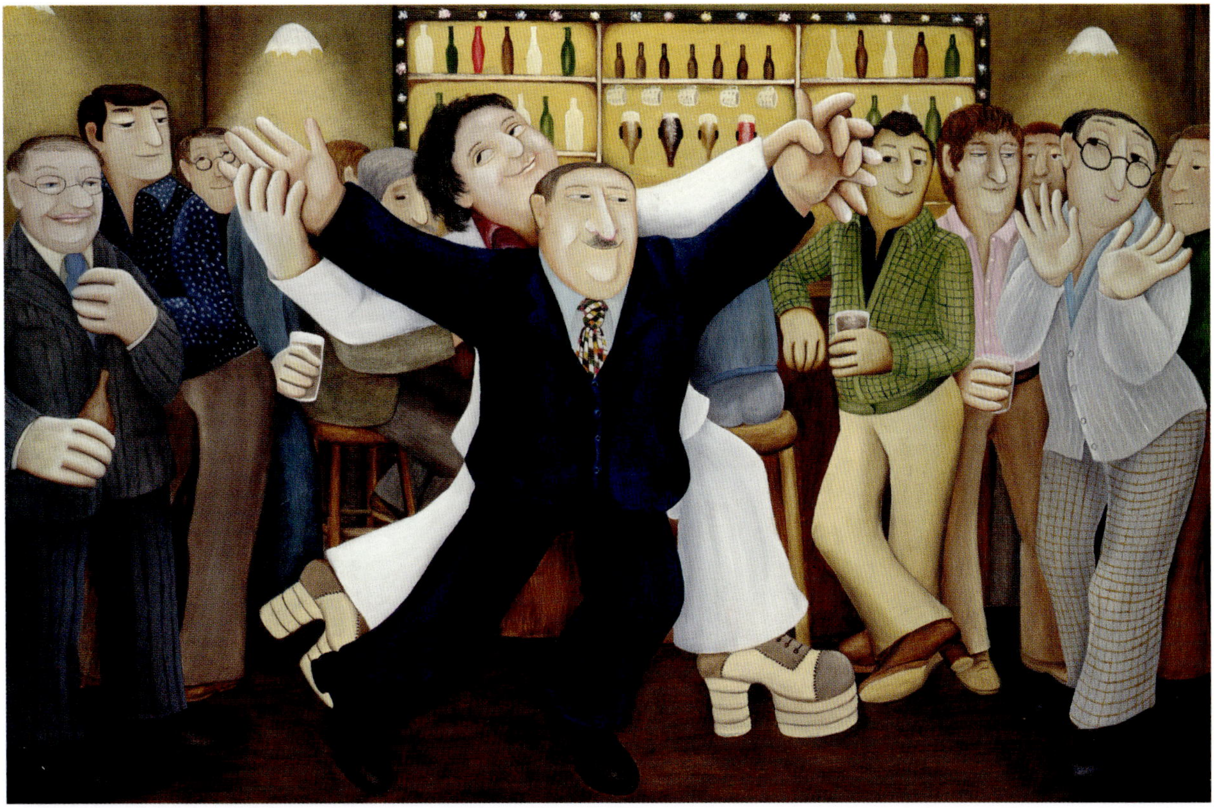

Tom Dancing

(c 1975). Brian Pearce has swept Tom Wilde, the landlord, into a dance. Tom has allowed himself a small grin. Brian is wearing wonderful platform shoes: footwear remained a much-loved subject for Beryl.

When the clubs closed, Diamond Lil's was the place to be. It was run by impresario Ronnie Potter, and in Beryl's time 'Diamond Lil' was Tammy Williams, a female impersonator who recalled, 'All the seasoned matelots would push the rookies to the front and we used to decimate the first four rows. The more hecklers there were the better it was . . . "The Farting Opera" to the tune of "Old-Fashioned Girl" was a popular number, as was "These Boots are Made for Walking" with me in a long alluring evening gown with hobnail boots underneath.'[4] Tammy had gender-affirming surgery at the age of 35 and may have been the inspiration for Sylvia, who Beryl said 'used to be a man but is now a lady'.

Beryl, John and Tony would sit in the Castle (the front bar of Diamond Lil's). The club was extremely sticky. The ashtrays were nailed to the tables and the tables to the floor, in case a fight broke out. A contributor to a Royal Navy Forum remembered:

> Diamond Lil's had a bar attached to it, I think it was called the Castle. It used to stop serving drinks when Diamond Lil's opened. If you were lucky you could go from the Castle to Diamond Lil's without having to pay the cover charge. The place was run by a guy called Ronnie who played the organ, his wife used to sing (mainly blue songs). Ronnie Potter on the organ, Kim Taylor singing 'Blanket on the Ground' – or hosting the 'fun-game' where you had to name that tune – or dance if Ronnie played the hornpipe. If anyone went to the toilet (that was situated behind the stage area) during the stage show, Ronnie would ask them as they came out 'Could you hear us all right back there – cos we could hear you . . .' The last song was always 'The Stripper' and you had to do the actions to win a free drink. Just don't ask for cider or you'd get the special 'scrumpy' from the plastic barrel that was behind the bar – containing all the dregs from the previous night.[5]

Many remember the epic fights that broke out at closing time, but by then the Cooks had safely returned home.

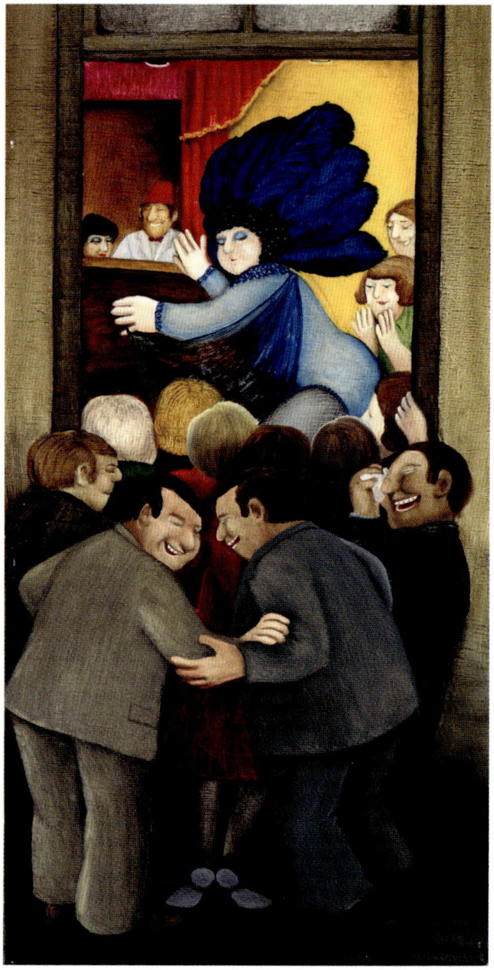

Brian Entertains
(c 1973–5). Here is Brian as his alter ego Ruby Venezuela, seen through the window of the Lockyer Tavern. At the back is Brian's accompanist Len playing the organ; Beryl stuck sequins on Brian's headdress in her painting, just as Brian had done when making his costume.

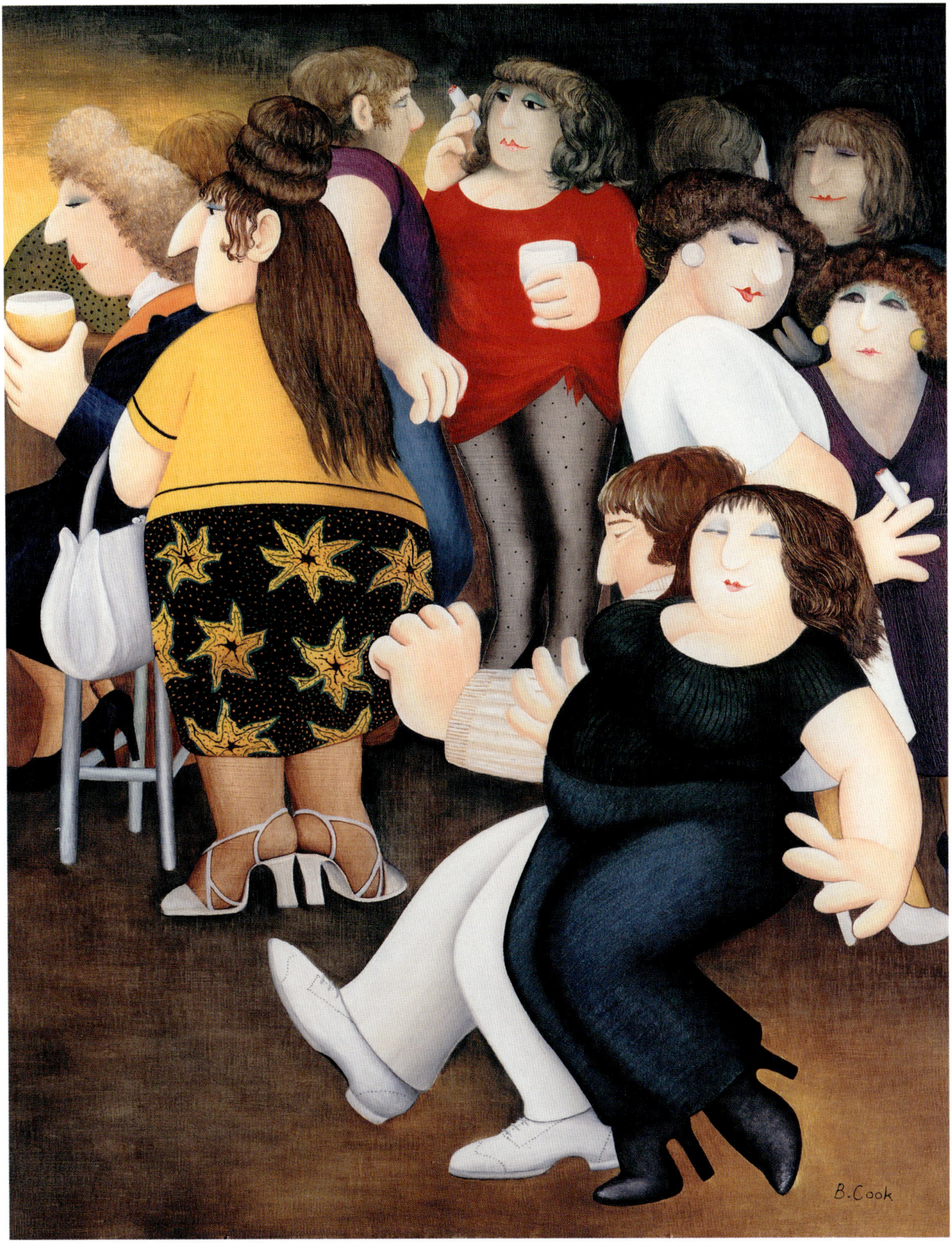

Union Street

(c 1978–9). The new owner of this painting wrote to Beryl in 1980 to ask for more details about it. Beryl replied that it was an amalgamation of the various bars and clubs they had visited on the Street, and that the 'big fat person in the flowered skirt is Mary', whom they often saw on Friday nights.[6]

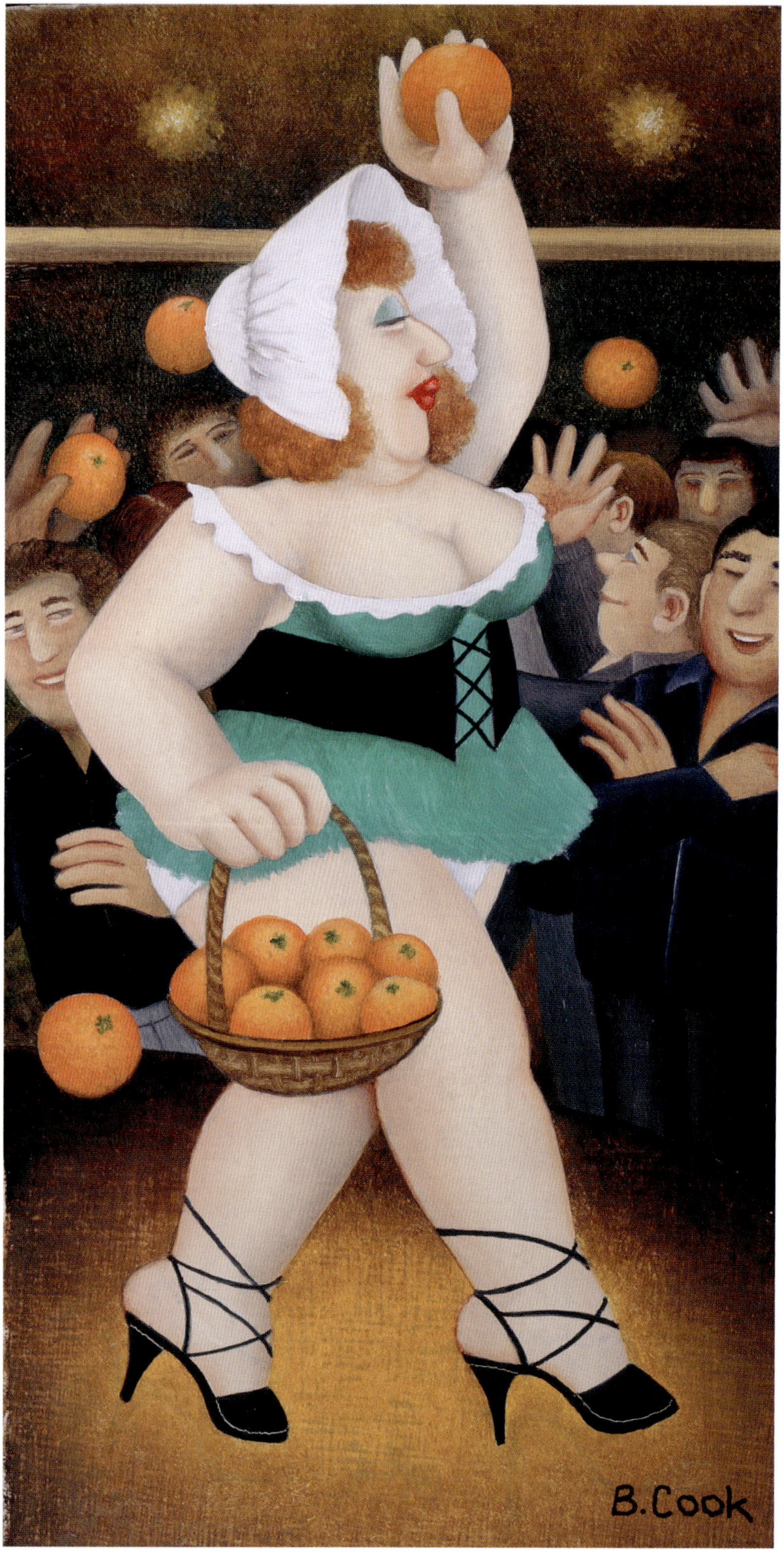

Big Julie as Nell Gwyn
(1980s). Nell Gwyn (1650–87) was rumoured to have been a prostitute and orange-seller, before rising to become a famous actress and long-term mistress of King Charles II.

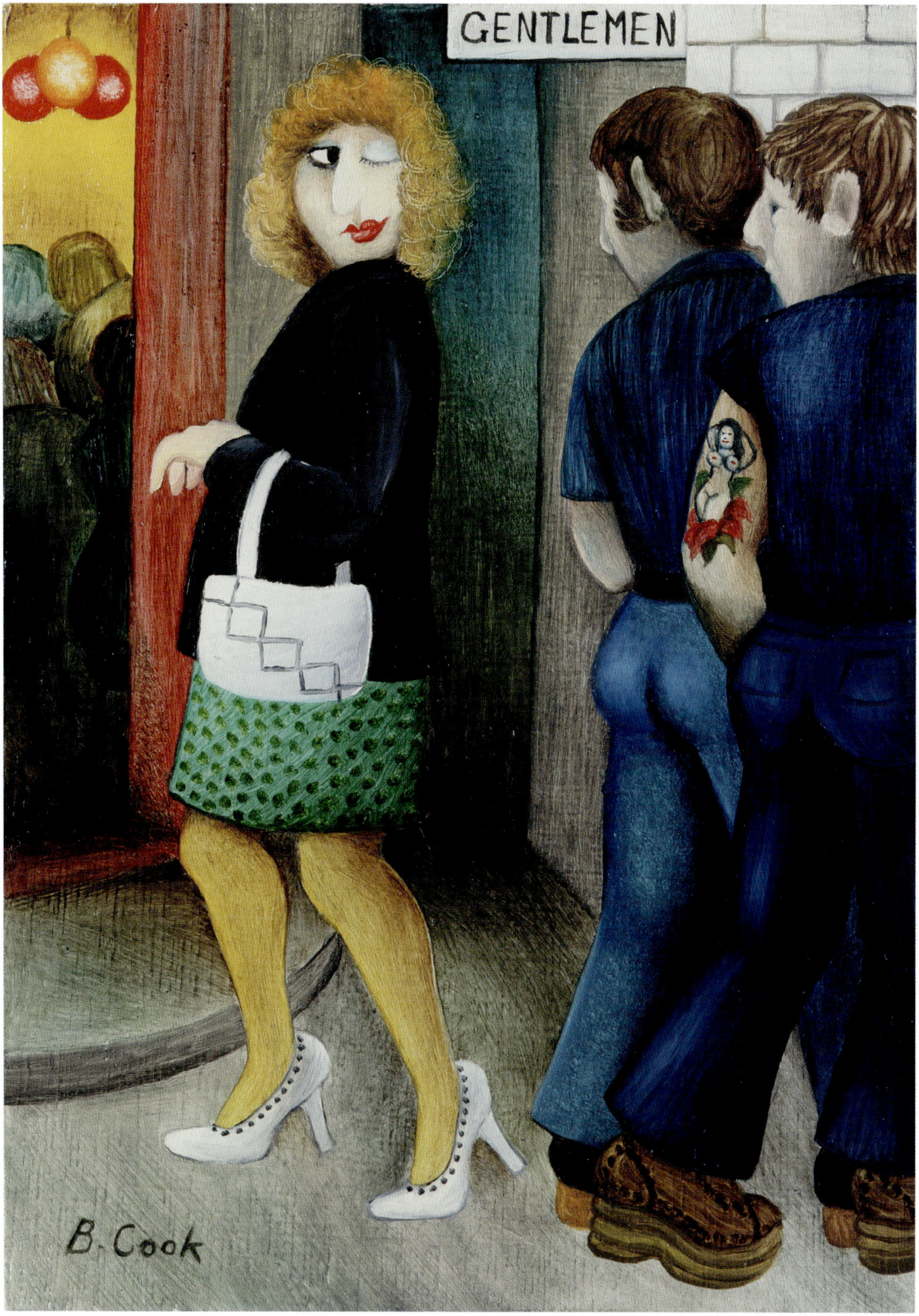

Sylvia
(1968–78). Beryl enjoyed painting the sailor's tattoo almost as much as she did Sylvia's hair.

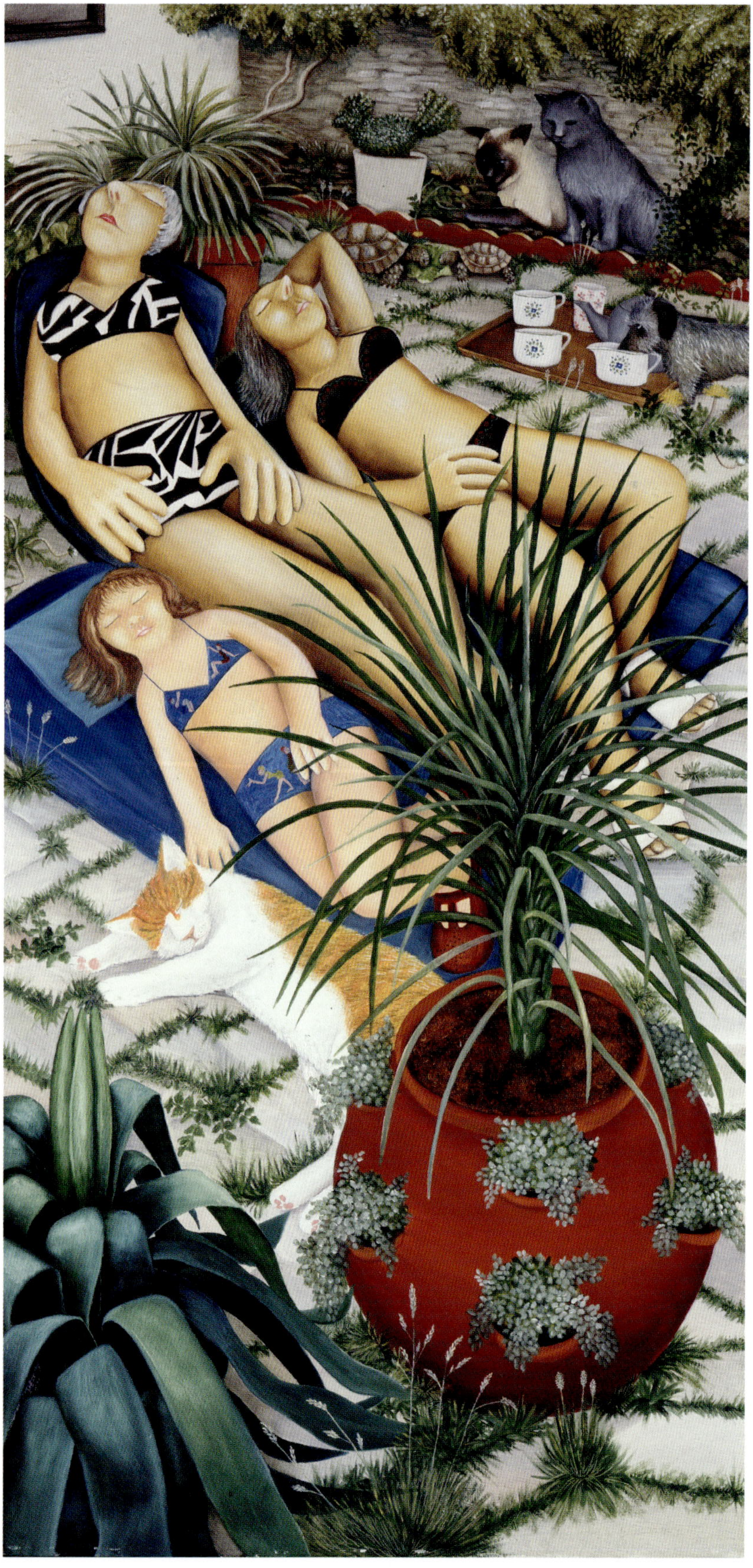

04

The Seaside Landlady

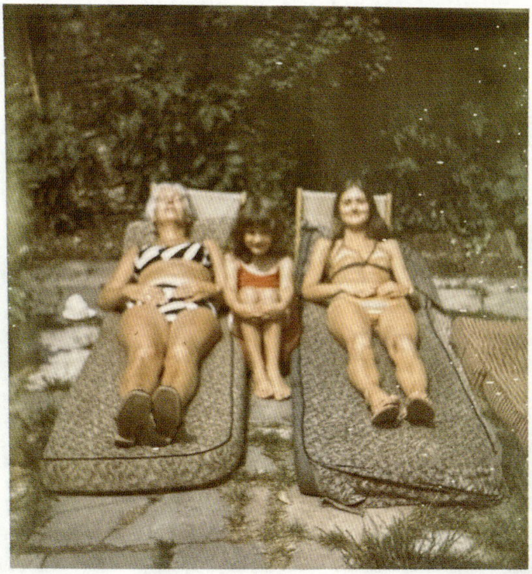

Family photograph of Beryl, Alexa and Teresa sunbathing (c 1977)

LEFT
Sunbathing
(1977). From top to bottom, Teresa, Beryl and Alexa in the small courtyard garden of Glanville House. The Cooks' pets were very much part of the family. At the top of the painting, Siamese cat Lottie and grey-coloured Smokey watch the tortoises, Hercule and Desiree. Bonzo the dog is drinking from the milk jug. Cedric is asleep next to Alexa.

Athenaeum Street, where Beryl's B&B was located, was part of a development by John Foulston (1772–1841), who from 1810 created neoclassical terraces punctuated by grand buildings such as the eponymous Athenaeum, The Royal Hotel, a theatre and chapel. These were mostly demolished before or during the Second World War. Some escaped, but the Cook's house was badly bombed and the rear part rebuilt.

It is a big house. The basement and top floor were let out, and Beryl and John lived on the ground floor, with the living room at the front. They used what would have been the dining room as their bedroom. There was a small room for painting, which doubled up as an ironing room during the season. At the back was a very rudimentary kitchen. They shared the bathroom on the first floor with their guests, something that was quite usual at the time – Glanvillle was very modern in having washbasins and televisions in the guest bedrooms. On the first floor, the big front room had been divided into two single bedrooms and there was also a double room. John Junior and Teresa, who married in 1969, moved into the basement flat in 1973 with their daughter Alexa.

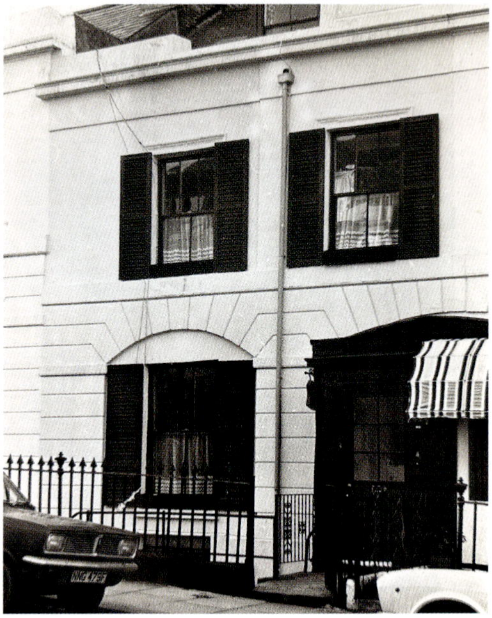

Glanville House, Athenaeum Street, Plymouth, to which the Cook family moved in 1968 (photo c 1993)

Beryl wrote, 'I never did any housework on sunny days in summer, nor did Teresa, my daughter-in-law, or Alexa. Luckily we had a tiny patch of garden at the back of the house which caught the sun, so we lay there lazily all day with the animals. We dreaded that we might one day be liberated, and have to go out to work instead.'[1] Beryl was not a typical B&B owner. She was extremely shy, so there was no communal dining room. Instead, guests were served their cooked breakfasts literally in bed. 'I tried to avoid taking people on their own, particularly women, because they were bound to be lonely and would want to chat with me . . . I did enjoy having visitors, though. I loved seeing the bedrooms looking nice, and the breakfast trays. My fried eggs were something to behold.'[2]

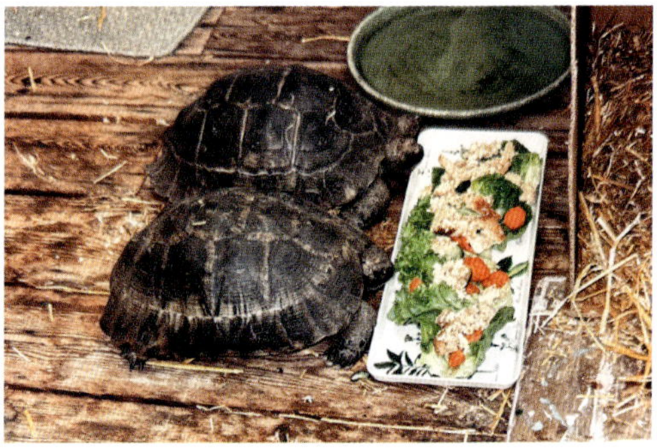

The tortoises, Hercule and Desiree. Desiree was bought to be a companion for Hercule, but turned out to be male as well.

She was quoted as roaring with laughter, saying that 'by mid-August I've just about had enough, so I get my own back by painting them. I transformed three guests into pigs in one of my paintings – well, that was how I saw them . . . and I did another of myself down on the beach stabbing holiday makers as they lay in the sun.'[3] As Teresa says, 'Thank goodness she liked me!'

When the season finished, painting started. Paintings accumulated. Beryl was so driven, that if she ran

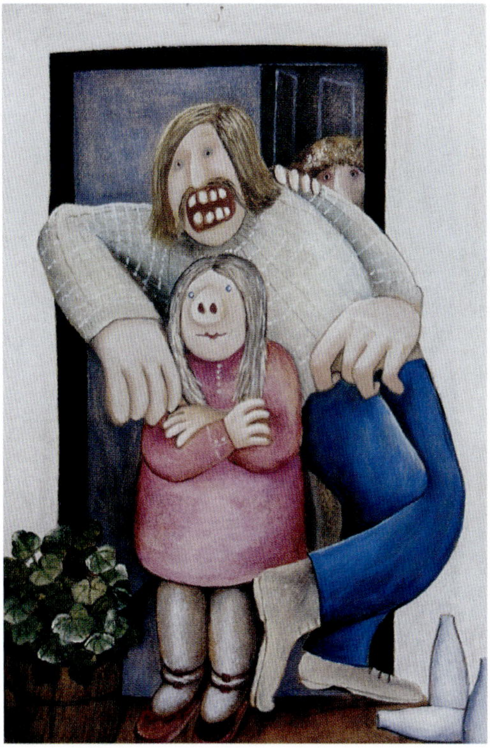

Untitled
(1973–5). Either annoying B&B guests or annoying tenants. Beryl later said that she thought it had been bought by a psychiatrist.

out of panels, she would paint on the reverse of pictures or even on the toilet seats (see page 57).

Added to this, she knitted, sculpted, embroidered and sewed, and read – and read. The walls filled up, paintings were hung on wardrobes and doors, stacked in cupboards and behind doors. Other spaces filled with an ever-growing assortment of knick-knacks bought in charity shops and on Plymouth market, usually for one pound or less. Some of these were props for paintings, some for display and some cannibalized for parts to be used in the works of art.

Joe Whitlock Blundell, editor of *Beryl Cook, The Bumper Edition*, remembered his first visit:

> The house was filled with an astonishing array of bric-a-brac – art deco lamps and teapots, Bonzo memorabilia, dozens of cruets, egg-cups and ashtrays, and several gems of the advertiser's art – plaster toucans offering Guiness for Strength, a sailor in bas relief complete with real Player's cigarette, and a shapely figure demonstrating the merits of a brand of male corsetry. Their two diminutive yet vociferous dogs and two cats were always in evidence around one's feet.[4]

These pets were dogs Minnie and Lottie, and cats Percy and Felix.

In 1975 Tony Martin offered to relieve the pressure by displaying some paintings in his (then empty) antique shop in Looe. The handful he took were very quickly sold at about £20 apiece, and we now have no record of what they were. However, the spaces very soon filled up again.

For the guests, the subject matter must have been an eye opener. Many were created especially for family and friends and could be extremely saucy. Presumably the Karma Sutra series and vicious portraits of guests were kept private, but others were inspired by their holidays in places like Paris and Amsterdam, where she took a great interest in the red-light districts (see page 58).

The effect was extraordinary – and polarizing. Many guests asked about the works, and if Beryl sensed that they didn't approve she would claim that her son painted them. Other guests were convulsed.

Among the guests were three actors who stayed at Glanville House in 1973: these were Joanna Tope, Martin Duncan and Peter Benson. They were appearing at the Plymouth Arts Centre in John Arden's *Armstrong's Last Goodnight*.

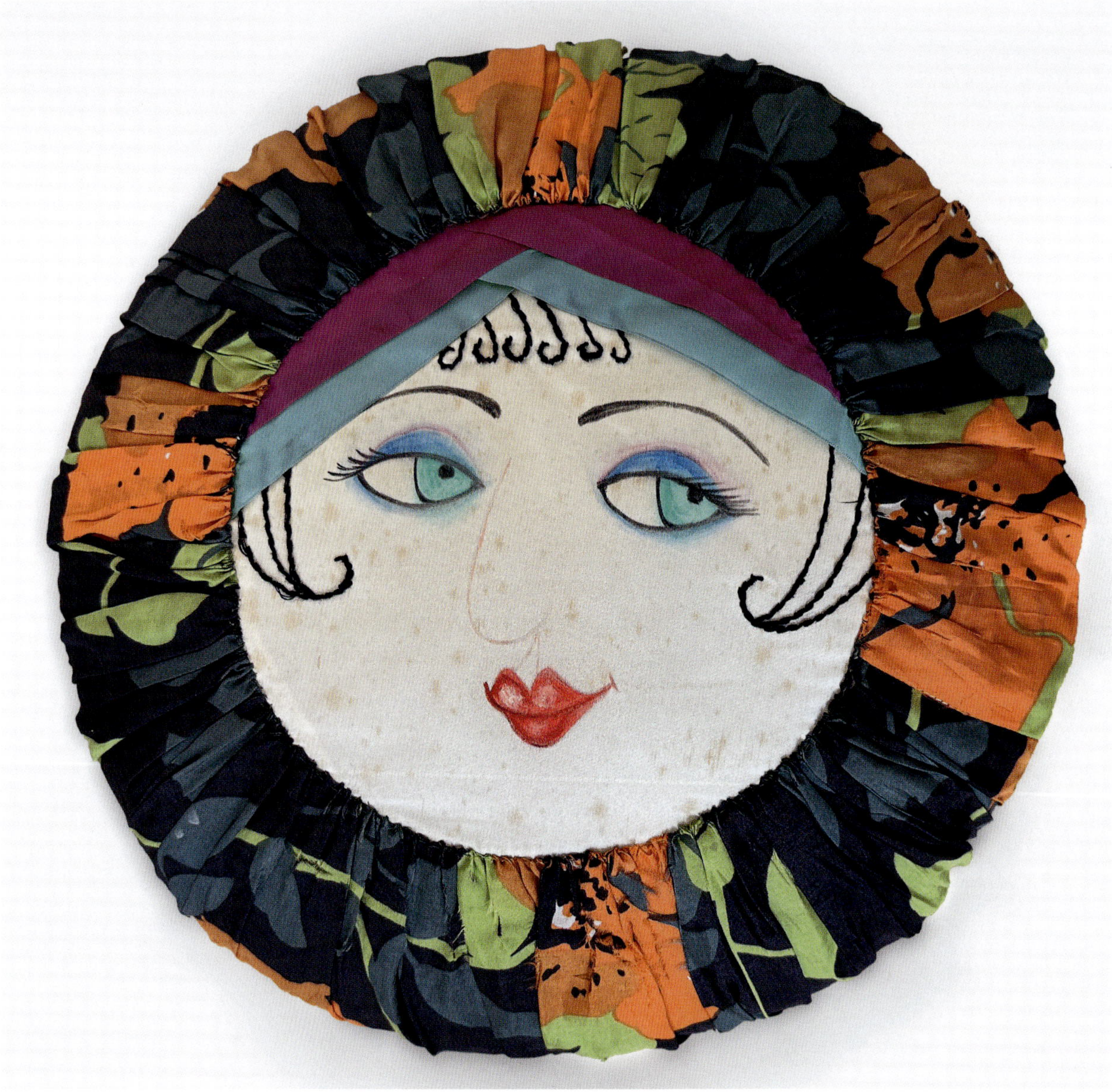

Cushion
(c 1968). The design reflects Beryl's love of art deco.

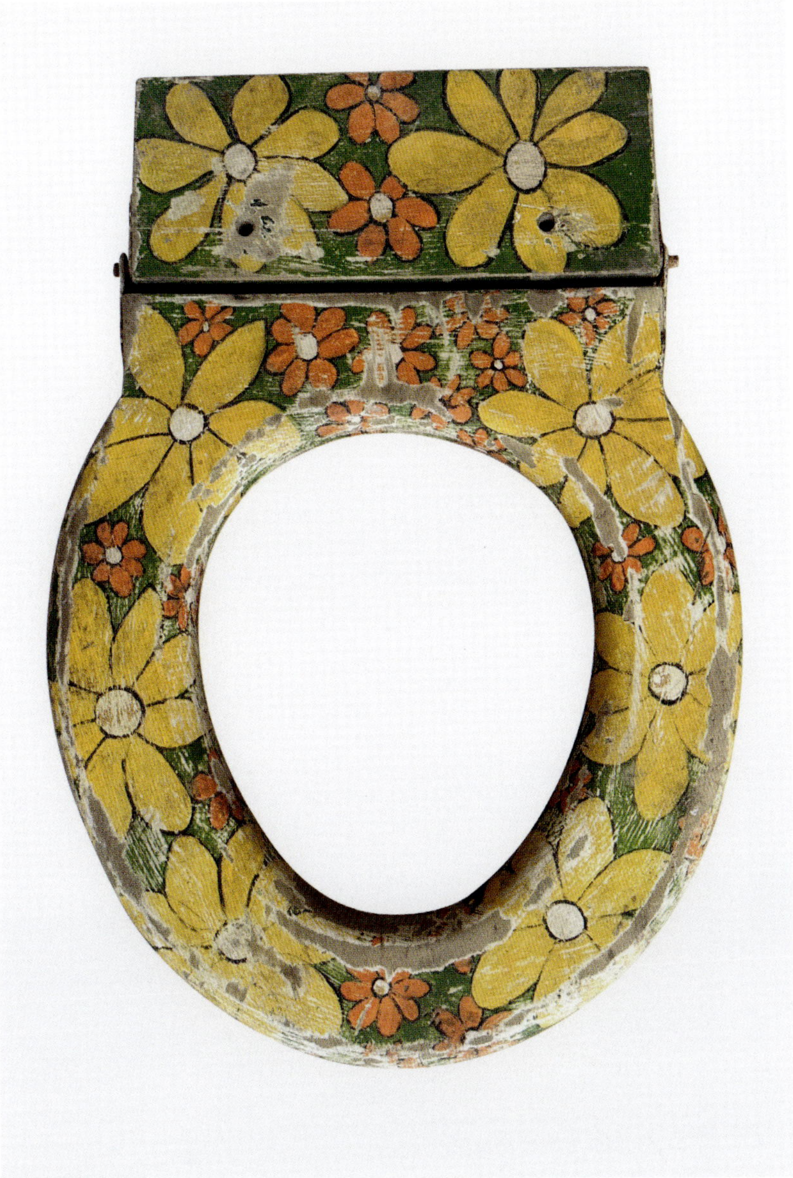

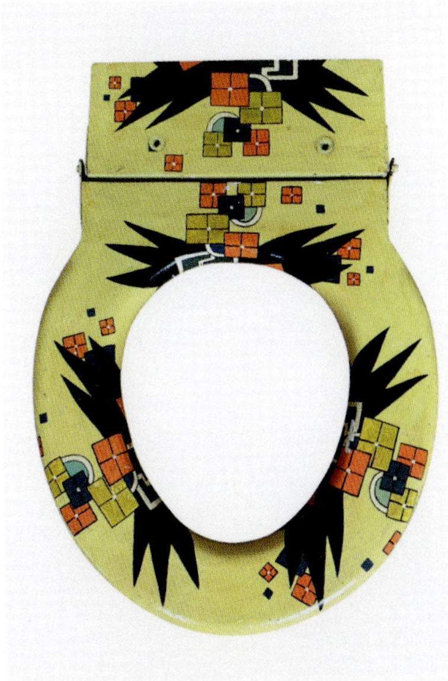

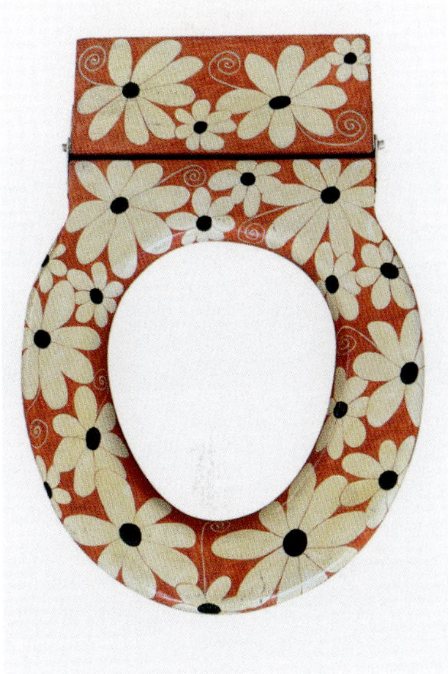

Toilet seats
(1970s). When she ran out of panels, Beryl would resort
to painting on toilet seats.

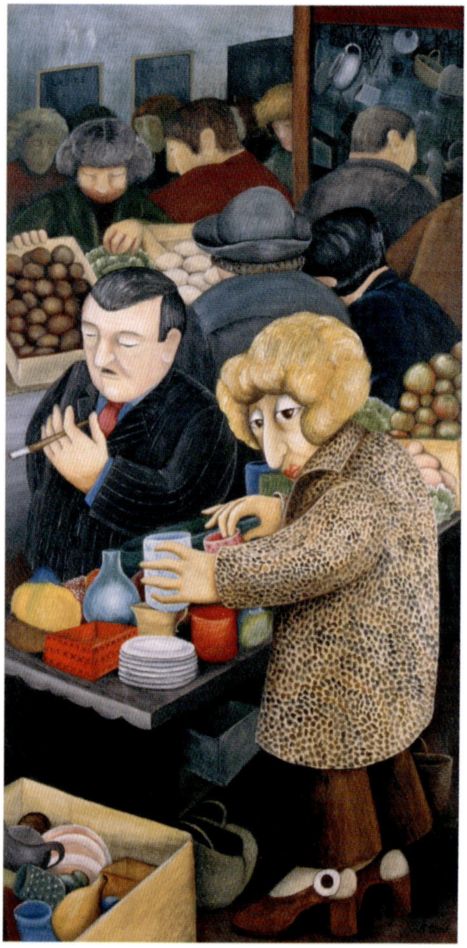

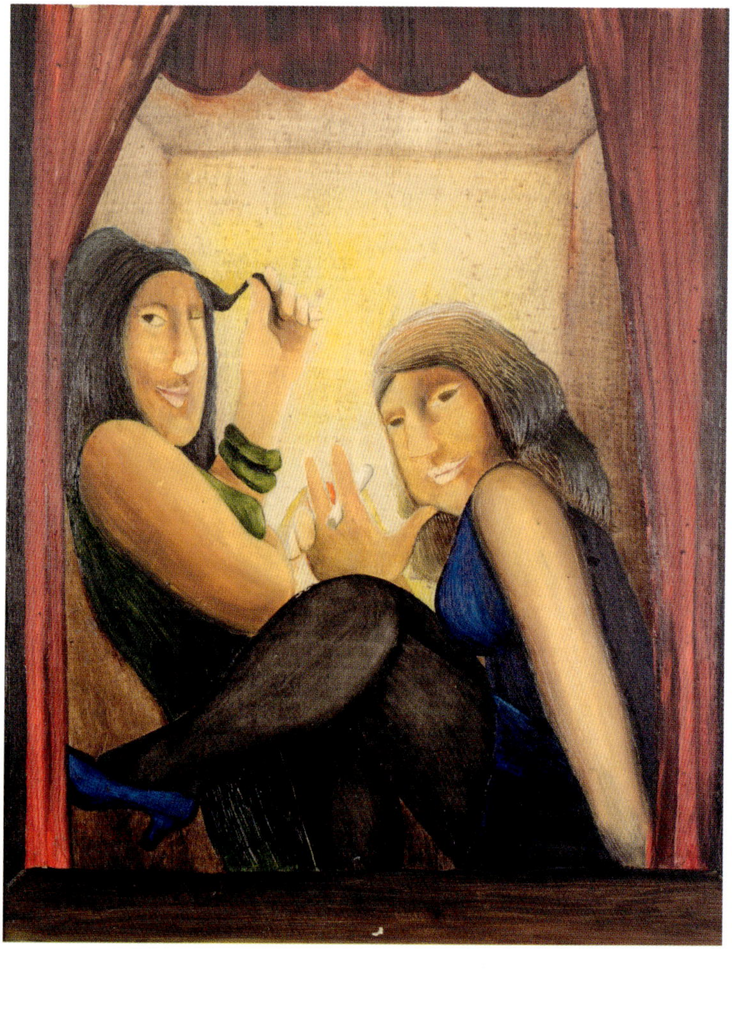

The Pannier Market
(c 1975). One of Beryl's favourite stalls is featured here: bric-a-brac. The Pannier Market still exists and is well worth visiting.

Red-light District
(1975). An interviewer later wrote, 'When she goes on holiday, to places like Paris or Amsterdam, she takes a special interest in the red-light district. She doesn't always like what she sees, but she likes to see it.'[5]

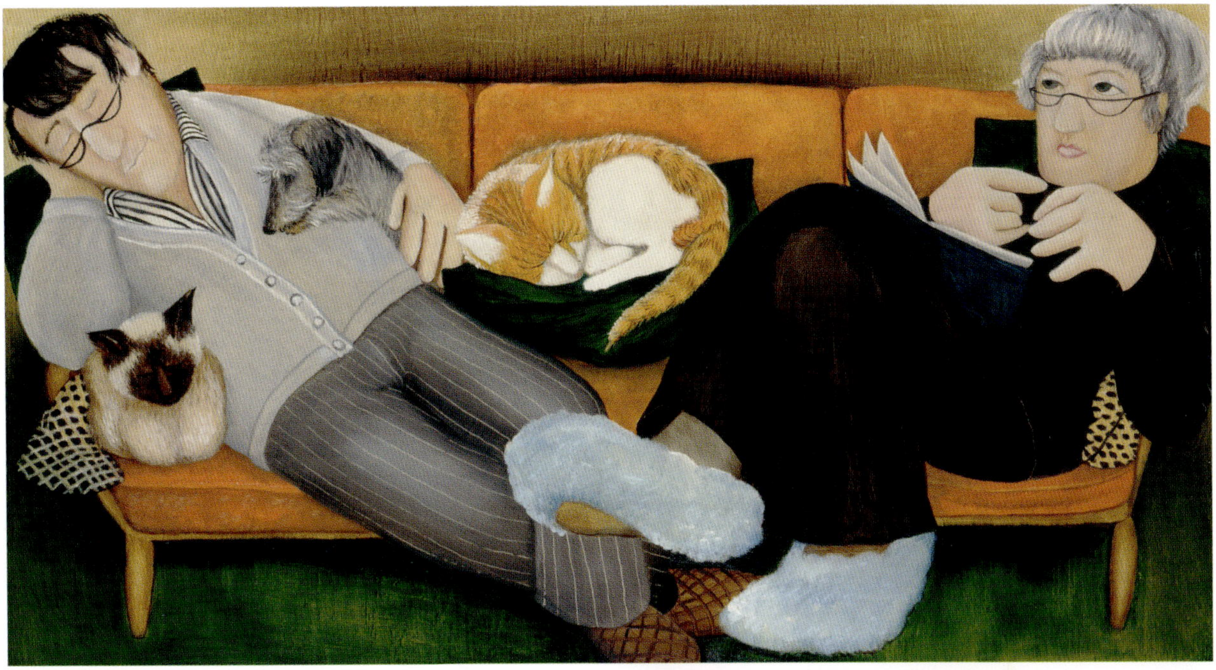

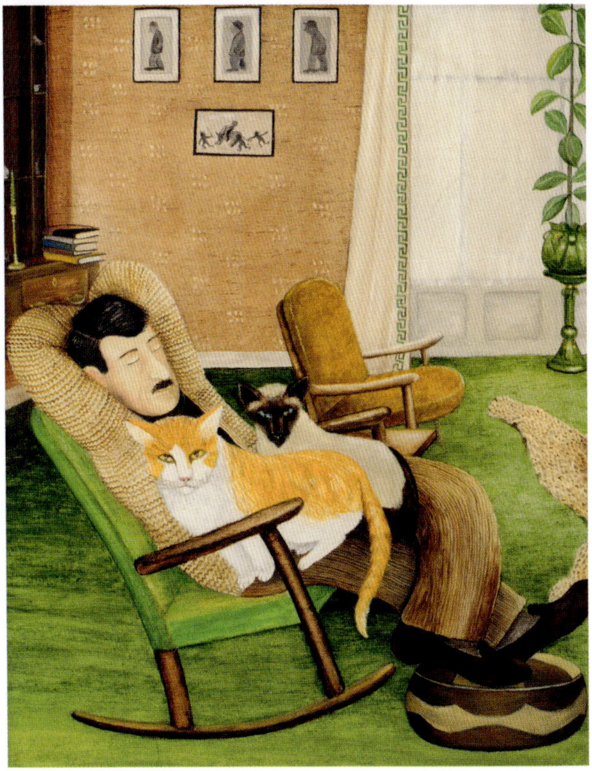

Watching Television
(1973). Beryl's hands were never still, unless she was asleep. As well as watching TV, she would be reading or knitting. If she ran out of knitting, she might unravel an earlier project and re-knit it.

John and Cats at Athenaeum Street
(c 1970). The green carpet and leopard rug were brought from the cottage in Looe. The three pictures in the top row on the wall are *Vanity Fair* 'Spy' cartoons. Cedric (ginger) was not very clever, perhaps because he had an oddly shaped head.

Joanna was a frequent visitor to the Plymouth Arts Centre, ten minutes' walk away from the B&B. She mentioned Beryl's work several times to its director, Bernard Samuels. When he telephoned, Beryl was polite and willing for Bernard to visit, but in no hurry to suggest a date. Eventually the fact that the centre was holding an open exhibition prompted him to try again. John brought in the painting later titled *Sabotage* (see page 69). Bernard was welcomed at Glanville House where he saw almost everything, apart from those paintings in Tony Martin's windows, and some saucy private paintings. He wrote:

> I soon became very keen to show the work. Mrs Cook on the other hand was diffident in the extreme. She seemed very apprehensive about possible public reaction to an exhibition. There was a number of sexually explicit jokes in the pictures I saw and I had premonitions of rather silly publicity.[6]

Eventually Bernard quashed his fears, and persuaded Beryl to go ahead by saying that that it would be her only way of getting all her work out and seeing it in one place. She agreed, on the proviso that there was no publicity, no catalogue, no hand outs and certainly no private view. John crammed the pictures into the boot of his car – not the way art should be moved. Some had jerry-made frames, some were without frames at all, some had been painted on both sides or nailed to the wall, none was glazed, and all were of varied shape and size. The exhibition was very difficult to hang, and complicated by the inclusion of objects such as a pair of cinema seats painted by Beryl, a sculpted head under a dome, garden ornaments, embroideries and plaques. People kept dropping in as word got round even before the opening. The exhibition, The Collected Works of Beryl Cook, opened in November 1975.

Recreating the exhibition would be a puzzle. There is no complete list of exhibits. There are tantalizing photographs of some parts of the exhibition, partial loan lists and some receipts for paintings that were sold. Some excited purchasers wrote to tell Beryl what they had bought and how much it meant to them, or seeking further information. Titles of paintings have changed – *One Bowling Lady Giving Another Bowling Lady a Surprise* is now more snappily titled *Sabotage* (see page 69). But the location and images of many are now unknown. How I would love to see *Two with Shrimps, Parrot and Potty, Man at Door with Child, Thoughtful Schoolgirls* and *Happiness is Egg-shaped*.

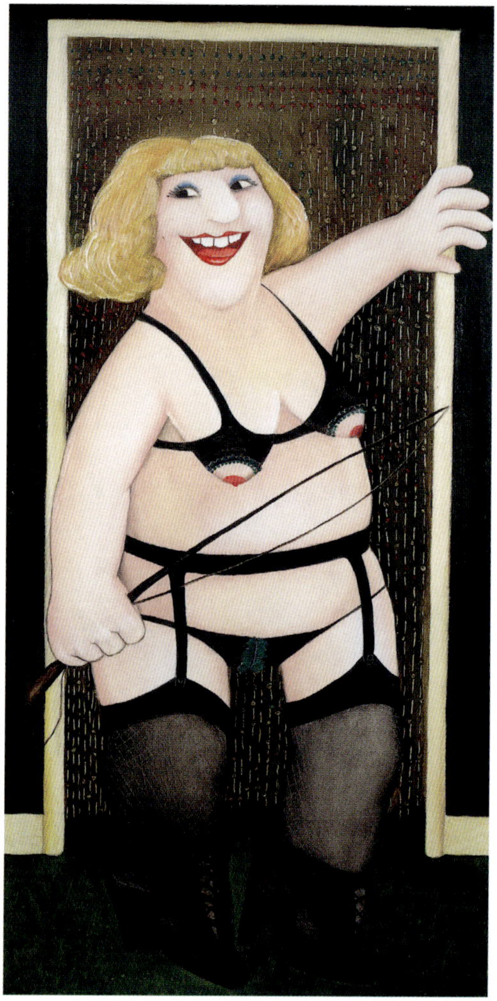

Anyone for a Whipping?
(1972). This was painted for husband John's birthday. He had asked for a great big outrageous nude – and got one.

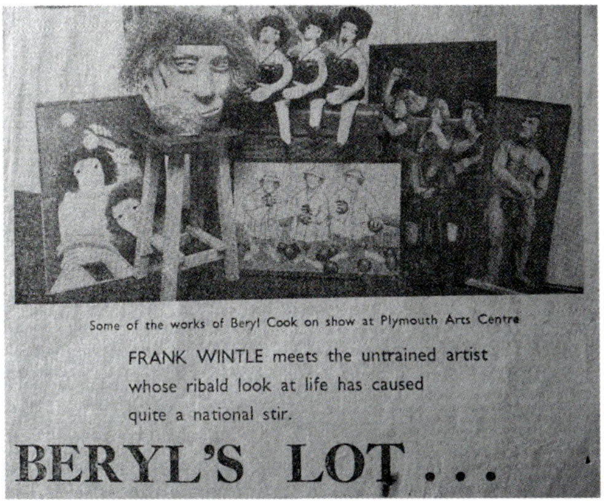
Some of the works of Beryl Cook on show at Plymouth Arts Centre

FRANK WINTLE meets the untrained artist whose ribald look at life has caused quite a national stir.

BERYL'S LOT . . .

An assortment of exhibits, including the *Three Dancing Ladies*, were featured in a *Western Morning News* article, but Beryl refused to be pictured.

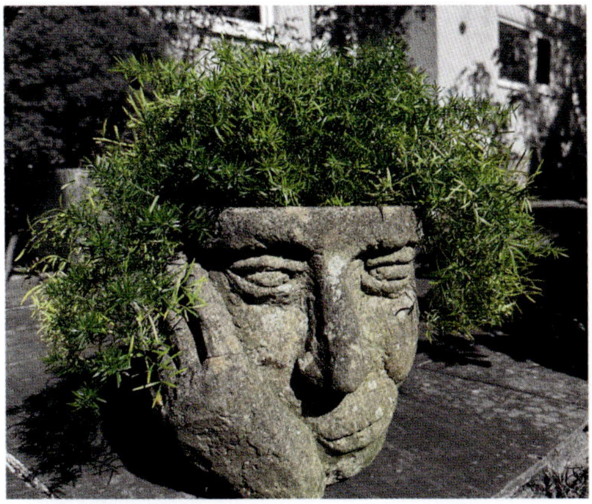

Chive pot (c 1975). The plant pot which featured in the newspaper cutting remains in the family and is used for chives, grass or other suitable hair-like foliage.

Bernard recounted:

> In no time the public were coming in large numbers to look at the exhibition. There were a few who did not take to the work but most were immediately won over. I had never known an exhibition which had generated so much laughter. I had to help one person out of the gallery who was, literally, quite helpless with mirth.[7]

Beryl was very reluctant to sell her pictures, but she did need the space to produce more. As a compromise, the right-hand side of the room was hung with ones she wished to keep. The ones on the left-hand side were for sale for between £30 and £40, with one or two 'daringly' put at £60. The Bank of England inflation calculator gives the 2025 equivalents at £233, £311 and £467 respectively. Some 27 paintings were sold and Beryl started frenziedly painting more to put on the walls. Among the sales were three acquired by the Plymouth City Museum and Art Gallery. Beryl received two thirds of all sales but was then – and forever remained – uninterested in the commercial value of her work.

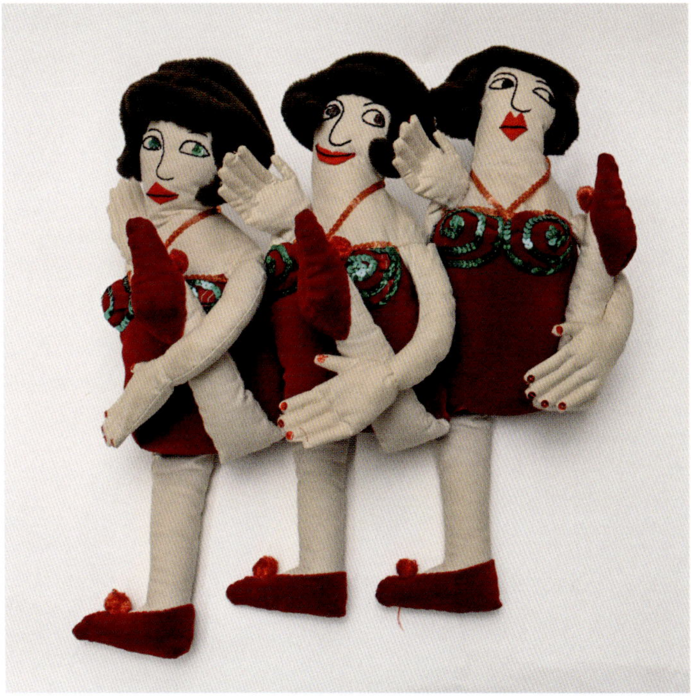

Three Dancing Ladies
(1974). This cushion is made from cloth, velvet and sequins. Unusually for Beryl, she has given the ladies fingernails. It is beautifully made; Beryl was an accomlished seamstress.

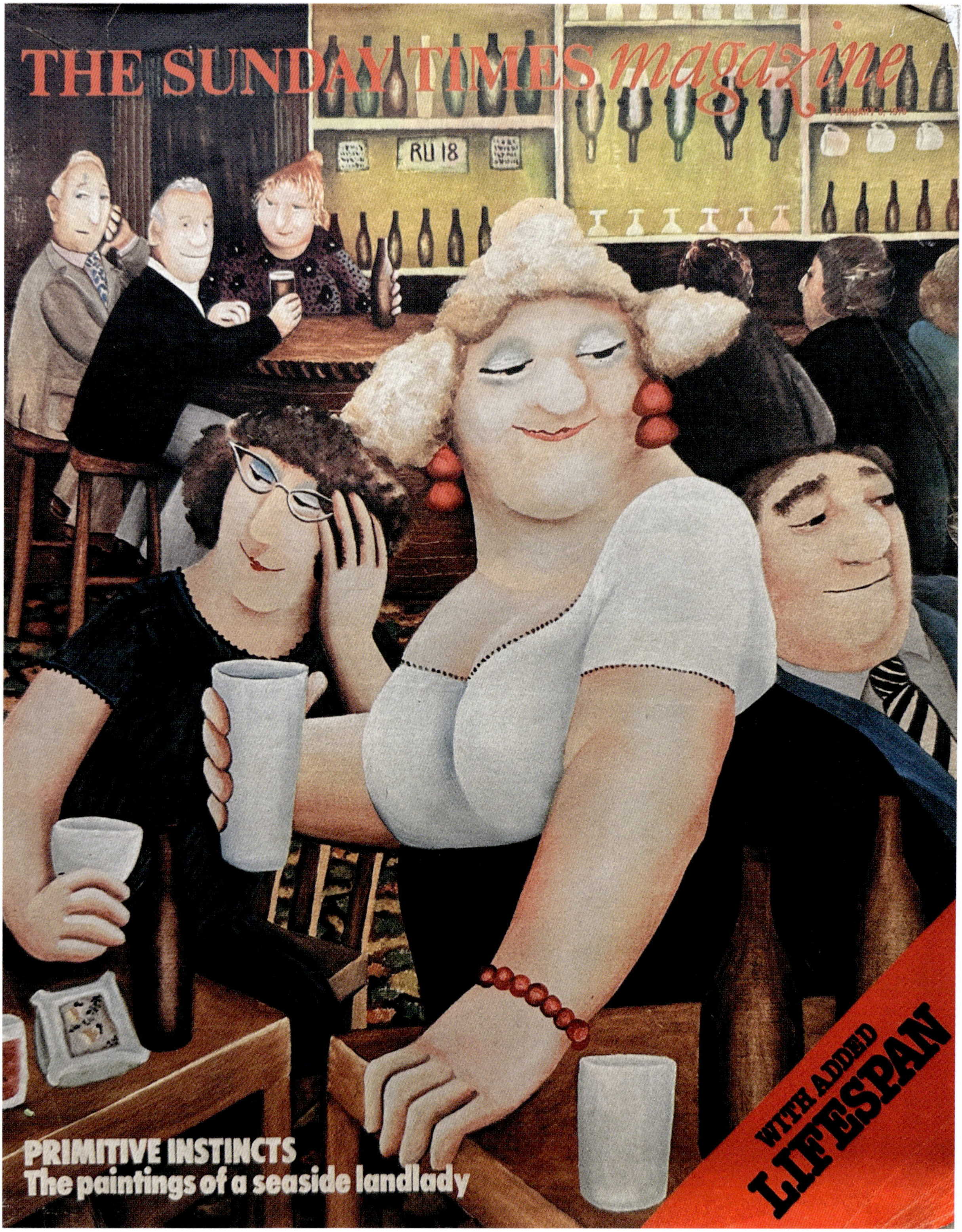

The *Sunday Times* supplement
which changed Beryl's life

Bernard found it impossible to stick to his promise of no publicity. In the first week, Frank Whittle of the *Western Morning News* managed to interview Beryl, but she refused to be photographed. 'I want to preserve my anonymity at all costs,' she said. His article, dated November 21, called the exhibition 'the most extraordinary ever to have graced the walls of the Plymouth Arts Centre' and described Beryl as 'a discovery in every sense of the word.'[8]

The Guardian's West Country theatre critic Allen Saddler had been visiting the theatre to see the American comic Ray Hassett, who was late, so Saddler wandered upstairs to where Bernard Samuels was hanging the exhibition. His short review appeared on 25 November 1975. These were not Beryl's first published reviews. *The Cornish Times* published a short piece as early as November 1972 reporting that it had acquired two large works by Beryl, whom they christened 'the Looe Wonderwoman'. One they had found by chance in Liskeard – where John and Teresa were at that time living – and then they had snuffled out the second. Unfortunately, few people read *The Cornish Times* so they were unaware of its scoop.

A piece on local television followed the *Guardian* article. Saddler also wrote for *The Sunday Times*, and he arranged for them to do a picture spread in their *Sunday Magazine*. Their feature writer George Perry and photographer Nick Mason came down to Plymouth and were so bowled over they bought works for themselves. Allen Saddler interviewed Beryl and 'Primitive Instincts, the paintings of a seaside landlady' made the front page of *The Sunday Times Magazine* on 6 February 1976.

Bernard wrote, 'Our phone rang for weeks. Letters came in from all over the world. The great and famous pleaded for pictures of which there were no longer any for sale. There was a constant flow of enquiries from dealers and the media, which went on for several years.'[9] Beryl's wish for anonymity was well and truly thwarted.

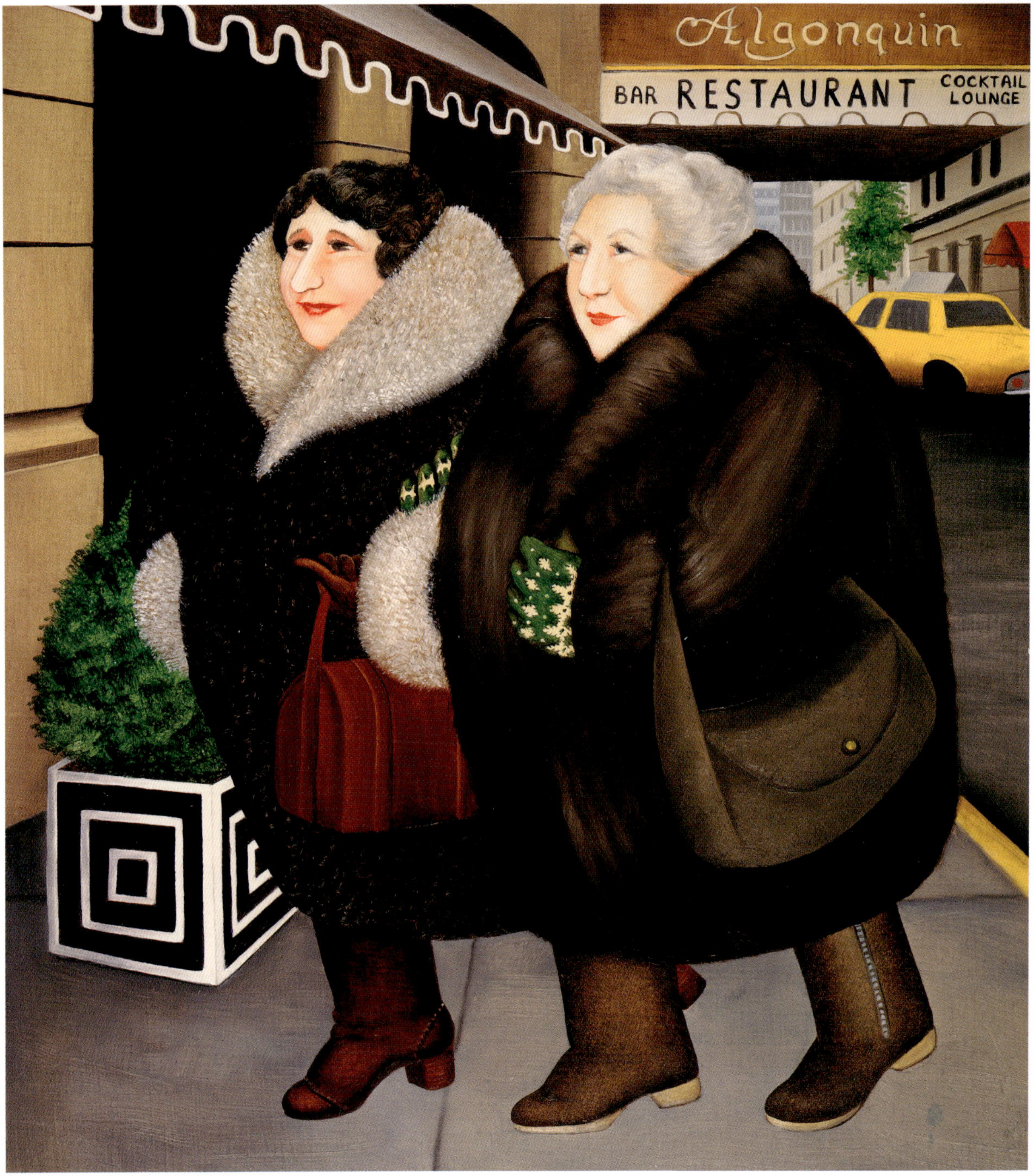

Bar & Barbara

(1984). This painting of Barbara Key-Seymer (right) and her partner Bar Roett is how Beryl imagined their arrival at the Algonquin, the famous hotel. Bar's aunt had died and left a Persian lamb coat, a mink coat and all her jewellery to a friend in New York and Beryl portrays them delivering the bequest. The Algonquin was a suitable location as in the 1920s it had hosted a circle of writers, critics, actors and wits, including Dorothy Parker, Tallulah Bankhead and Noel Coward.

05

Overnight Success & Lifelong Friendships

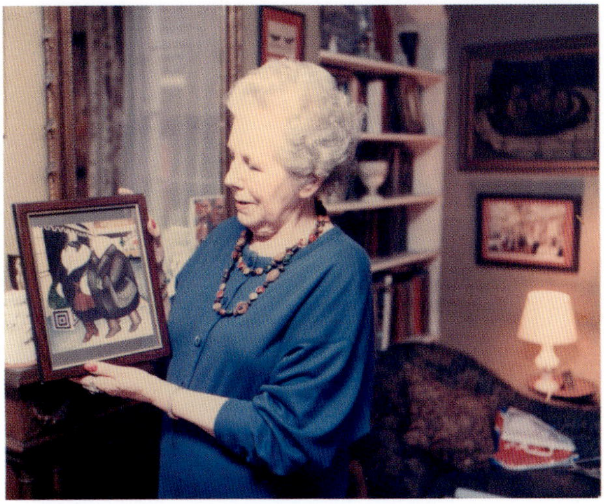

Barbara proudly displays *Barbara and Bar,* gifted to her by Beryl.

The five-page colour article and cover illustration in *The Sunday Times Magazine* on 6 February 1976 caused a sensation. With a circulation of 1,382,000[1] many people would have eaten their weekend breakfast confronted by the brightly coloured painting of a buxom woman in the front bar of the Lockyer Tavern. Some no doubt choked on their toast, but the majority were enchanted and amused – at least one person laughed so much that they fell out of bed.

Beryl had painted everything in the exhibition for herself and her family and friends. Thanks to her astonishing visual memory, people she had seen in the pubs, clubs and on the Hoe had no idea they had been immortalized – she didn't need to set up an easel. Very nervously, Beryl took an advance copy of *The Sunday Times Magazine* into the Lockyer to see what they thought. The result was electric. 'Joyce, who was in the background, nearly went berserk. She thought it was absolutely marvellous, and she also rang up Liz and Mac who were also in the picture and got them to come in . . . they absolutely loved it to our great relief.'[2]

From then on, unless the person had asked or agreed to be portrayed, she changed their appearance in the paintings. This didn't stop many people claiming to recognize themselves or others, mostly to their great pleasure. And a surprising number of people have claimed to know Nigel, the subject of the graffiti in *Eating Chips in a Municipal Shelter.*

Allen Sadler's article is written with style and panache. It conveys Beryl's sense of humour and sources of subject matter, both innocent and vulgar. Moreover, it established a set of facts about Beryl that was to be repeated ever after. She is a seaside landlady, a 'new and original primitive painter'. Her early life included a 'miserable, self-conscious season as a chorus girl'. She produced her first painting, *Hangover*, in Rhodesia (see page 21). She is painfully shy and she worries.

One painting featured in the article was *Wedding Photograph*. Fifty years after this was painted, Terah Walkup (curator of art at The Box, Plymouth) tracked down the bride who said that the groom was wearing a wig, which would have delighted Beryl. The family were Maltese and many of the guests flew over specially. The painting became part of Bernard Samuel's own collection, and was bequeathed by him to The Box.

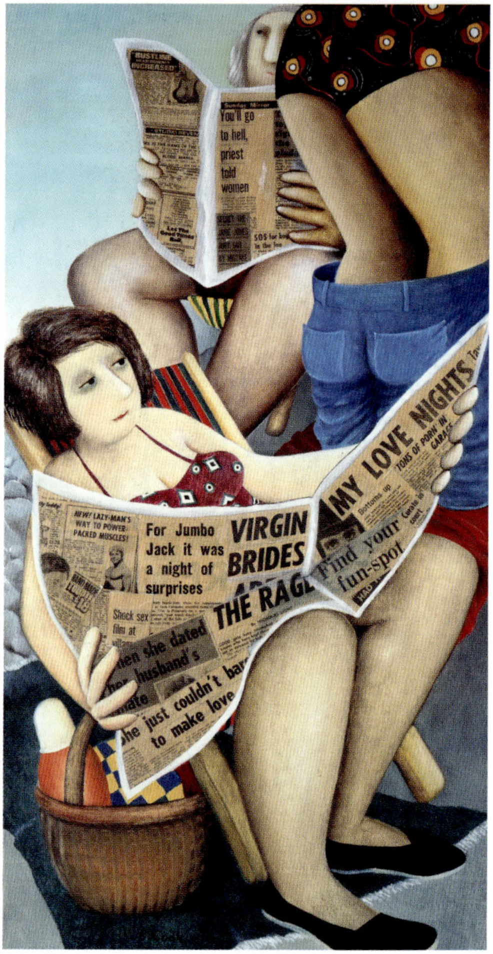

Reading the Sunday Papers
(1973). This picture was owned by Beryl and John's friend, Tony Martin, and then acquired by The Box, Plymouth City Council.

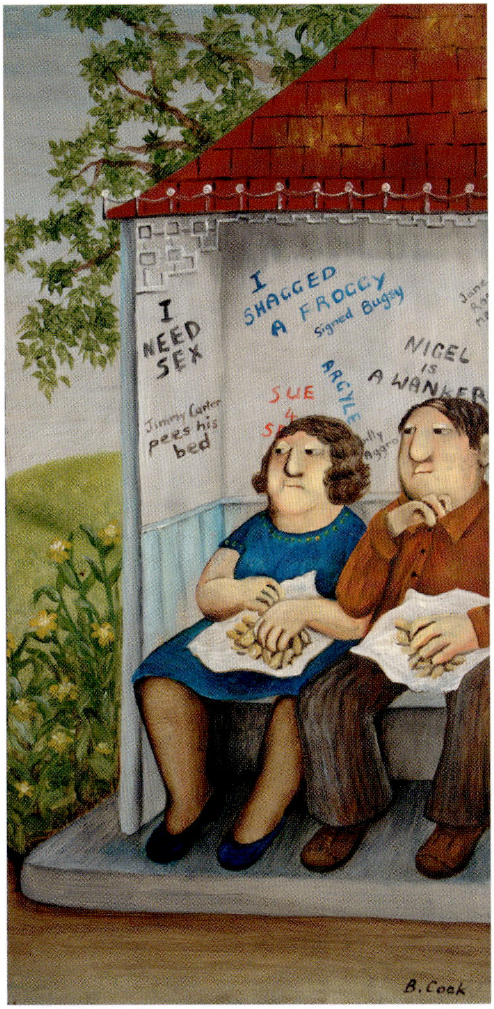

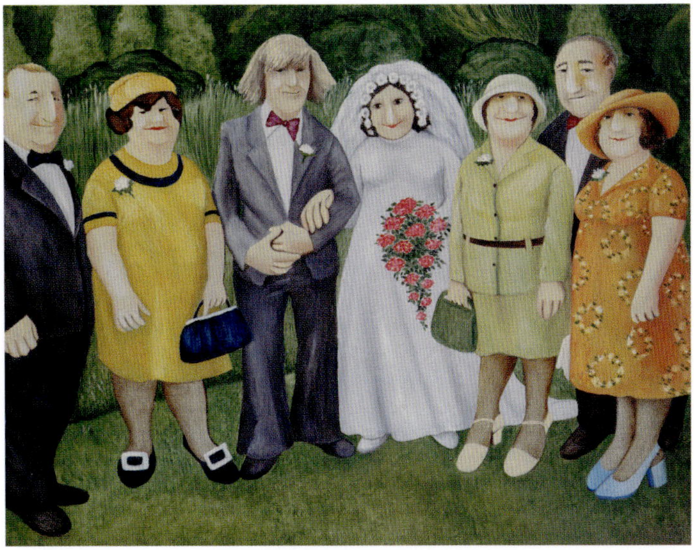

Eating Chips in a Municipal Shelter
(c 1975). All the graffitti shown is authentic.

Wedding Photograph
(1975). This was based on a photograph in the local paper.

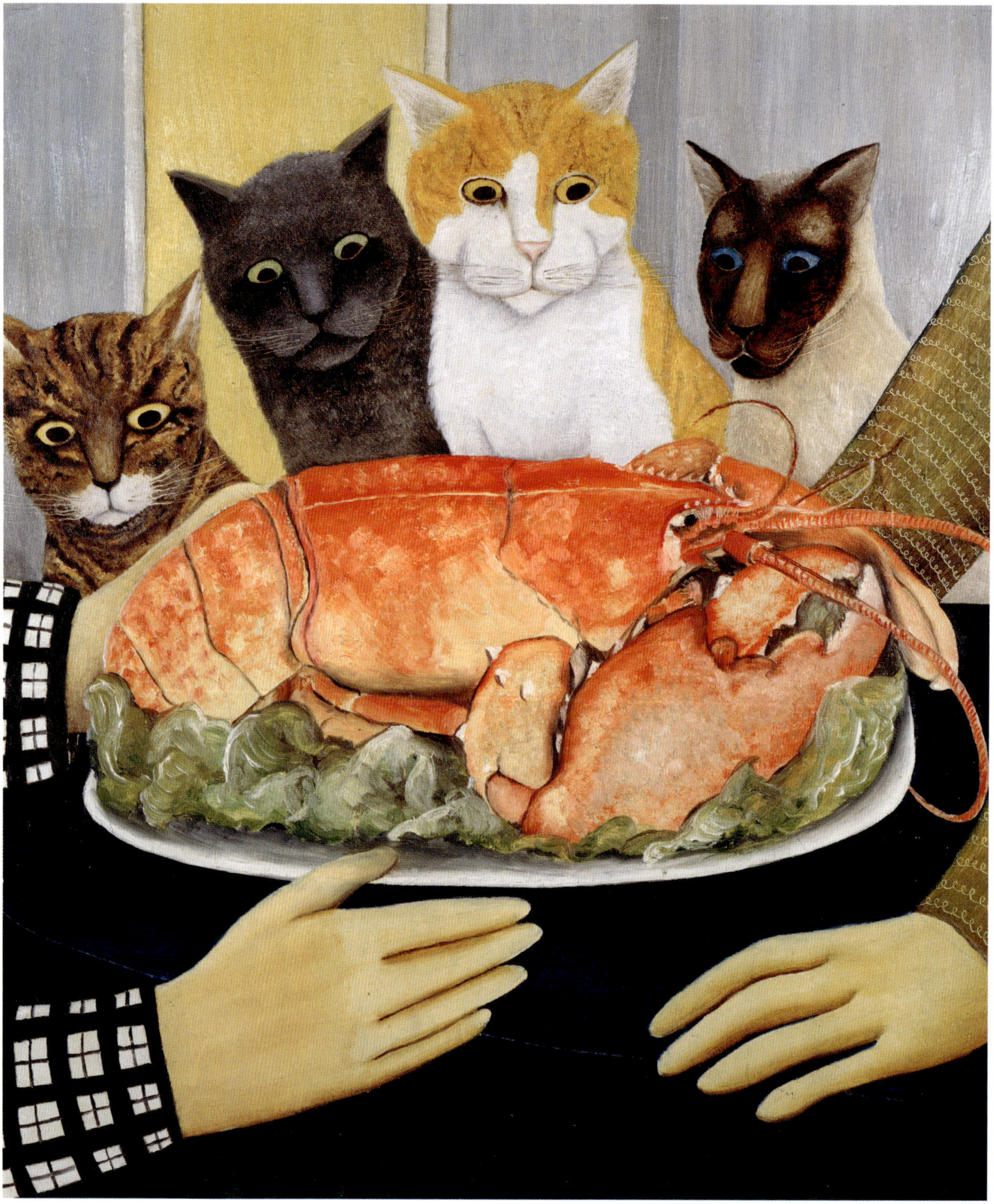

Four Hungry Cats

(c 1975). From left to right: Nipper, from next door, and Smokey, Cedric and Lottie, John and Beryl's cats. John Senior was very fond of seafood, and Teresa bought this lobster for his birthday. It was so huge they had to cook it in the twin tub washing machine.

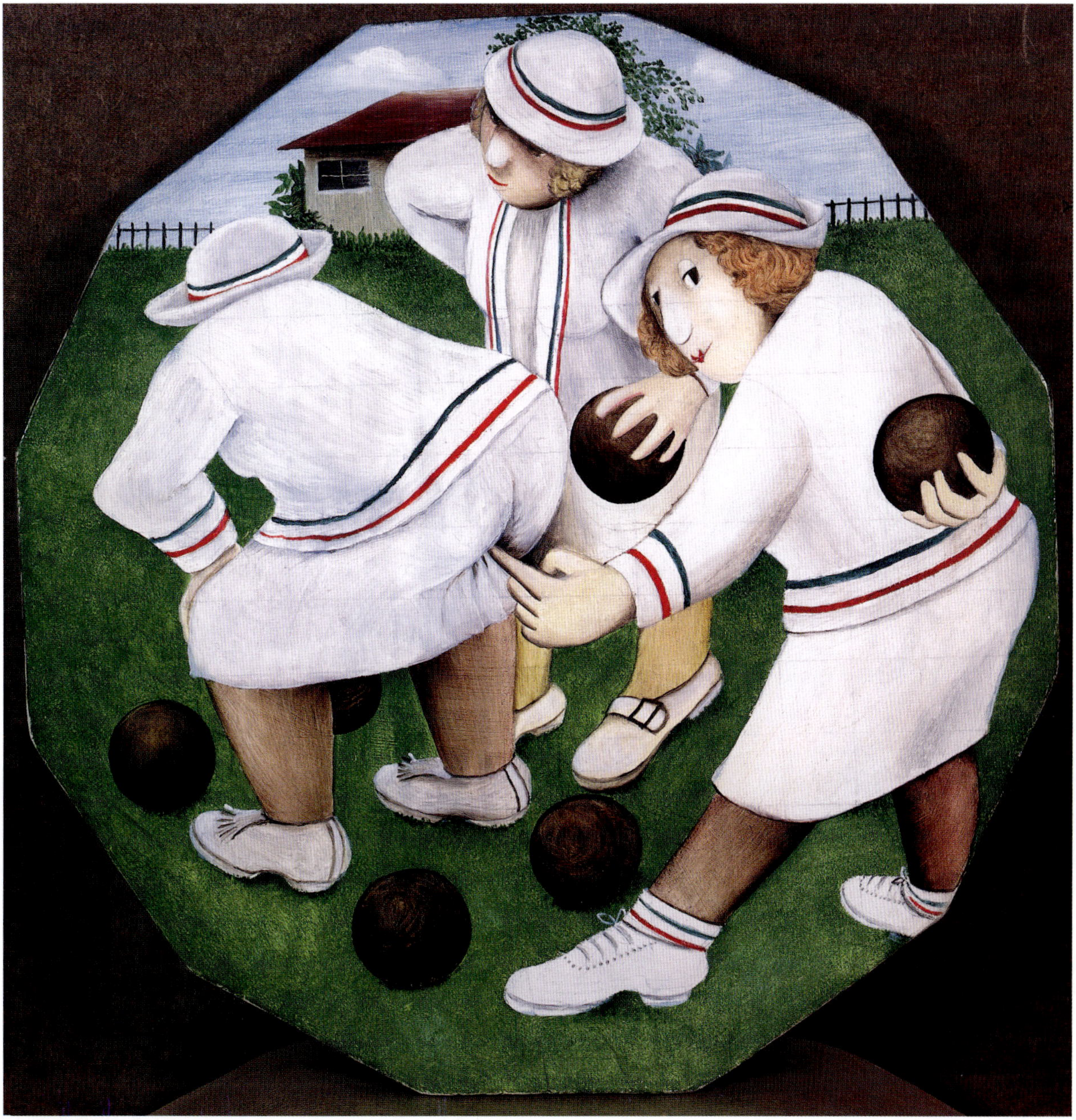

One Bowling Lady Giving Another Bowling Lady a Surprise
(1974). Oil on breadboard. This picture is now rather more snappily known as *Sabotage*.

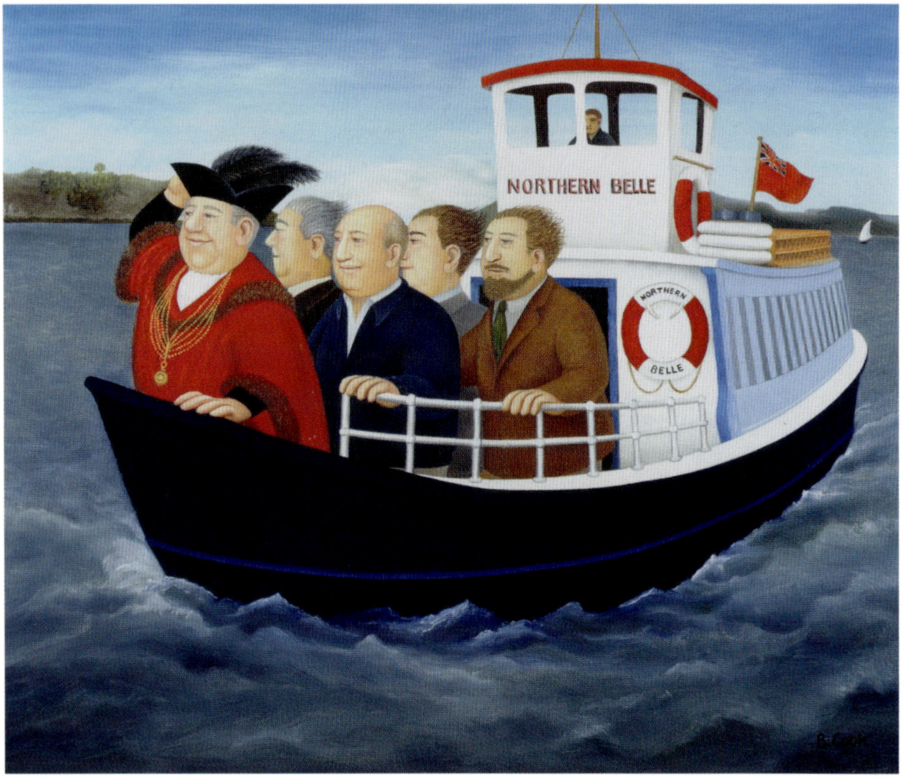

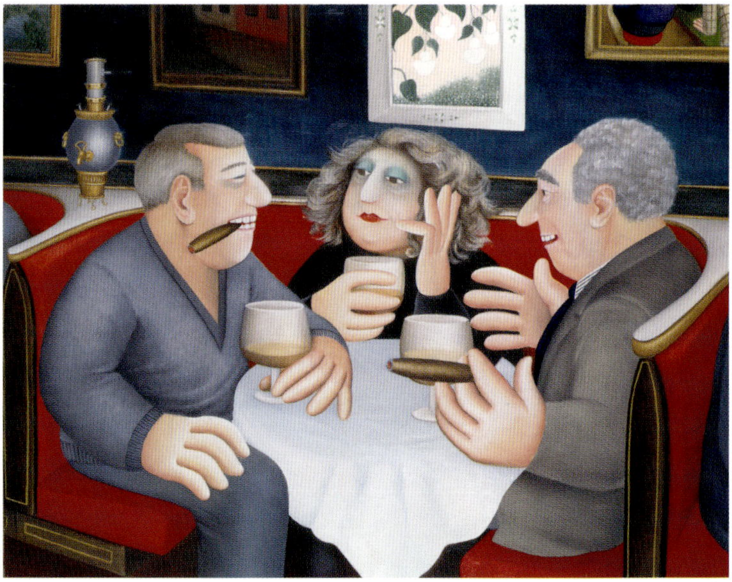

Going Towards Art
(1990). Bernard is in blue behind the Mayor, and they are taking the passenger ferry across the Tamar to Mount Edgcumbe to see an underground installation that formed part of a city-wide art project.

The Russian Tea Room
(1983). The Russian Tea Room, owned by Faith Stewart-Gordon, was famous for its intellectual clientele such as Leonard Bernstein and Dustin Hoffman. Beryl's paintings joined the art collection on the walls.

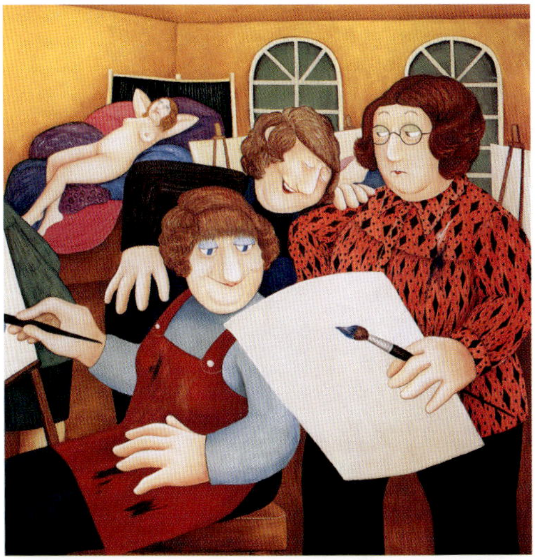

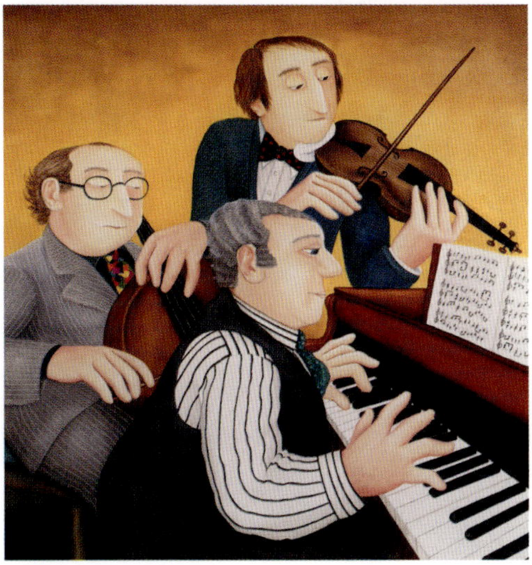

Other paintings really appealed to readers. Letters began to flood in, enquiring whether the paintings were still available to purchase. *Four Hungry Cats* (see page 68), *Sabotage* (see page 69) and *Eating Chips in a Municipal Shelter* (see page 67) were particularly in demand.

Even more people wanted to know where the paintings could be seen now that the exhibition had closed. Fortunately, staff at the Whitechapel Gallery in East London had also seen the article, and wanted to recreate the exhibition as a matter of urgency, due to uncertainty as to whether the newly appointed incoming Director – Nicholas Serota, later Director of the Tate – would approve.[3] The Whitechapel exhibition ran from 23 April to 14 May 1976.

Beryl never forgot what she owed to Bernard Samuels, Tony Martin and Joanna Tope. All were life-long friends. Beryl also supported the Plymouth Arts Centre by donating works for them to sell for fundraising, and she painted them a wonderful sign which for many years hung outside their premises in Looe Street.

Another early lifelong friend was Faith Stewart-Gordon, who ran the famous Russian Tea Room in New York for more than 30 years. She saw the article and wrote immediately. On her next trip to London, she came down to Plymouth by train and bought two paintings right away. She wrote, 'I was crazy about Beryl and John from the moment we met. They are two pixies with a fey sense of humour, a generous spirit, a droll manner and a shyness that's endearing.'[4]

By now, demand for paintings was so great that Beryl was able to give up the B&B and use one of the bedrooms as her studio to paint full time. John Senior moved his job from Bodmin to Allen's Vauxhall Dealership, very near their house, and he and John Junior were pressed willingly into service to help answer queries and fan letters. These increased in number enormously in 1979 when ITV's *The South Bank Show* featured her work. The fan letters and draft replies have all been kept, including the following, life-changing exchange:

Art Class and *Musicians* (c 1980), the two sides of the sign Beryl painted for Plymouth Arts Centre

March 26, 1979

Dear Mrs Cook

I am writing to say how very much I enjoyed the programme on you and your paintings on *The South Bank Show* last night. I was most interested when they showed a painting of Edward Burra's on the screen and said that your paintings resembled his.

I was a really close friend of Edward Burra from the time we were at Art School together, until his recent death. When I first saw your paintings reproduced in *The Observer* supplement I was very taken with them and thought at once of Edward and how much he would enjoy them, so took the copy of *The Observer* down to Rye where he lived. He was delighted and loved the paintings. There were some reproductions recently of the cards made by Gallery 5, and a fellow art student of ours rang me up from Birmingham and said she'd seen them and said 'I'm sure Edward would have loved that ladies [sic] paintings,' so I sent her one of your cards (the Picnic) which I bought in Cambridge of all places, and told her that Edward had indeed been a great admirer of your work. You may never have seen his early paintings which are mostly in private collections. I think you must look at things with the same eye.

I simply love your paintings, which of course I have seen at the Portal Galleries [see Chapter 6]. They are absolutely fresh and straightforward and quite unique, and what is more, they can be really funny. I was laughing out loud last night. I think if you did a series of postcards (the ones that have been done are marvellous, but cost 25p, rather too much for ordinary postcard buyers) what I call 'seaside postcards' they would be a terrific success, and unlike Donald McGill, would need no captions, as they are witty enough as they are.

I do wish you every success, and hope you will go on giving us pleasure for many more years.

Best wishes from Barbara Ker-Seymer

This was Beryl's reply:

I am writing straight away to tell you of the immense pleasure your letter gave me when I received it from Lionel (Portal Galleries) this morning. I didn't know a great deal about Edward Burra until I bought a small book by John Rothenstein about three years ago when I saw immediately that it is exactly how I would like to paint, were I capable of doing it. Not only did I love the paintings but he seemed to be such an appealing man, and I rushed to get the book as soon as I got your letter and

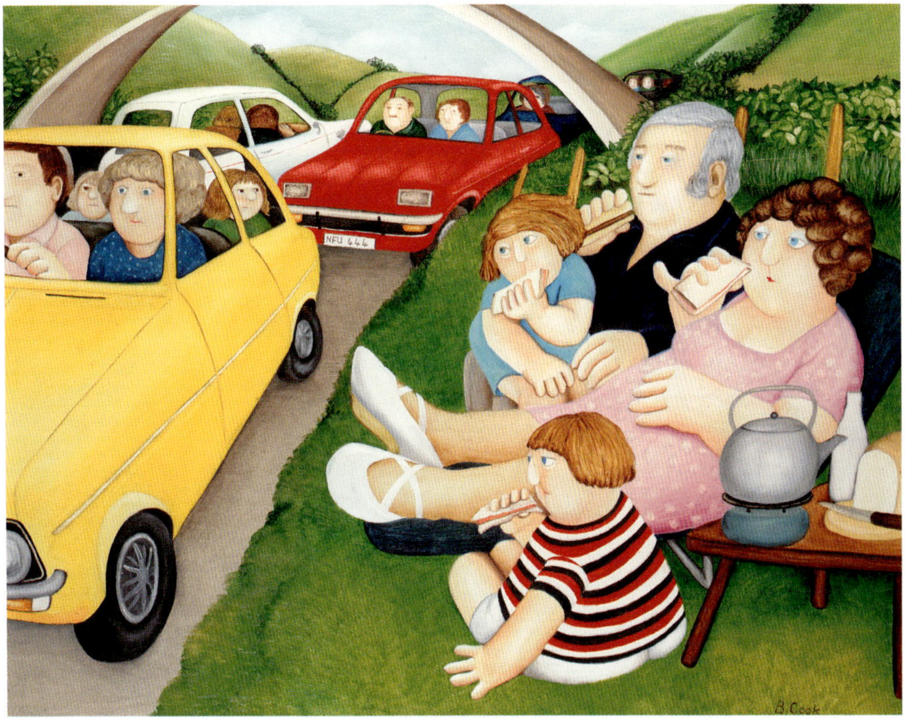

Picnic

(c 1977). In 1980 Beryl wrote to Barbara on a Gallery Five card of this painting to say how much the past year's correspondence meant to her: 'I'm forever troubled by lack of confidence and somehow you have put it all into perspective for me.'

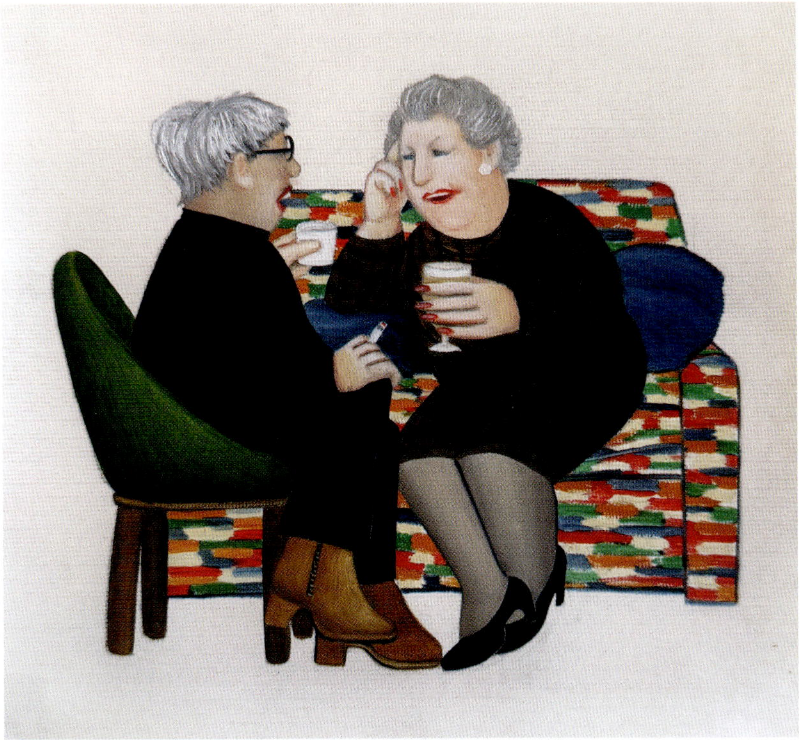

Untitled

(c 1982). Beryl and Barbara chatting, created especially for Barbara. Barbara was rather deaf and Beryl disliked using the phone, so when they were not together they preferred to write to each other. Beryl pointed out that she had – for once – painted her nails for Barbara.

> re-read his correspondence to you. I had been feeling rather harassed about the quantity of mail and calls I get until I saw your letter and I knew in a flash that everything is worth it in return for the pleasure and excitement other people bring to me. I do thank you for writing also for telling me you had shown Edward Burra the magazine, I feel I can go upstairs and tackle a large painting of 'Tescos' now with renewed vigour!

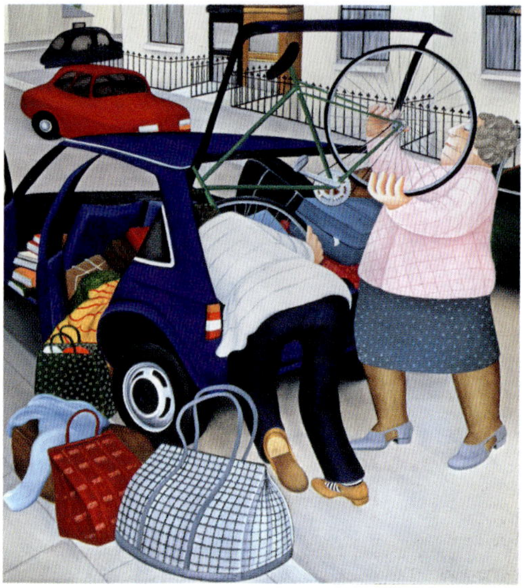

Packing the Car
(c 1988). Barbara and Bar packing their car outside their home in London. In her caption for this painting, Beryl points out the large pile of books 'ready to fall off the front seat'. Beryl and Barbara exchanged book recommendations and analysed the books in their letters.

Thus began a long and close friendship. As well as seeing each other regularly, they wrote at least once a week, with additional letters and cards for birthdays and during illnesses. Even when either was abroad the letters continued, despite the vagaries of the post. The result is in effect a diary kept by both, with Beryl frequently telling of her difficulties in painting, nervousness about being interviewed or filmed, and which paintings she is working on. Barbara in turn describes her daily life – far more social than Beryl – and the doings of her partner Barbara (known as Bar) Roett. A generation older than Beryl, she had been one of the Bright Young Things and a gifted and vivacious professional photographer: her subjects included Evelyn Waugh, Margot Fonteyn, Jean Cocteau and Vita Sackville-West. Her friends were a bohemian, free-thinking and free-loving network of actors, dancers and artists. Her reminiscences are quite eye opening, and often very funny. To be admired and supported by someone with this background and art knowledge was very special to Beryl, who made sure to tell her so in her letters.

Bar Roett returned Beryl's letters when Barbara Ker-Seymer died, and so they were reunited with the other half of the correspondence. Without this archive of nearly fifteen years of letters we would know much less about Beryl Cook the person, as she guarded her private life so carefully.

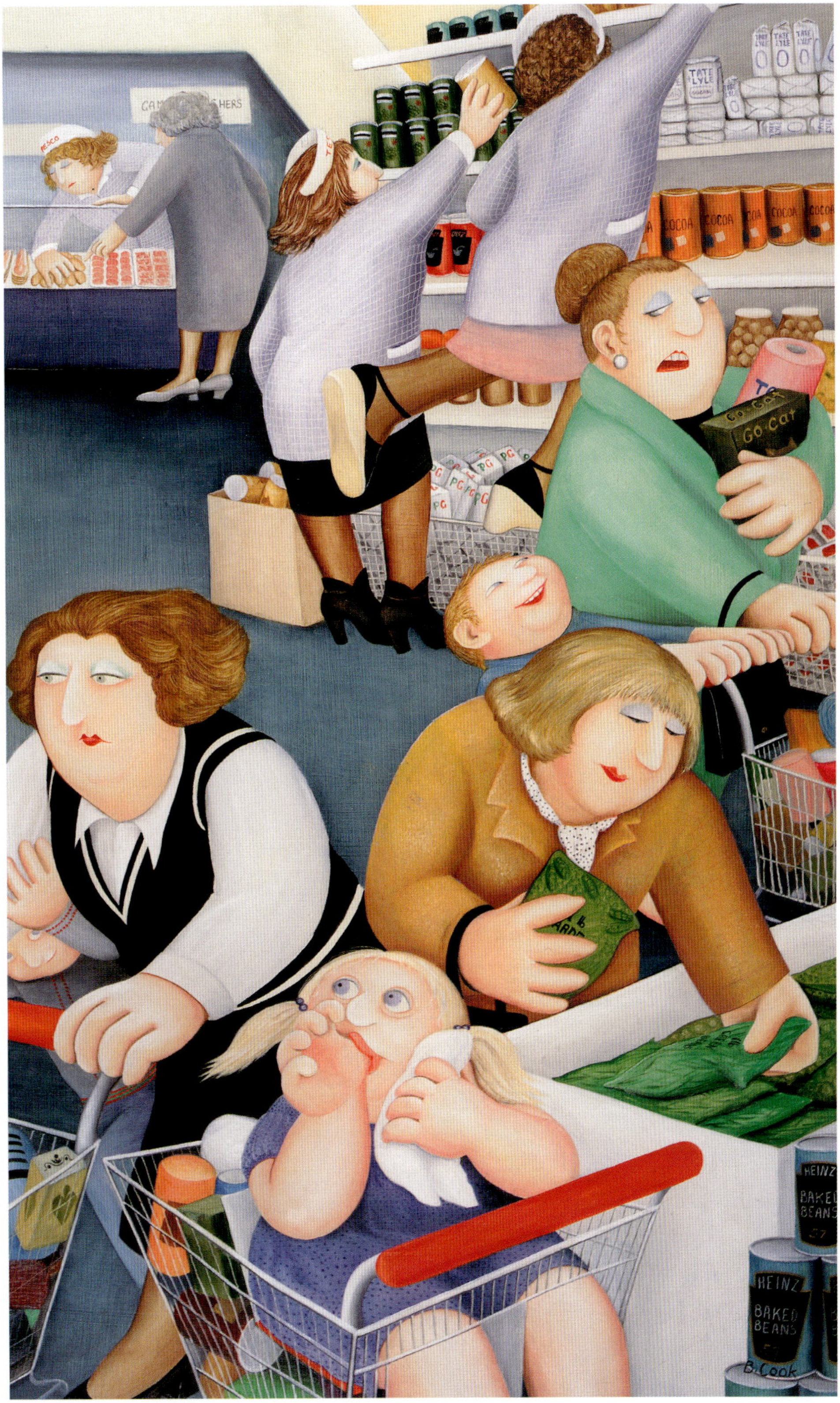

Tesco

(1979). This was probably the painting that Beryl was working on at the time she started her friendship with Barbara Ker-Seymer.

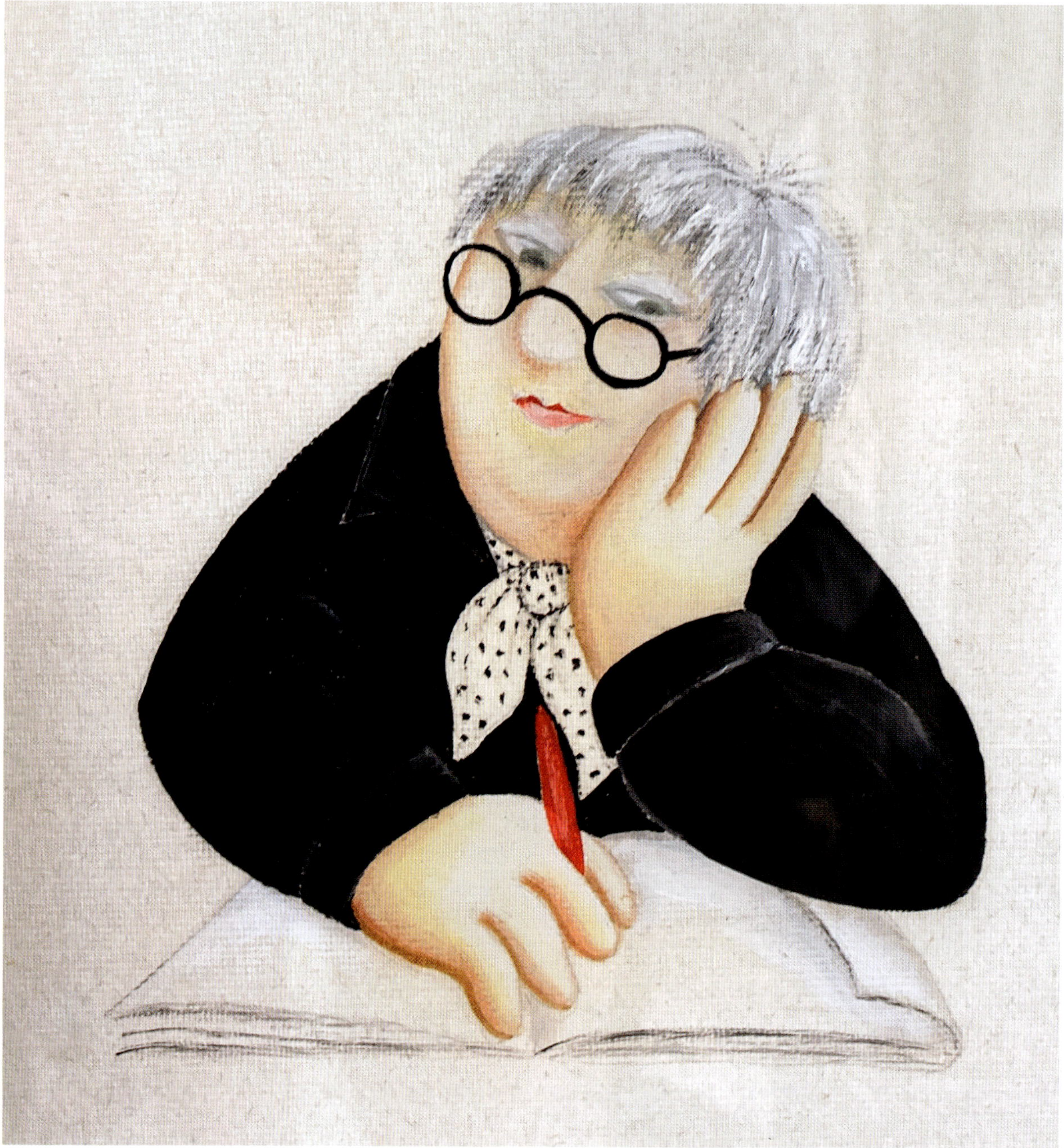

For her book *Private View* (1980), Beryl's self-portrait shows her signing books, which was not an activity she relished. She has shown herself in the sort of clothes she actually wore. Many of these were bought in Littlewoods, which she loved so much that she said she wanted her ashes scattered there. Unfortunately this proved impossible; it closed in 2005.

06

Managing Success

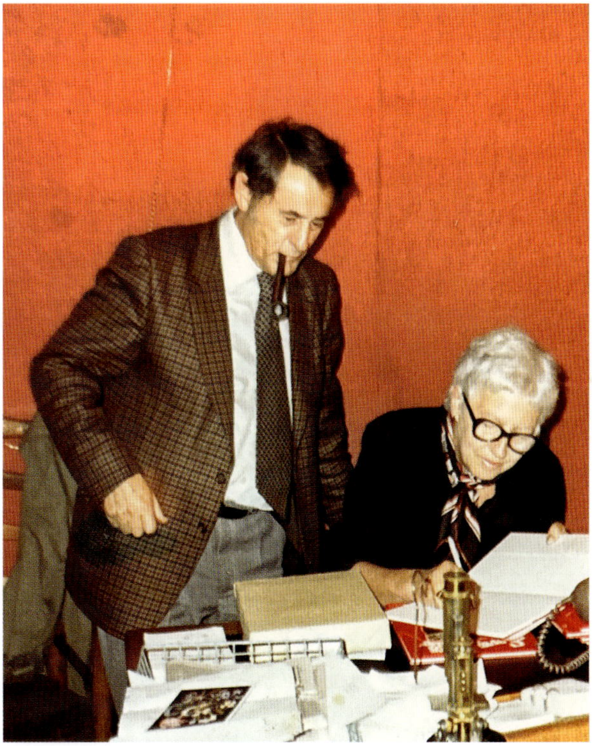

John Senior and Beryl busy with some extensive administration

In 1976 Beryl described herself as bourgeois and as a boarding-house keeper, but fate had decided this would change. *The Daily Mail* said that in 1978 Beryl made £6,000 from her art, the equivalent of £326,895 today[1]. I have no idea if this is true, but in any case, the new level of activity could no longer be run from the kitchen table; it required a network of professionals to meet the demands of would-be owners, the media, potential commissioners and, of course, her fans.

Financial Weekly reported that in the same year:

> [Beryl's] commercial stakes were raised. It must be said that unlike many artists she is not consumed with ideas of wealth, then again she is not complaining. The price of her pictures doubled to the £400–£800 range; Gallery Five, the card manufacturers, produced a sell-out edition of ten; publishers John Murray produced The Works, by Beryl Cook, which has already sold more than 10,000 copies. In addition, a limited edition of a print has been produced by a Bristol Gallery.[2]

Knowing about the finances worried Beryl, and she was in the happy position of not having to rely on the money, because she already had everything she wanted. A large part of her didn't even want to sell the paintings, because she missed them when they were gone. Fortunately, John Senior proved an exceptional business manager. He coordinated all the partners' activities, ran Beryl's diary, acted as her chauffeur and travel companion, and kept track of which painting was where. He cooked their meals and prepared Beryl's panels. He acted as company secretary, doing tax returns and dealing with official correspondence. Beryl was fully aware how much she owed him and the rest of her family and friends; she always said that it was because of them she was able to paint. Beryl's fans were aware too, because they had read about their strong partnership and often addressed letters to both of them. Interviewers noted how they finished each other's sentences. Maybe they sensed the most important role of all – providing reassurance and guidance, and shielding Beryl from interruptions and critiques, so that she could follow her own path as an artist.

Several people contacted Bernard Samuels after Beryl's overnight success, offering to be her art agent. With his help, Beryl and John selected the Portal Gallery in Bond Street to handle sales and give her a presence in London. Lionel Levy, its director, had specialized in

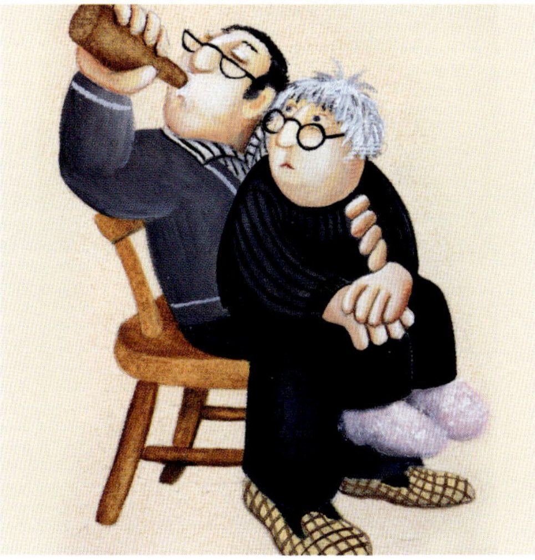

Still Life with Husband (1980s). Beryl is John's ventriloquist dummy; he is doing the trick of speaking for her whilst drinking a bottle of beer.

naïve painters for twenty years and Beryl fitted well into his stable of quirky artists. Beryl and John developed an excellent working relationship with Jess Wilder and Mary Bee at the Gallery.

Beryl's first Portal show was in 1977. It included some works already seen at Plymouth Arts Centre (borrowed back from their owners) and fresh paintings. Lionel Levy said, 'She's an absolute original: not only is she unique as an artist but she's a chronicler of her own world and time. Not only do we rarely have any of her pictures in the gallery now, but there's a waiting list, including other galleries.'[3]

Beryl was extremely loyal to her business partners, despite being approached by others, and the last Portal show she did with them was her eighteenth, in 2006, when she was 80 years old.

The Mayfair location meant that even the most London-centric art critic could drop by and the shows were well reviewed. Where possible, they coincided with a Beryl book publication. The Portal also commissioned its painters to paint a special piece of art each year for Christmas. This could pose a challenge for Beryl who was not particularly au fait with bible stories, but she rose to the occasion. She found it much easier when the themes got broader.

In return for their commission of 50 per cent, the Portal also not only showed her works in a very prestigious location, but handled publicity, including the tricky business of negotiating interviews and television appearances. When a museum wanted to borrow paintings, the Portal was responsible for negotiating the loan from the new owners – whose names were of course kept confidential if they wished. However, it was public knowledge that Jackie Collins, Rodney Bewes, Clare Frances, Chris de Burgh, Whoopi Goldberg and Yoko Ono had bought paintings.

An early visitor to the Portal was David Walser of Gallery Five, the greetings cards company. He too signed a contract with the Cooks and immediately produced ten cards, including *Sabotage* (see page 69) which became a best-seller. 'I am bored with nostalgia and romance in greetings cards,' he said. 'When I saw Mrs Cook's paintings I thought, "How vulgar!" They are not at all pornographic; just a rare belly-laugh vulgarity.'[4] Soon fans were obsessively hunting down new cards and the calendar, which was produced every two years or so.

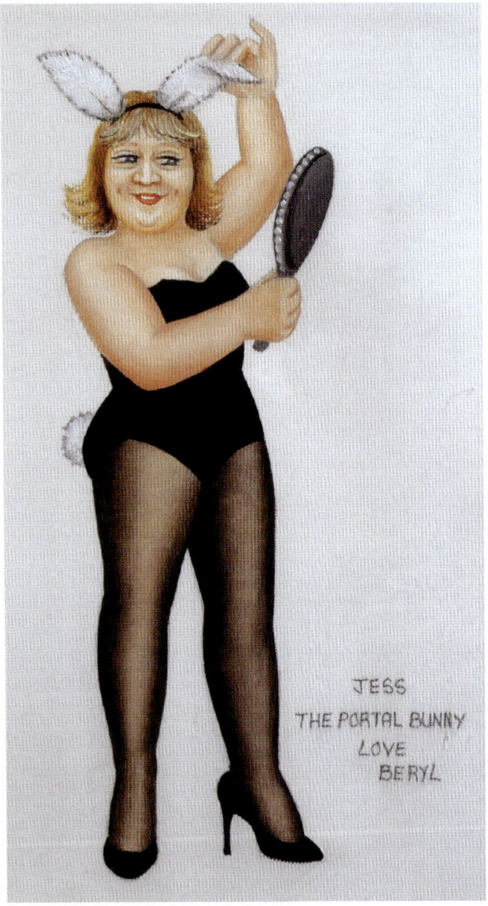

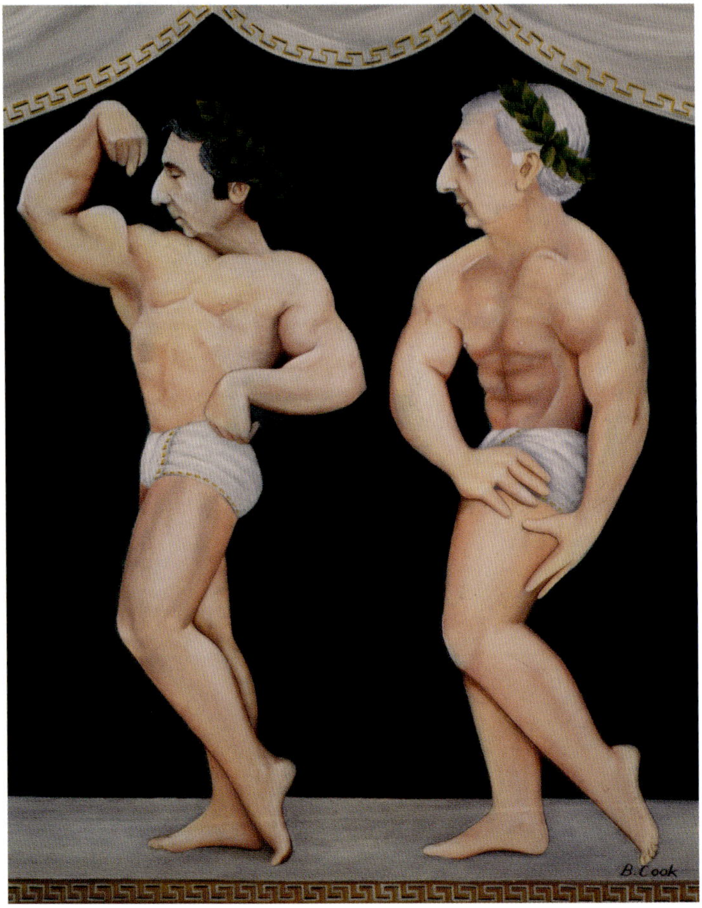

Jess the Portal Bunny
(1999). This was painted as a private gift (and joke) for Jess.

Two Greek Gods
(1980s). Lionel and his business partner Eric of the Portal Gallery, based on a newspaper cutting of a Mr Universe contest

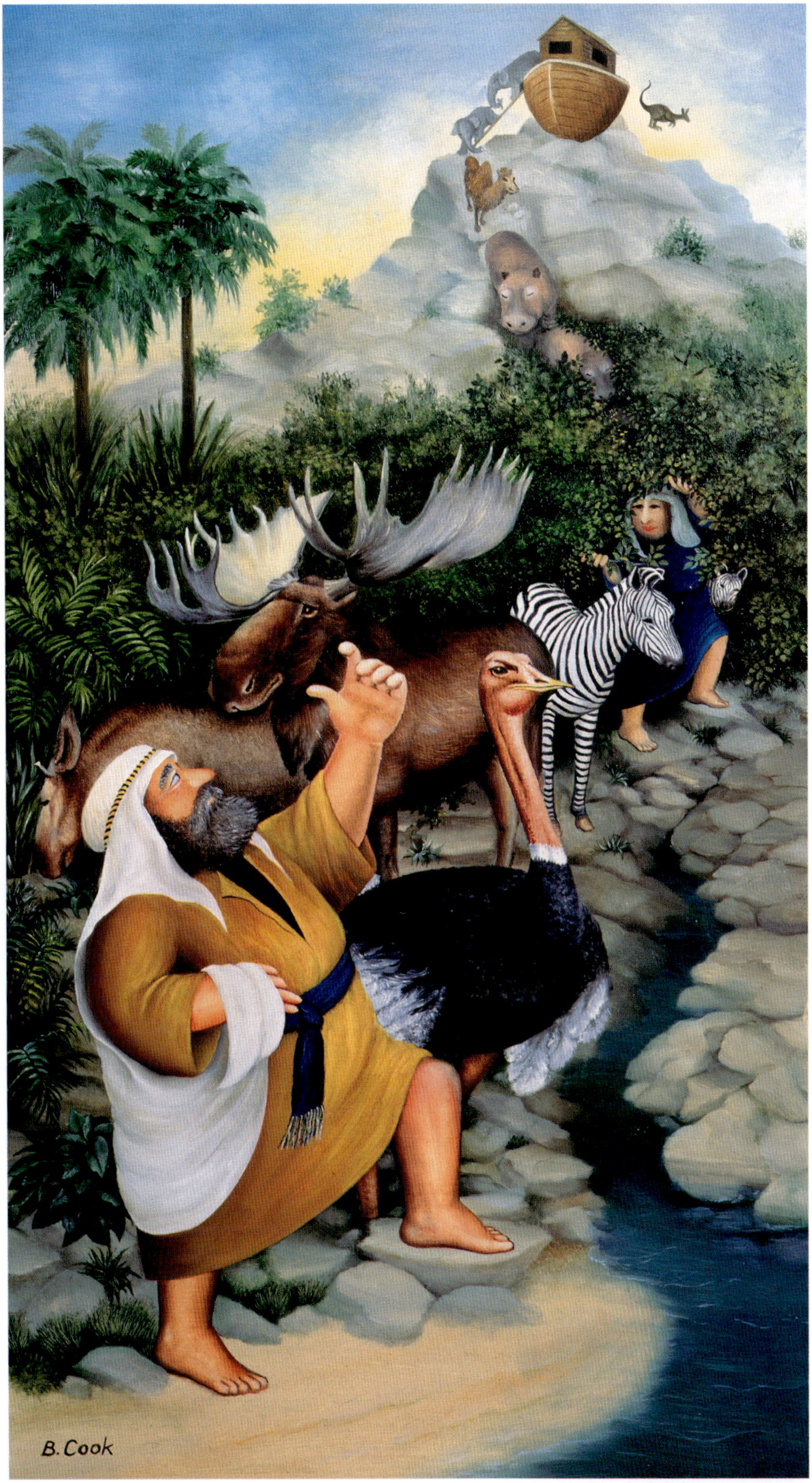

Noah's Ark

(1990s). Beryl explained that she had problems in painting Noah's wife who looks like she is wrestling with the undergrowth.

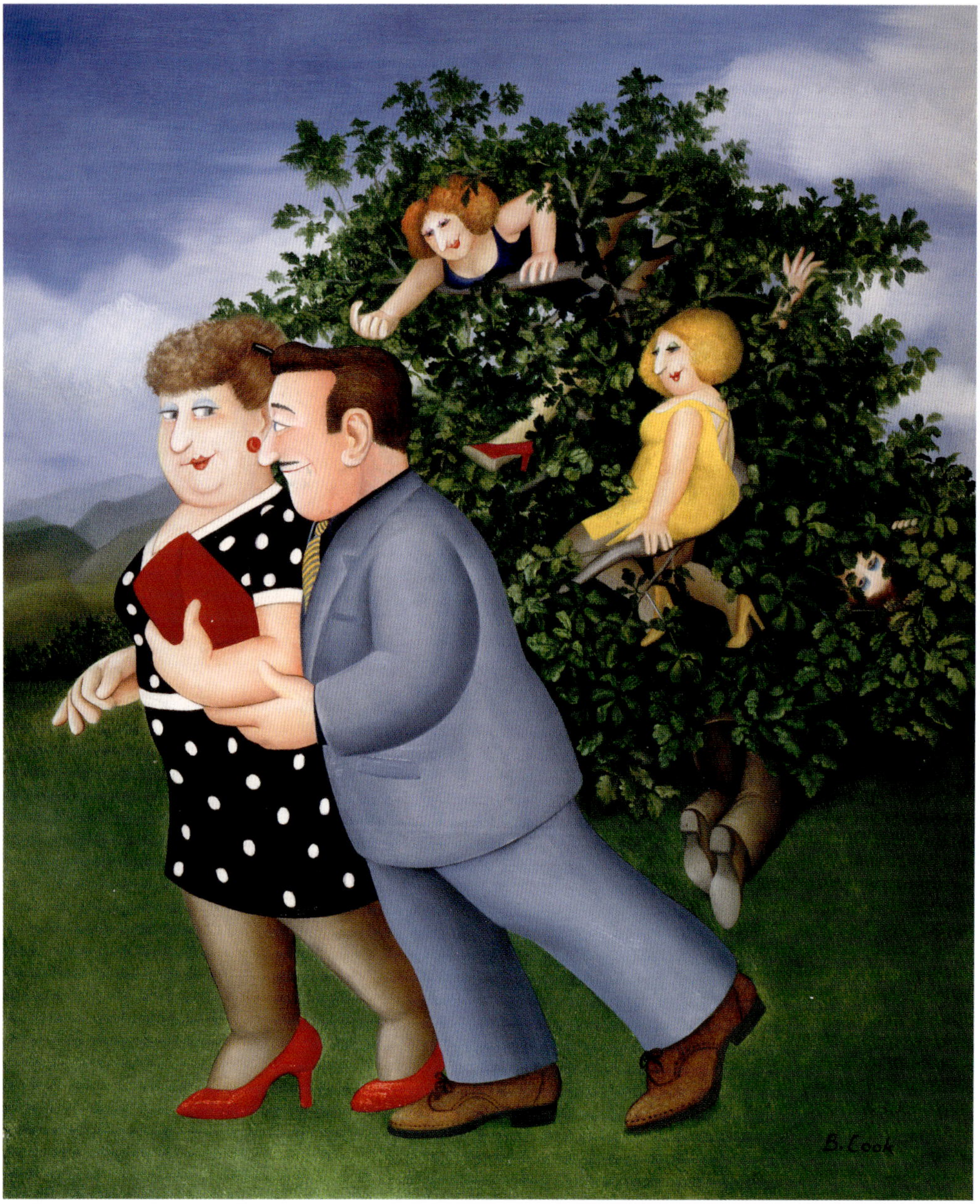

ABOVE

A Bird in the Hand

(1984). Painted for the Portal Gallery's Christmas Show, the theme of which was Aesop's Fables. This is a very typical Beryl interpretation, playing on the double meaning of the word 'bird'. The man seeking the 'birds' in the bush is going in quite the wrong direction.

RIGHT

No Man is a Stranger to His Valet

(1995). Beryl's version of this little-known proverb centres on the gentleman's awful secret – his pink girdle. She loved corsetry, whether on men or women.

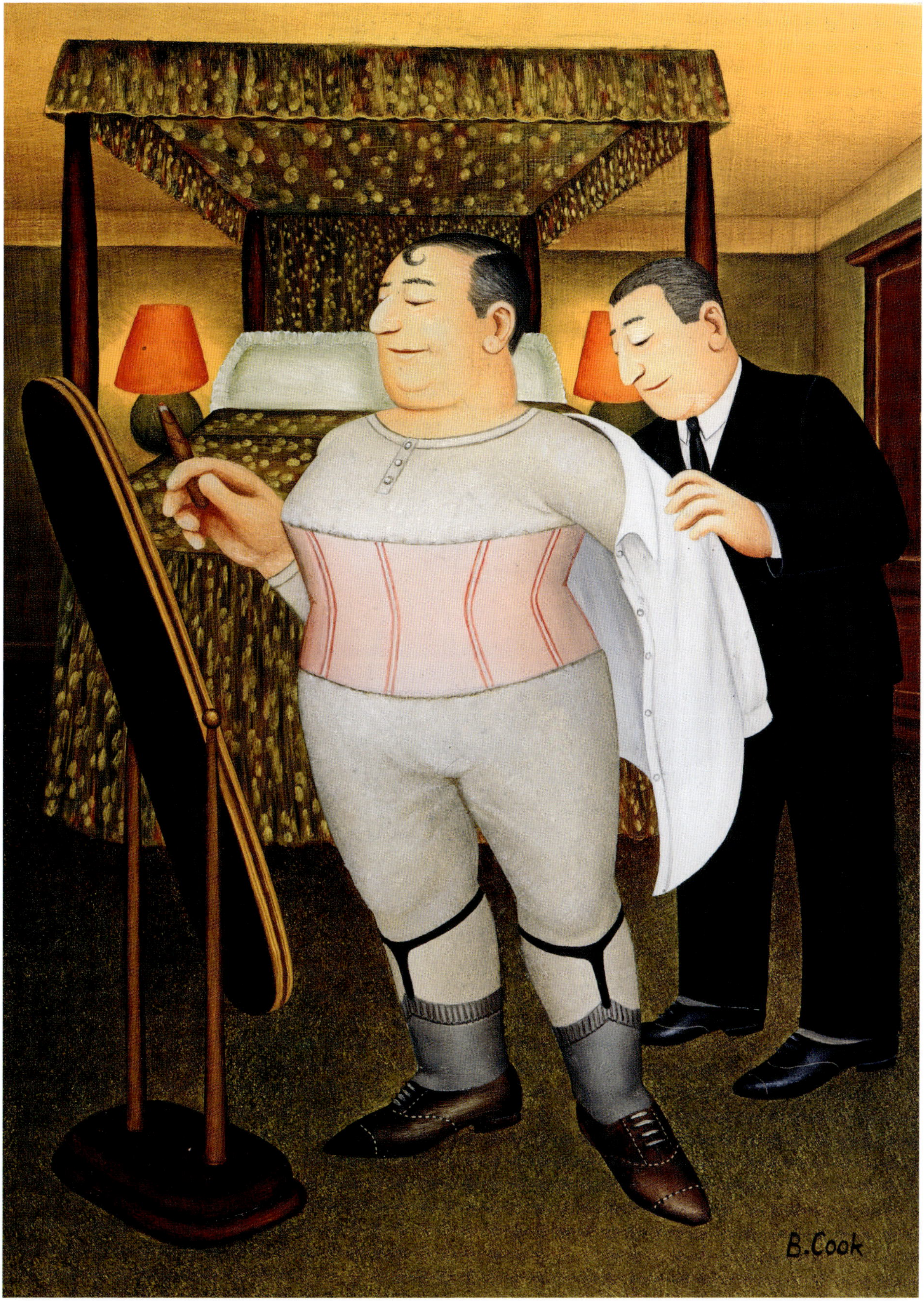
B.Cook

Those with a slightly higher budget could collect Fine Art Prints produced by The Alexander Gallery in Bristol. The first was *Four Hungry Cats* (see page 68) which was initially sold to help raise money for Plymouth Arts Centre. These were high-quality limited editions, signed by Beryl and stamped with the approval of the Fine Art Trade Guild.

The John Murray publishers offices were near the Portal Gallery, and one of their young editors, Joe Whitlock Blundell, was another early visitor. As he recalls, 'John Murray's was not the most obvious publisher for Beryl's colourful, sometimes camp, subject matter. They were more famous for Byron and Darwin, John Betjeman and Kenneth Clark, but Jock Murray was immensely tickled by Beryl's work.'[5] It was a good decision, because sales of the first book, *The Works* (1978), were impressive, and a reprint was soon required.

Altogether Joe worked on 12 books with Beryl. The pattern was the same for nearly 30 years. Joe would arrive at the Cooks' for a weekend and be shown to Beryl's studio, where she had laid out the new paintings – such an exciting moment, with Beryl alternately proud and worried. There followed drinks in The Dolphin and a few other pubs, during which the book would not be mentioned. Next morning, a remarkably fresh Beryl would produce a perfect cooked breakfast, and after a cigarette the discussions about the book began. Saturday night might also involve a trip to another pub or Diamond Lil's. The weekend was rounded off with a Sunday roast.

The captions are an important part of Beryl's books, much appreciated by her fans. They explain the inspiration behind the paintings and some of the difficulties Beryl encountered in producing them – Beryl is very honest when she feels something has not quite worked. At first Beryl told the story behind each painting to Joe, who wrote the first draft for her to correct. Soon the roles were reversed, with Beryl handwriting the captions and Joe editing them where needed. The paintings were photographed in Plymouth and transparencies flew backwards and forwards to London, and between publisher, printer, Portal, the Alexander Gallery and magazine picture editors. Beryl always checked the proofs (but not the forewords written by others) and was very particular about the accuracy of the colours.

The Works was followed two years later by *Private View*, with a masterly foreword by the art critic Edward Lucie-Smith. The book contains many new paintings, again mostly inspired by Plymouth, family and friends.

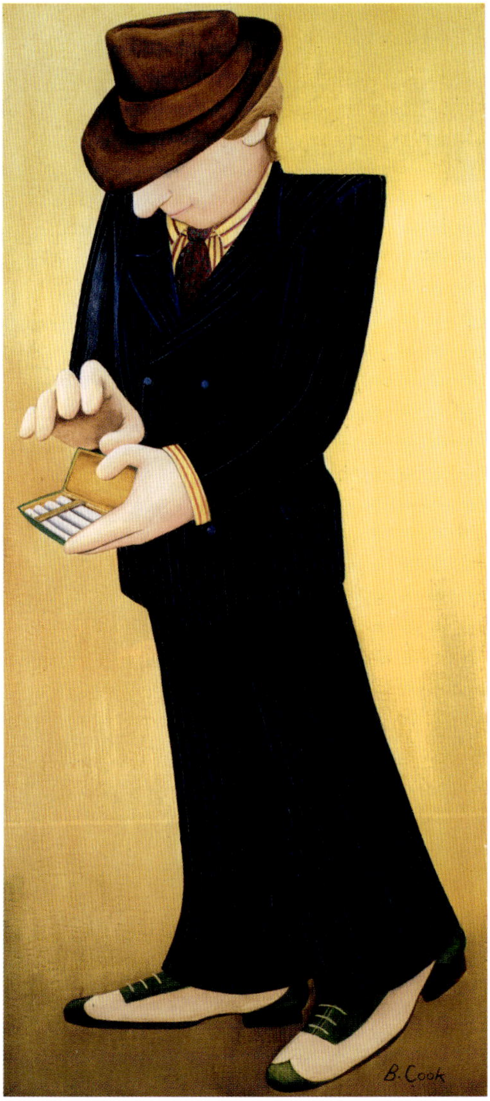

Joe's Shoes
(c 1978)

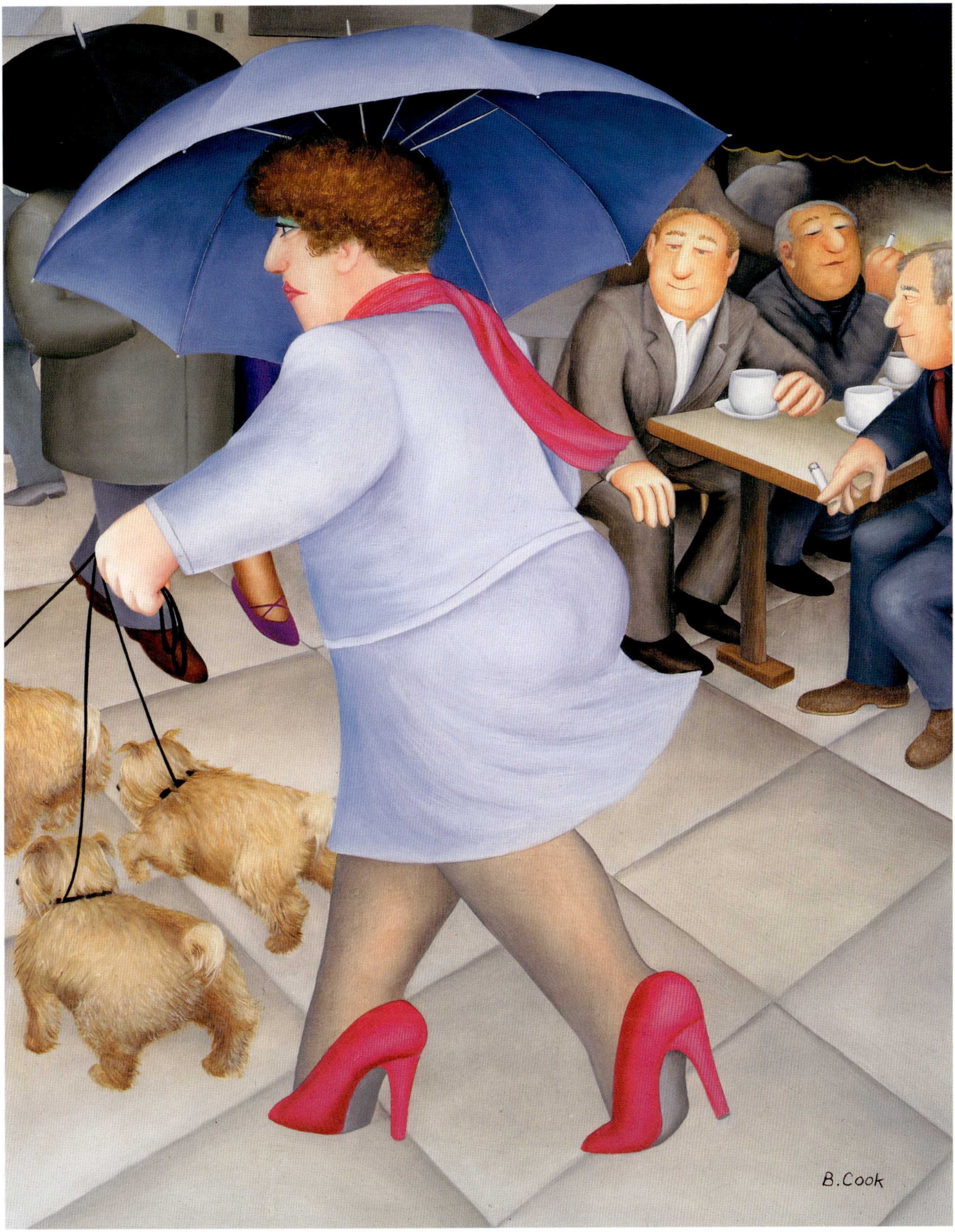

Albemarle Street

(c 1988). The Cooks often stopped for coffee on their way between the Portal Gallery and the offices of John Murray publishers.

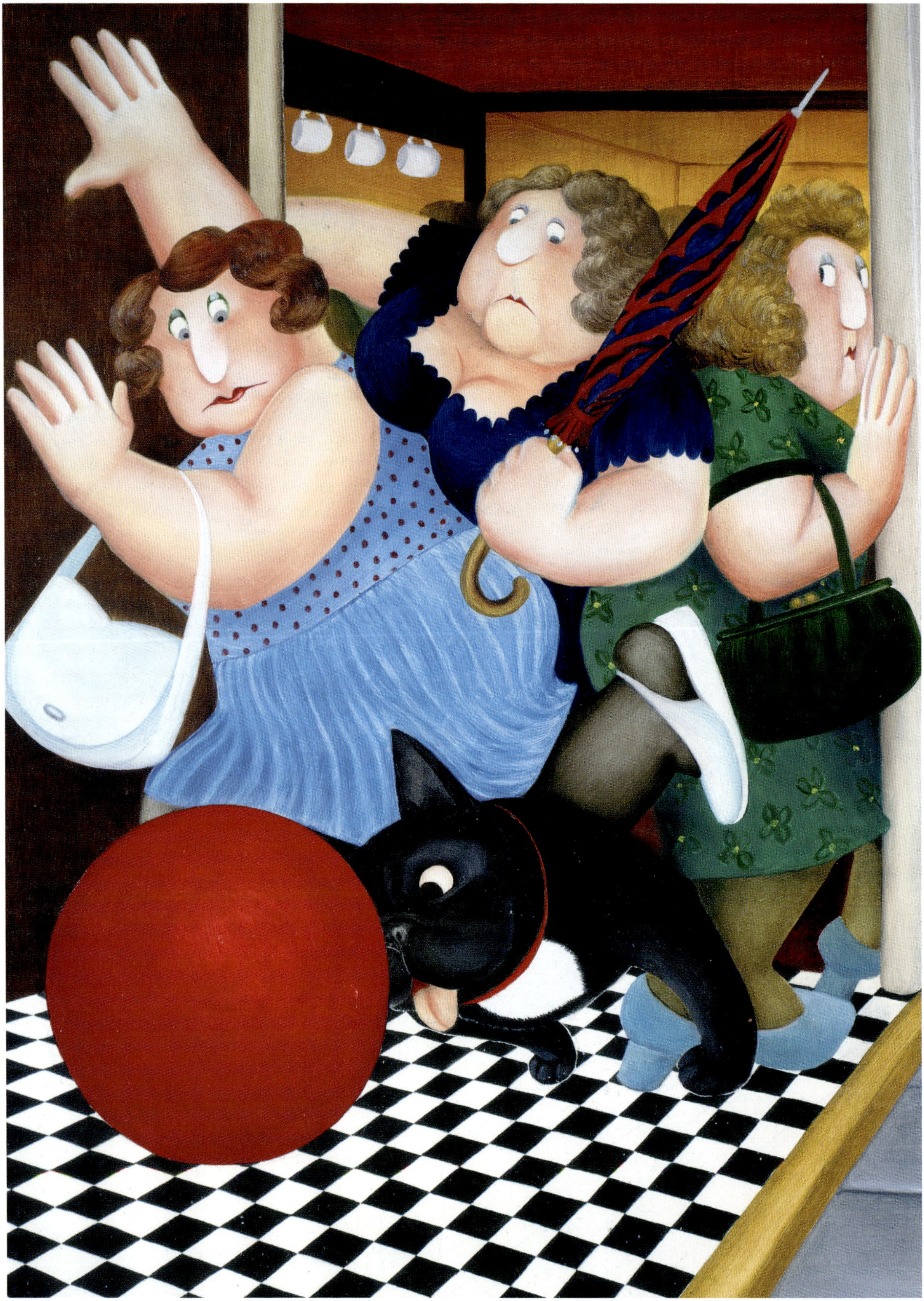

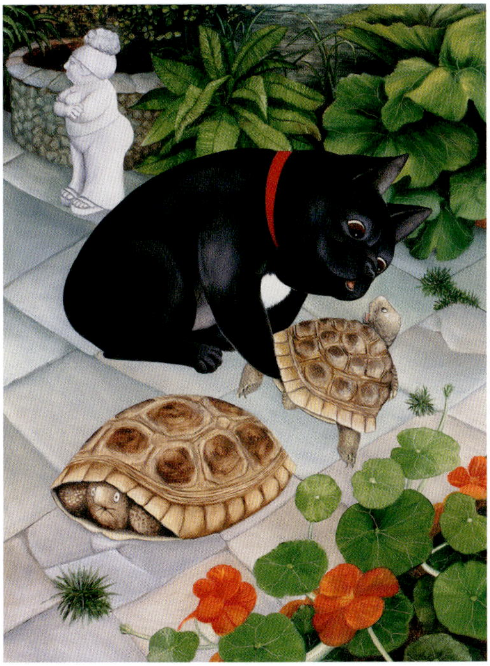

Bertie and the Big Red Ball (John Murray, 1982) was a collaboration with Edward Lucie-Smith and Bertie. Ted was an early and influential supporter of Beryl who became a friend, and Bertie was his French Bulldog whom she had already painted from memory.

Bertie terrorized children on the beach by chasing their balls, hence the idea of the book, which covers his adventures across Plymouth and the ensuing mayhem. It doesn't include the occasion when Bertie bit one of the Cook's tortoises and John Senior had to mend its shell with superglue.

Beryl Cook's New York (John Murray, 1985) reflects the growing market for Beryl's work in the United States. John and Beryl spent just over three weeks in New York in 1983. Beryl was an extremely nervous traveller and her letters to Barbara involve discussion of the exact combination of Valium and alcohol required to keep her calm on the plane. The itinerary was suggested by Norman Henry, her American agent, who produced his own line of Fine Art Prints under the name of Flanagan Graphics Inc. It included a trip to Atlantic City, a slightly run-down casino town, where Beryl's roll of quarters lasted two days so she felt confident she didn't have a gambling problem. In New York, they were able to visit Faith Stewart-Gordon at the Russian Tea Rooms, as well as the Roseland Ballroom and Coney Island, and dine on oysters at the Oyster Bar in Grand Central Station.

It was back to London for Beryl's last book with John Murray, *Beryl Cook's London* (1988). By now Beryl and John were often in London, sometimes with so many business commitments that they didn't have time to visit their friends. They did enjoy staying in hotels and especially eating at Langan's Brasserie and Joe Allen's Covent Garden restaurant, both popular with celebrities. Daniel Farson (another friend, see page 103), Barbara, Joe and others suggested inspiring places to visit. These included the stickier spots of Soho, Harringay Greyhound Stadium and Smithfield Market, unlikely to be on most tourists' lists.

Beryl's next five books were published by Gollancz but still with Joe as Editor. While they include work inspired by Beryl and John's home life, *Bouncers* (1991), *Happy Days* (1995) and *Cruising* (2000) open a whole world as the Cooks travelled in search of inspiration. Beryl described these trips as holidays in her letters, but they were in fact work too – and fortunately the tax man finally agreed. The potential sticking point was a trip to the USA where they travelled out by Concorde and back on board

ABOVE
Checking Up
(c 1982). Bertie vs the Cooks' tortoises

LEFT
Bertie in the Pub
(c 1982). Bertie causes chaos at the pub in pursuit of his red ball.

the *Queen Elizabeth 2* ocean liner. It was understandably hard for John to get enough annual leave for this amount of travelling, so he retired to become Beryl's full-time manager in 1986.

Beryl's final book was *Beryl Cook, The Bumper Edition*, produced in 2000 by Gollancz. It is indeed a bumper book. Fans found much to enjoy in the thematically arranged chapters, perfect for dipping into. But even at the age of 74 Beryl did not allow a photograph of herself to appear.

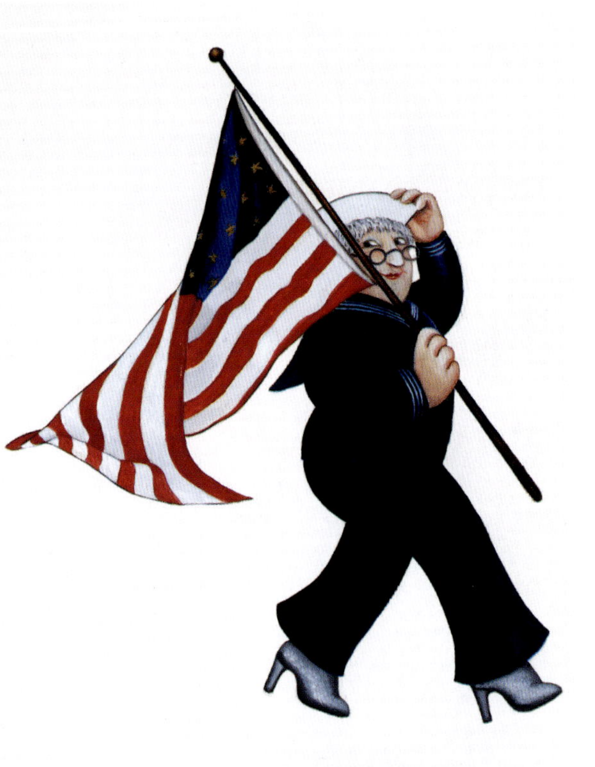

Self-portrait with Flag
(1985). Beryl's self-portrait for *Beryl Cook's New York*

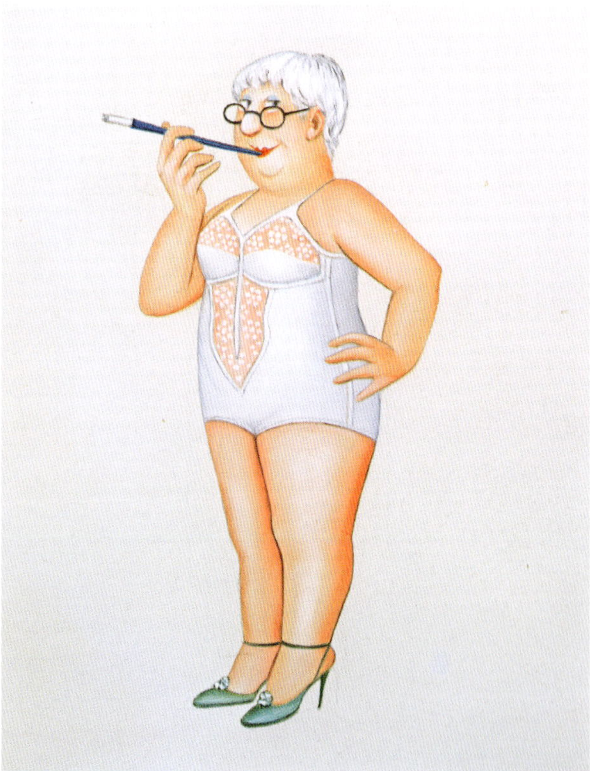

Self-portrait
(1988). Beryl's self-portrait for *Beryl Cook's London*

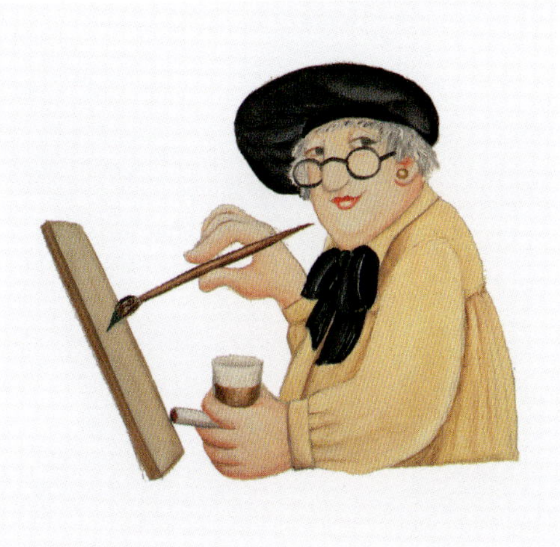

The Artist
(c 1978). Beryl refused to have her photograph in *The Works*, and provided this portrait instead.

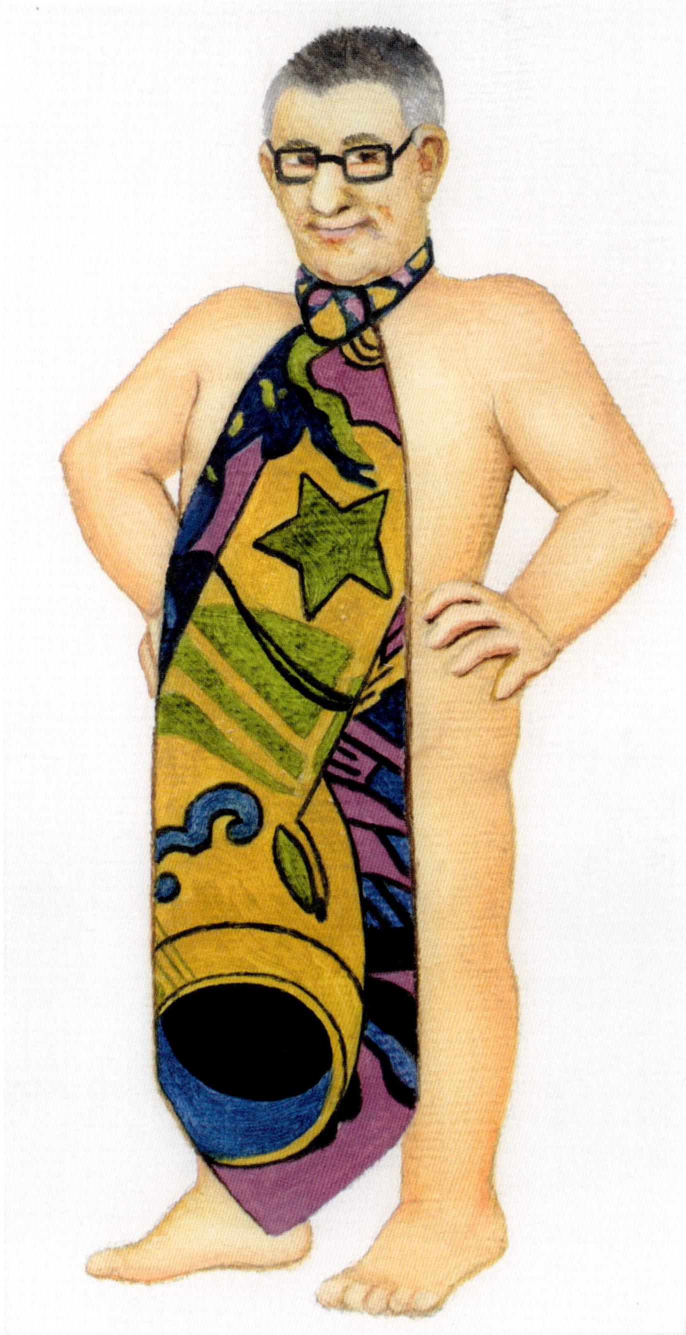

The Tie
(1990s). Beryl bought this silk tie for John's birthday, but he spilled something down it the very first time he wore it.

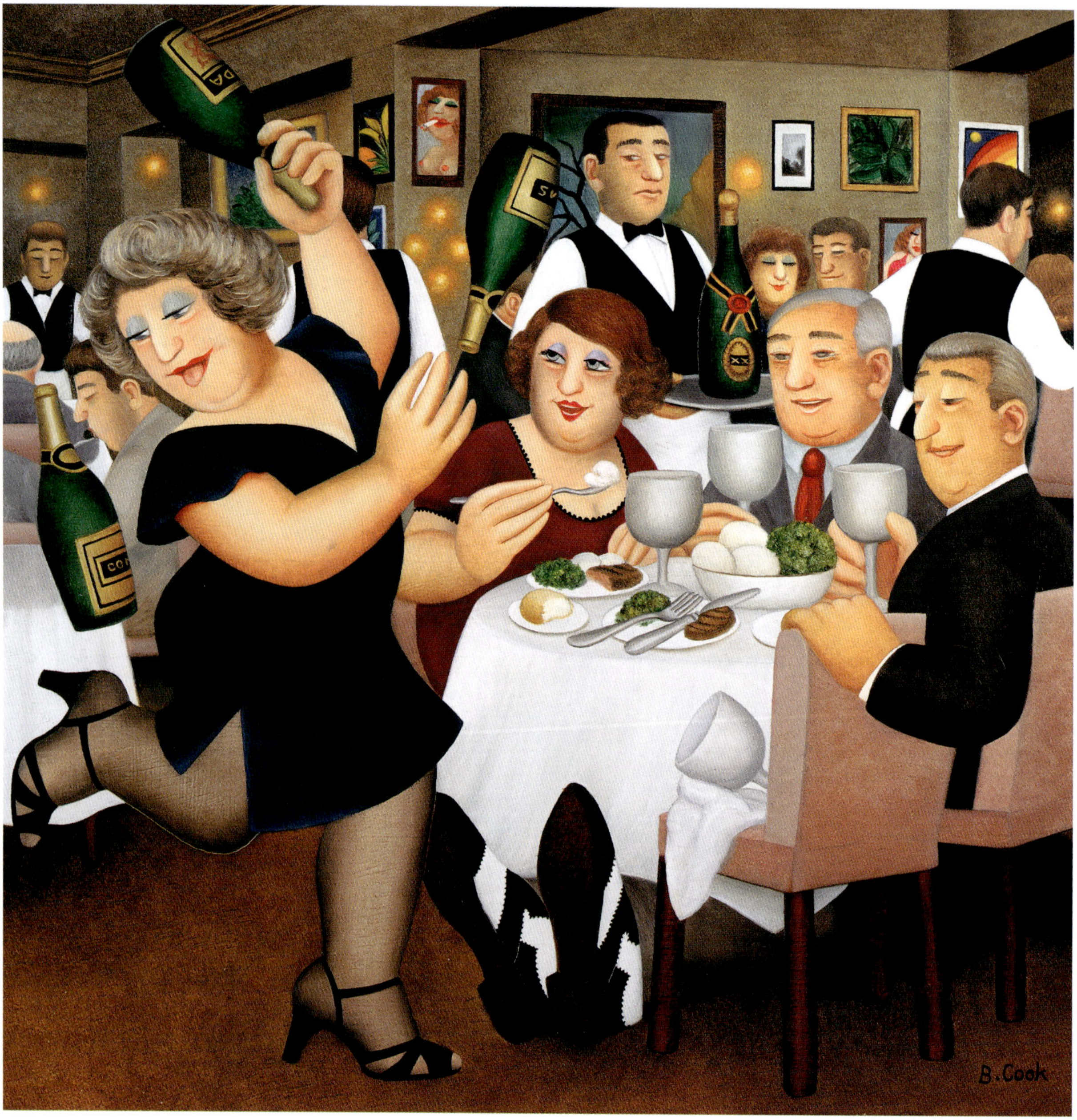

ABOVE

Dining Out

(1994). This was painted for the Portal Gallery's Christmas Show, on the theme of 'Eat Drink and be Merry'. It was inspired by Langan's Restaurant, a celebrity hangout whose owner, Peter Langan, was sometimes found passed out under a table. It was one of the few restaurants Beryl enjoyed going to during their business trips to London.

RIGHT

Paddington Station

(c 1988). The Cooks had to travel increasingly frequently to London on business, but at least they were now able to afford to go first class.

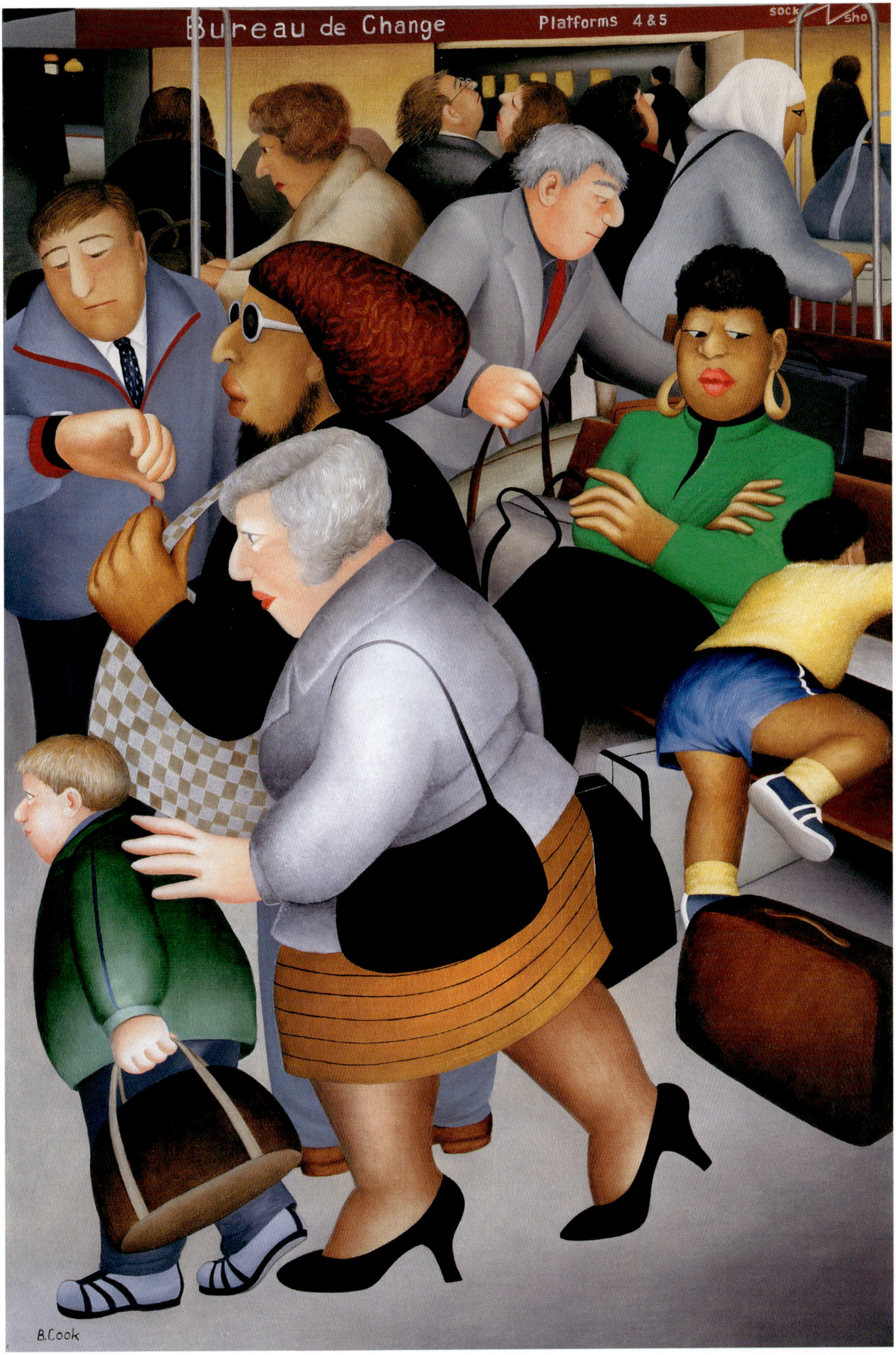
Bureau de Change
Platforms 4 & 5
B.Cook

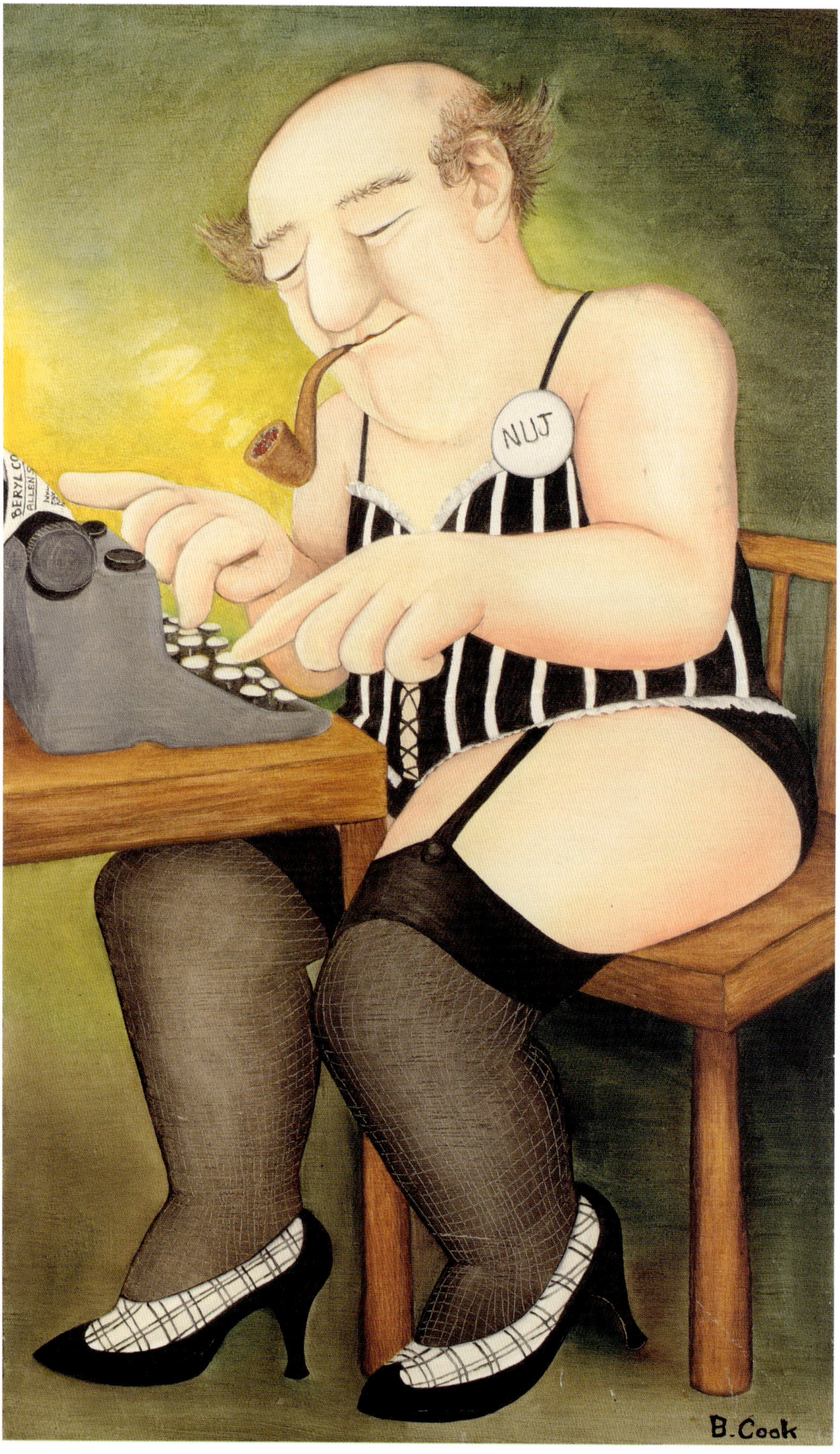
NUJ
B.Cook

07

A Flash of Genius – Critical Reaction

LEFT
Untitled
(c 1977). Beryl's revenge picture of Allen Saddler. On the back is written: 'This picture was painted over 30 years ago in the middle 70s. It is of a journalist named Alan Sadler [sic], a really nasty piece of work. He visited my second exhibition in the Arts Centre at Plymouth, took a look round, then went away and composed an absolutely vicious review for a London paper. I was horrified, never spoke to him again (although he tried) and never, never read anything written about myself from that day to this. I invented this outfit, I hope it is something he would loathe.'

I was really very surprised when the paintings were taken seriously by reviewers ... but I didn't read anything that was written about them until someone said that the piece in *The Guardian* mentioned a sinister aspect in my work. I was so worried I didn't sleep – but when I read the review I was very pleasantly surprised.

Frank Wintle quoting Beryl Cook in 'Beryl's Lot', *Western Evening Herald* 3 December 1975

Thus began a love–hate relationship with the press, and with art critics in particular. Hate because the slightest negative comment hurt Beryl terribly, and love because a few of those who reviewed her became very good friends.

Allen Saddler wrote both the 1975 review that Beryl read in *The Guardian*, and the 1976 *Sunday Times* article that propelled her to fame the following February. The first is not as nice. Visitors loved the humour, but Saddler saw 'raddled tarts in Plymouth pubs, all with sharp, red Clara Bow lips', 'go-go dancers nobody would want to go with', and 'women with fey expressions of gentle madness, more than tinged with malice'. Overall, however, he found the exhibition 'enchanting and very personal; at first jolly and exhilarating, but after closer examination, slightly sinister'.

I think this early review affected Beryl more than she admitted. From then onwards (at least in public) she avoided anything sinister, even if the subject matter (such as a morticians' or a fight at a wake) might have merited it.

The following summer the Portal Gallery's first Beryl Cook exhibition was reviewed by the poet and art critic Edward Lucie-Smith on *Kaleidoscope*, BBC Radio 4's arts programme.[1] Lucie-Smith's enthusiasm was palpable; the patterns of shapes, the 'fat roly-poly people doing nice roly-poly things', the verve and humour – all entranced him. While he acknowledged the debt to seaside humour, he paid Beryl the enormous compliment of taking her work seriously rather than lazily labelling it 'primitive' or 'naïve'

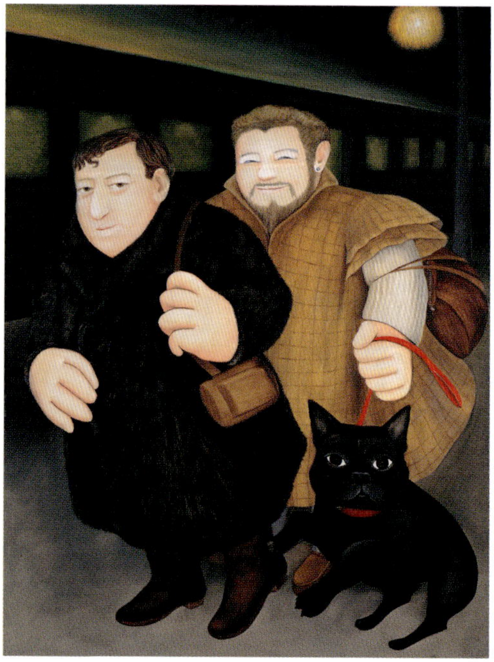

Ted and Heinrich
(1979). The couple arriving at Plymouth station to stay with the Cooks. Bertie is looking distinctly devilish. When the couple split up, Beryl offered to paint a flap with an alternative face on it.

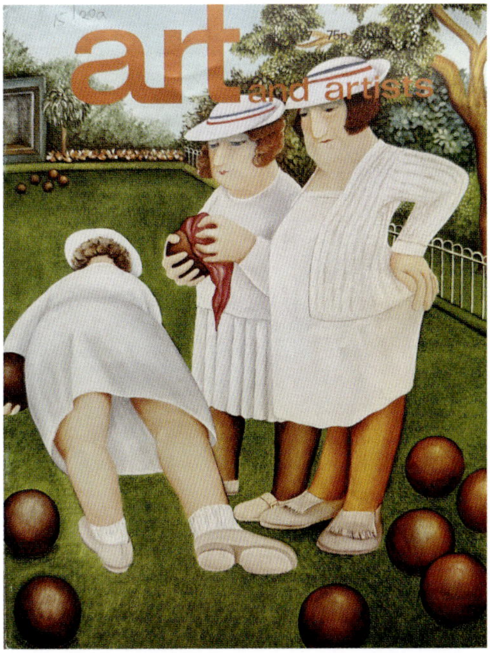

Art and Artists magazine cover (July 1977) showing *Ladies Bowling* (c 1977). In discussing this work on *Kaleidoscope*, Lucie-Smith commented on the mountain of bottom and two very odd legs sticking out at the bottom of the bottom.

and thus unworthy of deeper study. Indeed, Lucie-Smith questioned the whole concept of a primitive artist: 'If for example, Beryl Cook had been a Florentine painter of the 1400s she would have been regarded as being perfectly professional, in fact many of her compositions are awfully like art of that kind.'

While Lucie-Smith saw an interesting edge and lack of sentimentality in Beryl's cat portraits, he was less enthusiastic about her fantasy pieces such as the pigs in *Come Dancing* (see page 218) and preferred her 'hard observation of [an] unillusioned look at humanity, but managing to preserve a real liking for it'.

Edward Lucie-Smith also wrote for *Art and Artists* magazine, and the cover of their July 1977 edition featured the bowling picture that he had discussed on *Kaleidoscope*. His short review began 'If "serious criticism" made its way to the Portal Gallery, at the time when Beryl Cook's exhibition was on view there, no doubt it drew back in alarm'. Yet if serious criticism wants democratic art, here it is, he says. Again, he praises her use of figures to create compositions with movement, and to fill spaces in surprising ways. Like Peter Blake and Edward Burra, she relishes low life – 'which is one of the things that democracy is about'.

Beryl wrote to Edward Lucie-Smith to thank him for both the magazine and radio reviews. They met in the autumn of 1978 and thus began another life-long friendship, which extended also to John George, the editor of *Art and Artists*. Their correspondence is preserved in the Cook Archive and, as with Barbara Ker-Seymer, it lasted a lifetime. I believe that Barbara, Tony, Ted and John Senior were the only people whose opinion Beryl valued about her work. They certainly provided reassurance, took her and John on tours of London to find inspiration, and suggested overseas trips that would fuel her imagination. Each had the stature to be confident in their taste, rather than disconcerted by the perceived vulgarity.

Beryl's work was appreciated by other art critics, too, such as Charles Spencer on Anglia TV in 1978 and Waldemar Januszczak on *Kaleidoscope* in October 1978. This and many magazine and newspaper articles were inspired by the publication of Beryl's first book, *The Works*.

But some serious critics did indeed 'draw back in alarm' as Ted had predicted. They were horrified by the vulgarity and overcome by snobbery. It is easy to forget the class obsession of 1970s and 1980s Britain. Even though Thatcher's Britain believed in rewards for hard graft, there were plenty of books advising about etiquette, covering how one ate, got in or out of a car, dressed, decorated or even planted out one's garden. TV sitcoms such as *The Likely Lads* (a Cook family favourite), *To the Manor Born, Keeping Up Appearances, Steptoe and Son* and even *The Good Life*, played on social anxiety. Was something kitsch, or just bad taste?

Snobbery when it came to Beryl's paintings wasn't just confined to the art world. In an old folder, marked 'warning, warning, mad person', there is a single letter addressed to Beryl, from the Devon County Ladies' Bowling Association.

My own mother disapproved of lace curtains, tomato ketchup, milk bottles on the table, applying makeup in public, red lipstick, eating in public, pierced ears, tattoos, hoop earrings and generally making a scene. Daytime television and the whole of ITV were beyond the pale. I feel anxious even remembering these things. Leopard-print was associated with prostitution and Bet Lynch in *Coronation Street*. And we were thin. Anyone who has tried on a vintage Biba piece can attest to the smaller size of people then. Larger people – who of course did exist – should have been doing keep fit in legwarmers, not disporting themselves in loud clothing on the beach.

Beryl showed the joy of people who were not at all self-conscious, wearing what they liked and not trying to adopt the trappings of the upper middle or middle classes. This made Adrian Searle, Art Critic for *The Guardian*, queasy in 2007. 'Her art depresses me. I thought I would be able to summon some sort of enthusiasm for its Englishness, its playfulness, its sauciness. But I can't.'[2] His official beef seems to be that she lacks ambition, but what he writes about is the sauciness, the shoe fetishism and the whipping. He accuses the Baltic Gallery Gateshead, who were hosting *The World of Beryl Cook,* of pandering to popular taste. They had undermined their position by leaving the task of writing an introduction to Jess Wilder of the Portal Gallery, who is – shudder – Beryl's commercial dealer. Beryl's work is clichéd, not affirmative; soap opera without depth; Mike Leigh without humour; art for people who don't like art. Liking it diminishes Lowry.

I want to shout at him, did you actually *look* at her paintings? Can you not see what I see? And why should good art be anxious and miserable anyway? Just slink off and join Brian Sewell in the nearest branch of Café Rouge. Fortunately, Beryl was completely unaware of what Adrian Searle or anyone else wrote, as she never read reviews and articles. Instead, she passed them to John to read.

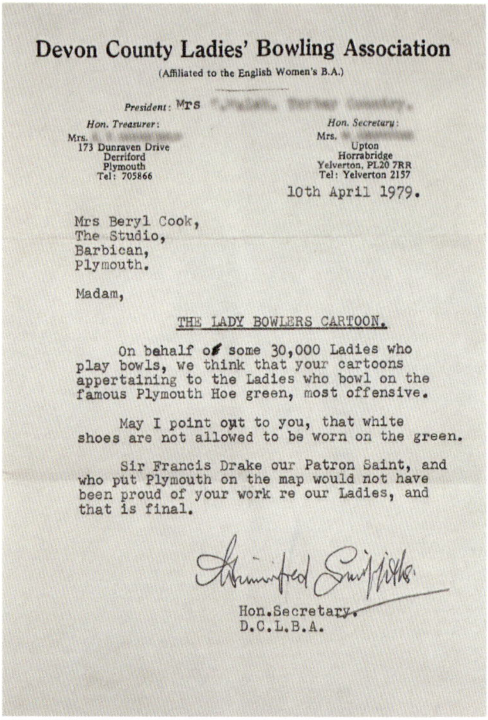

Devon County Ladies' Bowling Association
(Affiliated to the English Women's B.A.)

President: Mrs

Hon. Treasurer:
Mrs.
173 Dunraven Drive
Derriford
Plymouth
Tel: 705866

Hon. Secretary:
Mrs.
Upton
Horrabridge
Yelverton, PL20 7RR
Tel: Yelverton 2157

10th April 1979.

Mrs Beryl Cook,
The Studio,
Barbican,
Plymouth.

Madam,

THE LADY BOWLERS CARTOON.

On behalf of some 30,000 Ladies who play bowls, we think that your cartoons appertaining to the Ladies who bowl on the famous Plymouth Hoe green, most offensive.

May I point out to you, that white shoes are not allowed to be worn on the green.

Sir Francis Drake our Patron Saint, and who put Plymouth on the map would not have been proud of your work re our Ladies, and that is final.

Hon.Secretary.
D.C.L.B.A.

A letter of complaint from the Devon County Ladies' Bowling Association

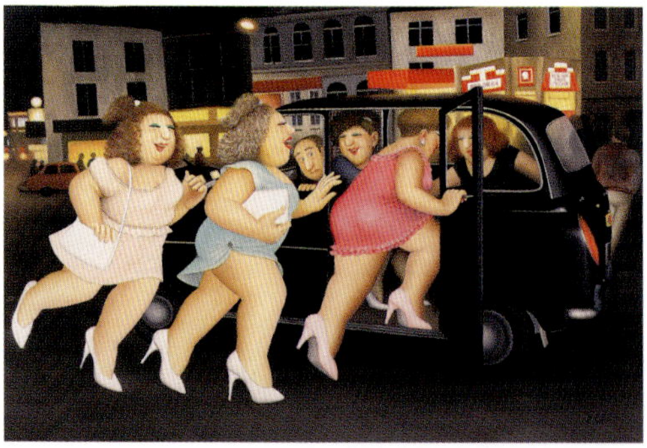

Girls in a Taxi
(1991). Happy women piling into a tax on Union Street, with Kentucky Fried Chicken in the background. Saddler said 'you feel for the springs'.

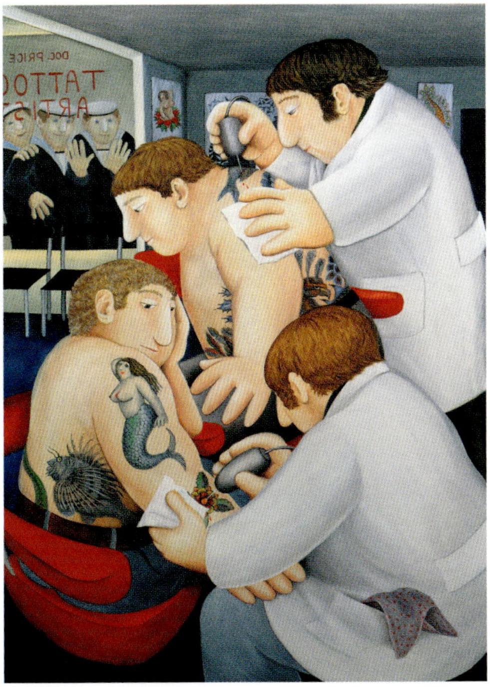

Tattoo Artists
(1979). Two sailors are having traditional tattoos done at Doc Price's on Union Street. Even though tattooing has a long and honourable history, especially for sailors, it was for a long time considered socially unacceptable and was banned for some professions such as the police. Today, one in five people have a tattoo.

She would run out of the room if something about her came on television or the radio. This was because she had been deeply hurt by one review in particular, ironically by Allen Saddler. She took her revenge (see page 92).

I have been unable to locate the offensive review, but a later one was published in 1995. That year, Plymouth Art Centre mounted a Beryl Cook exhibition to celebrate 20 years since their first. It was opened by Sir George Christie, Chairman of Glyndebourne, a huge fan of Beryl's work. Allen Saddler was back again, but in acidic mood:

> Seeing nearly a hundred paintings in the Cook collection made me think that Cook can be jolly, but also unkind. There are lumpy ladies everywhere. Is it a celebration of lumpiness? Large cutouts of bulging women in skimpy underwear welcome visitors at the doors. Their pointy nipples have punched a hole through their bras and their bellies sag over their fantastic fun-set knickers. Is it possible that Cook's eye enlarges the human figure? Is this lumpy liberation? Even in homely pursuits – like three girls getting into a taxi – you feel for the springs. A woman jogging is a hopeless case. Sitting on a male knee in a bar gives cause for alarm. A stripper is big value for money. If it all started with Cook's Adam and Eve, we are in for a strapping time.
>
> Another feature is the expressionless characters, always surprised by the intrusion when eating their fish and chips, playing tennis, in hospitals, in a bible class, looking particularly uninspired. There are the same blank-faced lumps in the Gare du Nord. Most of Cook's ladies have thick cupid lips, although the dominatrixes smile thinly as they brandish their whips.

But most offensive of all:

> And 20 years ago Cook gave my wife a painting of two holiday visitors, sitting dough-faced in a bus shelter on Plymouth Hoe, surrounded by graffiti.
>
> We had the painting for 15 years, but when we moved it didn't seem right . . . I put it in a local auction with a reserve of pounds 200. The auctioneer rang me up. 'What do you think you're playing at?' he said. 'I can't put this up for my clients to see.' I had forgotten about the graffiti – 'Nigel is a wanker. I shagged a Proggy. I need sex!' he ranted on indignantly. I took the painting away and then took it to London; via the Portal Galleries it got to Bonham's auction where it sold for pounds 4,000, and we went on a cruise down the Danube. Thanks Beryl Cook . . . .[3]

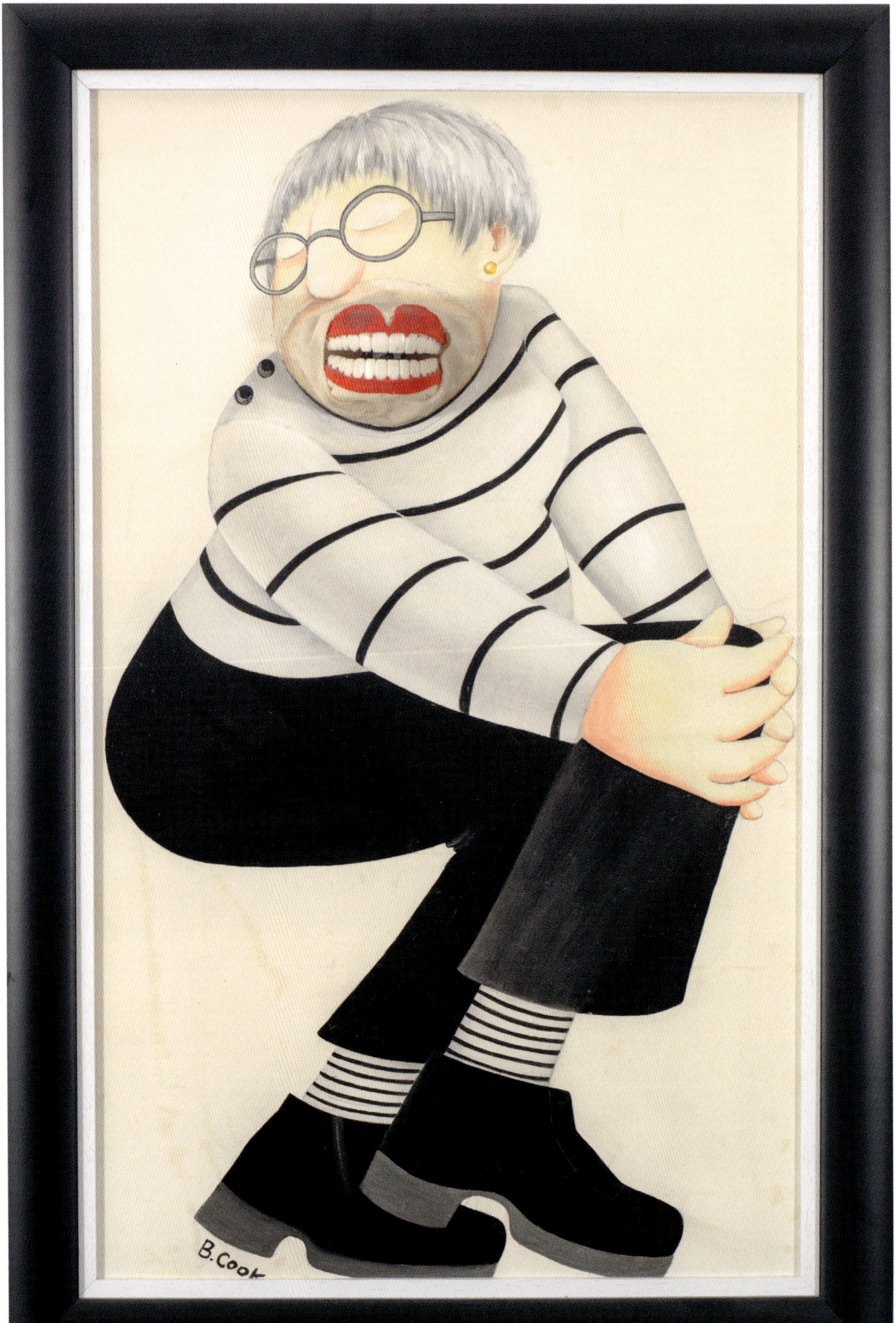
B.Cook

08

Media Coverage

LEFT
Chatterbox
(early 1980s), complete with wind-up teeth

As an extremely shy person, Beryl avoided interviews with newspapers and magazines as much as she could. However, she knew that she had to help promote her shows, publications, prints and cards, and that her fans wanted to know more about her.

She had a tendency to turn the tables and interview the interviewer, or to return to the old set of facts; her early life, first painting in Southern Africa painting for her family, visiting pubs, a bit about her technique, how her paintings never turned out as good as she had imagined them . . . no wonder she thought of herself as a chattering head repeating facts on a loop.

Beryl preferred newspaper and television interviews to take place in Plymouth. If it went well, the interviewer might be invited on an evening out. *Company* magazine's Alex Hamilton was taken on a pub crawl:

> Her favourites are The Dolphin, a fisherman's pub; the Antelope in Union Street, considered rock bottom but very interesting; the Prince Regent; and the Gypsy Moth, full of gays. She catches gays marvellously, and the old ladies who go out in a pack, and the carpenters and tradesmen, and especially the matelots, for whom she feels sorry because the girls available are not very young, even if very willing. She loves anywhere where there's a mix, and hullabalooing, and getting a bit drunk, so long as it's not trendy. But she says, trendy in Plymouth is different from London – it's a grounded set![1]

Gay Search interviewed Beryl for the *Woman's Journal* in September 1979 and got further than most. She clearly understood the important role that John Senior was already playing in Beryl's artistic career, and the importance of her family and pets. One gets the sense of a flowing conversation rather than a series of questions and answers, and Beryl comes across as amusing, self-deprecating but also extremely grateful for her luck. She is definitely someone who has had fame forced upon her, and cannot believe it will last – and won't mind if it doesn't, because it hasn't changed her.

Shortly afterwards *Woman* magazine asked Gay to report on the newly arrived phenomenon of men stripping for all-women audiences. The stripper didn't want his teenage daughters to know what he did, so Gay couldn't bring a photographer. Gay immediately thought of Beryl, whom she had so recently interviewed. The result was one of the most famous and popular of Beryl's works, *Ivor Dickie*, also known as *Ladies Night*.

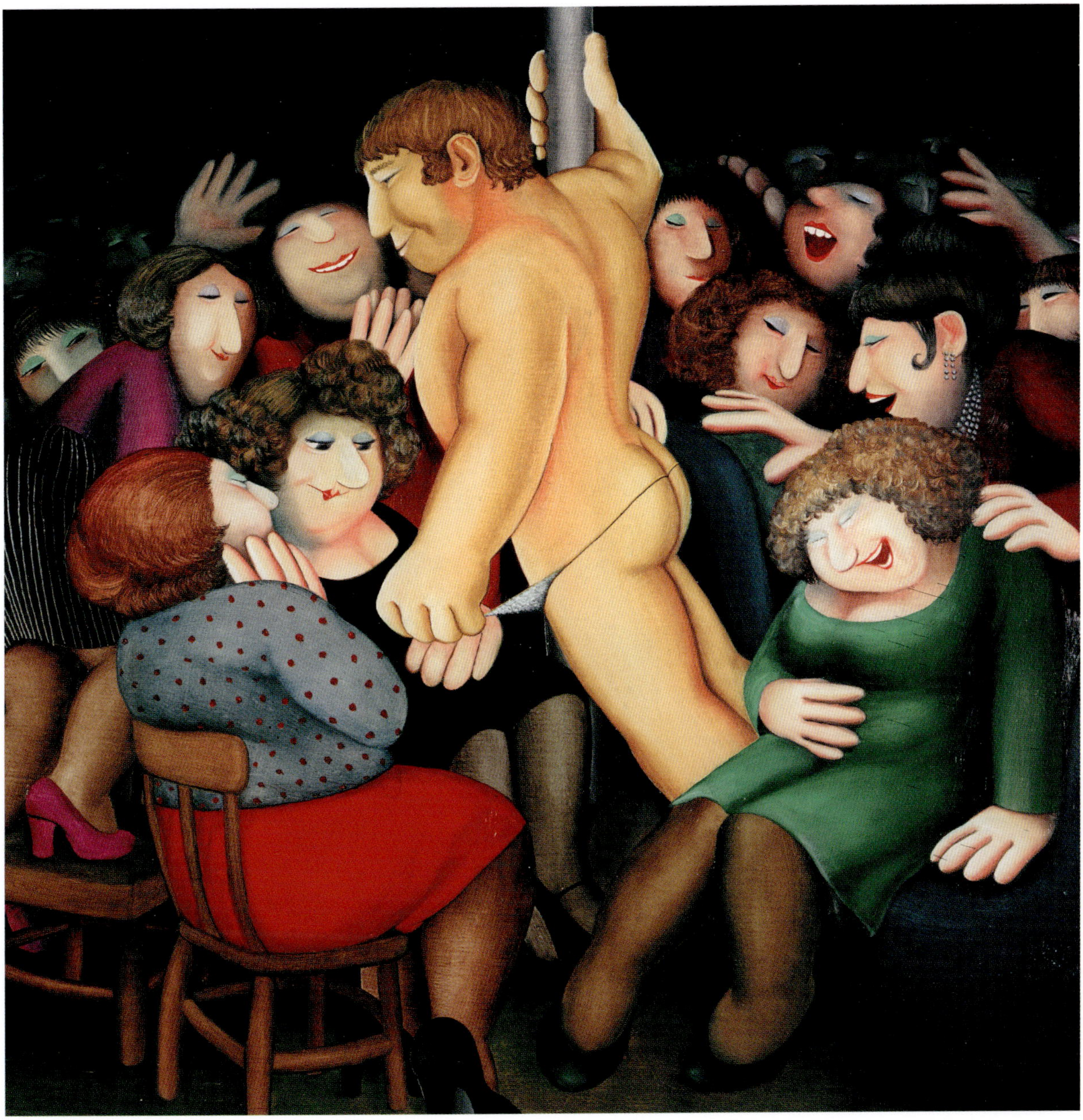

Ladies Night (Ivor Dickie)
(1980). Commissioned by Gay Search for *Woman* magazine and one of the most popular images to be reproduced as prints and cards.

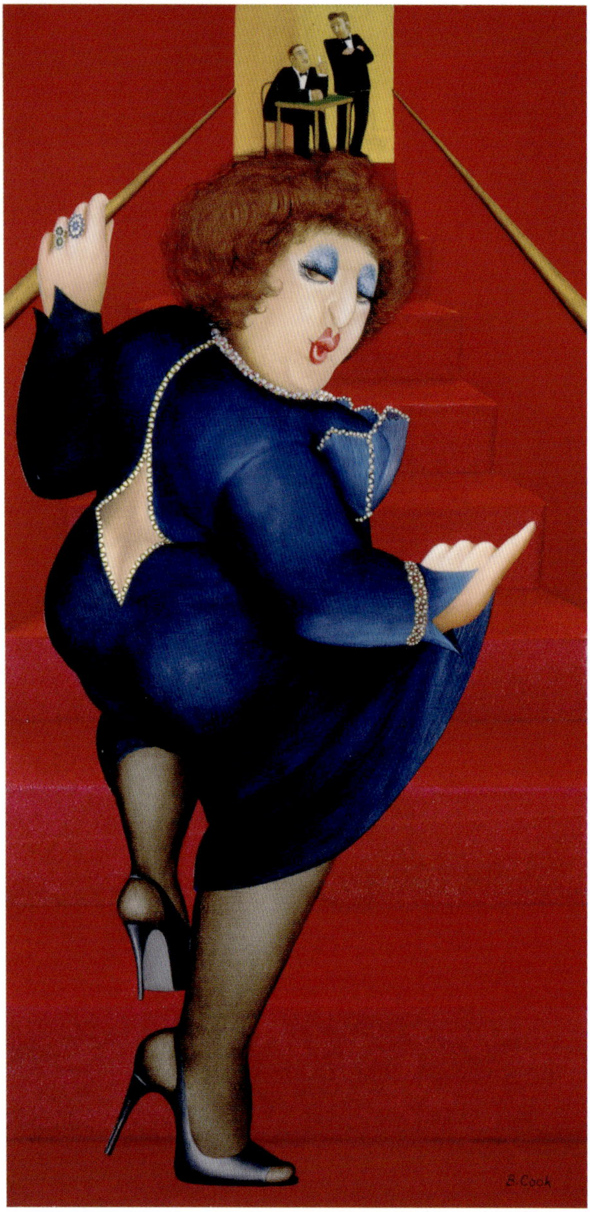

Ruby Venezuela
(1987). Ruby leading the way to the piano bar after her performance at Madam Jojo's. Here anyone could sing at the piano – but sometimes only once.

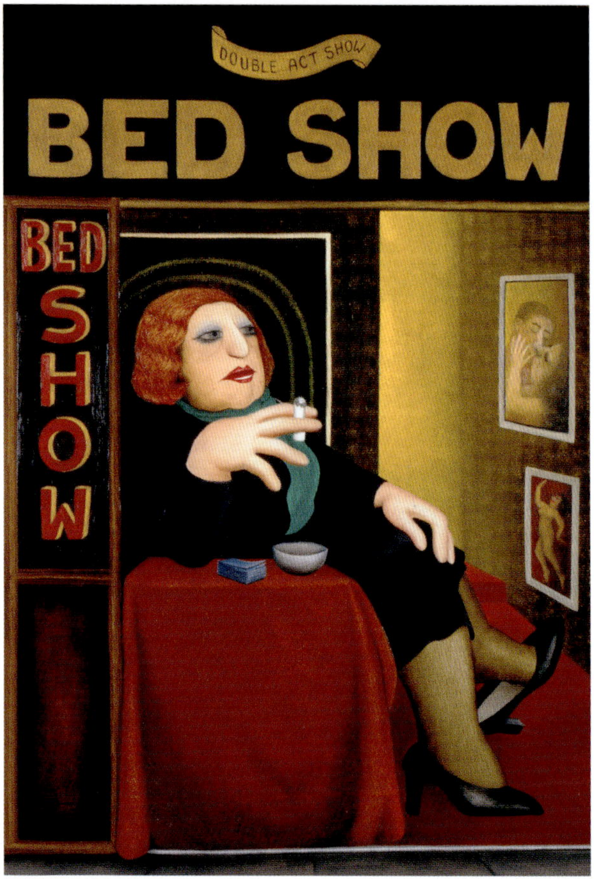

Bed Show in Soho
(1986)

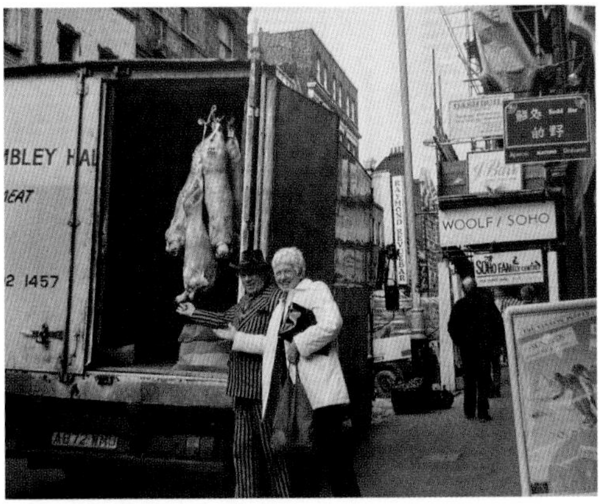

Beryl with George Melly, from Dan Farson's book *Soho in the 1950s*

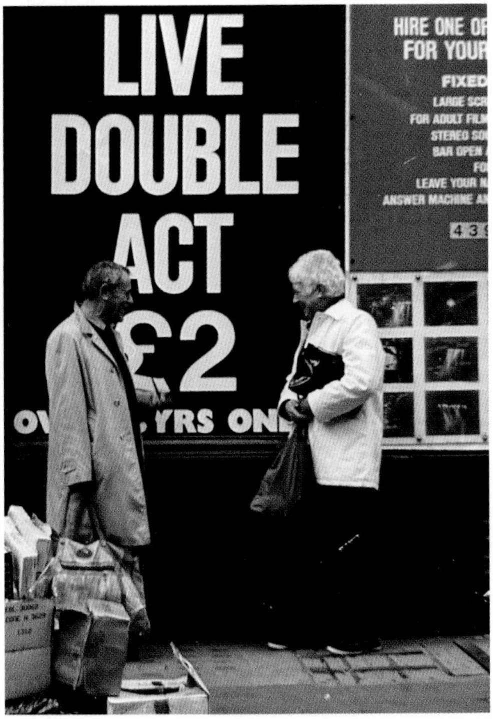

From a composite Christmas card sent to Beryl and John by Dan Farson in 1987

In *The Bumper Edition*, Beryl says she had joined in with the cries of 'Get 'em Off!' and that, for once, she was very happy with the painting. She particularly liked the expression worn by the lady in black, and how she had got in all the hands stretched towards Ivor.

I can now reveal what they saw when he did 'Get 'em Off'. 'He was wearing knickers with eyes on the back and a tassel on the front,' Gay Search later wrote.[2] In a private letter to Beryl, however, she said that he was not only nude but was 'helicoptering'. Apparently, the stripper was thrilled when he saw the painting – and after all that, complained that the face didn't look like him!

A newspaper interviewer who became a good friend was Daniel Farson. Farson has been described as photographer, writer and drunk, whose time in bohemian Soho fascinated Beryl. He was about the same age as she and John, and about 20 years younger than Barbara Ker-Seymer but he and his friends carried on the same traditions of a dissolute and occasionally inspired life.

Like Burra and Beryl, Farson was an observer, at places like the notorious Colony Club where the regulars were too drunk to notice or care. As he was blotto too, a great deal of what he claimed had happened was imaginary, but it had the ring of truth.

The first Beryl Cook interview I can find by Dan was published in *The Mail on Sunday* in September 1985. This coincided with the Portal's *Beryl Cook's New York* show, and the publication of the book of the same name by John Murray. During his visit to Plymouth, Beryl and John took him to a pub called The Bank. As its name suggests, it had been converted from a bank in 1982 and was on two levels, joined by a staircase. Dan said it was 'the best bank I've been in! And Union St such fun. I knew I would like you both, but had not expected such an immediate rapport. I hope it does not sound presumptuous if I say that I think of you now as friends. . . . It was a perfect visit.'[3]

Fortunately it seems the feeling was mutual, because in 1987 Beryl and John visited Dan in London. They enjoyed lunch at Langan's Brasserie in Mayfair, and were joined by George Melly, who insisted she go to a transvestite nightclub at midnight – this was Madam JoJo's, where 'a large man advanced towards her in a wig and false breasts and joined her table. On stage he had just appeared as "Ruby Venezuela playing Tweetie Pie", but he turned out to be a neighbour from Plymouth.'[4] Altogether Beryl and John had a fine old time, and George Melly became another friend. Dan's book,

Soho in the 1950s, includes a picture of Beryl with George Melly. Dan also sent one of Beryl and John standing outside a Soho porn show advertising a 'Live Double Act' which 'kept them tittering for hours'.[5] The resulting paintings featured in *Beryl Cook's London*, published the following year. Beryl had watered down the attractions that were advertised on the front of the *Bed Show in Soho* – choosing rather less explicit ones.

Barbara, who knew Dan and his circle of old, was concerned: 'He is first and foremost a journalist and would sacrifice his best friend for a story. You are wise to meet every journalist with "no comment". Particularly after reading that book about journalists . . . Dan Farson is getting rather unreliable as he drinks too much and is probably a bit desperate now for a "good" story (i.e. a "bad" one)'.[6] Beryl replied that she was weak as far as he was concerned, because she so admired his photographs. He was also very entertaining.

Barbara's attitude was completely understandable. This was the era of tabloid journalism, paparazzi and intrusion. The public's appetite for sleazy stories and celebrity scandal knew no bounds. Beryl collected the more amusing clippings, some of which were incorporated into her work. But she had no wish to be the subject of prurient interest herself.

The main reason for this was the crippling shyness which led to days and nights of terrible anxiety before recorded or live interviews. Nobody would have known, because she was highly amusing and full of anecdotes. A reviewer described a Radio 3 interview with Beryl as 'one of the most hilarious three quarters of an hour that my radio has given me for some time'. This was one of Edward Lucie-Smith's *Conversations with Artists* series, so it probably helped that she knew her interviewer. The review continued:

> Beryl Cook, Plymouth boarding house landlady turned painter, again behaved as if there were no microphone, while confessing between hoots of laughter to the curious selection of objects that turn her on and stimulate her to paint . . . why these act upon her as they do she was quite unable to say and Lucie-Smith applied his professional-critical questioning in vain. To his credit he quickly realized that it was going to get him nowhere and began to let the conversation run itself.
>
> There was quite a lot to be learnt of both parties from the fact that he had never heard of The Flintstones – one of Mrs Cook's sources of inspiration – while she, when asked what she used for references, had no idea what he meant.[7]

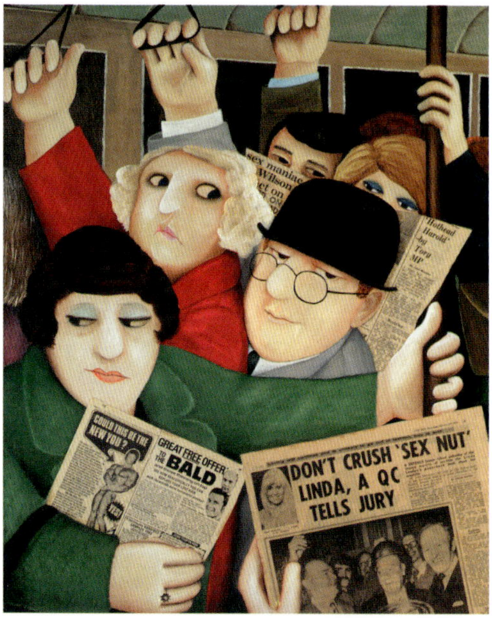

Togetherness
(1977). Featuring newspapers from Beryl's collection

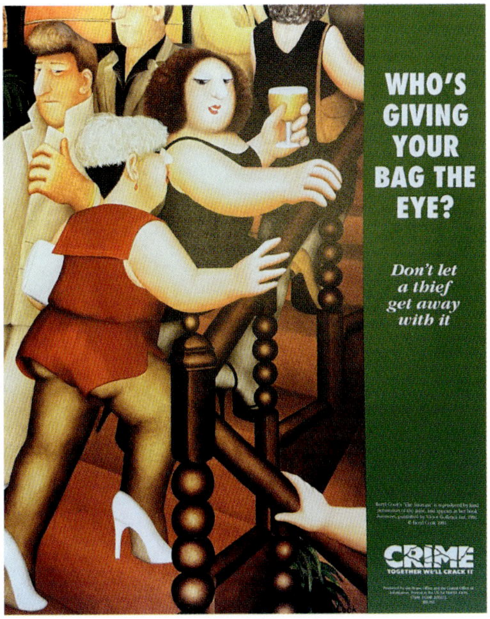

Poster using Beryl Cook's painting *The Staircase* that caused a 'sex storm', according to the *Western Morning News* (1992)

Over the following years, Beryl made many television appearances and gave media interviews, usually coinciding with a new exhibition or book. It was never something she enjoyed, but it was something she knew she had to do. Obviously, she never read or watched any of them, but John wrote a thank you letter afterwards.

Meanwhile the press continued to try to stir up controversy if it could. Beryl wrote to Barbara that someone in Barrow-in-Furness had complained to their local paper about the print of *Lunchtime Refreshment* (see page 106) in the window of a shop. The press did try to get a quote from Beryl, but 'fortunately we are ex-directory and as you can imagine I had NO COMMENT.'

Barbara offered to write to the complainer 'saying that I am an elderly lady in her mid-80s who was present at the performance and I thought it was charming and delightful and everybody enjoyed themselves very much. The men were not in the least salacious and I am sure returned to their building sites well refreshed and able to get on with their strenuous jobs.'[8]

The *Western Morning News* of 5th September 1992 tried to whip up a story with the headline, 'Warning posters stir up a sex storm'.[9] It reported that there had been a complaint from feminists 'because she had allowed one of her masterpieces to be used in a "sexist" anti-crime poster'. An Equal Opportunities Commission spokeswoman said, 'This is very unfortunate. It's a pity that a Government Department can't put its message across in a non-sexist manner.'

Newcastle Police retorted that it was far more effective than a bland crime prevention poster of the past: 'One day last week half of all crimes committed in an area of Newcastle was handbag and purse theft.' The Home Office there had been an all-women research team.

The article continued: 'She [Beryl] was unrepentant yesterday, saying complaints about the poster were "a matter of complete indifference."' I should think she was less indifferent in private, as she had a very low opinion of strident feminists.

None of this would have cost Beryl much sleep, but there was an ongoing court case which dragged on and did upset her. A litigious neighbour (he had feuds with several people) next to their land in Cornwall accused them of having depicted his family naked (apart from hats) in *Tea in the Garden* (see page 107).

It seems likely that someone had seen the Gallery Five card of this painting and posted it through his door. He said that it undermined his reputation in Plymouth and his local area. He had also received an anonymous phone call where someone had gruffly asked 'Can I come to your next tea party?!'

It is true that the background of the original painting was based on the neighbouring house (Beryl often used photographs to help with backgrounds) but she had never seen them naked and the faces didn't look like them. And the neighbour undermined his position by talking to the press himself.[10] He dropped the case, paying all expenses. John and Beryl donated the payment to a local charity.

Nevertheless, as the picture was incredibly popular, Beryl repainted the background.

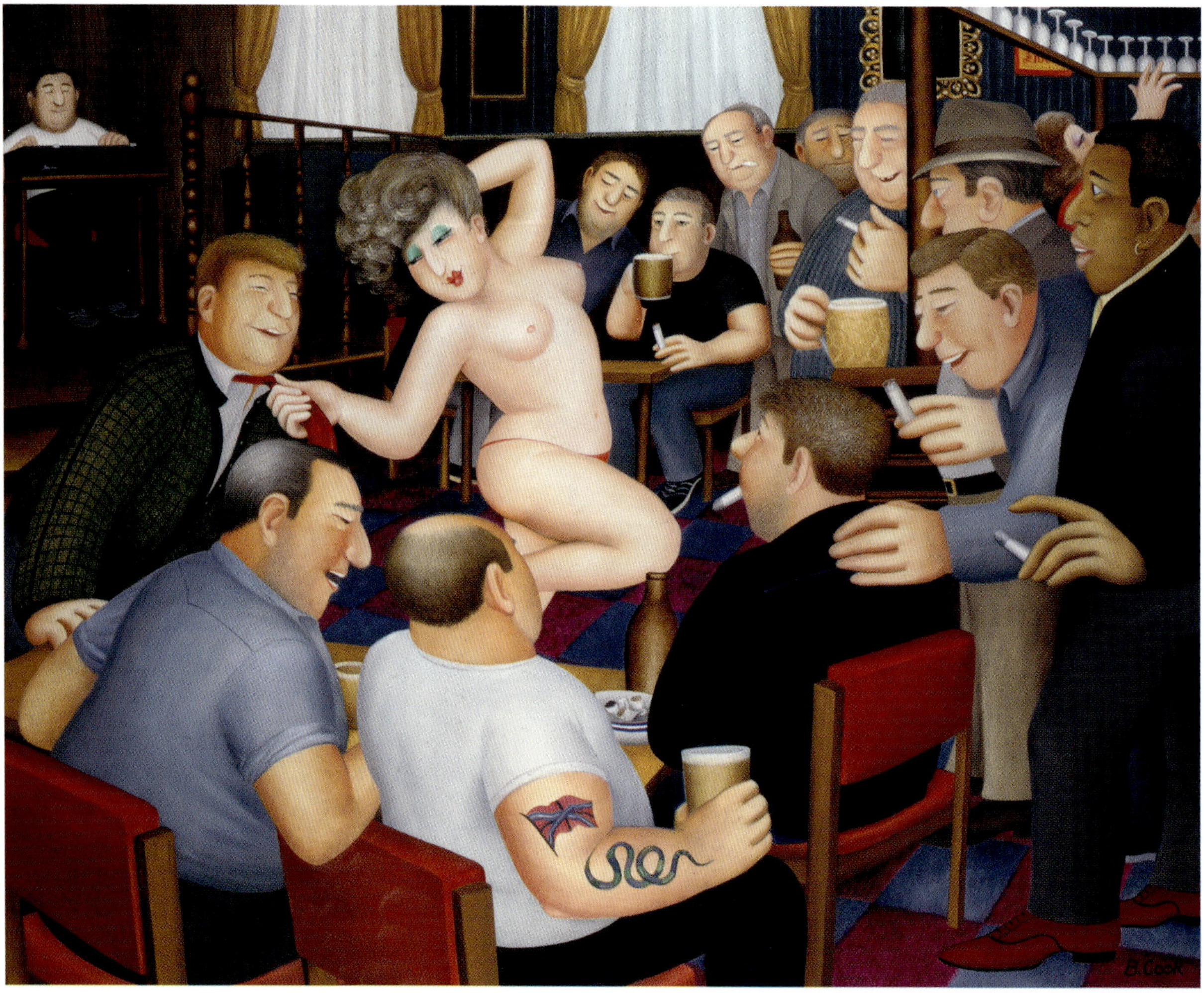

Lunchtime Refreshment
(1990). The Queen's pub in Docklands

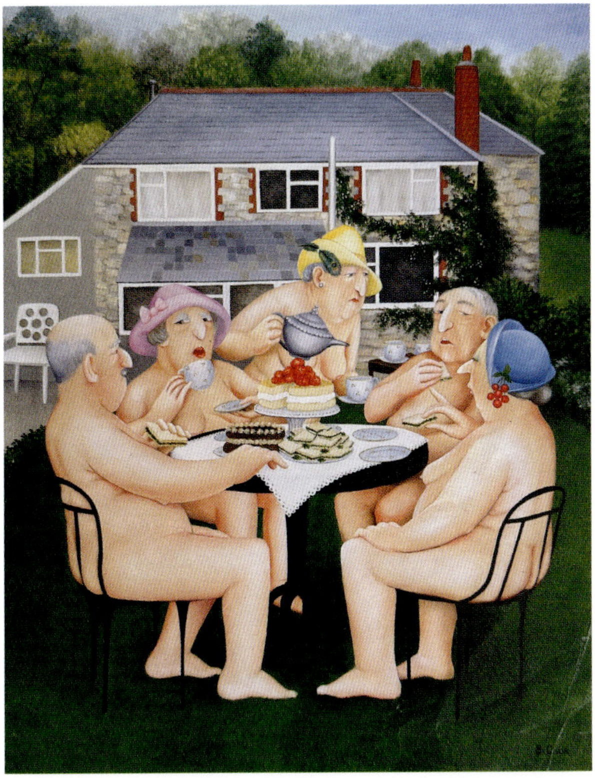

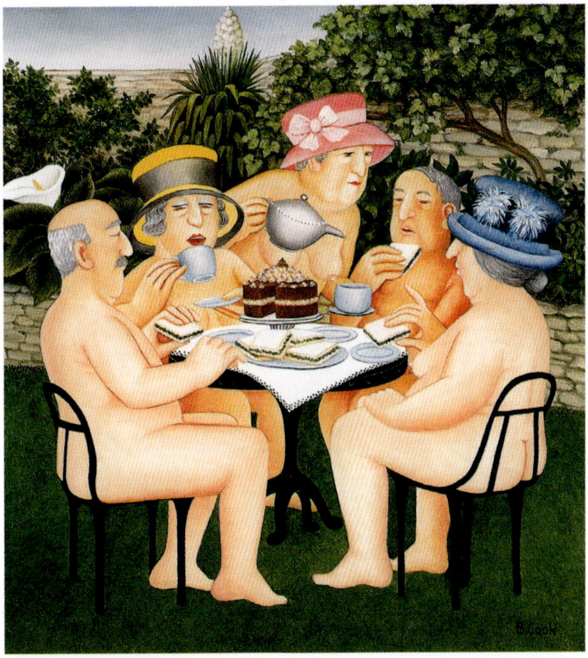

Tea in the Garden
The subject of a law suit, original (c 1985) and overpainted (c 1995)

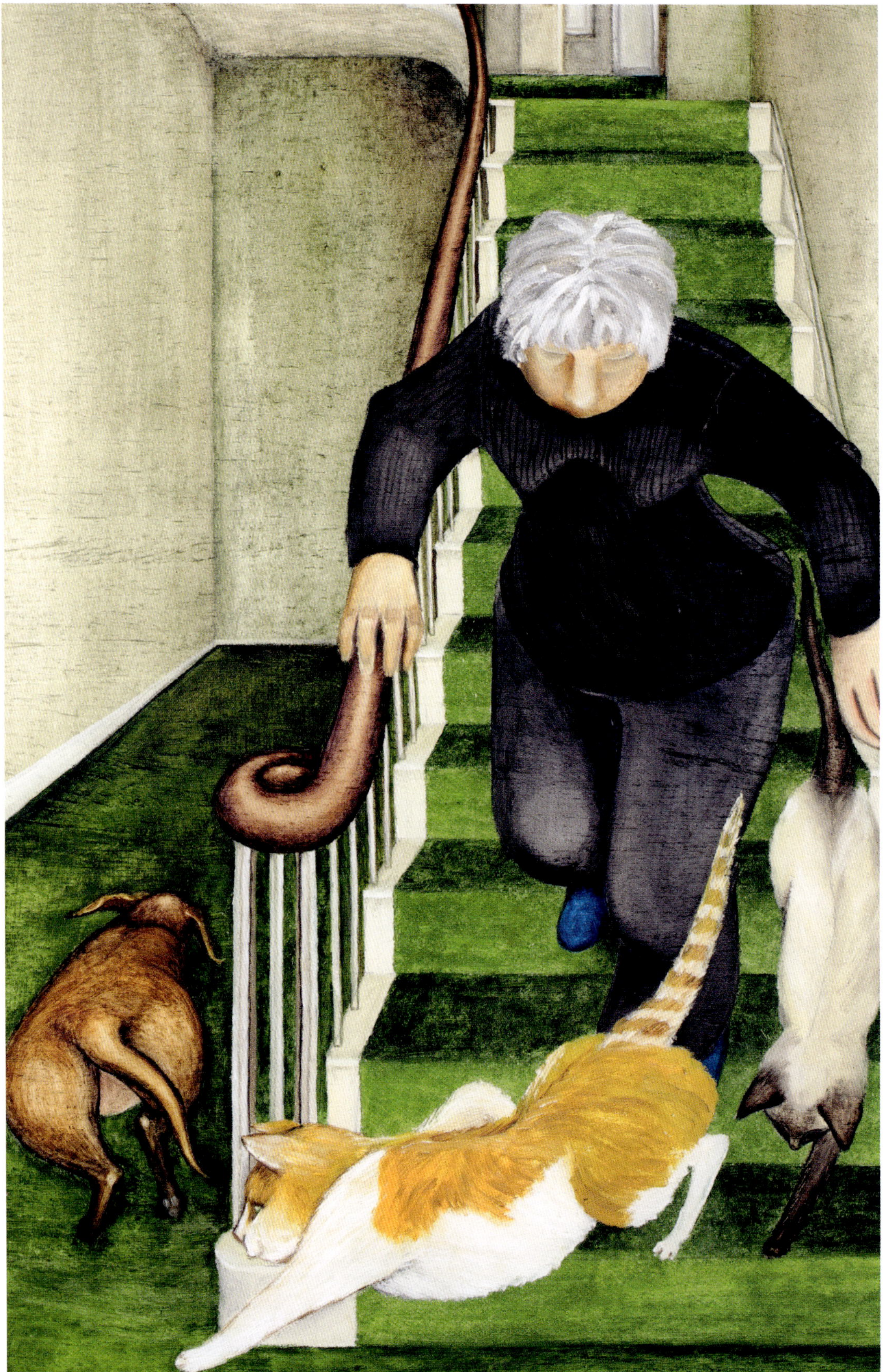

09

Life as a Painter

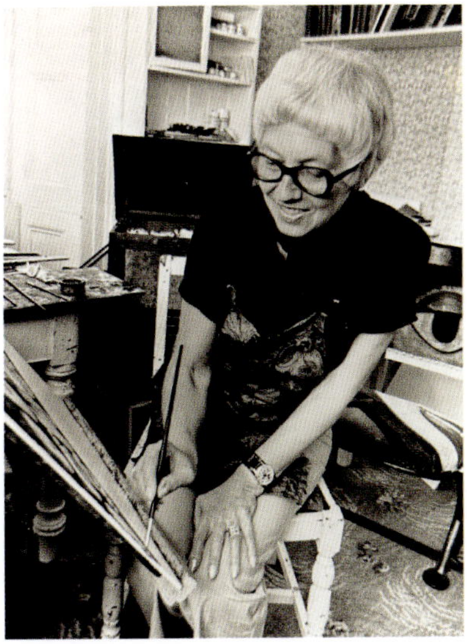

Beryl at work in her studio,
which had once been a guest bedroom
(late 1970s)

LEFT
Coming Down the Stairs
(1974), featuring Lulu the dog, ginger cat Cedric
and Lottie the Siamese

Becoming well-known has given me two great gifts – being able to write 'painter' on forms where it asks 'occupation', and the freedom to paint all day without feeling guilty about wasting time.

Letter dated 16 September 1984
from Beryl Cook to Chris Fassnidge

Almost immediately after her rise to fame, Beryl realized that she could give up the B&B business and work full-time on her art. She moved her studio out of the ironing room and into one of the guest bedrooms and she and John quickly established a routine.

Every day except Sunday, the teamaker beside the bed went off at half past six. After a bath and breakfast, she and John took Bonzo for a walk on the Hoe. Bonzo was notorious for not coming when called and, being afraid of larger dogs, he usually got home before them. By nine, they were back at the house. Urgent letters would be dealt with, unless there was a pressing idea developing in Beryl's head.

On three days a week Beryl went shopping. She loved the Pannier Market, where there were fruit, meat and fish stalls, and junk shops where she could look for bargains to add to her collection. Despite their newly found success Beryl did not splash out on expensive items or fancy clothes – she still enjoyed exploring charity shops and places like Littlewoods, where prices were low. Beryl was often first at the door when the supermarket opened and deft at arriving quickly at the tills. She was back at home by 10.30 a.m. and up the stairs like a gazelle.

Beryl painted until about 12.30 when she had a quick lunch alone unless John was able to join her – as he was when he got a job at Allen's Garage a few minutes away and after he retired to become her manager. Either way, she was back at her painting table by 1.15 p.m. and would paint for a couple of hours prior to an afternoon nap.

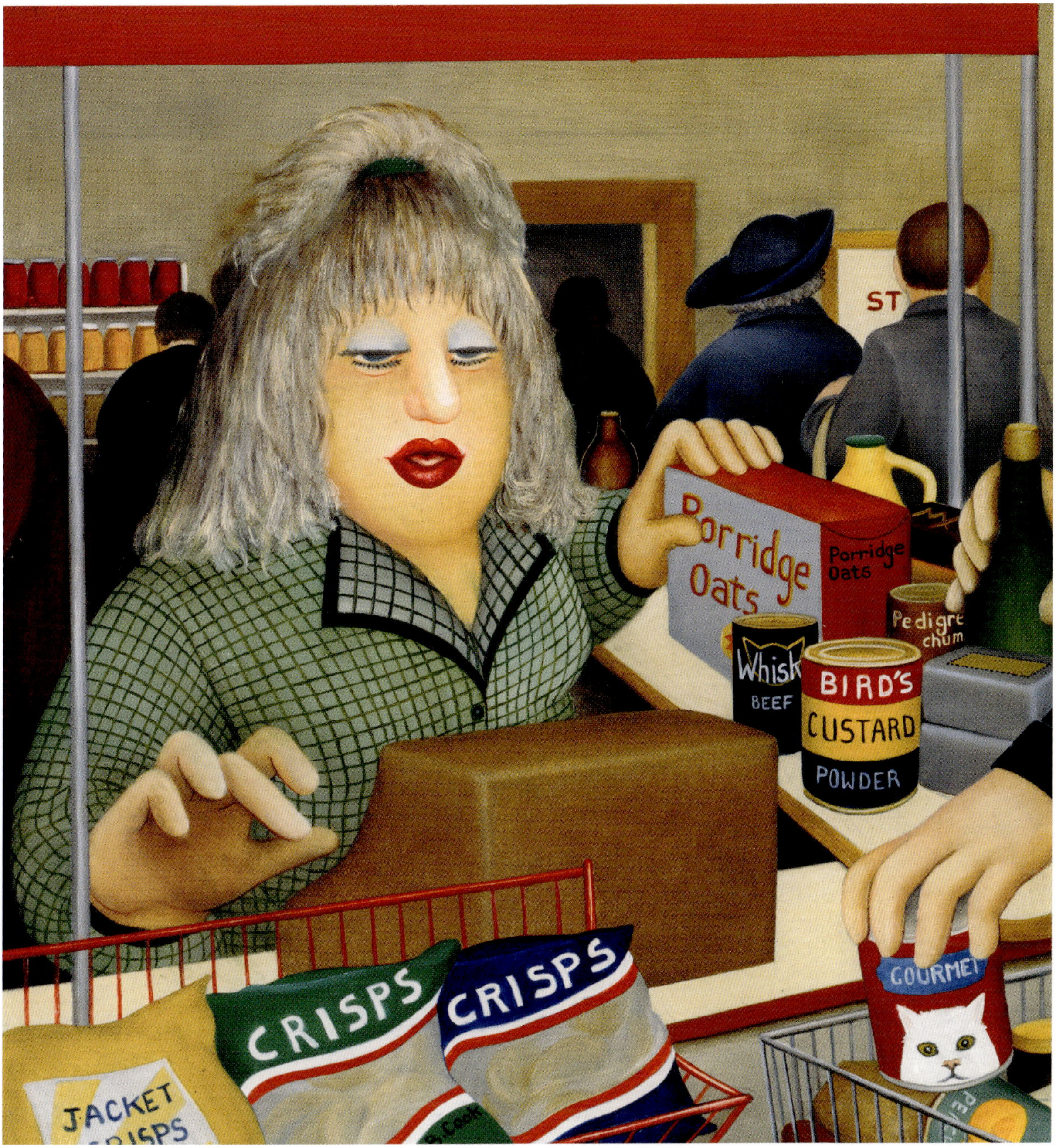

Checkout Girl
(early 1990s). This shows Beryl's favourite cashier, due to her perfect red, glistening mouth and her fabulous hair – sadly she left before Beryl had finished the painting.

Then more painting as long as the daylight held out, although she did like to be in the kitchen by six when John came home from work. The evening meals were prepared by John. On weekday evenings the couple would watch television after dinner, although Beryl often knitted or read at the same time. They avoided the news or anything unpleasant. Programmes they enjoyed included *Coronation Street*, *Stanley Baxter* and *Benny Hill*. There was quite a lot of wrangling with the new video recorder so that they could record programmes on art, but it often failed. They were in bed by 11.00 p.m. where Beryl read, preferably biographies of people already dead as she felt they were more truthful.[1]

Once a week, Beryl went to the hairdressing salon at the Co-op, which was part of Derry's Department Store. She wore her hair grey and fairly short but I think she enjoyed looking in the mirror at the more complex hairstyles. In her picture of the hairdressing salon she has indulged in her love of curls and also introduced the Head of Department, the only man. He was Giovanni Sponziello,[2] who had come to England in 1963 where he enjoyed a stellar career with Steiner before coming to the Co-op in Plymouth so that he could care for his family. He now lives in Tavistock.

Her hairdresser was called Sarah and Beryl was fascinated by her account of her hen party, which inspired the famous painting of the women arriving at The Dolphin (see page 46). The bride to be is dressed in a huge hat decorated with inflated condoms, as we would call them today. Beryl painted a smaller version for Sarah.

Beryl was also a frequent visitor to the library, which at the time was in the same building as the Museum and Art Gallery. She wrote:

> I love reading, and used this library for many years. Libraries can offer me books for pleasure, books to tell me about other countries when we are planning to travel, books to show me what a bassoon looks like if I should suddenly need to paint one, and even a book to teach me how to paint if necessary! For this painting I took notes of the bookshelves and furniture each time I made a visit so I could try to make it authentic. To get the books right I copied a pile of my own, artistically arranged on a nearby table.[3]

Beryl was an extremely quick reader. She would occasionally skip the boring bits and would then pass the book to John and Tony to read before returning it to the library. Maintaining a continual flow of books took more

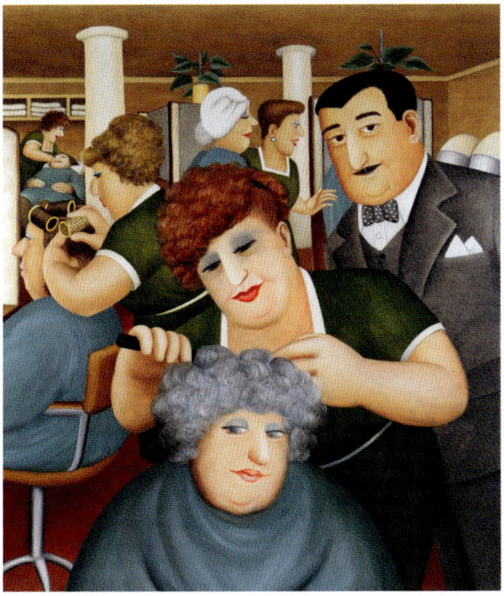

Hairdressing Salon
(1990). The salon was overseen by Giovanni Sponziello who is checking that everything is going well. Due to her love of painting hair, Beryl painted hairdressers many times.

effort than it would today. Some had to come via Inter Library Loan which could take several months, and others needed to be ordered through a bookshop. Many of the books were recommended by Barbara, and the two would exchange opinions about what they had read – with Barbara often knowing juicy snippets about the people in them which had not been included. Beryl rarely read novels.

On Friday and Saturday evenings, Beryl and John would visit the local pubs, just as they had before she became famous. On the whole Beryl could be anonymous but they would sit near the door so that she could escape if cornered by an over-familiar local, which did occasionally happen. Usually, these visits were fairly short unless something riveting occurred.

The Lockyer closed shortly after the *Sunday Times* article was published (see page 63). One of the regulars, who blogs under the name of Madam Arcati, wrote, 'the loss of our pub was a disaster for the community. There might have been bitchiness, fall-outs and gossip but it was a community; everyone knew everyone and we all had a shared sense of identity. Now we had no-where to meet, chat, share our stories and to escape what could be a very unfriendly heterosexual world'.[4] They set out to find a replacement, eventually arriving at the Gypsy Moth IV on the Hoe, where Beryl and John often joined them.

Sundays were the only days Beryl didn't paint. The day started with her sitting at the kitchen table and tackling the fan mail, and thereafter it was family time. John would prepare a traditional Sunday lunch for themselves and any family and friends who were staying. Guests could stay upstairs and would be sent home with prawn or crab sandwiches for the journey.

The task of dealing with the fan mail was a large one. It arrived even if it was addressed simply to 'Beryl Cook, The Hoe, Plymouth'. The number swelled enormously after a magazine article and even more after a TV appearance. Letters came from across the world, especially the United States.

Beryl told Barbara that she wished she could be like Edward Burra, whose special x-ray vision allowed him to identify the envelopes that contained cheques, after which he threw away the rest. In fact, fan letters were easily distinguished as they were usually handwritten.

Beryl felt a strong sense of duty to respond to every letter. Many could be answered with a signed Gallery Five card and a fact sheet giving a basic biography and information about where paintings, prints and cards could be obtained.

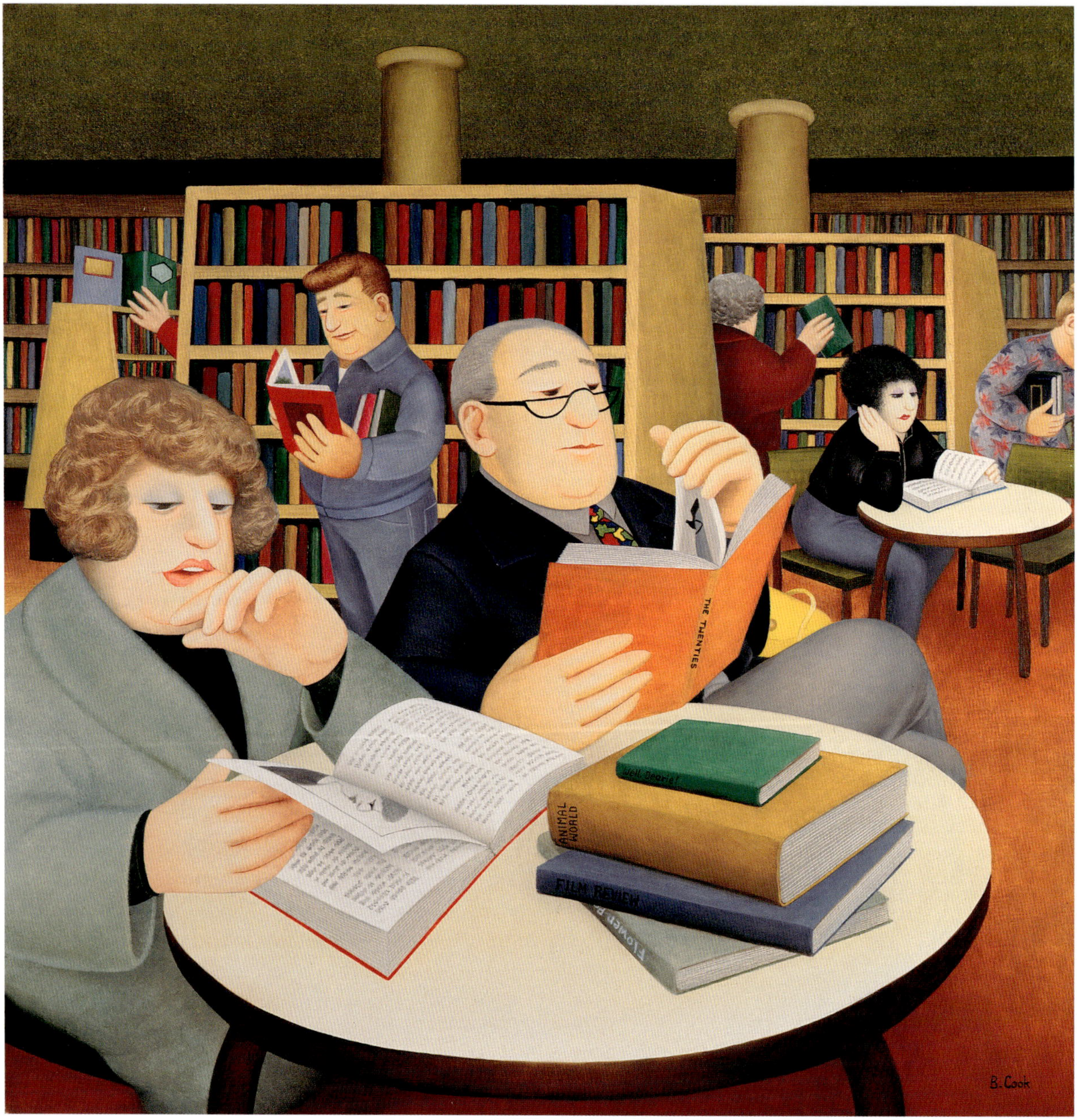

Public Library

(1980s). The man is reading *The Twenties*, reflecting Beryl's affection for the art, design and gossip of the period, and the little book on top is *Well Dearie: The letters of Edward Burra* by William Chappell, both friends of Barbara Ker-Seymer.

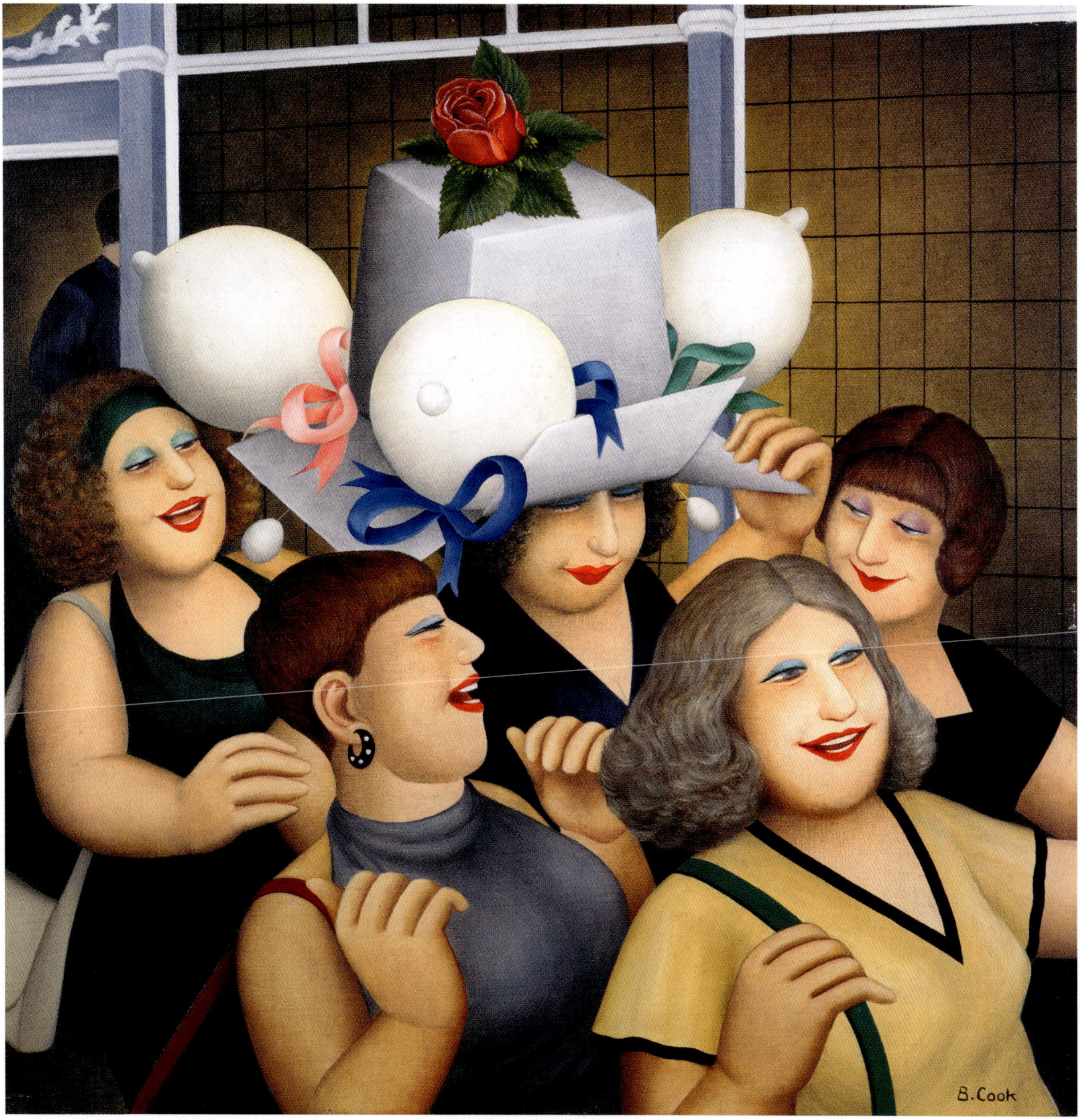

Hen Party 2

(1995). This is a second painting of the hen party also depicted on page 46, with some changes to both the hat and the girls.

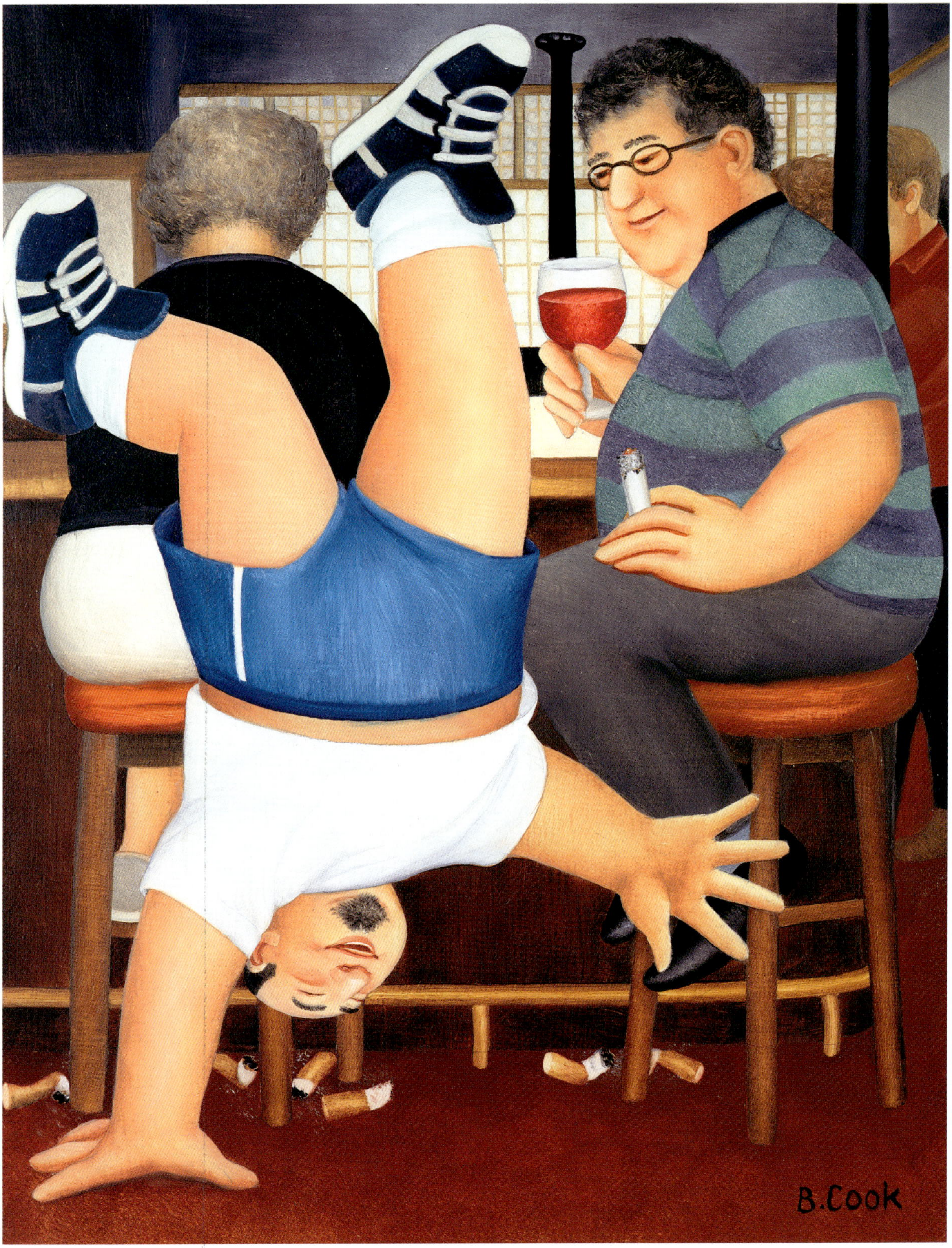

A Cartwheel for Billy
(1990s). Beryl didn't witness this incident in The Dolphin herself, but as soon as she heard about it a picture formed in her mind.

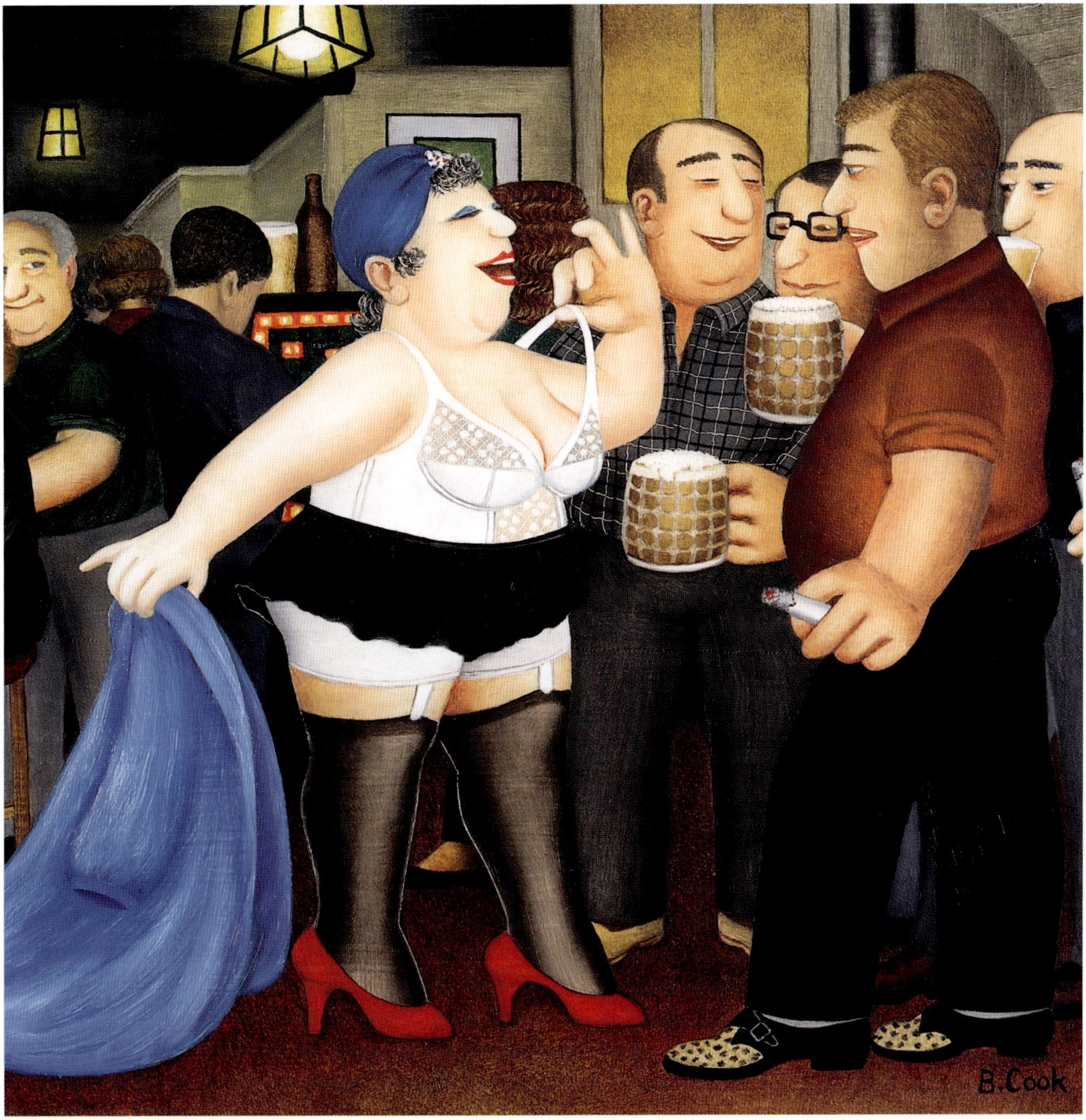

Strippergram

(1990s). Another event in The Dolphin – Beryl said she didn't know what the birthday boy made of it, as she was sketching the incident inside her handbag.

Requests for public appearances, talks, appearances on television panel games and invitations to openings were all politely refused by John on her behalf. However, a large number of the letters were answered by Beryl personally, in her own writing. A draft was stapled to the letter and filed.

Beryl's drafts and the final letters are neatly written, with few alterations, whereas John's are spidery and often require a family member to decipher them. Given that Beryl was also painting and drawing six days a week, as well as signing huge numbers of art prints, this is an amazing feat and must have contributed to her later arm and shoulder problems.

The letters provide a valuable insight into Beryl's life and what her work meant to people. People wrote to say how much they love her work and list exactly what prints and cards they had on display in their houses, as well as those they particularly admire. They are bursting to report 'Beryl Cook' moments, or to suggest topics for her: their tap-dancing class (lots of bouncing bosoms), Morris Dancing, wrestling or the Turkish baths in Harrogate. She and John are invited to tea, or to stay, if in the area, and fans ask to visit them. They enclose photographs of their families and pets, a surprising number of poems, and their own re-interpretations of her pictures. The writing paper is homely, decorated with flowers or bonneted girls. They list the books that bring them joy and comfort in difficult times.

Very often they say how much they enjoy the captions in the books, which explain the background to the paintings and some of the challenges she faced. Many of the letters show great perception, especially those who felt that Beryl's work had been overlooked or undervalued.

Other letters came from people who had bought her paintings, not having met the artist. They expressed their delight, and described where they hung, or the response of the person they had been bought for. I particularly enjoyed this one, from a vicar:

> Your marvellous, funny, truthful and colourful painting of Jonah [see page 120] is in loving and caring hands – mine! It can't be easy to part with masterpieces, especially when you've painted them . . . I finally decided to ring the Alexander Gallery at the moment of committal at a funeral! It's seen by vicarage visitors – prayer group, Church Council, Mothers' Union, etc. Not everyone likes him – he's a much more 'successful' work of art than mere universal approval could give: those who think he is superb outweigh those who don't. PS I get wonderful results from sending *Ladies Night* [see page 101] to unsuspecting fellow clergy!

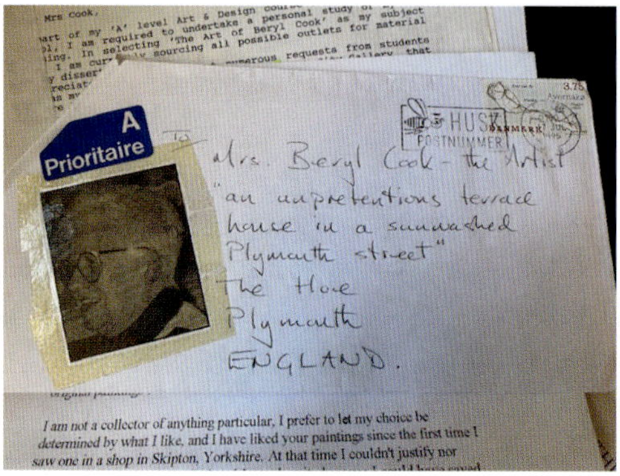

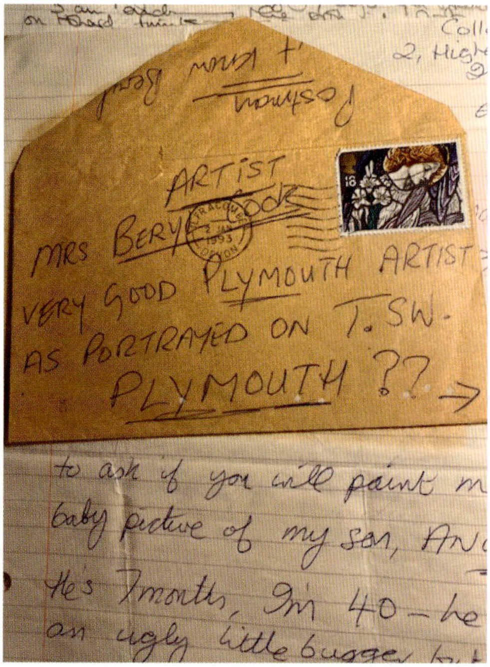

Letters that arrived despite being incorrectly addressed

There were many letters requesting a donation or a painting or print for a charity. Without being indiscrete I can tell you that the Cooks were very generous, although they had to be selective. They particularly favoured local charities for animals or sick children, and supported London Zoo by sponsoring an animal (a vulture called Beryl, and later a warthog called Basil (see page 121)). This reflected, perhaps, recognition of places that had provided inspiration for Beryl's paintings.

Beryl and John also supported requests endorsed by their friends. George Melly sent a circular from the Aids Crisis Trust requesting items for an auction to raise funds for Britain's first hospice and day centre for AIDs victims, the London Lighthouse Hospice. John wrote, 'Just a note on Beryl's behalf she is upstairs brush in hand. This is for the Aids Crisis Trust Auction. We both hope it raises a few pounds. It's of one of the acts at Madame JoJo's.' George sent a postcard in response, saying he 'loved the busy bee and the flowers' (see page 123).

Beryl received increasing numbers of letters from schools, where they had learned about her work (hopefully selectively – although there was one letter from a parent whose four-year-old son's favourite picture was *Anyone for a Whipping?* (see page 60) and produced their own, copies of which were enclosed). The number of enquiries from students studying her art at A level or as part of their degrees also increased. Many could be dealt with via the prepared biography. Beryl answered the others (or if she was busy painting or away, John would ask her and transcribe the answers). Only once did she suffer questionnaire overload:

> Q6: Surely at first your paintings looked wrong to you with their strange perspectives and inaccurate scales. Why did you leave them like this? Were you not tempted to make them look more realistic?
> A: I'm horrified to learn of the strange perspectives and inaccurate scales, I thought I was a realistic painter.

This questionnaire was from a sixth former doing a personal study on an artist that interested him and writing to her 'in her capacity as a naïve artist'. She answered all his other 40 or so questions with a straight bat – and it's quite a reasonable question really, though not tactful.

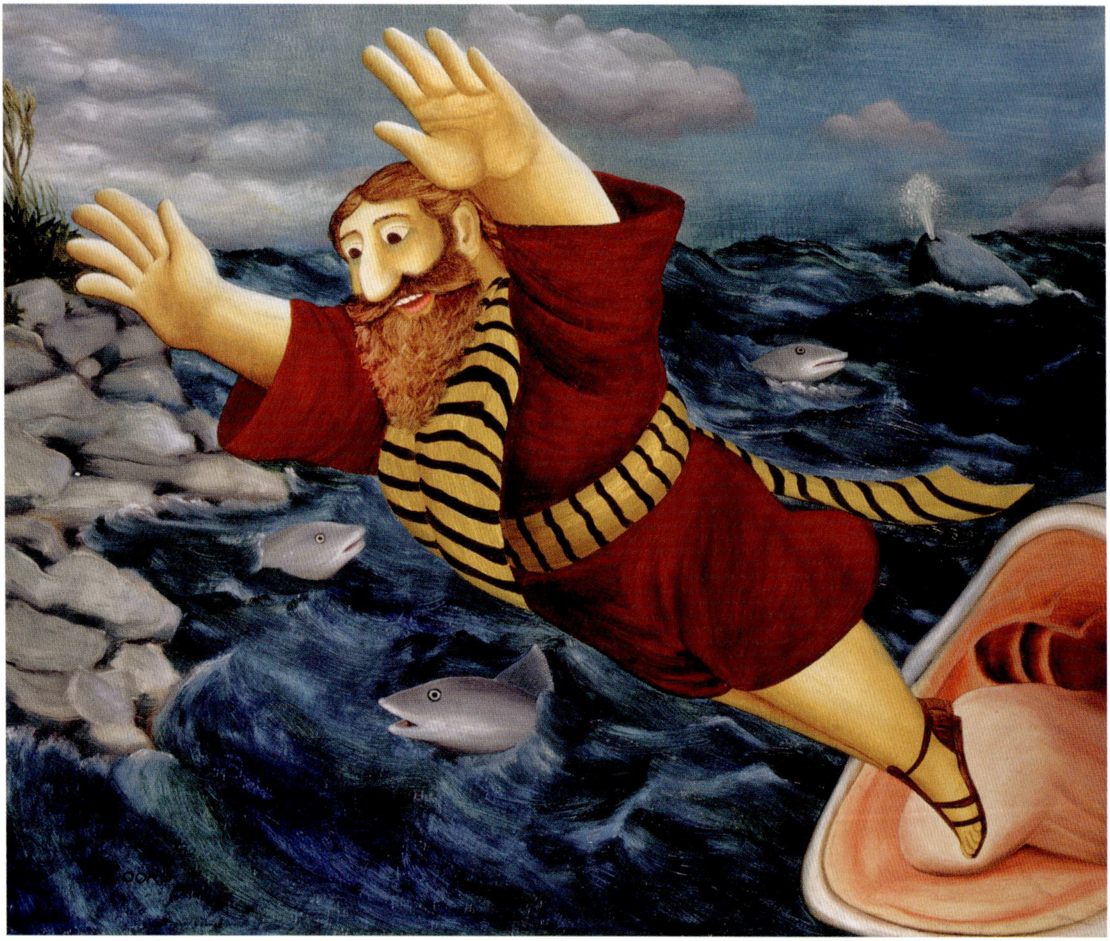

Jonah and the Whale

(c 1981). Beryl used a Victorian *Children's Book of Bible Stories* as inspiration. She said that the miracle was that Jonah emerged bone dry.

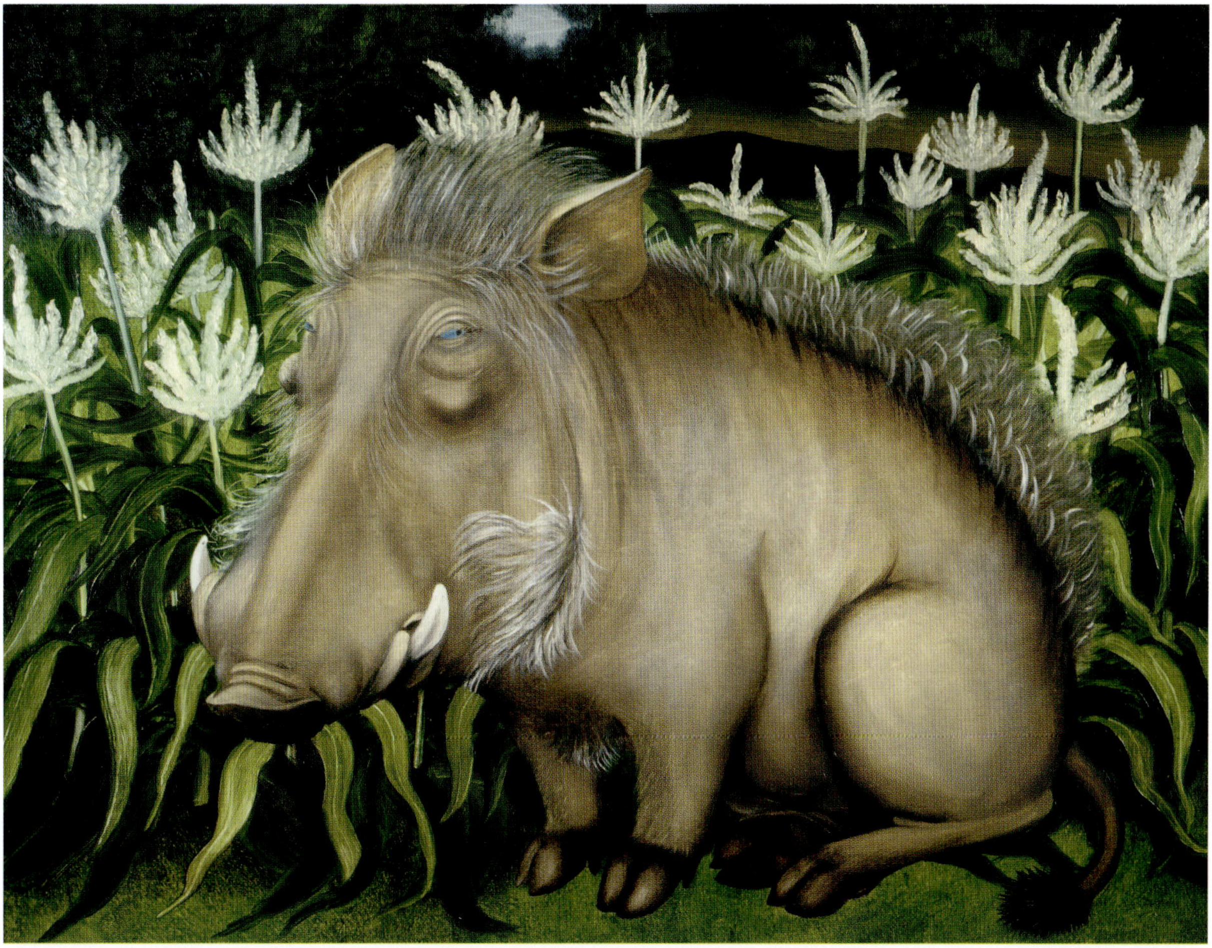

Basil the Warthog
(c 1980). Beryl 'adopted' a warthog at London Zoo because she remembered them fondly from Southern Africa.

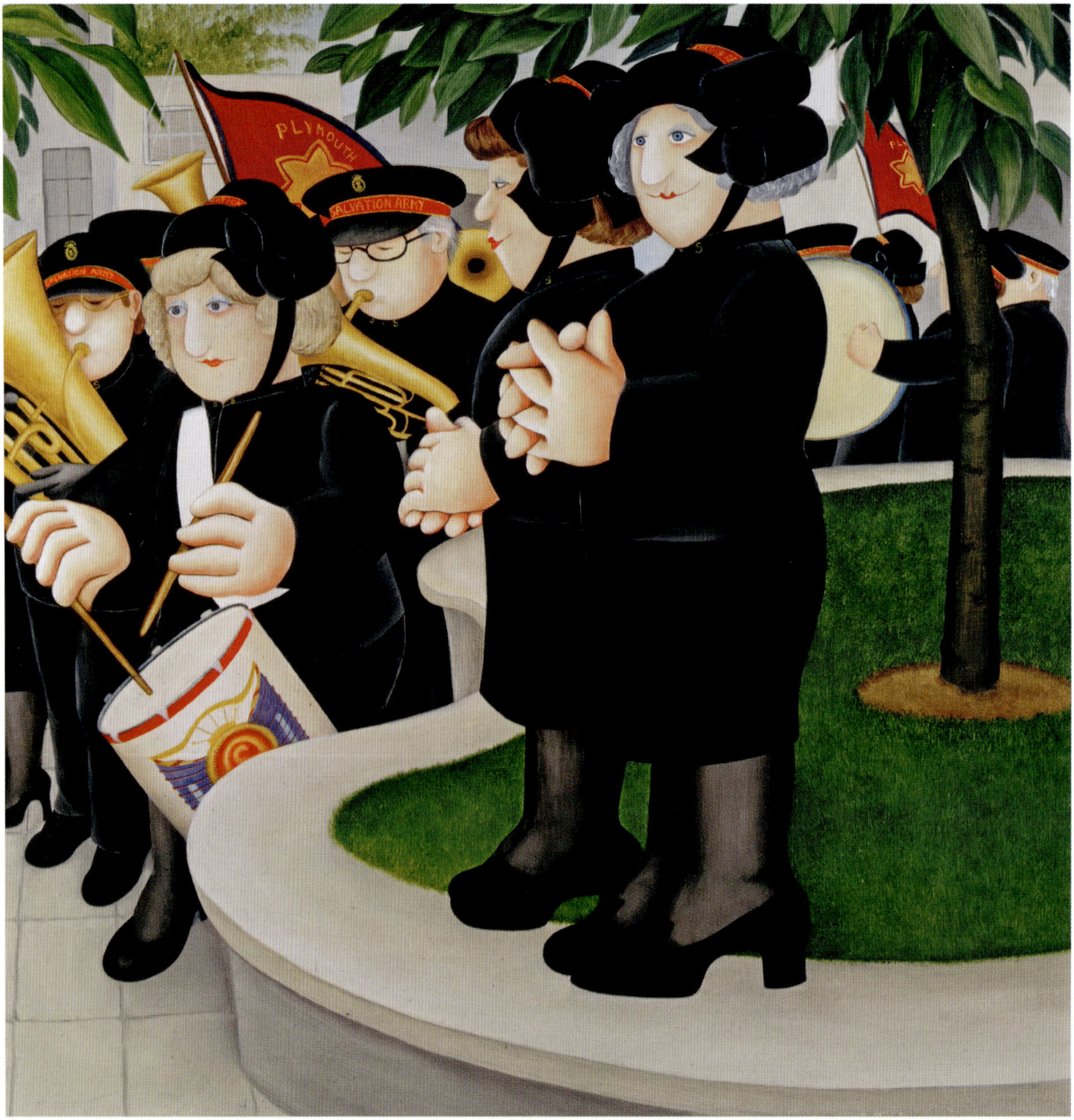

The Salvation Army

(c 1980). Beryl and John Senior were big fans of the Salvation Army and its work and knew some of the Plymouth members personally.

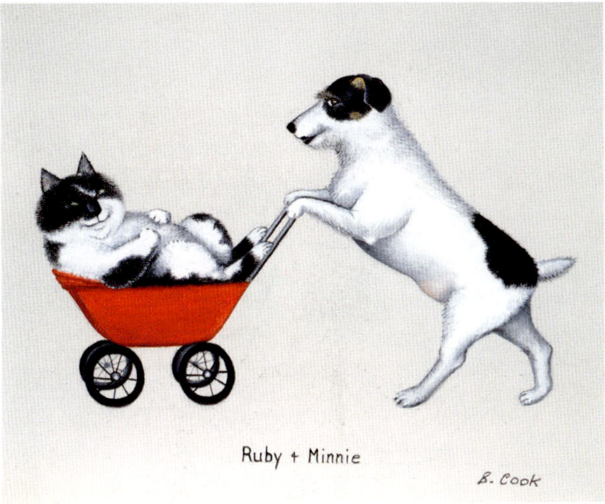

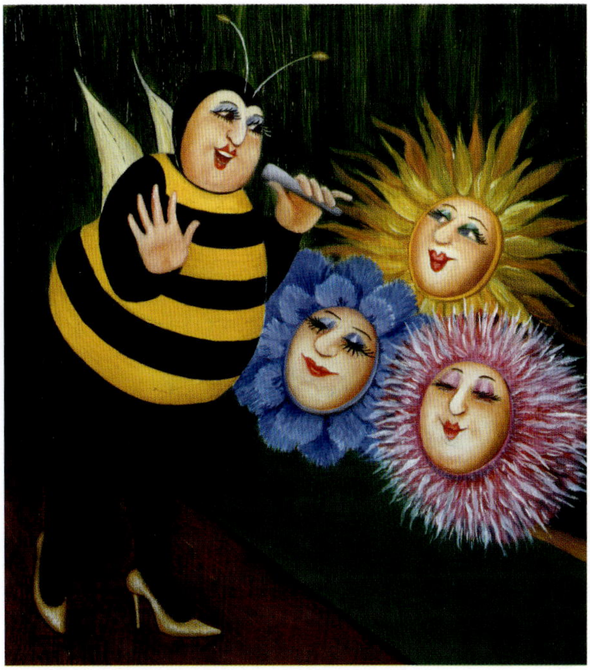

Ruby and Minnie
(early 1980s). Design for a card for Plymouth and District Dogs and Cats Home. Ruby was adopted from this charity, which is now called Gables.

Madame Jojo's
(1987). Painted for an Aids Crisis Trust auction. Madam Jojo's would no doubt have been well-known to bidders at the auction.

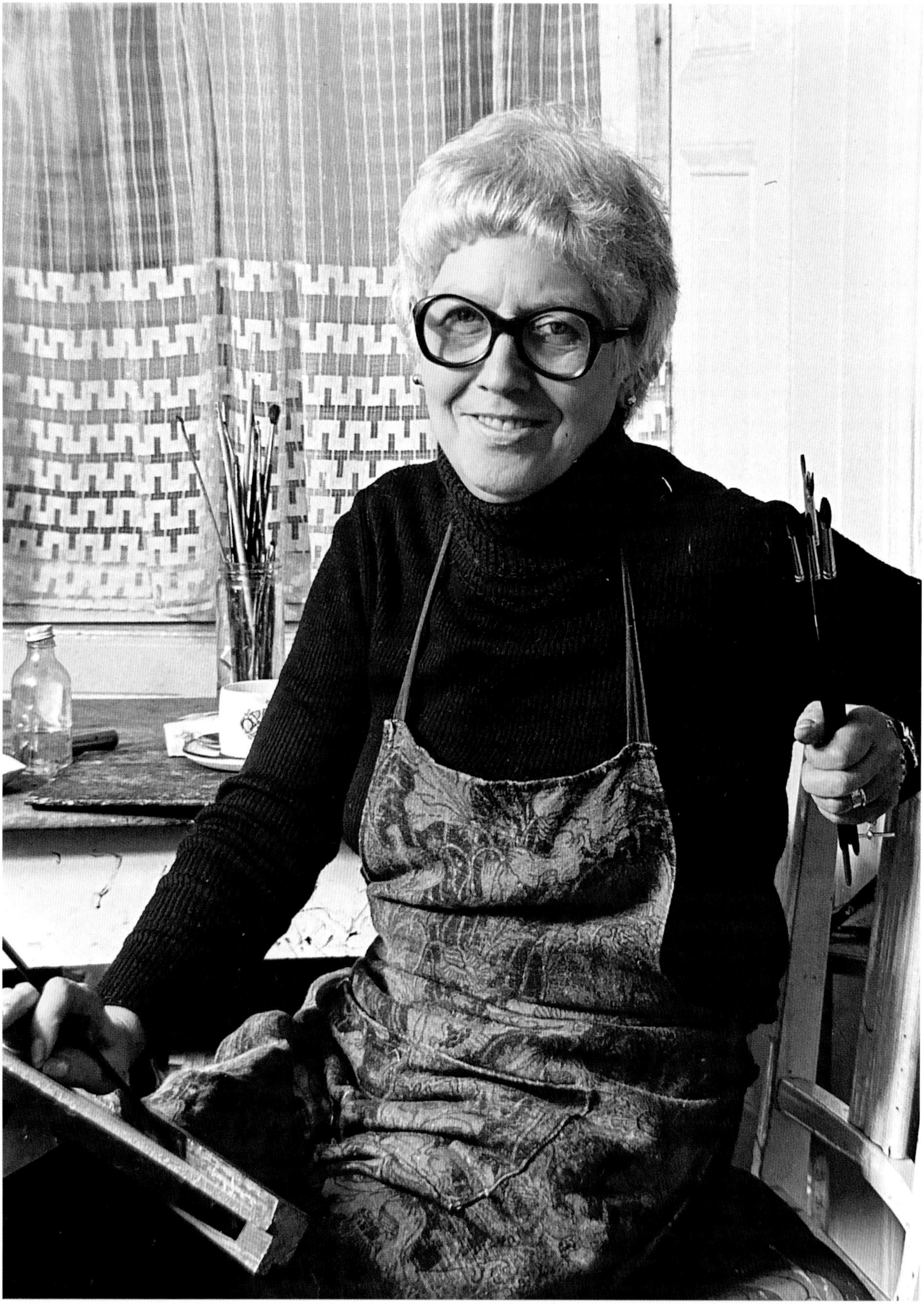

10

Painting Technique

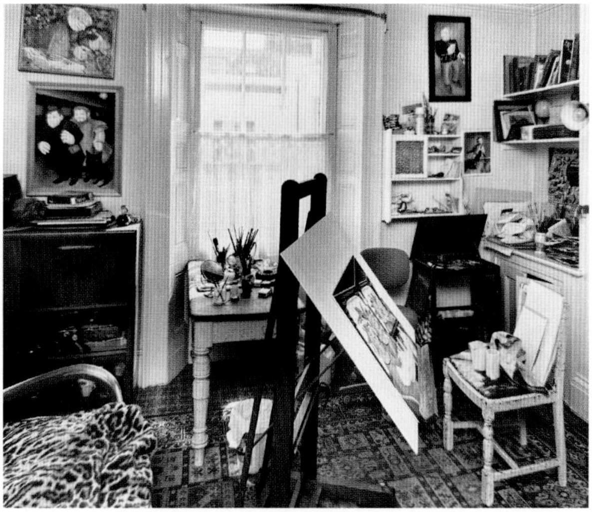

Beryl's studio, with a selection of pictures that she liked to have visible in order to reassure her that her paintings could turn out well. The dogs' sofa is visible front left (1970s).

LEFT
Beryl in her studio (1970s)

Painting took place in Beryl's old double B&B room – the original wallpaper and bedroom sink are visible in photographs. Everything was carefully laid out so as to be in easy reach, and BBC Radio 4 played in the background (unless *Woman's Hour* or some nasty news came on when it was hurriedly switched over to a music programme). Favourite objects and images crowded around the edges. A small sofa was covered with a leopard-print blanket on which the dogs slept. When the room was cleared for redecoration and double glazing, Beryl was shocked at the state of the carpet and the number of dog biscuits under the furniture.

By the time she was famous, Beryl had arrived at a technique that suited her. She still experimented, and she certainly developed her skills, but her attempts to paint on canvas were unsatisfactory and quickly abandoned. Small works, mostly produced for family, friends and charity auctions, were painted on oiled paper. Everything else was painted on three-ply marine plywood. This is made from waterproof glue and high-quality hardwood veneers, so it is more durable and resistant to delamination and warping compared to regular plywood.

John Senior would cut the ply to size and prepare it by painting it with emulsion, providing a translucence which is very apparent in her finished work. It also helps to explain why Beryl was free to use unusual shapes on which to paint, which is another part of the great attraction of her work – and a challenge for anyone hanging a show of her paintings.

Beryl could now afford to paint with expensive sable brushes. She applied her paint much more thinly than when she was painting on poorer surfaces such as driftwood or toilet seats. There were fewer paintbrush hairs to remove after painting, but quite a lot of cigarette ash and the detritus left over from frequent rubbings out while drawing the picture on the board. Beryl used oils, straight from the tube rather than mixed, (according to interviews), and loved black, even though she had been warned not to use it.

Beryl was inspired by the things she saw going on around her but rarely drew them exactly as she had seen them. She could recall what she had seen for months and even years later. This meant that she did not have to settle down with an easel in a pub or on the Hoe. She simply and unobtrusively made a tiny sketch on a piece of card under the table or behind her handbag, unnoticed by those she was observing. Indeed, when some of the 'girls' (as she called the prostitutes on Union Street) found out she was an artist she was really worried they might not speak to her again.

The sketch was not a full record of what she had seen, but had a key few reminders, such as 'puckered lips, red lipstick'. Some ideas were used immediately; others had to wait if there were urgent commitments. This could cause agony. 'For instance, there was a girl sitting in Union Street the other day. There were several girls in there, all sitting round a big table. Well, we were talking about going to America again. One of them was wearing the most wonderful red stretch nylon stuff. It started at the top and went right down to the ankles in folds, all draped in millions of folds. I turned to John and said: I don't know whether it's wise for us to go to America. I really mean this. I think it rather wrong for me not to be painting these things.'[1]

Other ideas came from magazine cuttings, such as her commission for *Art and Artists* in 1982 (see page 147), or the famous *Wedding Photograph*, which John had found in a newspaper (see page 67).

Thus, most pictures were put together from components. The way these were arranged by Beryl is the key to their impact and sense of movement. She might sketch figures – possibly drawn from a number of sources and sightings – and shuffle them around with magazine cuttings or ideas from postcards until she was happy. Backgrounds were created from photographs taken surreptitiously at the scene by either Beryl or John, or from postcards of places they visited abroad. This might take days until the arrangement somehow 'clicked' into place.

There are certain repeated compositions which pleased Beryl. Personally, I blame the breadboard, as *Sabotage* (see page 69) seems to me to be the start of Beryl's using the circular motif which she so enjoyed. There is a visceral pleasure in drawing rounded human forms – much more fun than angular bodies (while I am not an art historian nor an artist, when I tried life drawing, the rounded Brazilian twin was far more fun to draw than his thinner brother). This circular shape reappears in many of her public and private paintings, such as the eternity-ring of pets and *Strawberry Pickers* (see pages 130 and 131).

Another repeating shape is the tall rectangle, which Beryl used particularly successfully in her early work *Sunbathing* (see page 52). The shape suggests a shaft of sunshine moving across the courtyard at Athenaeum Street in the course of a day.

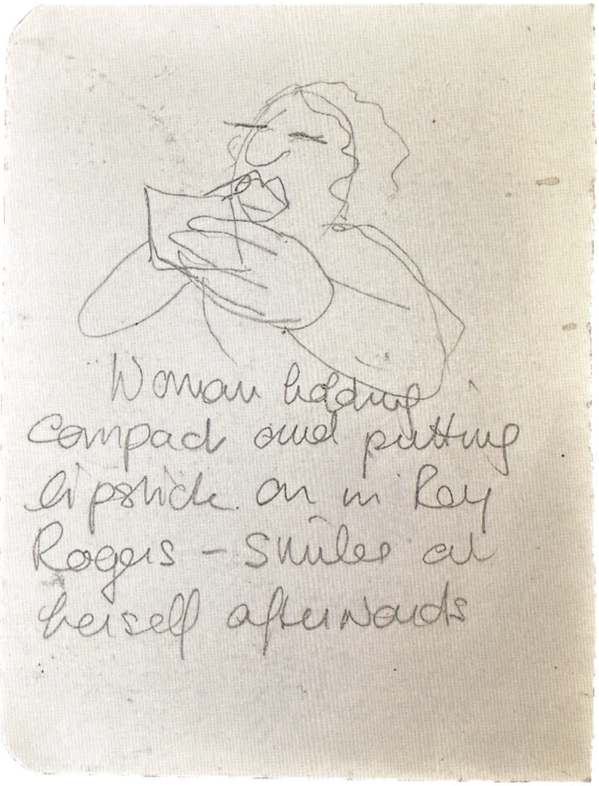

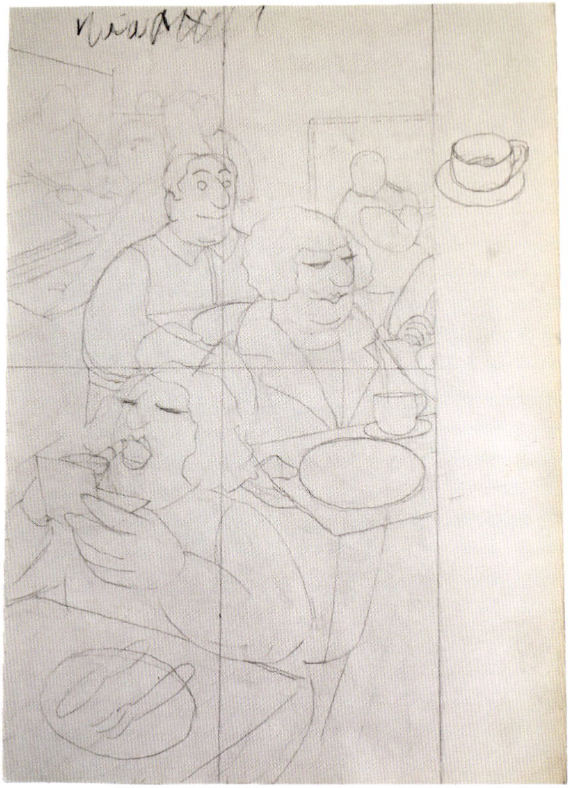

STAGE 1.
Handbag sketch of a woman in Roy Rogers, an American fast food restaurant. Beryl visited America at least three times – in 1982, 1988 and 1992 – and this could have resulted from any of these visits. In later years, when Beryl's visual memory was not as acute, she would use surreptitious photographs taken by herself or John.

STAGE 2.
The sketch incorporated into a completely different scene – Littlewoods in Plymouth. Beryl has used a favourite snaking arrangement in her composition, which she felt helped her avoid the perils of perspective.

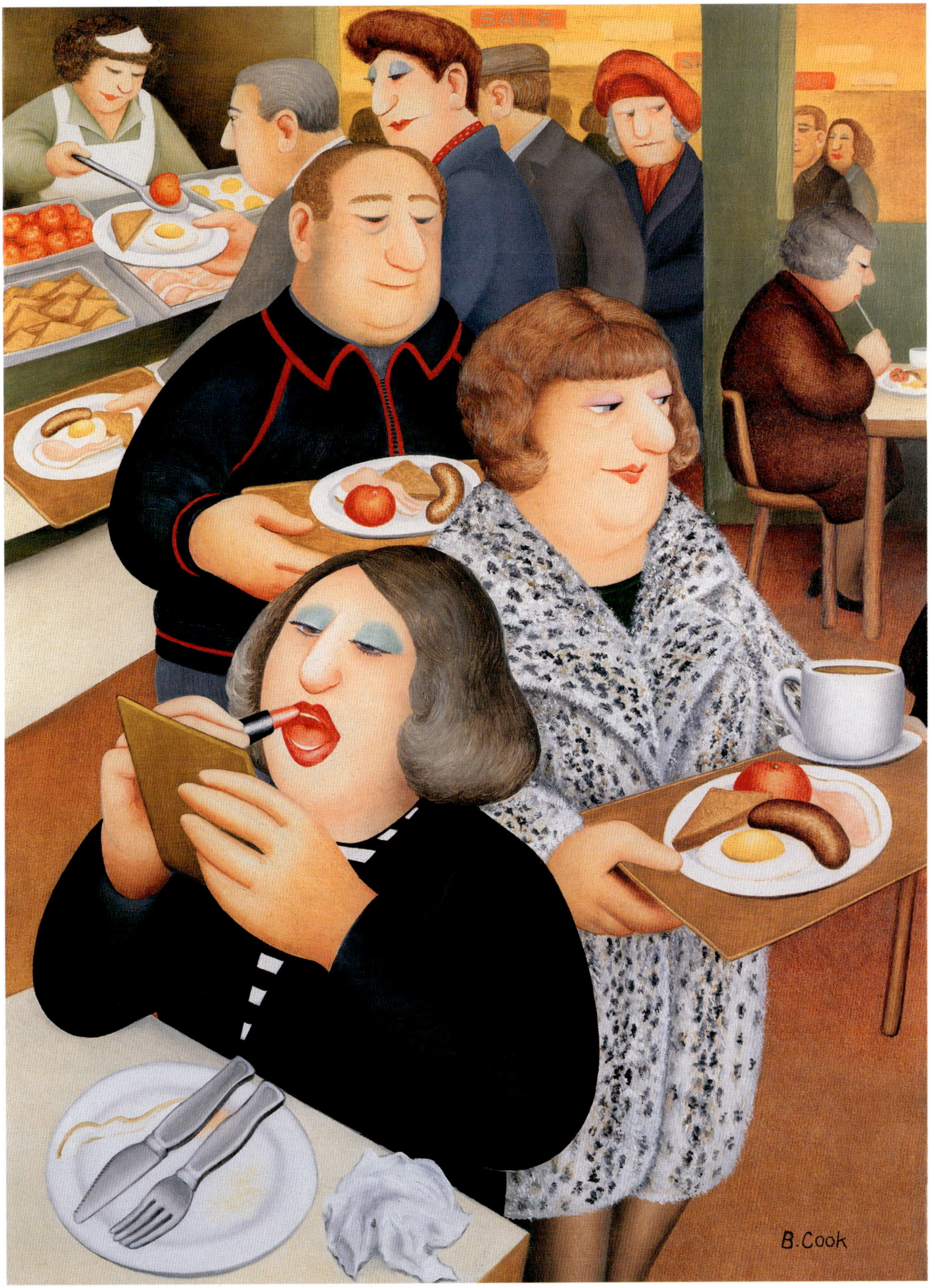

STAGE 3.
Breakfast Time
(1991). The resulting painting, made after Beryl had copied the squared-up sketch onto the plywood panel prepared by John

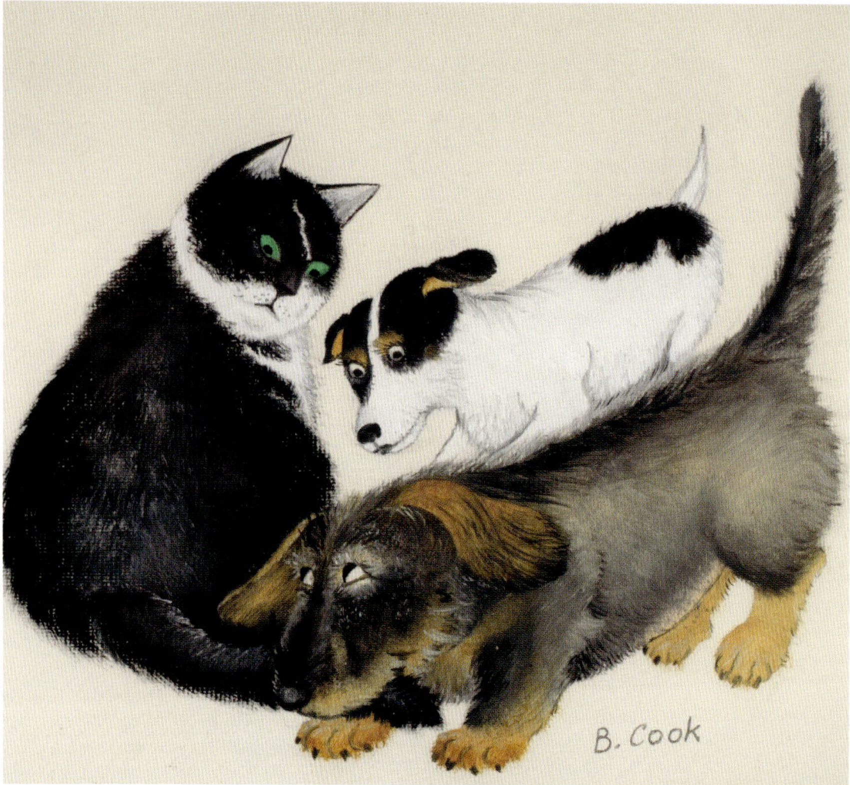

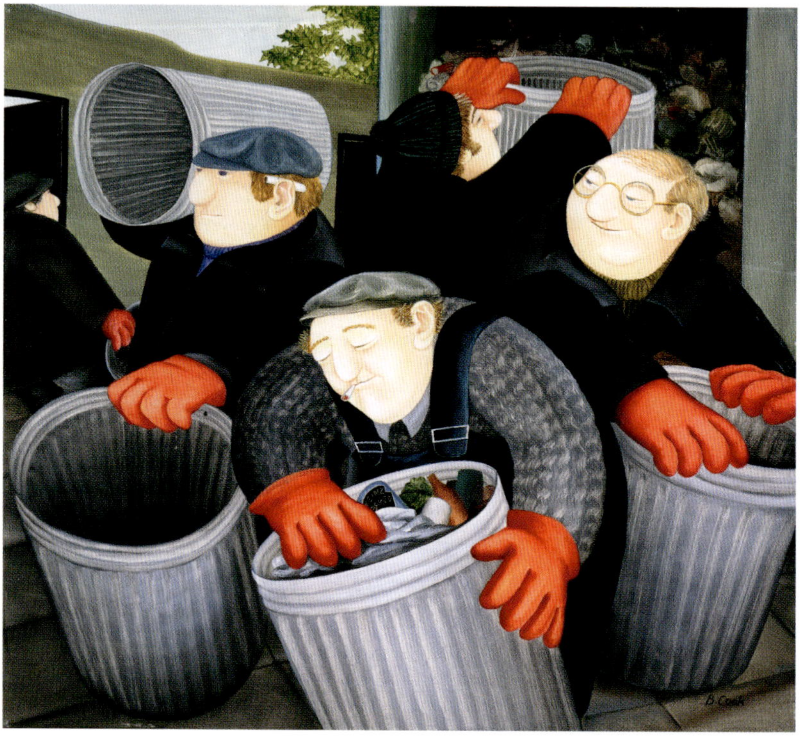

Ruby, Minnie and Lottie
(early 1980s). Each animal regards the next in a circle of reproachful gazes.

Dustbin Men
(1987). Beryl gave into her love of hands by exaggerating the size and redness of the cheerful dustbin men's gloves, which form a circle in this composition. They went on strike the next day.

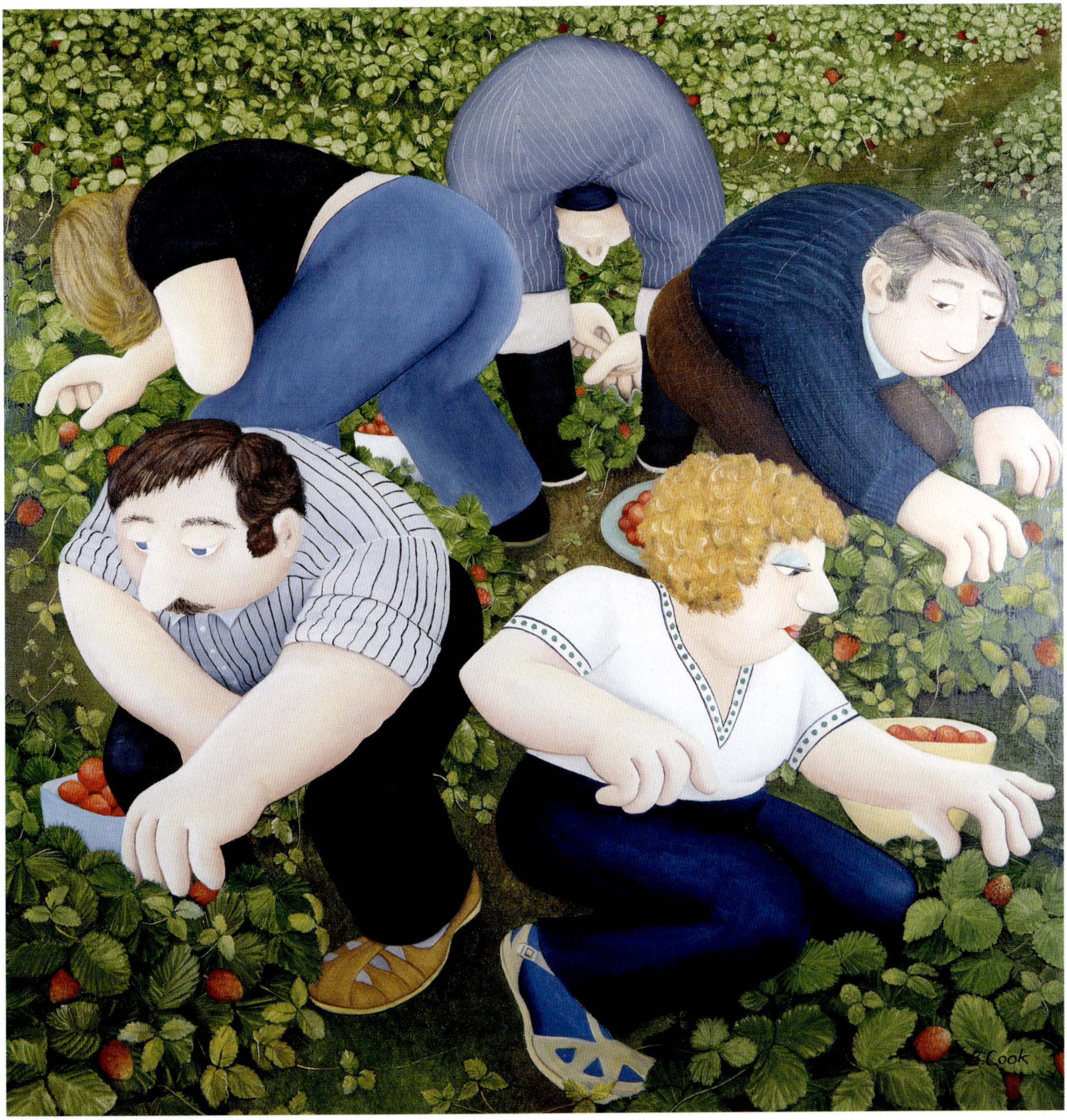

Strawberry Pickers
(early 1980s). Beryl painted all the strawberries from a single plant in a pot at home.

Beryl also found it allowed her to fit in as many faces as possible. This is particularly apparent in *Rowing Eight*, which incidentally was purchased by keen rower Rodney Bewes – who had acted the upwardly mobile Likely Lad in the TV series which had inspired *Juggling with Beer Bottles* (see page 31). Beryl used staircases for similar purposes.

Once happy with the composition, Beryl would transform it into a sketch. The sketch was then squared up and drawn on the board prepared by John. Arriving at this happy stage could take days, and much agony.

She considered this the most important stage: 'I'm very meticulous and I can't paint until I've drawn the picture: I do a lot of rubbing out, and after a week I end up with rather a grubby piece of board, but I have to get every detail right, especially the faces and the patterns into which I fit the arms and legs.'[2]

Beryl stated over and over again that her figures were big because she hated doing the backgrounds:

> Right from the start I painted figures, and not being too keen on doing backgrounds, I made the figures bigger and bigger to fill up the space. These days, when I'm doing a biggish painting, I make myself do the background first, partly because I have to, but also if I didn't, it would never get done. If you like, the background is the greens and potatoes, and the faces are the special bit of chicken that you save till last.[3]

Beryl told an interviewer, 'I paint like a painting book: I draw it and then colour it in. I start at the top and then rush rapidly towards the supreme favourite which is the whopping great figure in front. It's faces and hands I'm after.'[4] The backgrounds were certainly not rushed, however. They are painted with extraordinary skill and attention to detail, as for example in *Garden Centre* (see page 137).

Beryl struggled terribly with this background. On 10 June 1990 she wrote to Barbara that it was so big she had to stand up all day to do the top part. 'I'm just like Edward Burra, except in talent, I've had to draw every single thing up to and including each leaf of the plants before I could start painting'. A week later it was torturing her. 'I slept badly the other night, my mind restlessly painting leaves over and over again. And the awful part is that I know full well that all the hard work will not create a masterpiece.'

Barbara in reply reassured her that her treatment of leaves in *Birds in St James's Park* (see page 138) and *The Tiger* (see page 175) was masterful, but maybe she could paint

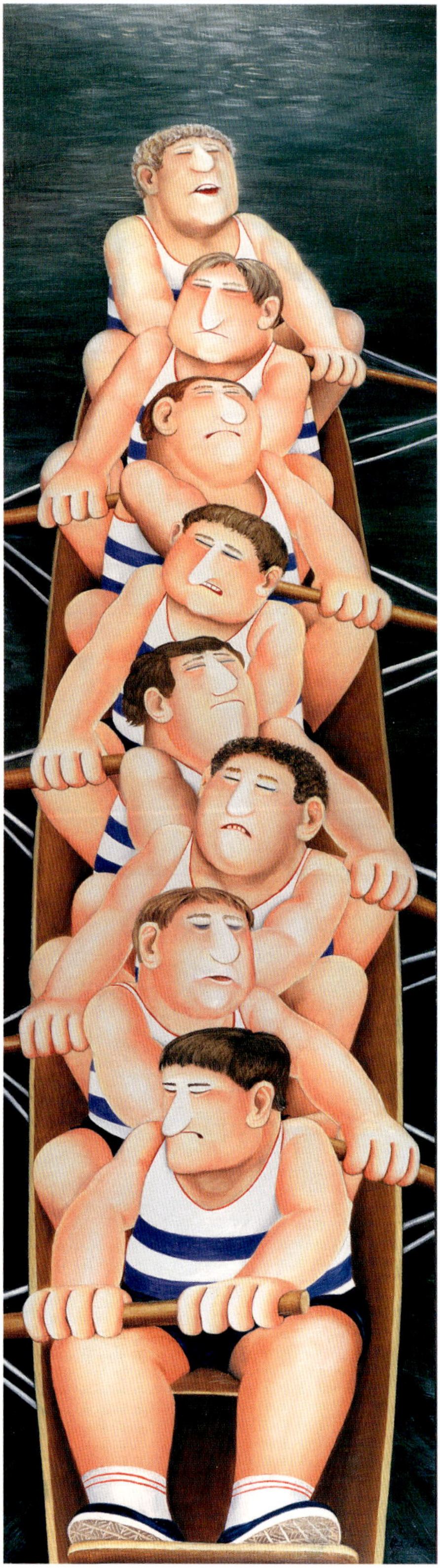

Rowing Eight
(1984). This painting was once owned by actor Rodney Bewes.

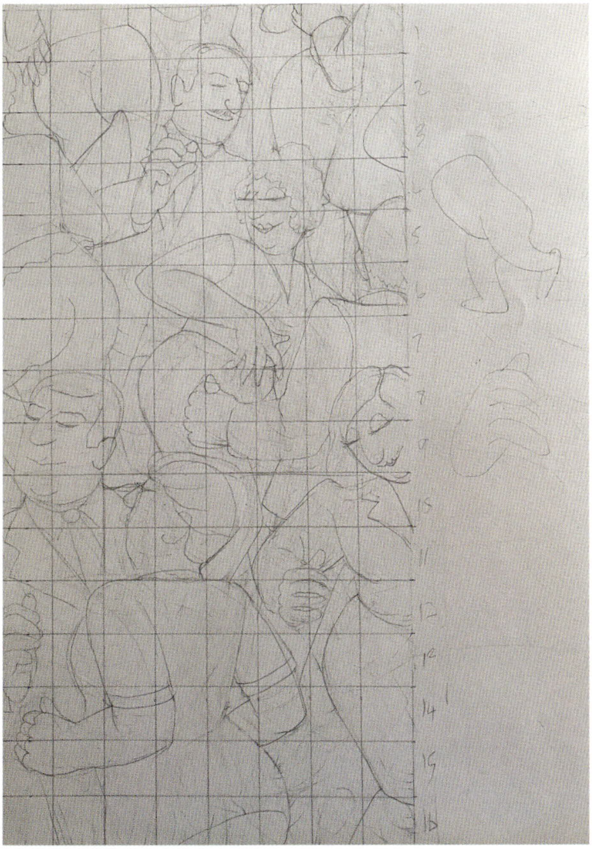

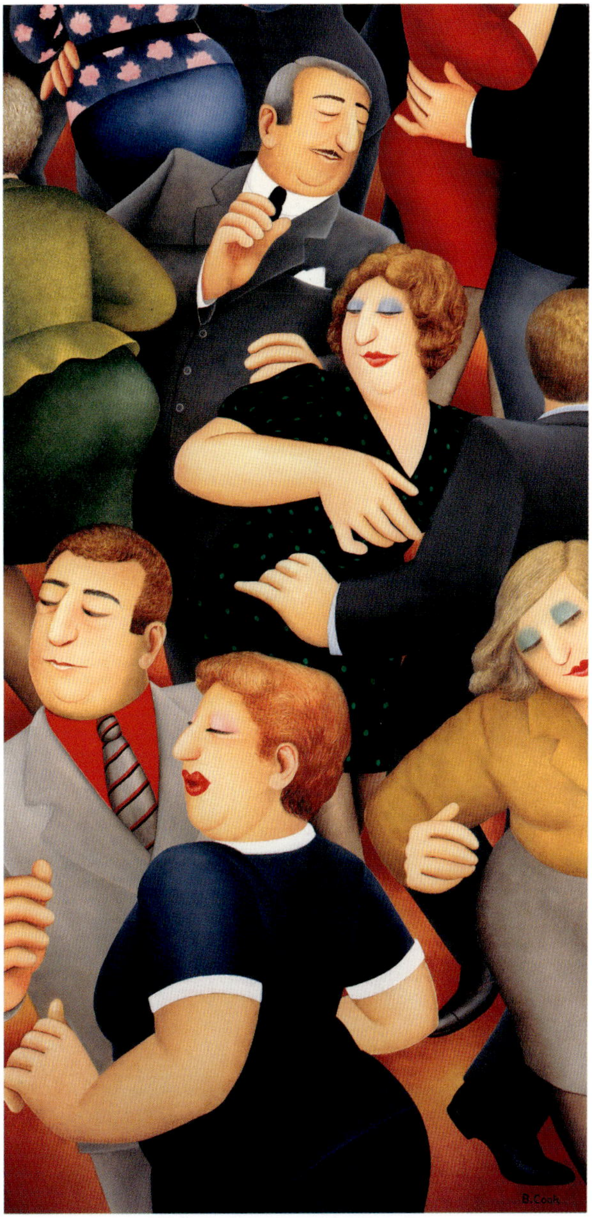

La Paloma Dancehall
(1990). Another complicated sketch and completed painting. Beryl has fitted the dancers into a tall rectangular shape. She has used a snaking arrangement to suggest the movement of the hips, further emphasised by the dancers' hands.

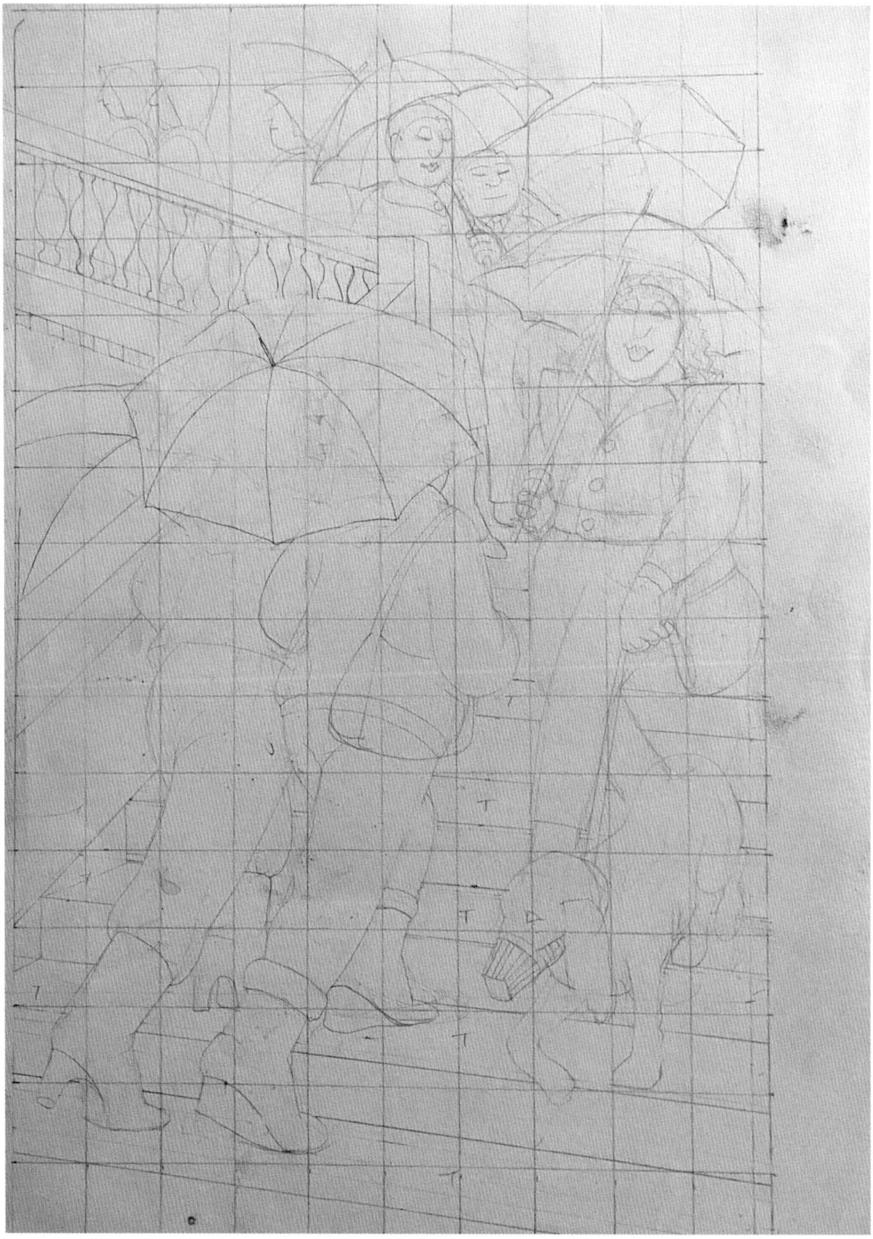

The Rialto Bridge

(1988). The squared-up sketch and the final painting

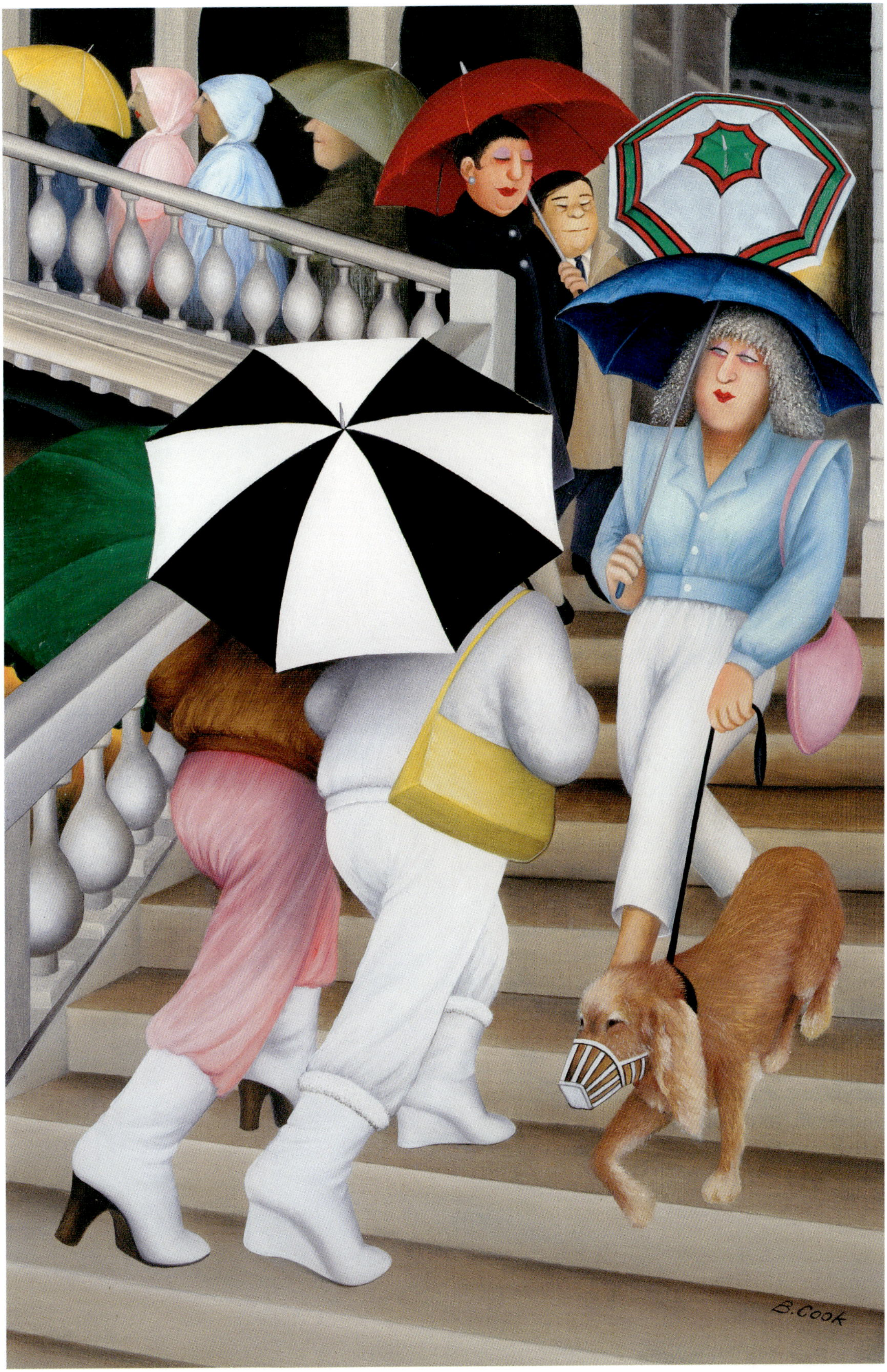
B.Cook

tropical leaves which are bigger and easier to paint. 'It will be a masterpiece.'

Beryl responded, 'I see my big mistake with the *Garden Centre*. The leaves are not nearly big enough', which I am sure is not what Barbara had meant. And Barbara was right – it IS a masterpiece.

On average, the actual painting would take about a week, depending on size and complexity. Faces were scraped off and repainted. She used 'dreadful swear words' when she was painting; '. . . . sometimes the things are so difficult to paint and I know I'm not going to be able to do it when I'm drawing them'.[5] But Beryl always pushed on and very rarely abandoned a painting. Completed ones were banished to the back of a cupboard and brought out after a few weeks or months, when Beryl would realize they weren't so bad after all. Sometimes she would prop them up in the studio to show her that she *would* be happy with her work – eventually.

> If I see a reproduction on a card or in a book, I say to myself: I wish I had that painting; I shouldn't have let it go. It's not that I ever alter them. Sometimes I worry that something will happen and I won't be able to do it again. And sometimes I'm anxious because, after I've painted them, I think they are so poor. It's only when I see them later I realize some of them are quite good.[6]

Beryl continued to use mixed media. She kept a collection of body parts and hair from dolls that could be used in paintings, such as *Man with Blue Eyes* (see page 140). His eyes came from a flea market in Amsterdam. *Queen Dancing* (see page 141) uses spray painted plastic flowers for its frame, and *Brian Entertains* (see page 48) has sequins on his headdress.

She also returned to the use of newsprint or magazine cuttings as a background, although she complained to Barbara that it had taken so long to arrange and glue down that she might as well have painted a background and got it over with.

Once you start to notice these compositional styles, Beryl's use of mixed media, and her brilliance with colour and detail, you appreciate more than ever the skill that goes into her work.

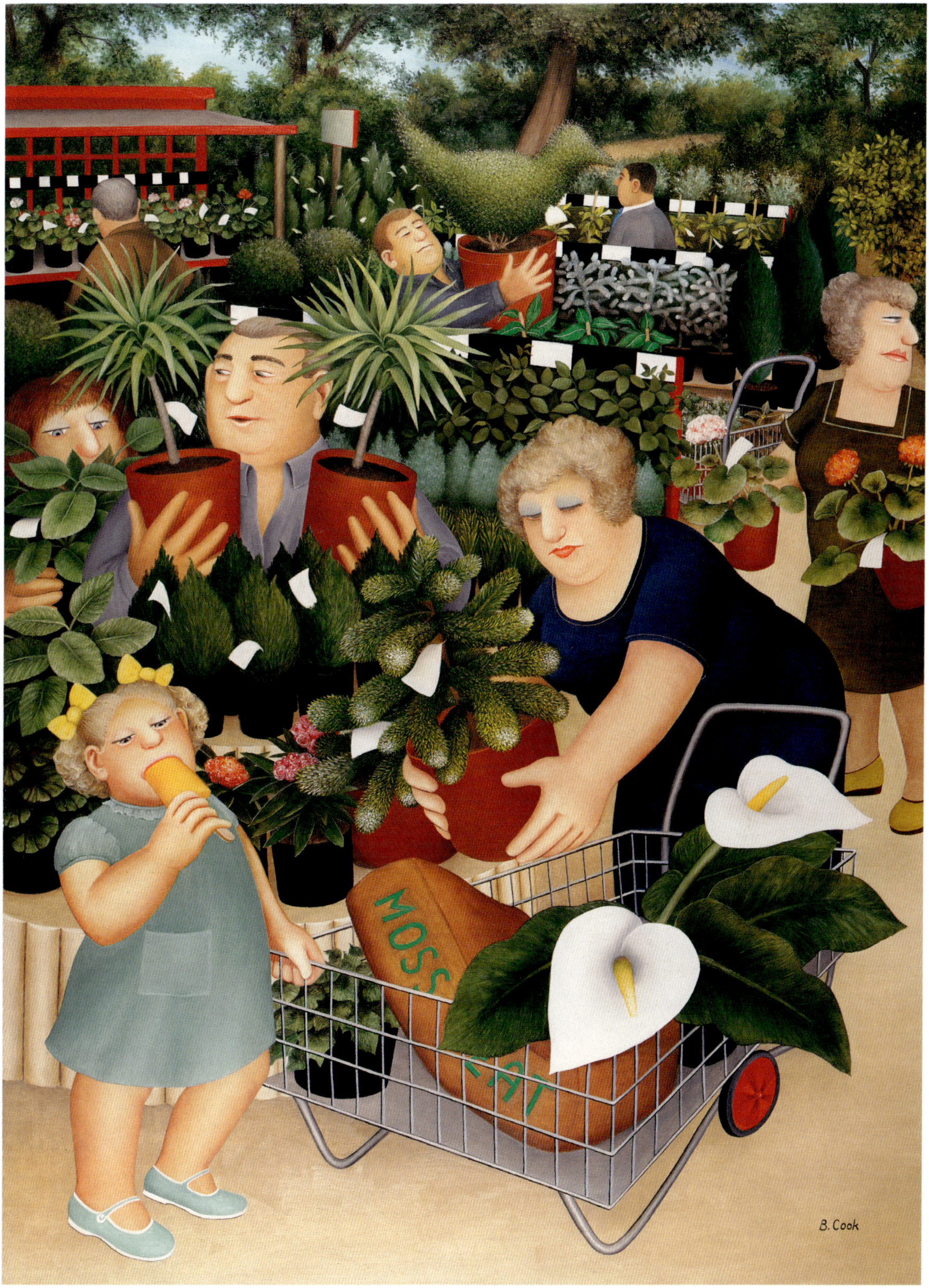

Garden Centre
(1990). The lily was dug up from the garden
and replanted after it had been painted.

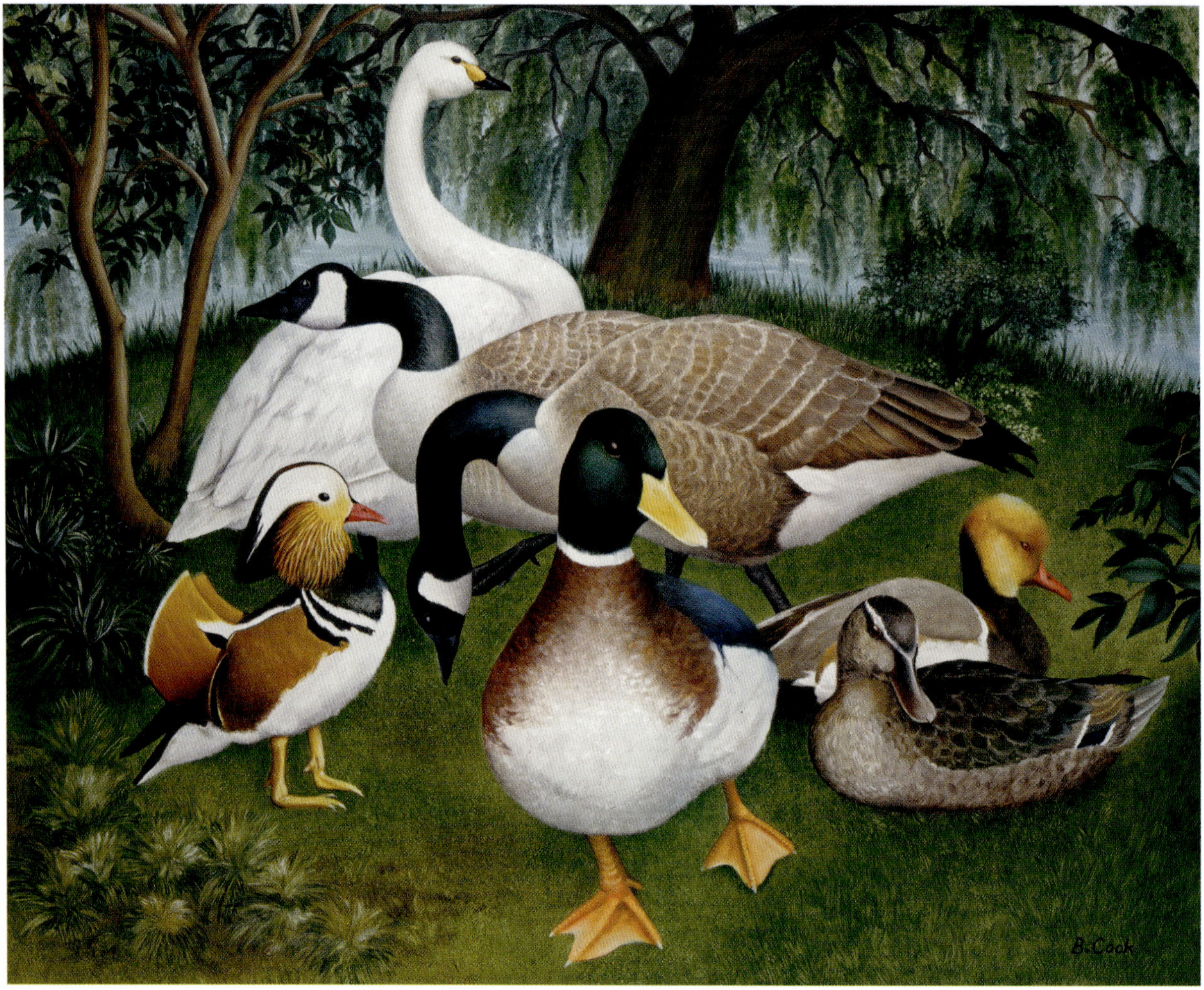

Birds in St James's Park
(1988). Beryl explained in *Beryl Cook's London* (John Murray, 1988) that the 'models were not entirely co-operative about standing together in a graceful group under a weeping willow', so she made a lot of notes and then arranged them to her satisfaction at home.

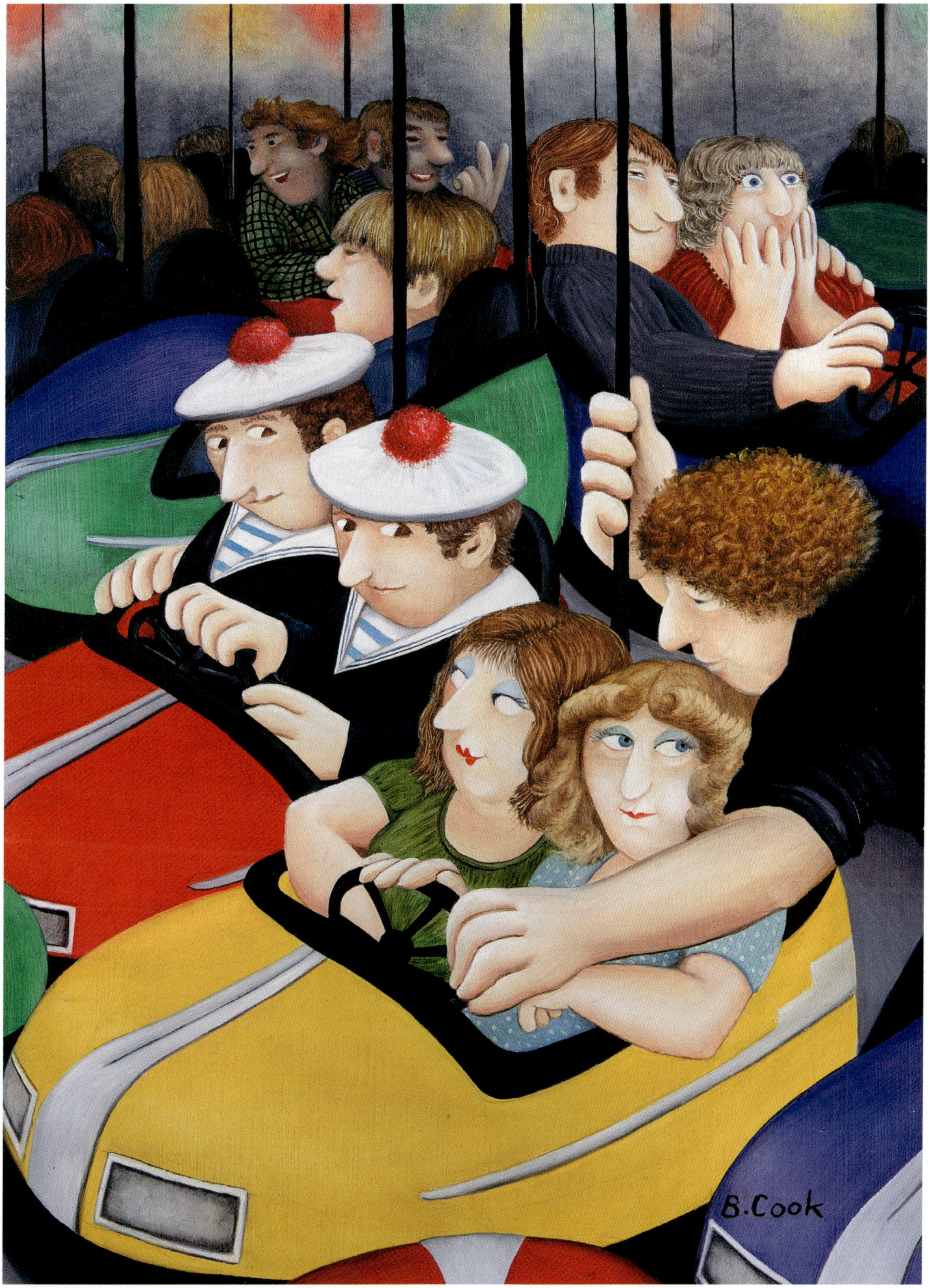

Bumper Cars
(1980s). This was one of the few paintings Beryl was happy with as soon as she had finished it. The sailors are French.

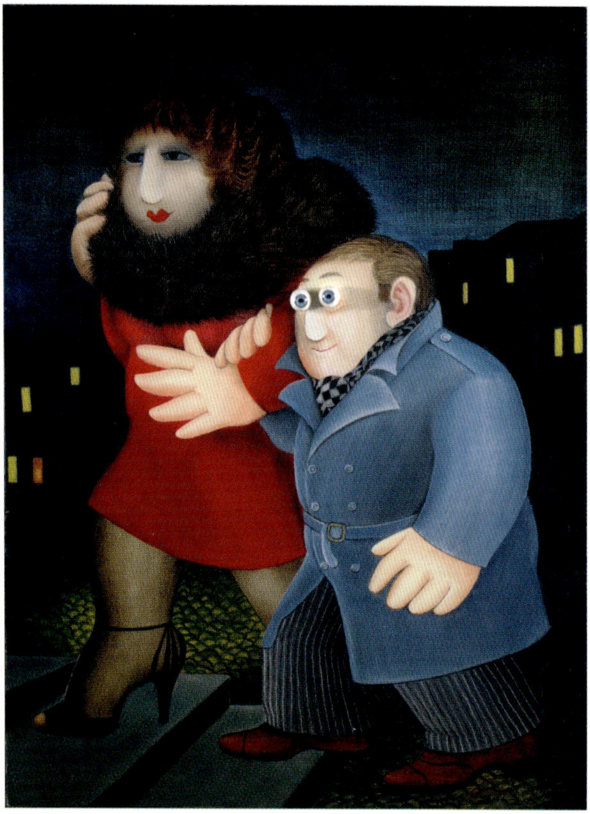

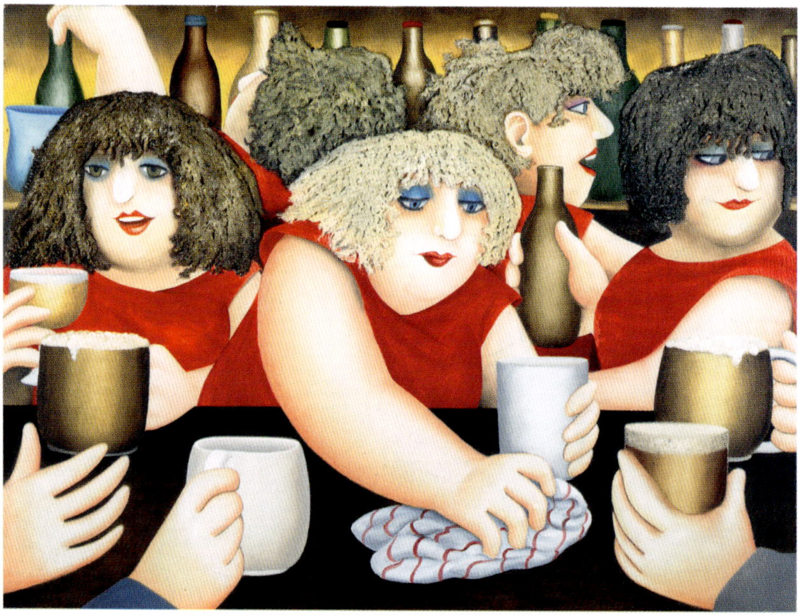

Man with Blue Eyes
(pre-1981). The doll's eyes came from a flea market in Amsterdam.

Mop Heads
(1985). Beryl used an actual mop head to form the hair of the girls in a bar in Union Street.

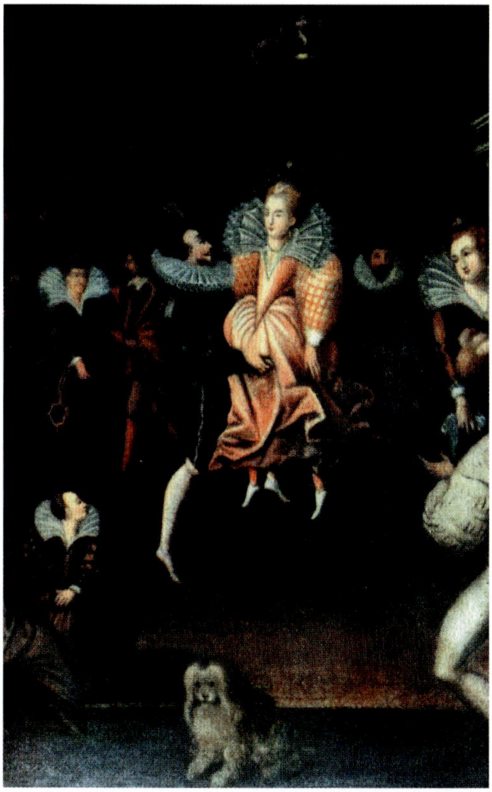

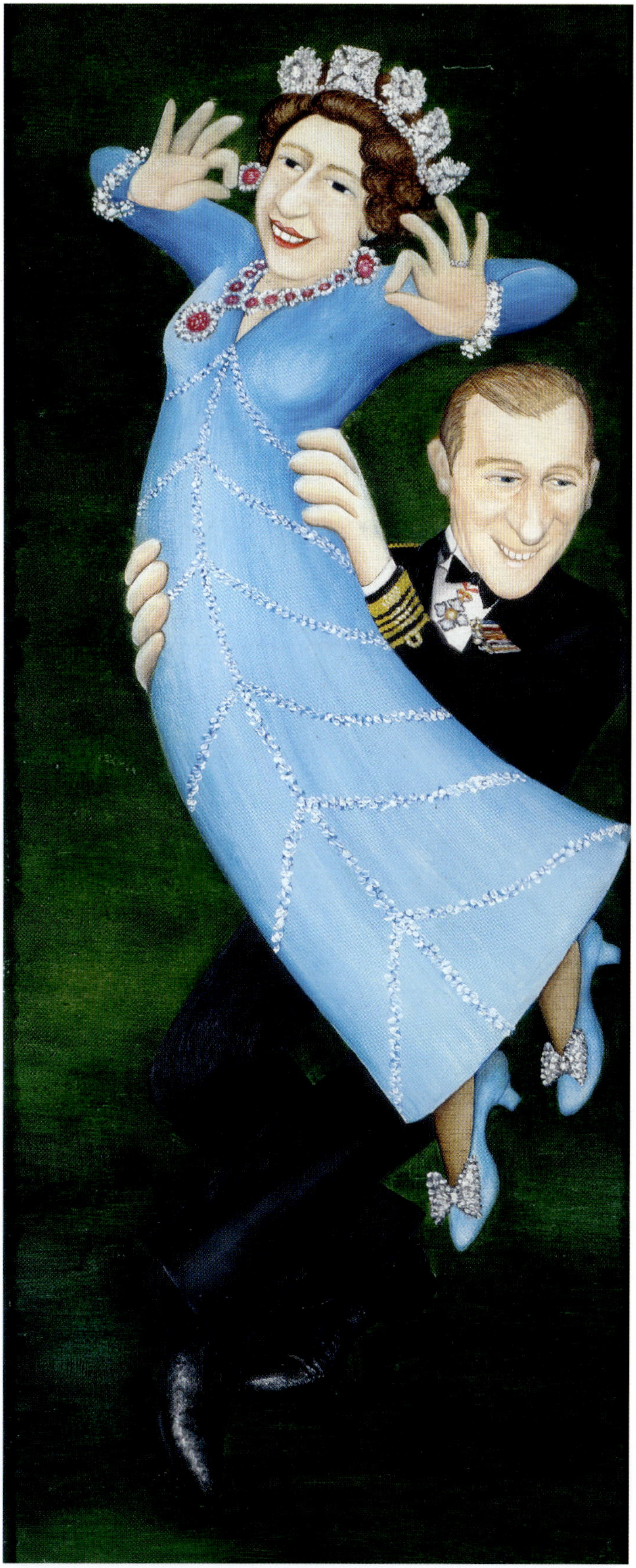

RIGHT

Queen Dancing

(1976). Painted for the Silver Jubilee and inspired by an old engraving of Queen Elizabeth I dancing the volta (c 1580, above). Recent research has suggested the historical painting is satirical rather than showing an actual occasion when Elizabeth danced with Dudley, her speculated lover. It is certainly suggestive.

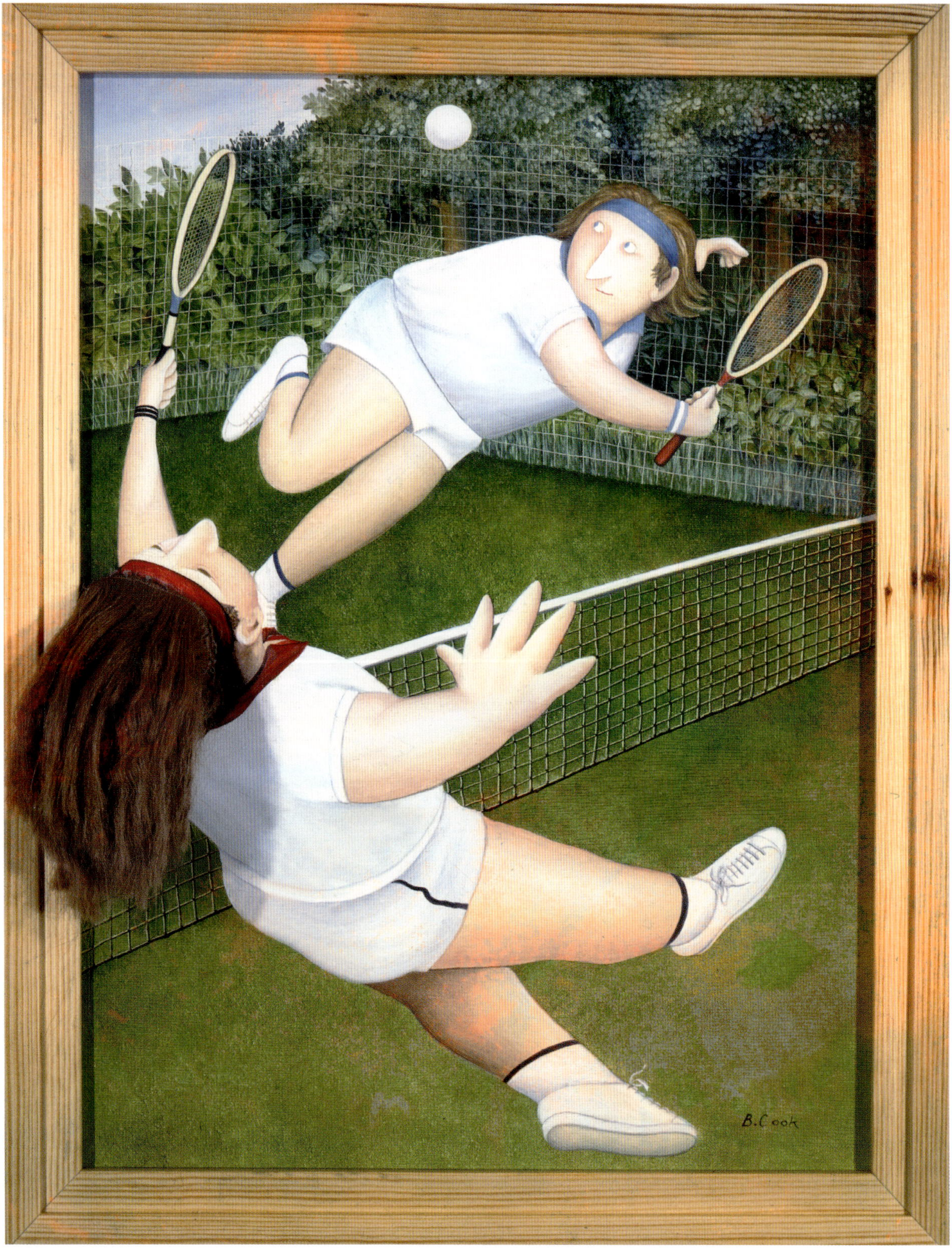

Tennis

(1979). This uses an old hairpiece of Teresa's – the opponent at the top is Tony Martin, who owned the work. The composition is magnificent.

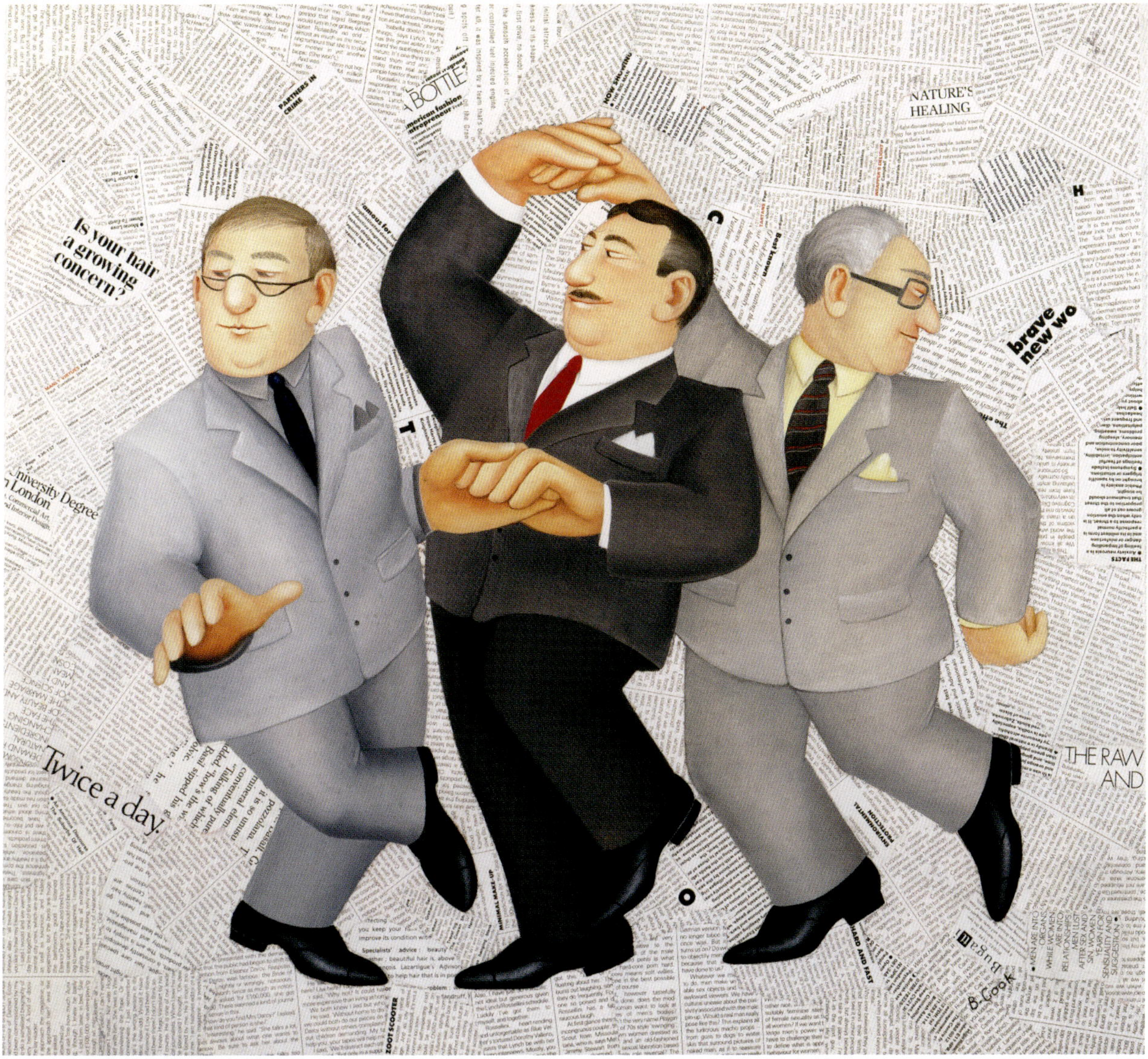

Three for a Quango

(1991). Another proverb painted for the Portal Gallery, an extension of 'It takes two to tango'. A quango is a 'Quasi-Autonomous Non-Governmental Organisation', something that was proliferating at the time.

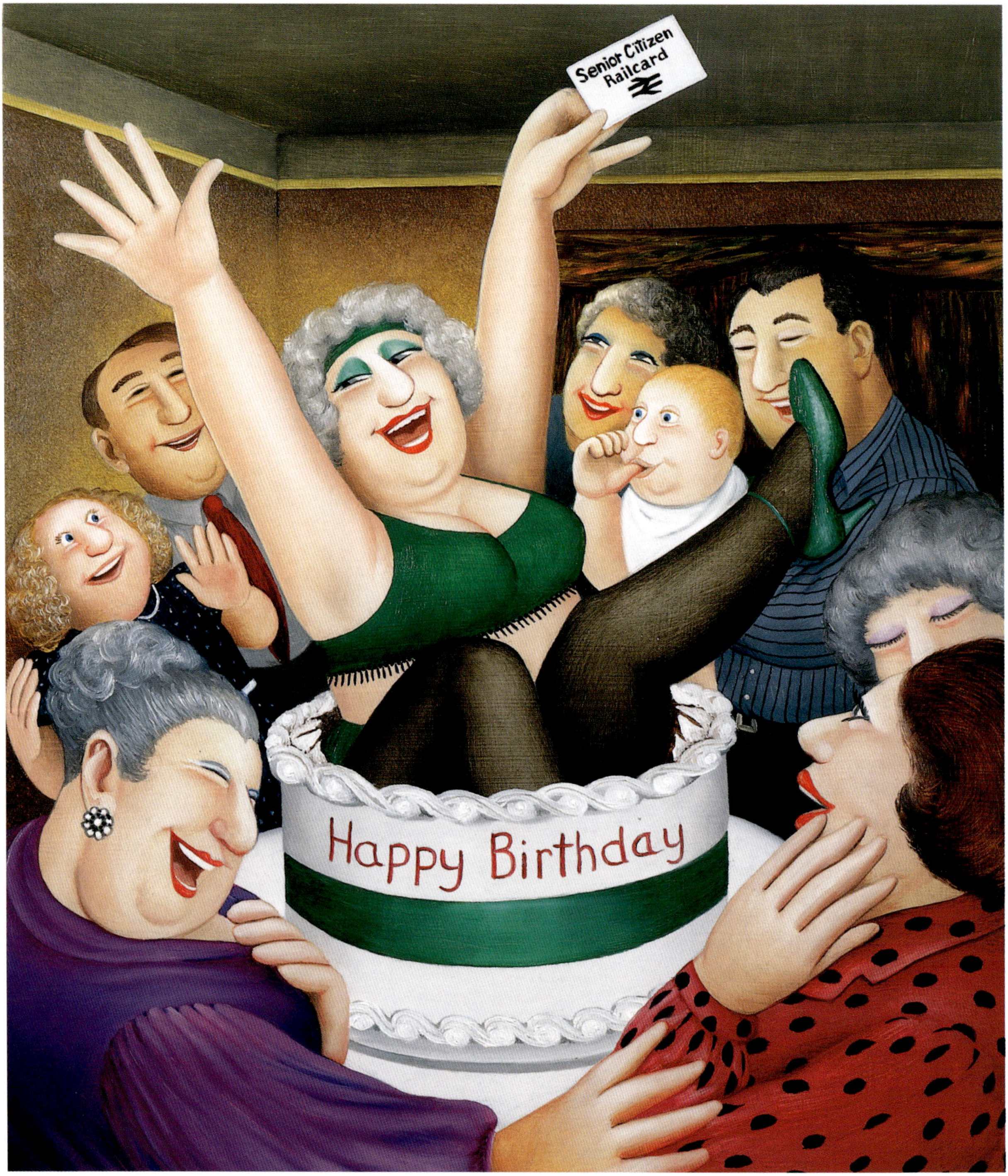

Senior Citizen Railpass
(1989). This was a commission for British Rail.

11

Painting to Order

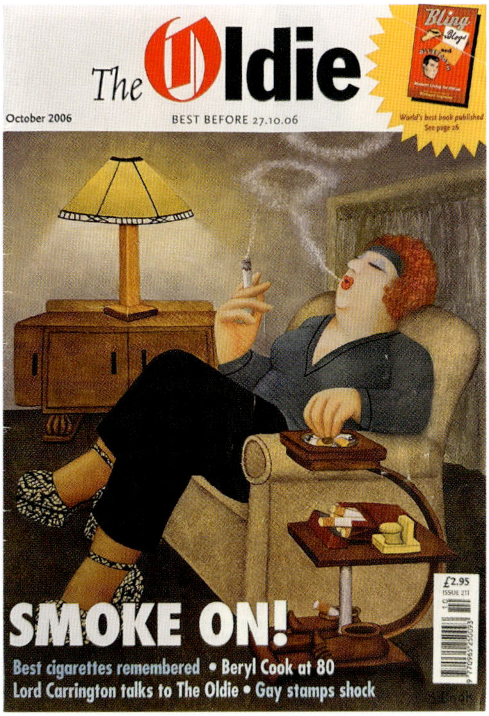

The Oldie
(October 2006)

Now that she was famous, Beryl was less able to set her own agenda. She *had* to paint for upcoming exhibitions and books. For some she could choose her own inspiration, but for others she had to reflect the demands of her growing fans in America, for example, or a subject matter agreed with the Portal Gallery or her publisher. The correspondence doesn't show this as an issue, because everyone worked well together and in any case John Senior was a master negotiator. Beryl occasionally felt the pressure but knew how long it would take her to produce the required number of works, as long as she didn't hit a block when painting them. She doesn't seem to report ever being short of ideas – indeed she often had a queue of scenarios of her own waiting for a gap in painting 'to order'.

Commissions did worry her, however. Many people approached Beryl asking her to paint portraits or pictures for them to give their partners or bosses. Beryl almost always refused; she would paint a portrait as a gift for a friend or family, but not for someone she didn't know in case, she would say, they didn't like it. However, she did accept formal commissions from magazines, publishers and for use as advertising. They still caused her concern, in case a suitable idea wouldn't 'appear'. Her solution was to do the painting on approval without any deposit, and only accept payment if the client was happy. Incidentally, Beryl usually retained copyright of her paintings whether commissioned or privately sold, so that she could use the images in her books. It made her very cross if she found that people had copied her work or used it without her permission.

In 1989 Beryl accepted a commission from the British Film Institute (BFI) to paint a picture for a poster. It was so long since she had been to the cinema that she had to pop to one to see what they were like. She wrote to Barbara, 'Have cobbled together my own (and Donald McGill's) scene of picture goers and realized at once that the darkness on everything but the screen would be a challenge.'[1]

The result was *At the Cinema* (see page 148), and you can see how Beryl left the back of the seats blank for the poster text. The BFI loved it, but said they hadn't worked out what was terrifying the heroine. Beryl replied:

> Many years ago a friend found himself in dangerous circumstances, a carving knife brandished above him and orders given that he should write a hundred times 'I must give stricter correctional treatment' immediately. Terrified (and

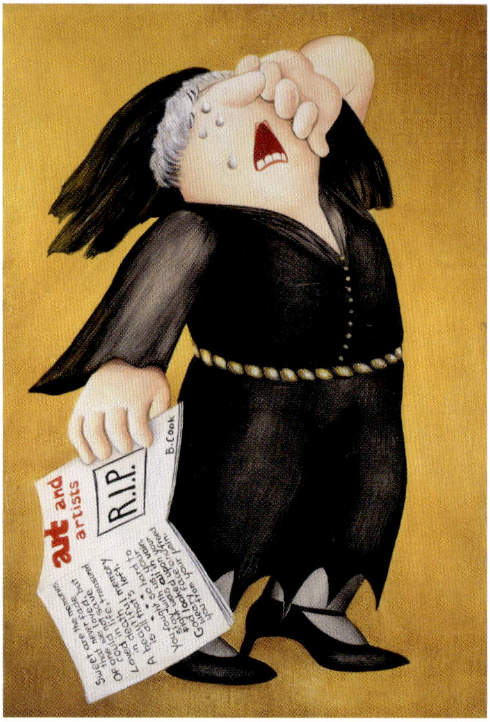

RIP to Art and Artists
(1980). Beryl painted this for John George, the editor of the magazine, when it temporarily closed down in 1980. She wrote, 'I've given Art & Artists a decent Christian burial for you, I am in full mourning'.[2]

wearing only underpants) he dashed to the typewriter deciding that handwriting would be too slow! I don't know if this was acceptable but he escaped in one piece to tell this me this story and I laughed so much (so did he) that I've never forgotten it. I changed him to her (which I'm better at).

Beryl said that this would hardly be suitable for publication, but I hope you disagree! At the same time as she was painting *At the Cinema*, Beryl was designing a poster for a new British Rail initiative, the Senior Rail Pass.

A similar cake had appeared in a design she did for the cover of *Art and Artists* in 1982. She accepted the commission because its editor, John George, was a friend, but she really struggled with his well-meaning suggestions. However, she told her interviewer, 'I tell you what, Judith, although I say I'm no good, I actually find when it comes to rock bottom, I can nearly always produce something'.[3] The picture was helped by a newspaper cutting of a family looking up into a tree. Once she remembered that she liked doing women – nude women especially – and liked people eating, she was well away. Barbara said the painting featured 'exceptional nipples'.

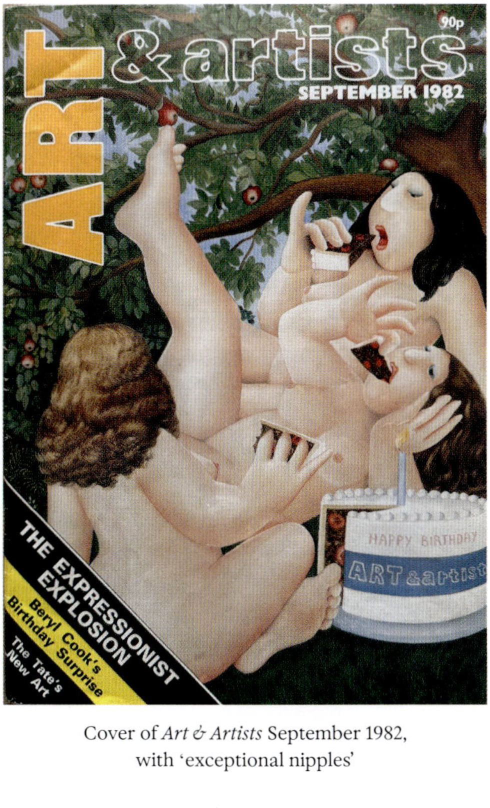

Cover of *Art & Artists* September 1982, with 'exceptional nipples'

The 1987 film *Personal Services* – about the famous brothel-keeper Cynthia Payne – was right up Beryl's street. She accepted with alacrity the request to design promotional posters for it (see pages 149 and 150). Beryl and Barbara had really enjoyed reading all about the police raid which had found 53 men partying and waiting to be spanked – including a peer of the realm, an MP and several vicars. Thousands of posters were produced for promotion in France but banned in the UK. Officially, it wasn't the image that was the issue: it was feared it would attract too much graffiti.

Beryl fulfilled commissions for covers for a number of magazines, including *Private Eye* (see page 148) and *The Oldie* (see page 149). One of the most striking adverts commissioned from Beryl was for Heineken which appeared on Father's Day in *The Observer* in 1984 (see pages 145 and 150). It was so unusual and well-produced that it won a silver award in the Campaign Press Advertising Awards of 1985.

Smithfield Market (see page 151), painted in 1985, was commissioned for the Alliance Freezing Works of New Zealand for its Boardroom. The Market has been trading for almost 1,000 years, first as a livestock market and then from about 1860 as a wholesale meat market, featured in Dickens'

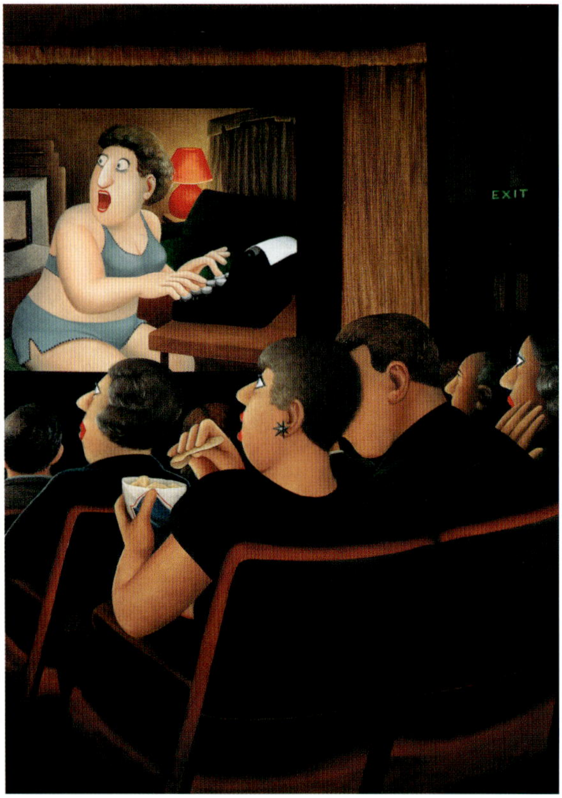

At the Cinema
(1989). This was a commission for the British Film Institute.

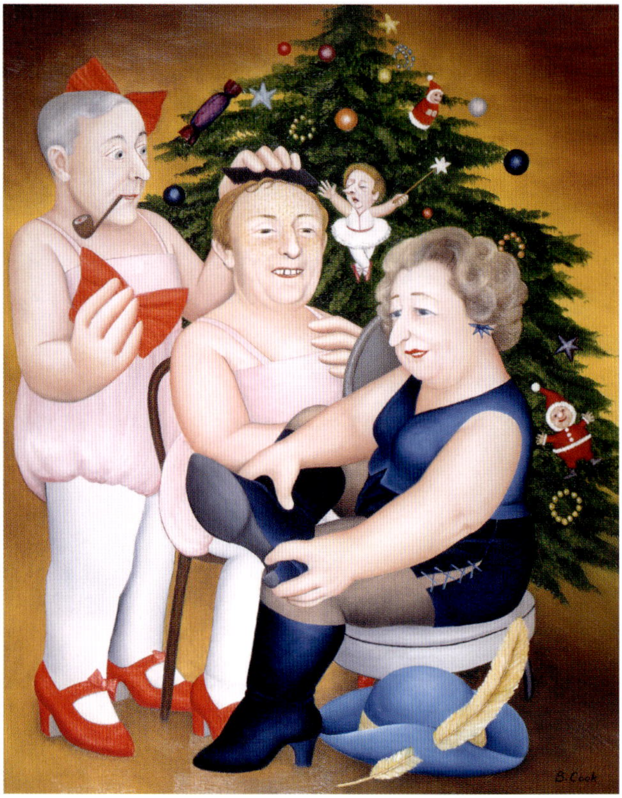

Private Eye
Cover for *Private Eye*, Christmas 1984 – featuring Tony Benn, Neil Kinnock (Labour politicians), Margaret Thatcher (Conservative Prime Minister) and a cut-down-to-size Arthur Scargill (leader of the 1984–5 miners' strike) in the tree. This was painted during the miners' strike. It did not originally have a background and it took Beryl two weeks to gird herself and do one.

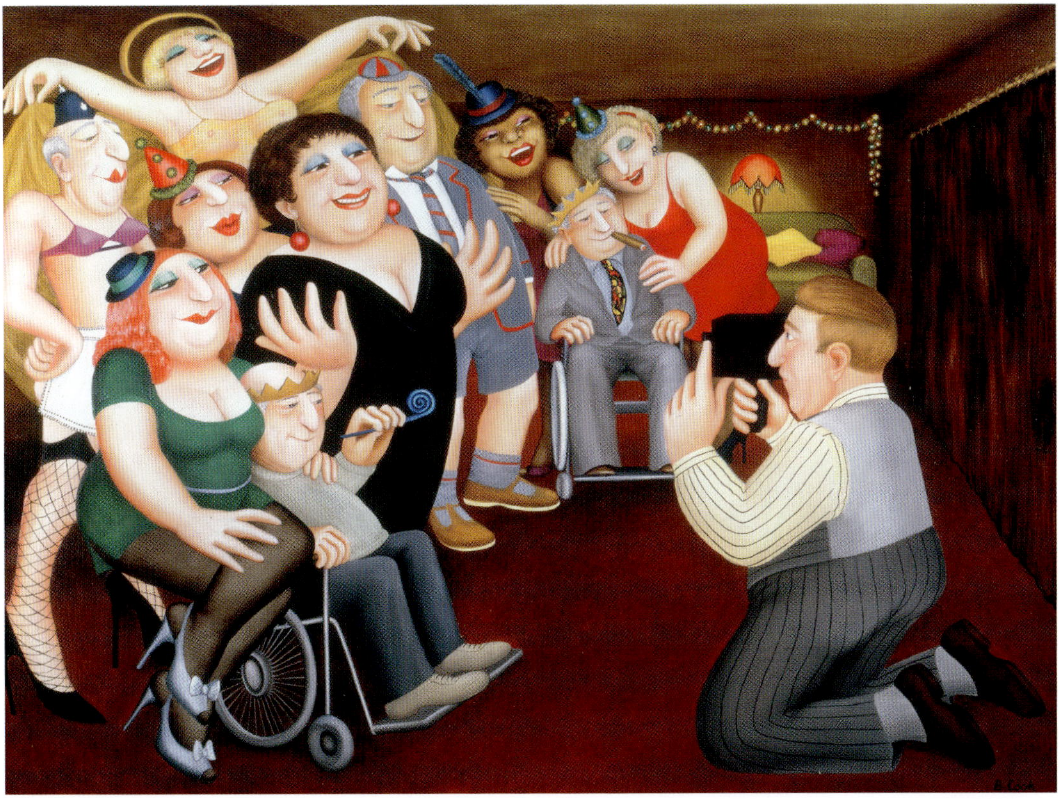

Personal Services 1
(1986–7)

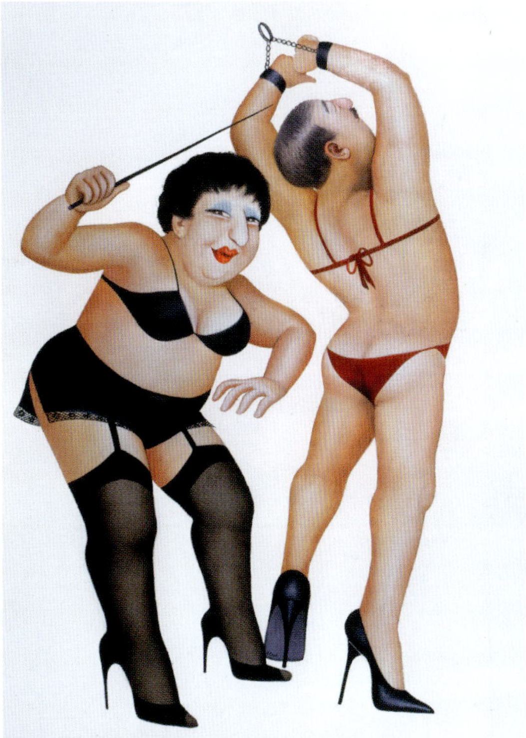

Personal Services 2
(1986–7). Beryl said, 'And here is someone with a problem'.

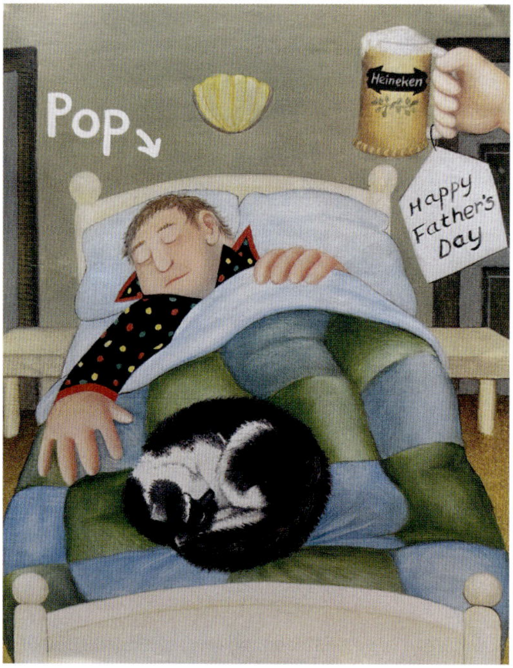

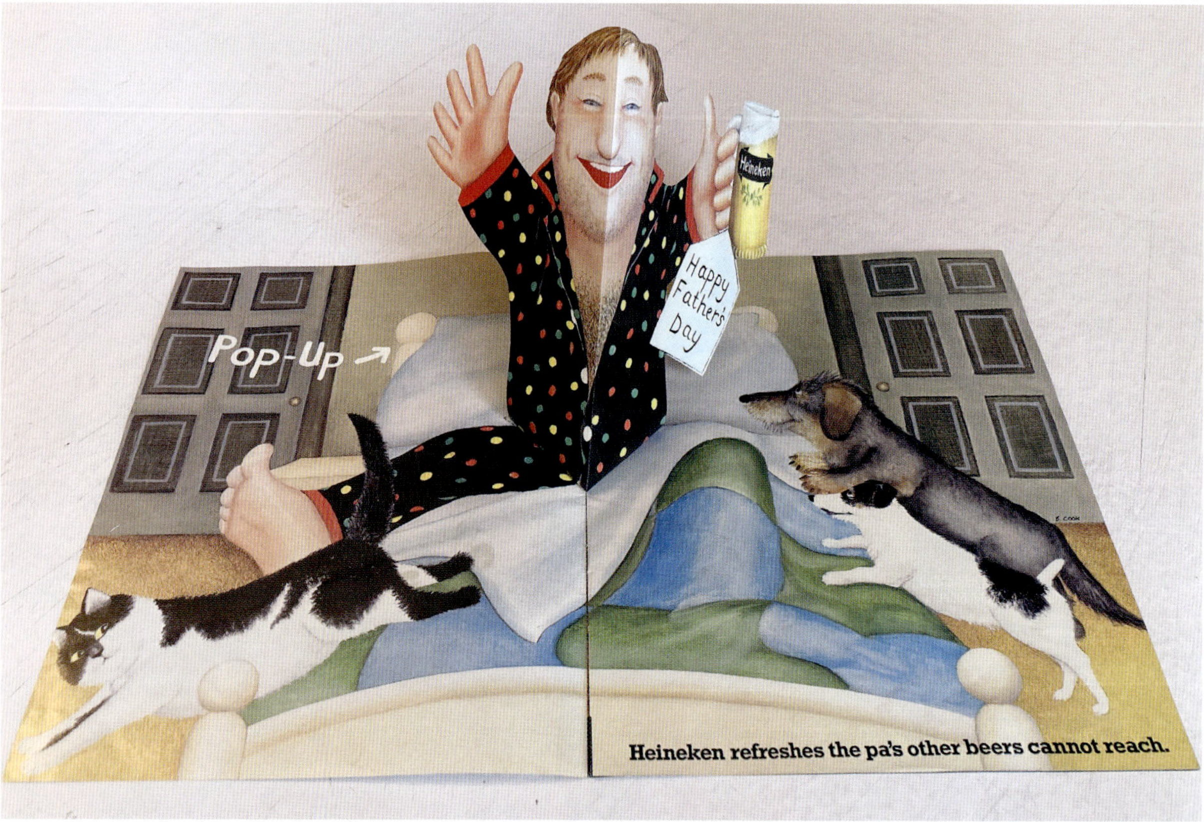

The original painting for the first page of the Heineken advert (1984), and the pop-up double spread which followed it in the *Observer Magazine*. The popular beer's catchphrase was very well known at the time.

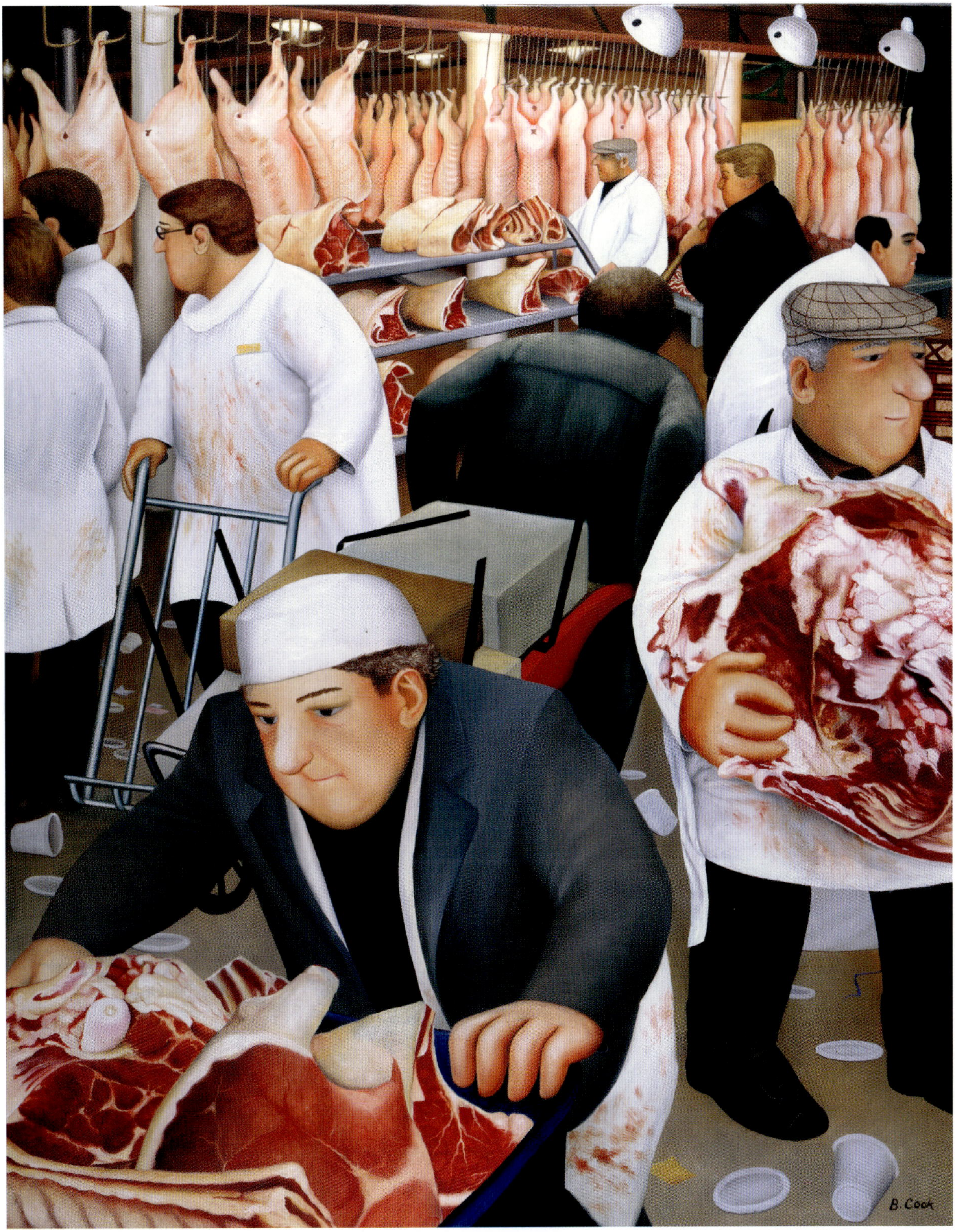

Smithfield Market
(1985). Commissioned for the Alliance
Freezing Works of New Zealand

Oliver Twist. It was already receiving frozen meat all the way from New Zealand, as well as Australia and Argentina, in the 1880s. Today, the meat deliveries begin at 10.00 p.m. and the cutting and processing by each trader begins, with selling starting at 1.30 or so in the morning.

Beryl went to the market twice, the first time with Barbara. Barbara wrote that on that occasion it was empty, and she couldn't imagine what Beryl could make of it. In fact Beryl used photographs, which Barbara assured her was completely acceptable, and that the finished work was a 'masterpiece'.[4] She also advised Beryl not to worry about the bloodstains, which Beryl felt were not lavish enough. Beryl put as many of the porters into the painting as possible and consulted her own butcher when painting the meat – afterwards eating a sirloin steak which she had purchased as a model. Beryl was a little stumped when an art student wrote to her to ask about the message in this painting. There is no record of her reply.

Two very good pictures were in fact rejected: *Percy at the Fridge* for a refrigeration company (see page 178), and *Poetry Reading* for the cover of a book of poems by Christopher Logue. Christopher Logue, CBE (1926–2011) was an English poet associated with the British Poetry Revival, who also wrote pop lyrics and plays. He had written to Beryl and asked whether she would paint a picture for the jacket of his anthology of verse for children called *Sweet and Sour*. He suggested a poetry reading, which inspired Beryl and she enjoyed painting it, even though she had never been to such an event. Logue was delighted, and wrote in a letter to Beryl dated 26 April 1982: 'How very kind of you to paint, with such alacrity, so charming and so accurate a picture.' I think its lovely, especially as there are two recognizable Beryl Cook paintings on the wall. Sadly, the publishers must have disagreed. I genuinely don't think Beryl minded at all – she said she missed her paintings when they went, anyway.

Things went better at Glyndebourne, the famous and very exclusive opera house in the grounds of a country house in Sussex (I applied for membership, and after a few years got a letter to check if I was still alive as the waiting list was so long). In August 1990 Sir George Christie invited Beryl to attend the opera and mingle with the audience, no strings attached. Though opera meant nothing to Beryl, Barbara told her she was very lucky to be invited, and Sir George sent so many possible dates that she and John gave up and attended a Michael Tippett opera, *New Year*.

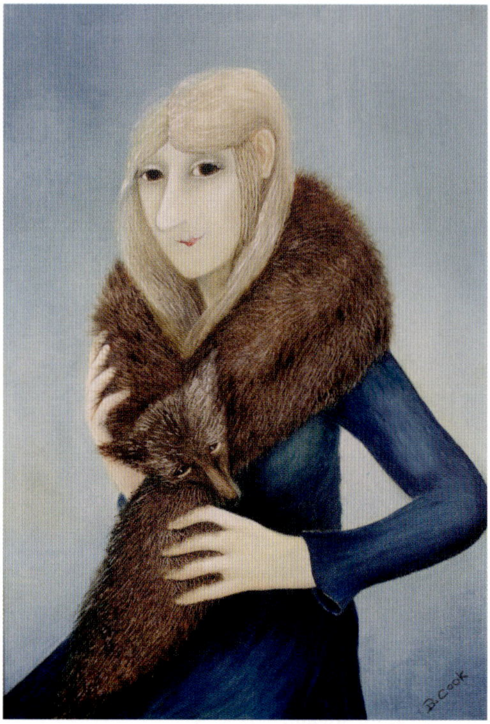

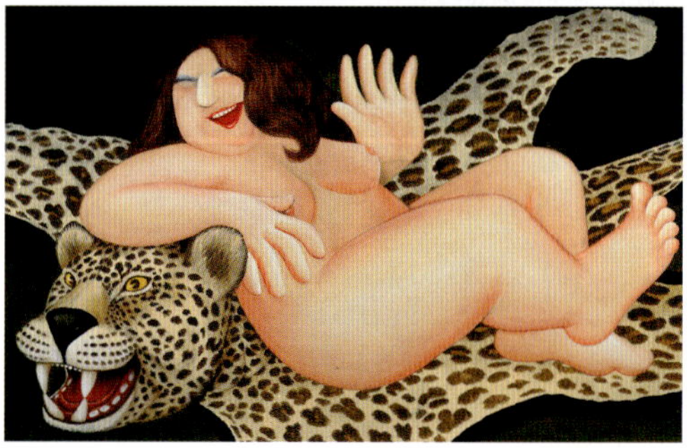

TOP
Teresa in a Fox Fur
(1972)

BOTTOM
Nude on Leopardskin
(1980), both in the background of *Poetry Reading*

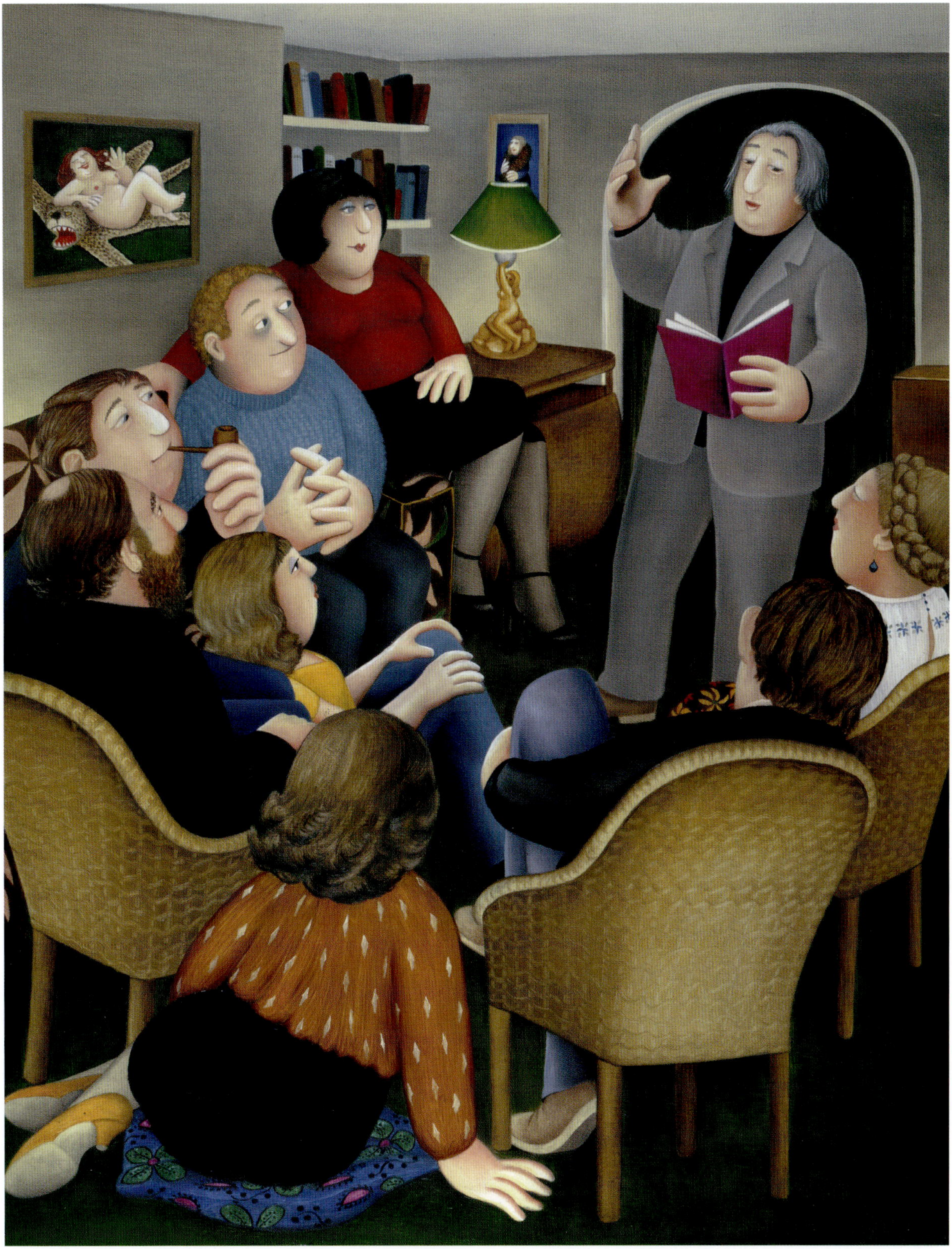

Poetry Reading

(1983). This was comissioned by Christopher Logue for the cover of his poetry anthology but was not used.

They sat right at the end of a row so they could escape if necessary, but in the event Beryl enjoyed the singing and the mock leopard skin coat that one of the cast was wearing. By January, Beryl wrote, 'I paint on, serenely. Am busy depicting the Opera at Glyndebourne, I forced myself to start painting instead of getting demented over the drawings.'[5] George Christie wanted to use the image for publicity and cards.

Beryl became very fond of George Christie and went to see Glyndebourne productions when they came to Plymouth. And although she may not have been invited to design for the ballet, she did really get on well with Wayne Sleep when she was asked to design a poster for him. She said he was a joy to watch and to talk to.

In 1986, Beryl's editor Joe Whitlock Blundell became Design and Production Director of the Folio Society. He commissioned Beryl to illustrate three of their books. At the time the Folio Society was a book club, and its members had to buy at least four books a year; they were not sold in bookshops. The books were exquisitely produced and the first title, *Mr Norris Changes Trains* by Christopher Isherwood (1990), appealed to Beryl who loved the 1930s setting in Berlin. She received advice from Barbara as to what a 1930s flat in Berlin would have contained, and she and John went to Berlin and Hamburg on a research trip Beryl wrote:

> As you know there is very little background in my pics but I've made it dark and had put a brass bedstead in the corner (which now worries me). The main thing is the Chinese screen he's standing in front of, my effort turned out to be somewhat crude despite help from Tony with a book and the one that he has. Just hope that no Chinese will be leafing through it . . .[6]

Beryl herself suggested the next book, *The Loved One* by Evelyn Waugh, and travelled to the Forest Lawn Memorial Park in Glendale, California, for inspiration. She wrote of this USA trip:

> We saw some marvellous things, froze to death in the mountains & desert, steamed and perspired mid-day in Flagstaff and California. What did surprise me is how beautiful the country was around Las Vegas which turned out to be a large town surrounded by pale mountains . . . Hollywood was in the middle of Thanksgiving for the last couple of days before we came home . . . having managed to get ourselves across to

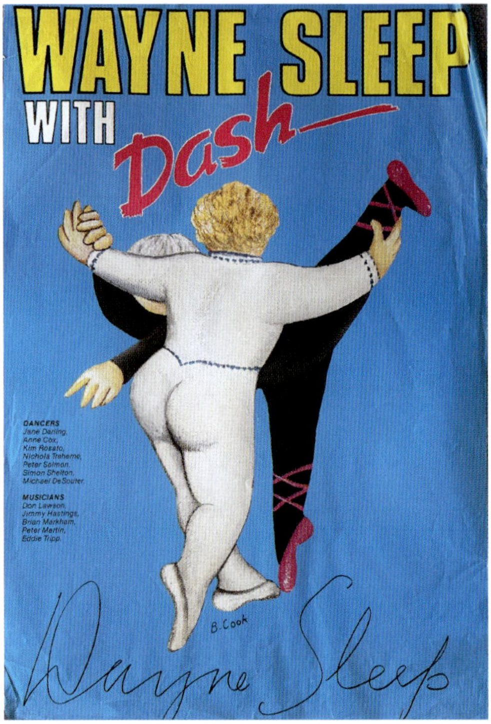

Wayne Sleep poster (1983). Beryl got on very well with her fellow Plymothian, and for once has portrayed herself in the painting.

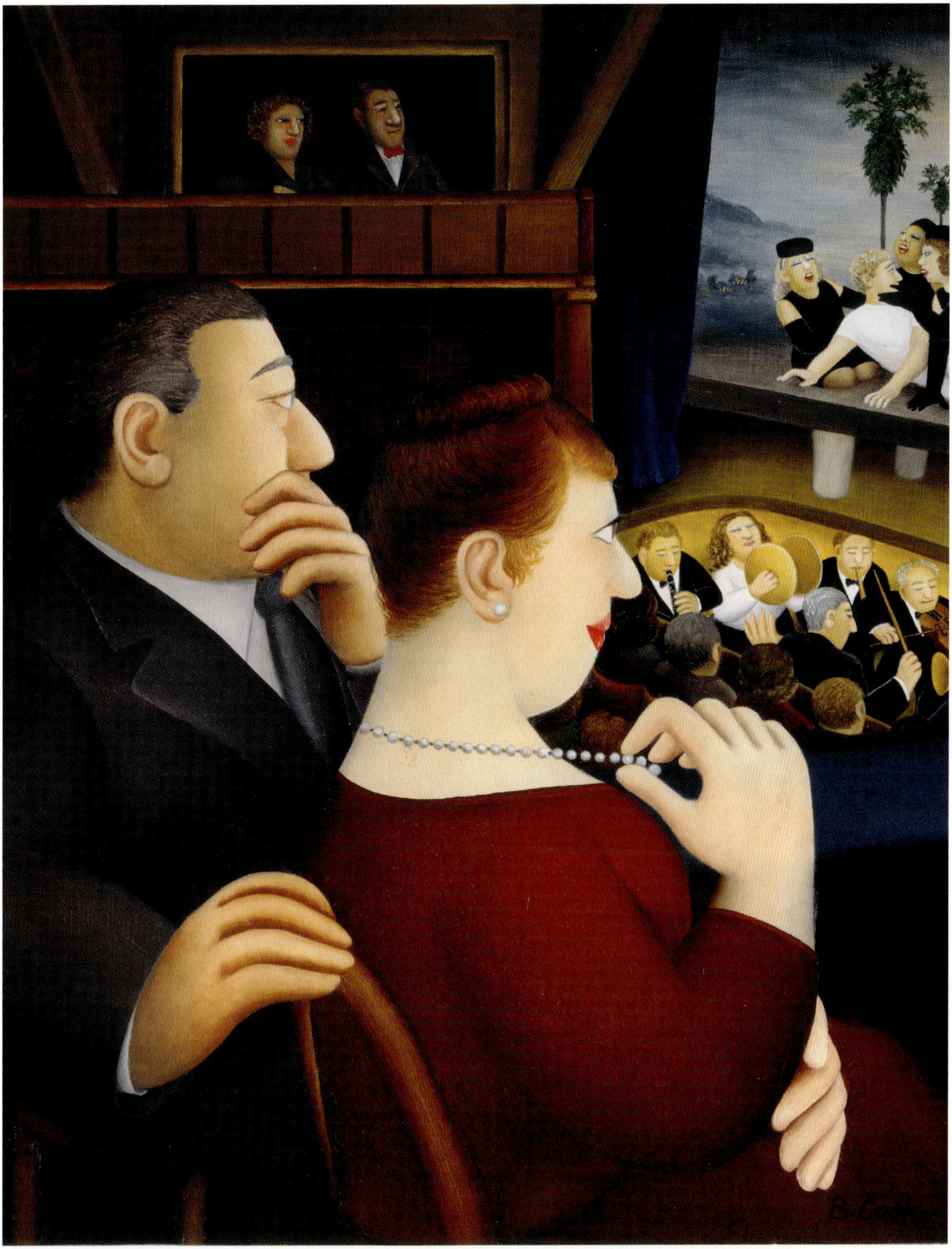

Magical Evening at Glyndebourne
(1991). The view from a Box. Beryl's paintings of performances often paid more attention to audiences than to the event itself.

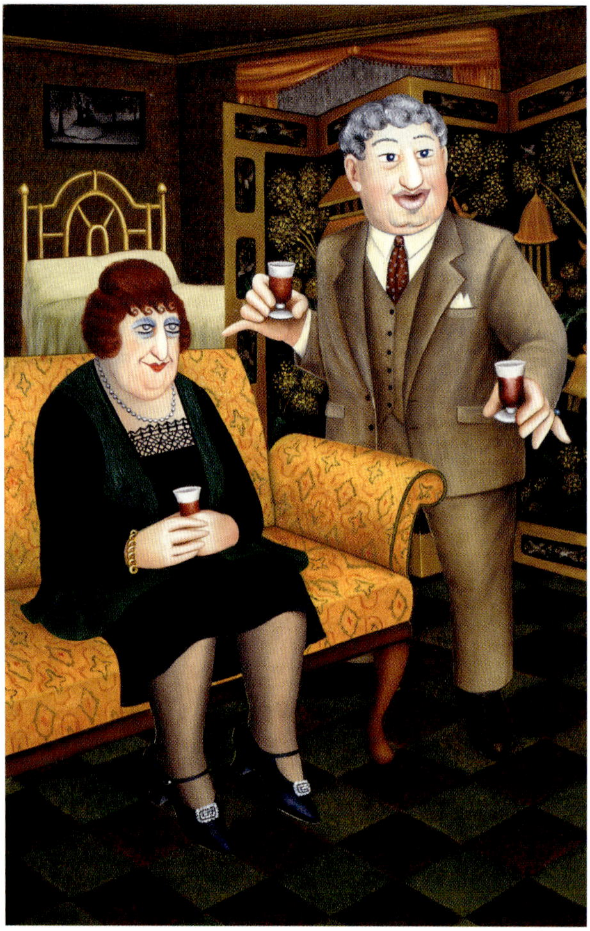

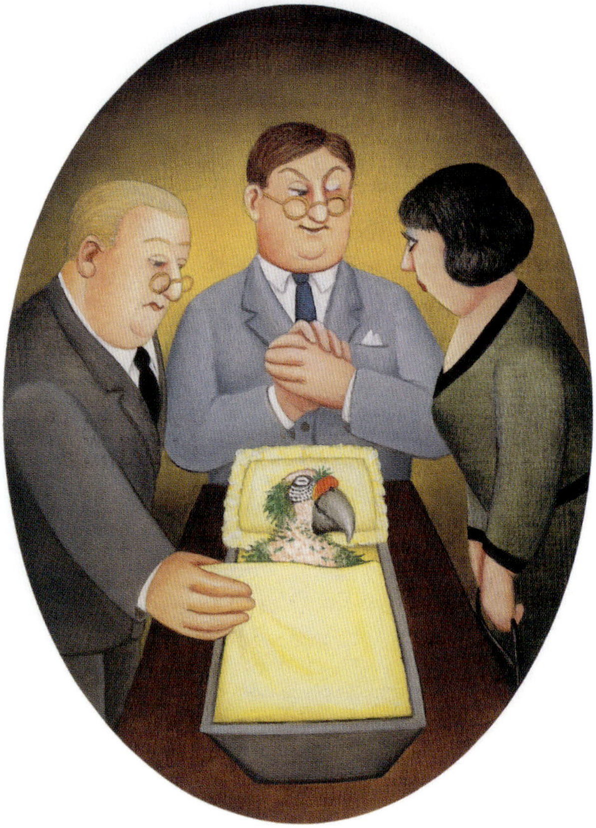

Illustration for the Folio Society edition of *Mr Norris Changes Trains* (1990). This was Barbara Ker-Seymer's favourite picture for the book: 'I do love her shoes so much (and the bags under her eyes)'.[7]

Original illustration for the Folio Society edition of *The Loved One* (1992). Beryl explained that 'the parrot is dead and lying in my version of a casket, NOT peacefully asleep in a cot as John just thought when he saw it'.[8] The parrot is destined for The Happier Hunting Ground, a pet cemetery.

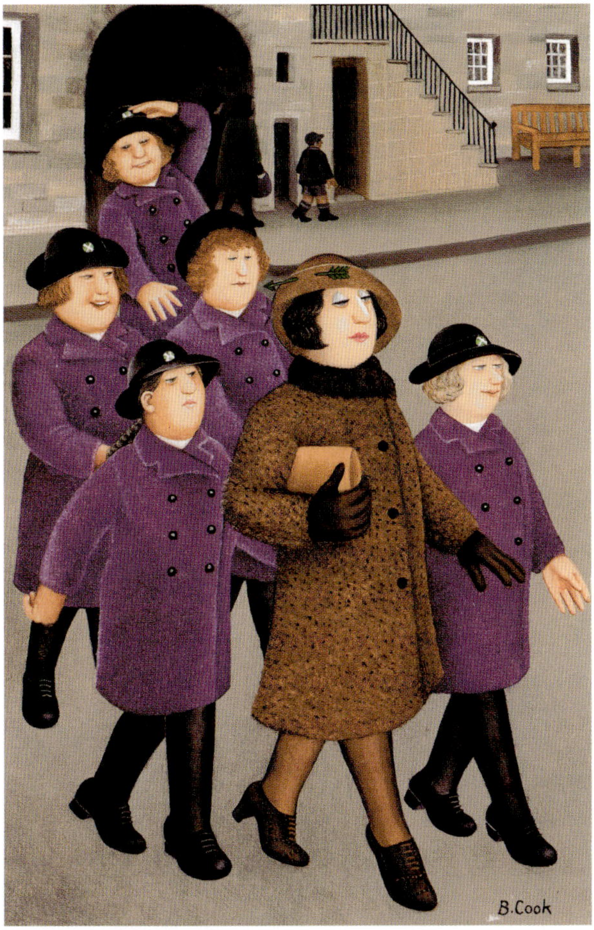

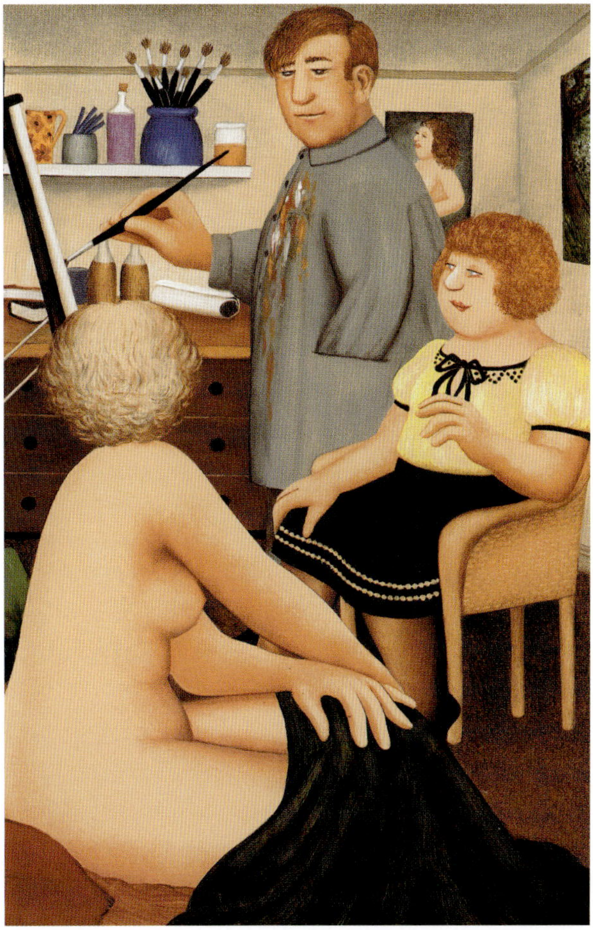

Walking in File
(1998). Illustration for the Folio Society edition of *The Prime of Miss Jean Brodie*. Miss Brodie is leading the girls, in their violet uniforms, through a slum area and they are trying to ignore the smells and shouted insults.

Sandy Sat with the Painter and His Model
(1998). Illustration for the Folio Society edition of *The Prime of Miss Jean Brodie*. One-armed Art Master Mr Lloyd is painting a naked Rose (wholly inappropriate) while pig-eyed Sandy looks at the result and realizes it looks more like Miss Brodie.

> Forest Lawns by bus (no less) we found it was acres and acres of green hills – thickly dotted with memorial tablets – and miles to walk uphill to the Wee Kirk O' the Green and others such like. This trip was abandoned and we sat for ages in the deserted streets to wait for another bus back to the Chinese Theatre. Then spent an interesting hour watching the seedy occupants of a café on Hollywood Bvd. The Dead Line tours had finished for the season by the time we got there, to my great regret . . .[9]

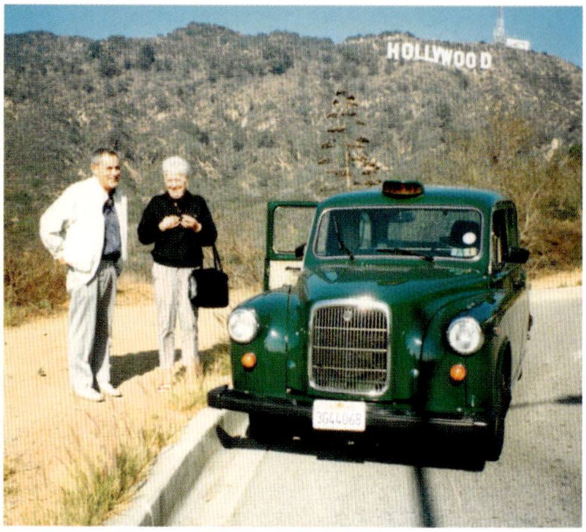

John and Beryl in front of the Hollywood sign, 1988

It is a rather macabre book but Beryl's illustrations avoid being sinister.

Beryl's third Folio book was *The Prime of Miss Jean Brodie* by Muriel Spark, an easier read than the other two. She drew on her memories of Kendrick School (see pages 16–17).

Beryl was particularly meticulous about the composition of each illustration, which was painted on board cut 20 per cent bigger than the printed size. There were still cries of despair and frequent scrapings off and repainting of faces. There was a further challenge, because the image had to extend a quarter inch beyond where it would be cut (a margin known as the bleed) in case of inaccuracies in the trimming process. This area had to be an extension of the background without having anything vital in it, which was against Beryl's instincts.

As well as commissions, Beryl's existing paintings were used for a myriad of other purposes, including record covers, adverts, postage stamps, jigsaws and pharmaceuticals. Pat White, of Rogers, Coleridge and White Literary Agents, handled such requests, always checking with Beryl to see if she was happy with the proposal.

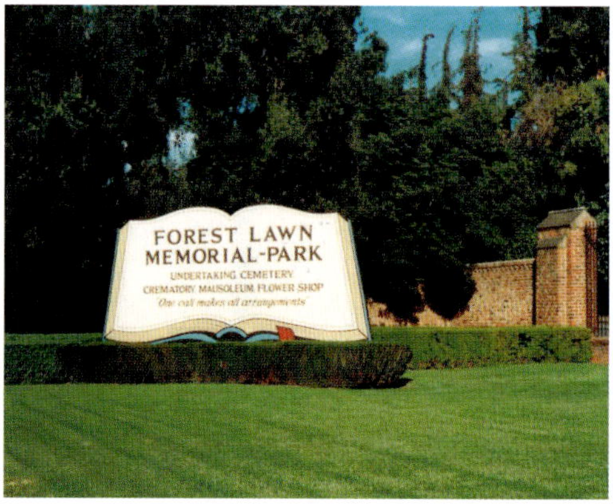

Beryl's photograph of Forest Lawn, the cemetery which became Whispering Glades in *The Loved One*

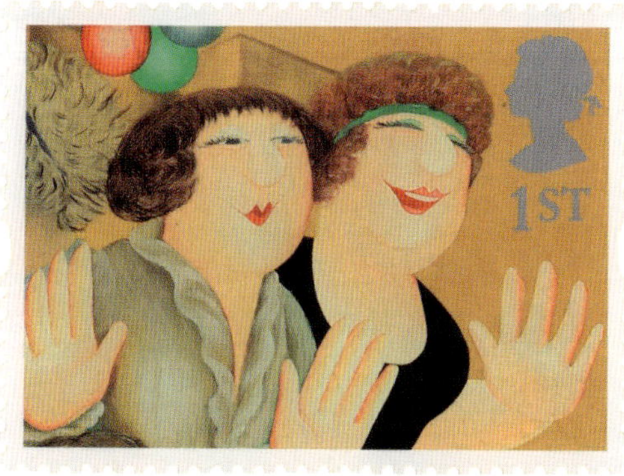

First class postage stamp featuring
Girls on the Town, 1995

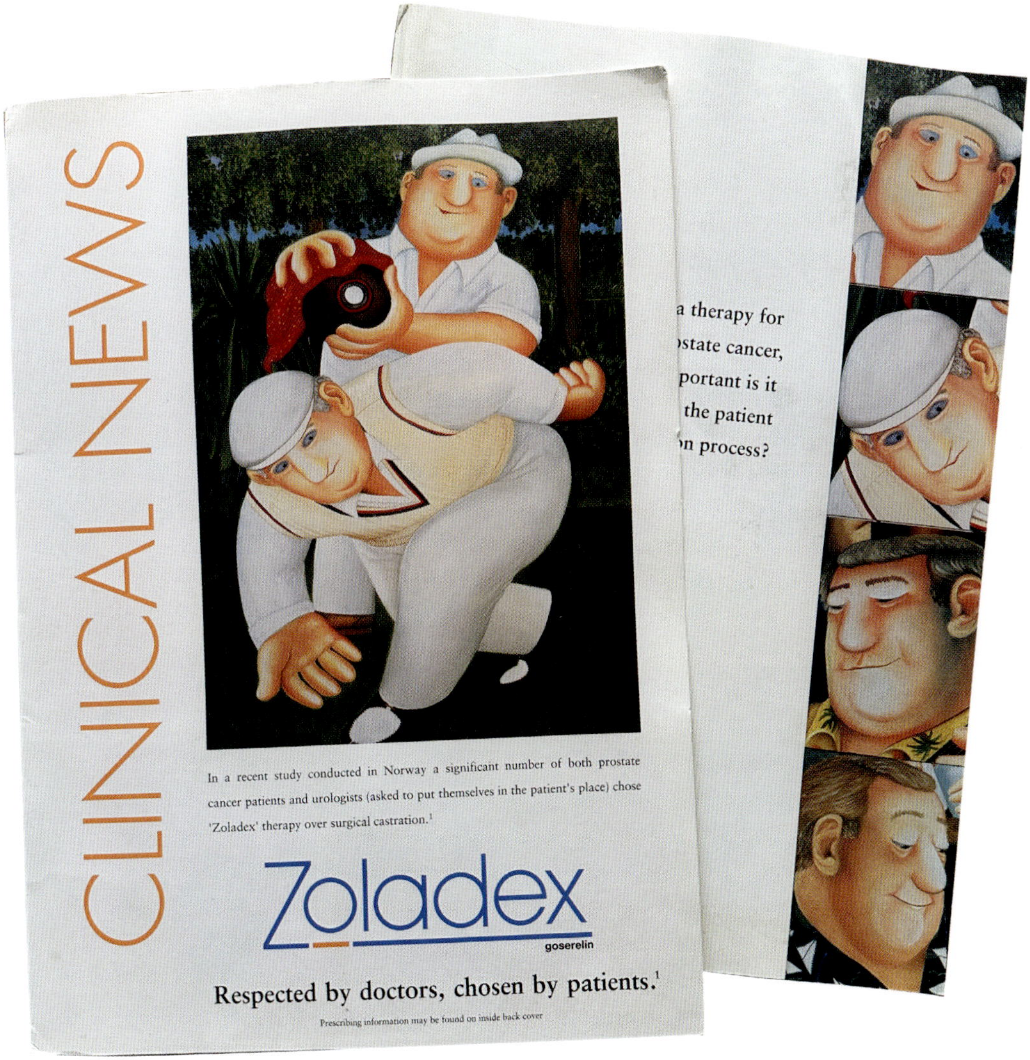

In 1992 two drug firms paid a considerable sum to use Beryl's images in their campaign (targeted only at the medical profession) for a prostate drug – it amused Beryl so she said yes. This one is an opportunity to see whether all Beryl's men look the same, as some people alleged.

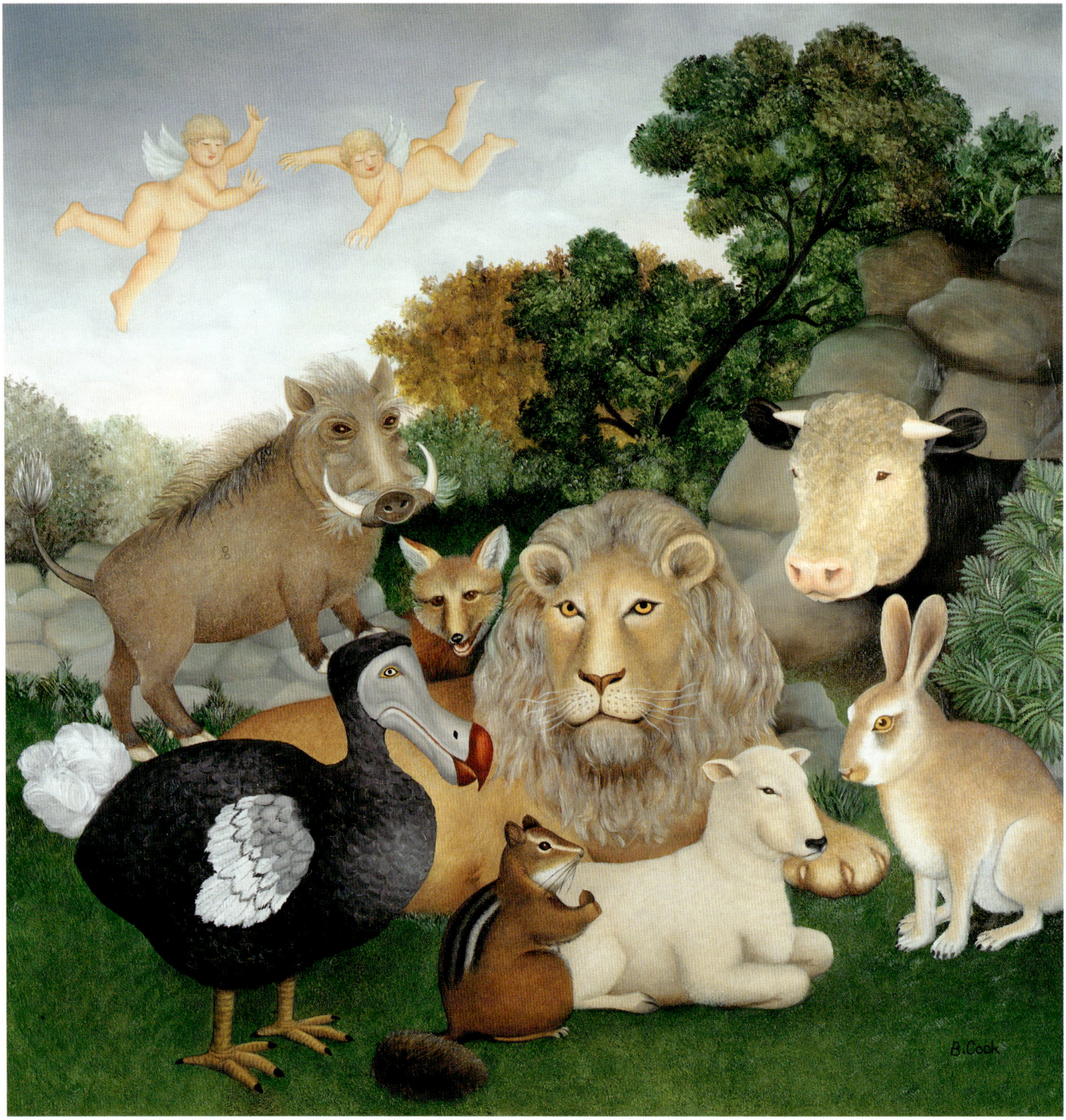

The Peaceable Kingdom
(1966) by Beryl, featuring Basil the Warthog whom
she had 'adopted' at London Zoo (see page 119)

12

Influences & Emulations

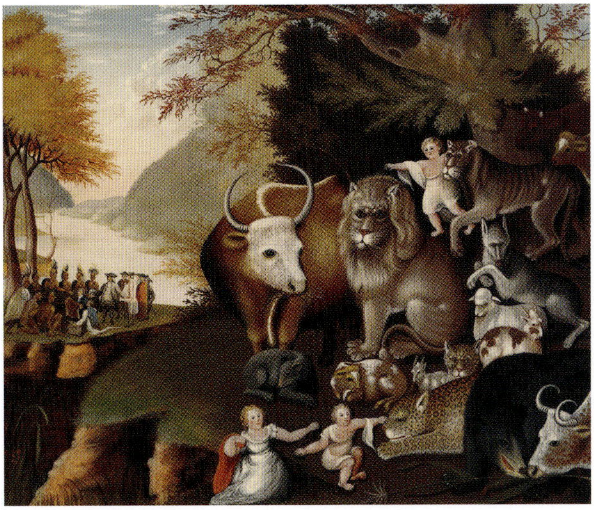

Peaceable Kingdom (1834) by Edward Hicks

In 2007 The Baltic Centre for Contemporary Art held a retrospective exhibition of Beryl's paintings. The catalogue includes reproductions of her paintings in date order, offering an opportunity to see how her art developed and became more assured, while staying true to her unique style and selection of favourite themes. At the beginning, the influences of other artists are clear, but she very soon starts to play with us by painting in the style of other artists for fun.

At the start of her fame, Beryl was quickly labelled as a naïve artist. This term, now outdated, was once applied to artists without any formal training in an art school or academy and, according to the Tate Gallery's website, it's typified by work that is simple, unaffected and unsophisticated.[1]

While it is true that Beryl had not received any art training, her work is certainly not simple, unaffected or unsophisticated. To paraphrase Dolly Parton ('It takes a lot of time and money to look this cheap'), it takes a lot of skill to look this artless.

Beryl probably didn't help by saying that two of her influences were The Flintstones and Donald McGill postcards. In fact, the same argument applies – it takes a lot of skill for a cartoonist to suggest so much in relatively few lines.

The influence shows in Beryl's economy of detail, such as the absence of fingernails, navels and shadows (once you start looking, there's quite a lot else missing or sparsely employed as well, such as nostrils). When Barbara pointed this out to her, she retorted that she could paint them – *if necessary*. Just as the Simpsons only have three fingers, her paintings read correctly and one scarcely notices. Ted defended her stoutly from any suggestion of inability, or – worse – faux naivety, and he and others disputed the naïve label anyway. She had just developed her own style. Beryl could always be naïve for fun; when her editor Joe missed out on an Alfred Wallis at an auction, Beryl simply painted him not one, but two. When Joe talked of publishing a book on Wallis, she said, 'Good idea. You write it and I'll do the pictures.'

In the past, paintings in this style were also sometimes called 'primitive', implying that the artist was unsullied by any association with Proper Art. Beryl had not grown up in an artistic vacuum. Her mother 'dabbled' in art herself, they went to art galleries and there were plenty of art books at home. Beryl liked a range of artists, but as we have seen, her biggest influence was Stanley Spencer.

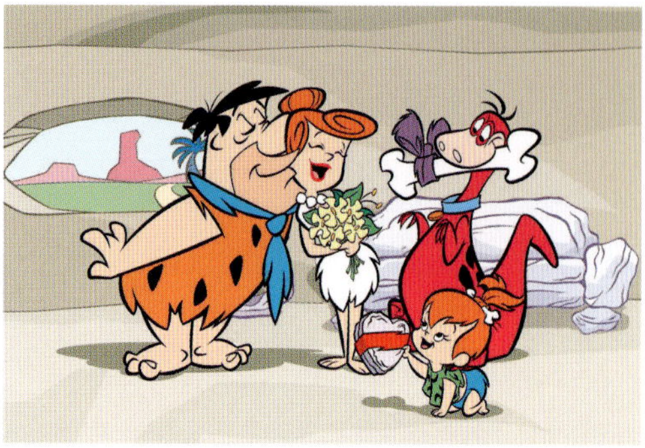

Beryl repeatedly mentioned the 1960s TV animation *The Flintstones* as a key influence. She said 'I used to go and look at cartoons, because they do it all so marvellously, don't they, in just those few lines'.[2] You can see the influence in her economy of certain details, such as fingernails.

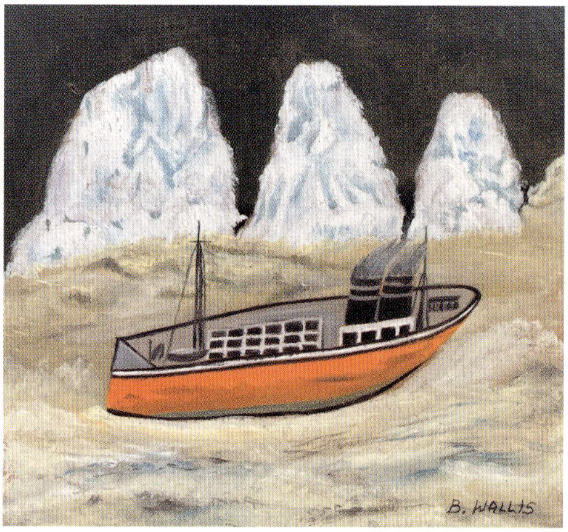

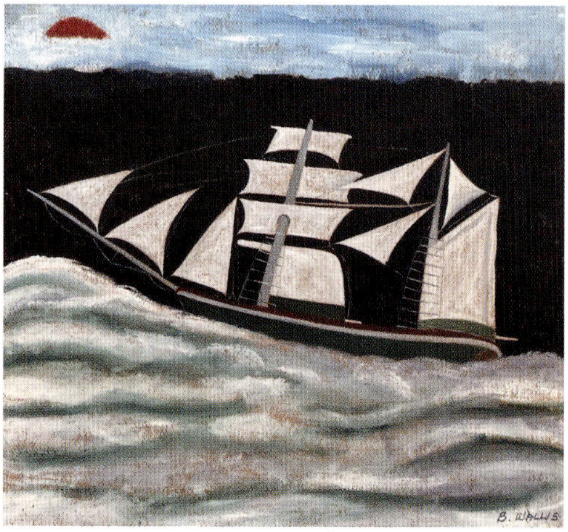

Beryl's versions of Alfred Wallis paintings, a commiseration gift for Joe (1981)

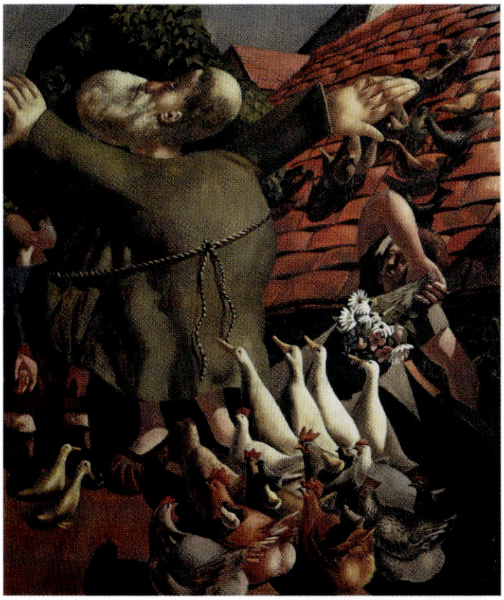

St Francis and the Birds
(1935), by Sir Stanley Spencer, Tate,
set in his home village of Cookham

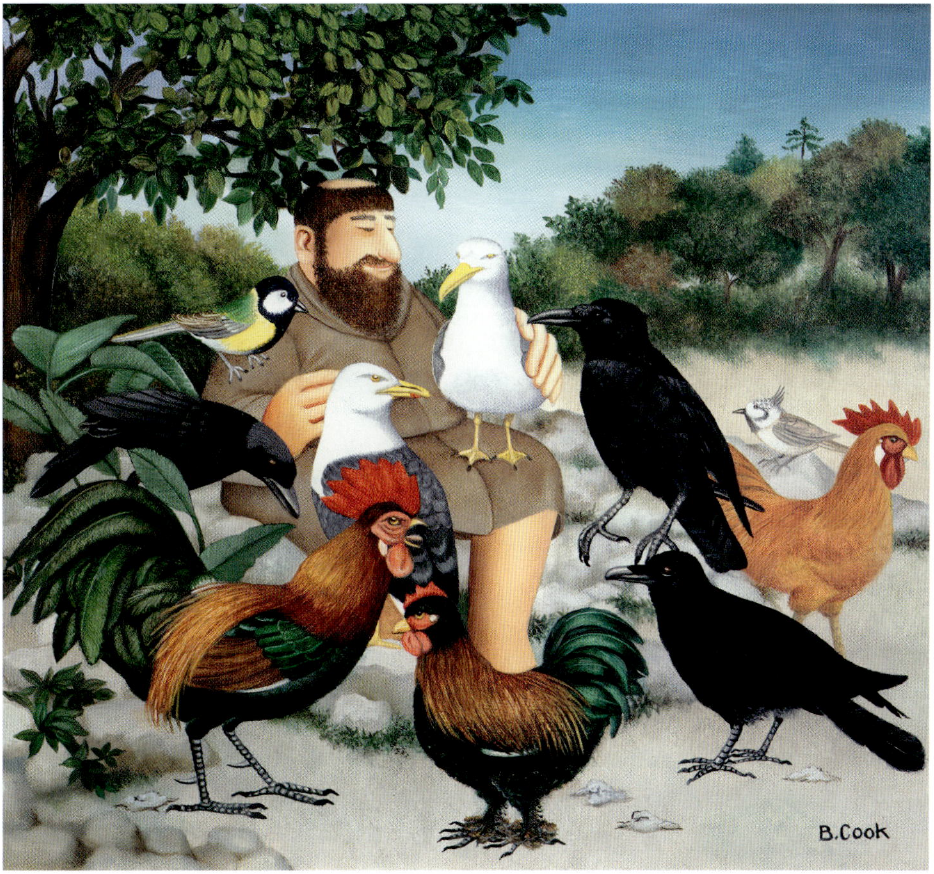

St Francis and the Birds
(1990). Beryl's version of the Spencer painting,
not set in Plymouth

There are so many parallels. Both artists populate their paintings with real locals and family members. Spencer's figures are distorted, seen from unusual perspectives, and have exaggerated limbs in impossible positions. However, the most obvious similarity is in the arrangement of figures and shapes, which cover the entire canvas, allowing for very little – if any – sky.

There was a key difference, however. Beryl insisted that her paintings had no meaning, whereas Spencer's subjects were driven by his personal philosophy of death, sex and resurrection, even if the meaning was somewhat difficult to follow.

The other big influence on Beryl's art was the work of Edward Burra (see also Chapter 5). Burra and Beryl's friend Barbara Key-Seymer inhabited the world of the 'Bright Young Things', the bohemian set of middle-class intellectuals who loved what they called 'slumming' among the working classes. No wonder Barbara was able to suggest itineraries for Beryl, who shared their appetite for jazz, seediness and theatricality but not their constant reshuffling of relationships.

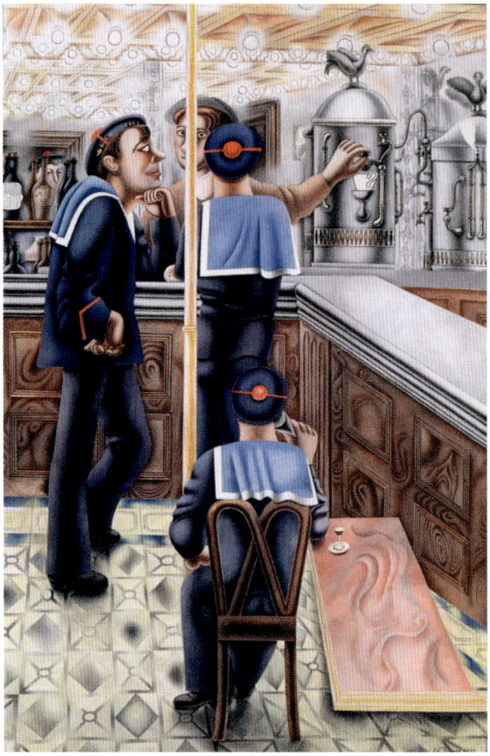

Three Sailors at the Bar (1930), by Edward Burra

Although Burra worked in watercolour and Beryl worked in oil, and Burra embraced the dystopian and downright deadly, while she celebrated joy, they had many similarities. Both painted from postcards where necessary, and 'borrowed' from other artists. Both began with pencil sketches to form what Ted calls 'an armature' for their work, rather than painting freehand. Both maintained a sort of childishness, and filled their picture with figures right to the edges, while playing with perspective and the human form.

Neither Spencer nor Burra was self-taught. However, both had comfortable, middle-class backgrounds which meant they could pursue their vision without having to compromise in order to earn a living. Burra sold very few paintings at first. Barbara and other friends encouraged him by buying his work and also rescued paintings that he had thrown out in despair, just as Tony had rescued Beryl's paintings from the skip.

Beryl and Burra both had photographic minds. Barbara wrote, 'He saw things and went home and when he came back it was as if he developed them.' Each surrounded themselves with cuttings, books, letters, jazz records, postcards and magazines. Both travelled the world in search of ports, shady cafes, red-light districts and general degeneracy. Both especially appreciated a sailor in uniform. In 1985 Barbara wrote to Beryl:

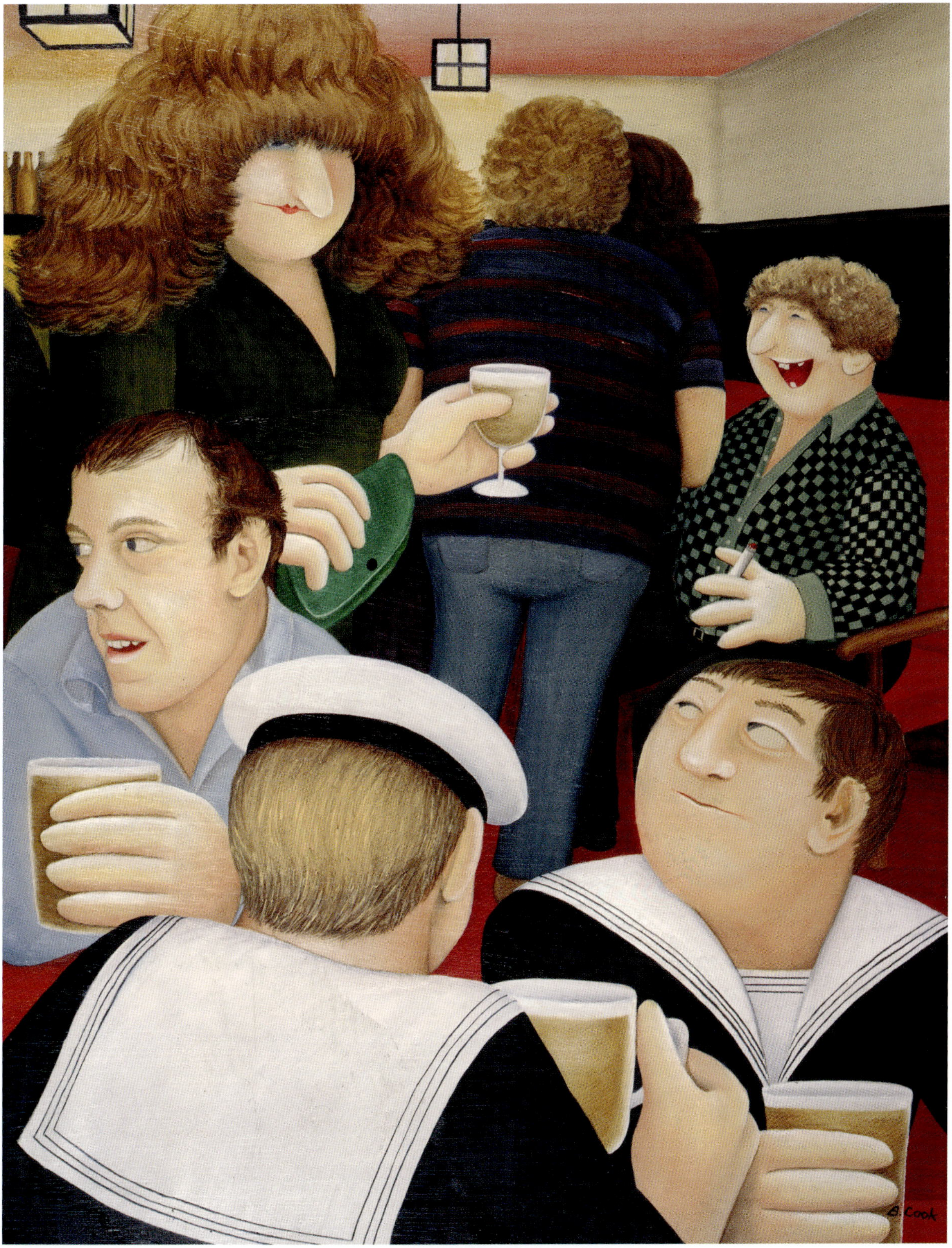

Hello Sailor
(late 1970s), inspired by
Edward Burra's *Three Sailors at the Bar*

> What you don't know is how alike you are to Ed in many ways . . . You are both observers rather than participators, in other words you prefer to sit in pubs and watch the people around you and noting everything for future use than sitting with people and being chatted to! Another thing is that you are very receptive and take an interest in everything that is said to you. You are a Godsend to me because after Ed died I had no one to write letters to in the way I wrote to him as you both have the same interests, another thing, Ed wouldn't dream of reading a notice of his work or go to an exhibition private view, so you see, you are very alike![3]

Barbara told Beryl about a Burra private view she went to at the Lefevre Gallery, and Beryl painted it for her, using pictures cut from the catalogue. The small man is Dustin Hoffman, a Burra collector, who was there in scruffy combat clothes, but with a huge chauffeur-driven Daimler waiting outside. 'He was looking at the paintings in the most intelligent way.'[4] The other guests are more interested in the canapes and drinks. Barbara looked at this painting every day, and it was hanging at the foot of her bed when she died.[5]

It's a reminder that Beryl used collage in quite a few of her works. She may not have been aware that Burra did this too – but only for about a year. It's more likely that she was influenced by Pop Artists such as Richard Hamilton, Kenneth Halliwell and Peter Blake.

Beryl and Burra both insisted that their work had no meaning, and hated art speak, (or 'F art' as Burra called it). Barbara said that 'I didn't notice any deep thoughts with Ed when I went to Barcelona with him.'

John and Beryl used Burra's travels as a basis for some of their own. They had already been to Amsterdam and Paris but got advice from Barbara about what to see in Marseille and Barcelona, Harlem and New York. A typical Burra voyage officially involved visiting museums and galleries during the day, and exploring the urban underworld at night, with a nap or swimming in the afternoon. Barbara knew the truth: he started drinking early on and then returned to his hotel to put his fingers down his throat so that he could start again later. Beryl liked a drink, but not to that extent.

Beryl and John loved Marseilles as soon as they got off the train. However, Beryl reported that 'There's not nearly enough Legionnaires about for my liking, we only found two or three although we loitered around that great big barracks

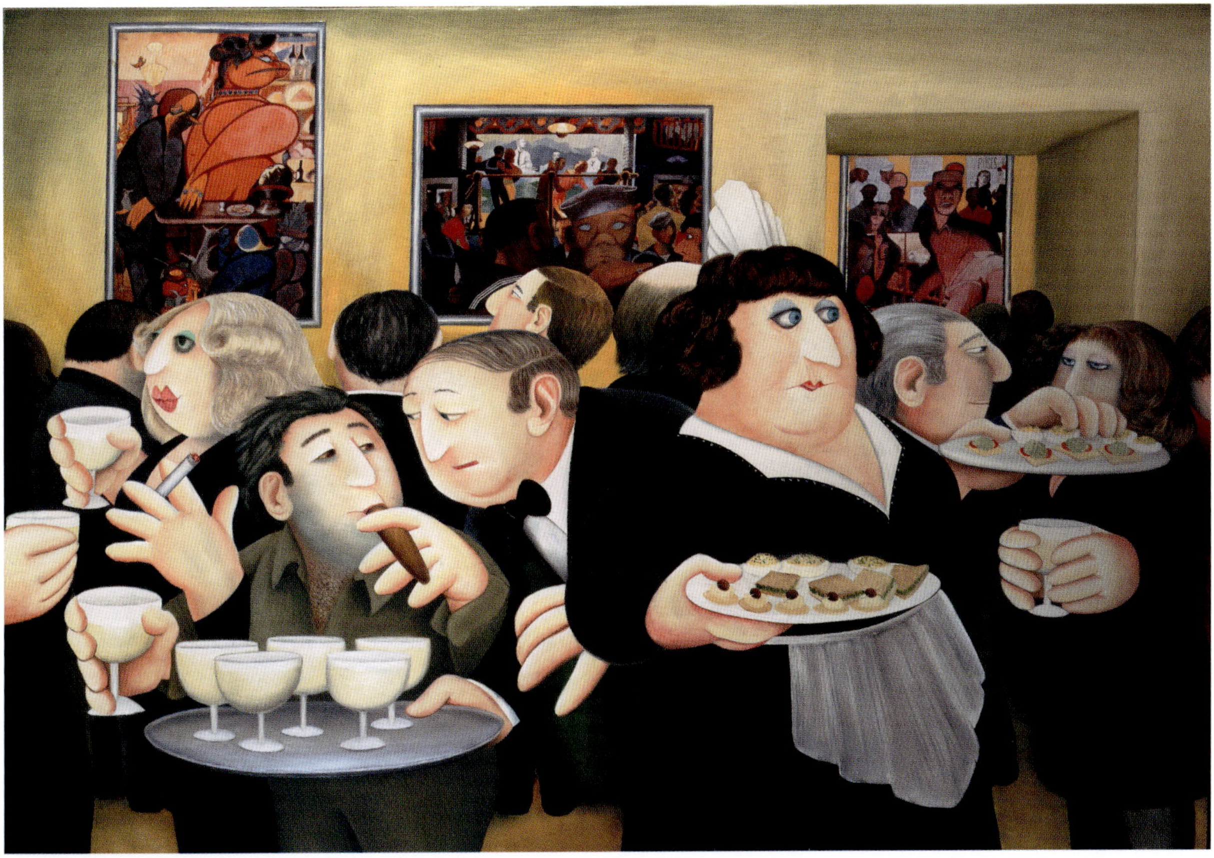

Private View
(1980). Beryl's depiction of the Edward Burra private viewing at the Lefevre Gallery

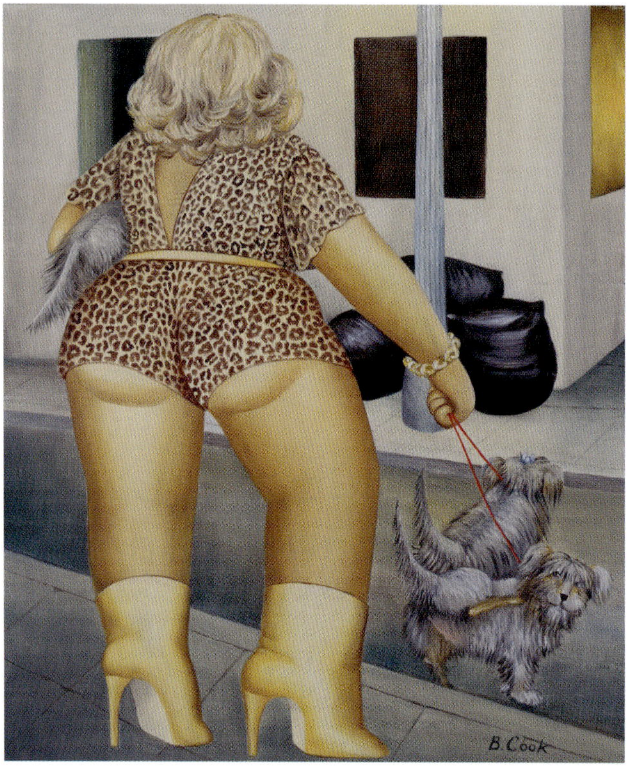

Lady of Marseille
(1980s), painted after a visit to Marseille in the footsteps of Edward Burra

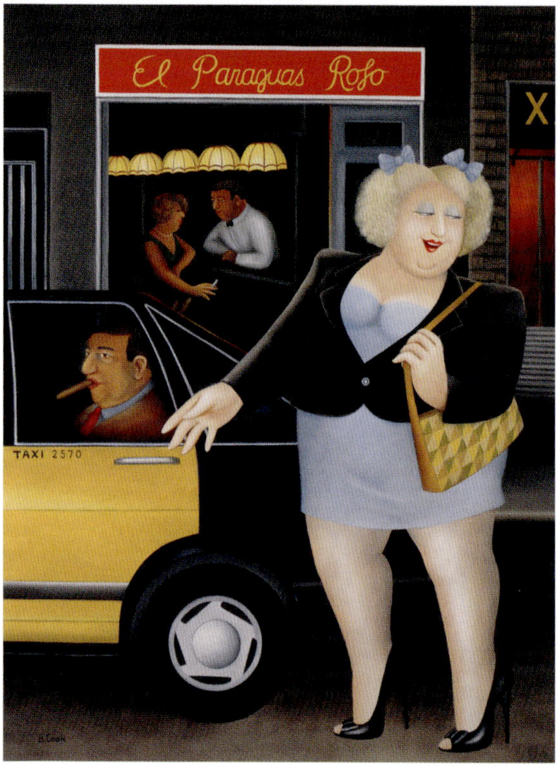

The Red Umbrella
(1991). This is Beryl's picture of Monica del Raval (real name Ramona Coronado Garcia, 1964–2024), a famous prostitute, in front of El Paraguas Rojo (The Red Umbrella) in Barcelona.[8]

where they recruit them. I raced upstairs and quickly painted a small picture of one of the girls as soon as we got home.'[6]

John and Beryl were inspired to visit Barcelona by a television programme they had seen featuring characters from freak shows and music halls across the city. Barbara said that Ed's favourite place was the Barrio Chino; before it was tidied up, it was a haven for artists, intellectuals, transvestites and prostitutes. Beryl and John's favourite bar was the Café Marsel: 'terribly seedy, where locals were playing various games and, I gather, sometimes keel over onto the floor to lie there, until they recover. Both the bar and the clients were in urgent need of renovation'.[7]

During the 1970s and 1980s art historians re-evaluated Spencer and elevated him to the group that includes Otto Dix, Diego Riviera, Balthus and Marc Chagall. This may explain why some fans and art historians saw similarities between their work and Beryl's. I am not an art historian, but I think it's important to differentiate between awareness and influence. Given how widely read Beryl was, I am sure that she knew a broad range of artists' work, and we saw her deliberately play with some of their styles when she first started to paint. Later we see her produce works inspired by Stubbs, Rousseau, Picasso, Modigliani, Botticelli and others, but these were for fun, to show that she could. She was not influenced by them in a way that forms or alters her development of her own artistic practice.

Beryl was introduced to the work of Tamara de Lempicka and Fernando Botero by Faith (see page 71) and Barbara respectively. While neither influenced her style, she was able to paint such a good Beryl de Lempicka for Faith that when Lempicka's agent saw it in the Russian Tea Room in New York, he thought it was an original (see page 171).

When painting *Fairies and Pixies* (see page 173), Beryl felt that her ex-Mabel Lucie Attwell painting desk was sending out vibrations. I think the vibrations might have got mixed in with those of Cicely Mary Barker.

The fairies multiplied enormously with the encouragement of John George of *Art and Artists* magazine, from whom Beryl had got the idea. Ted Lucie-Smith suggested she paint him as a little crop-haired motorcycle fairy, dressed in a thrilling mixture of sequins, gauze, Dr. Martens and black leather. So she did (see page 173).

Another favourite picture was *Peaceable Kingdom* by Edward Hicks (see page 161). It was very difficult to obtain a print and Beryl had to ask Norman to send one over from America. It was placed reverently in her studio.

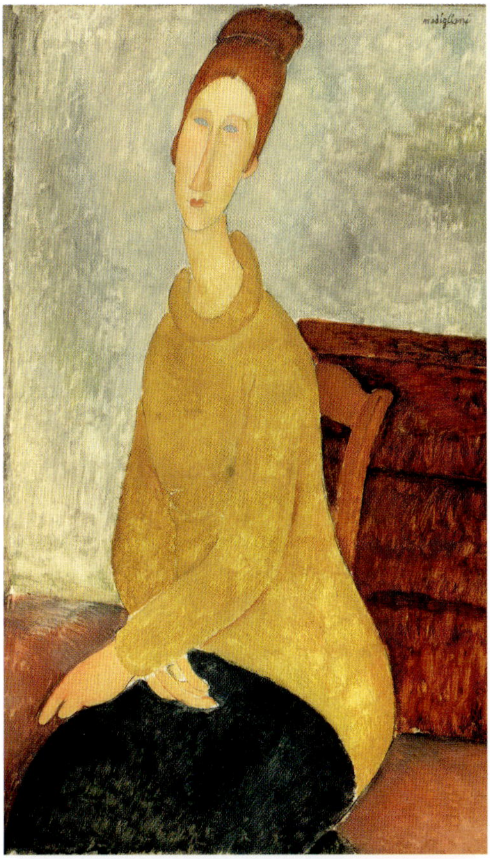

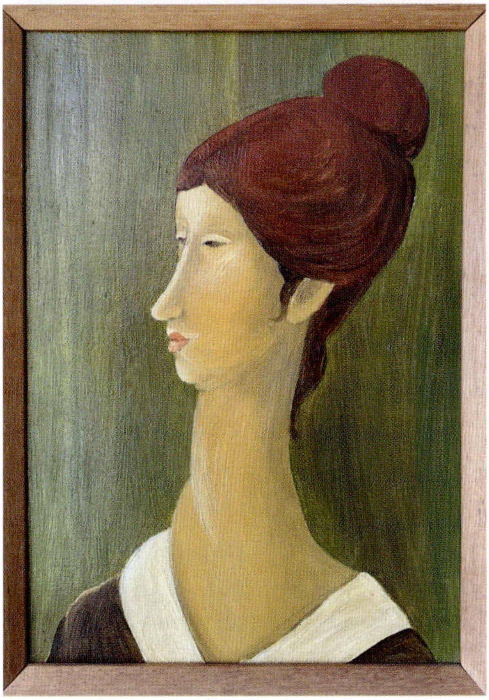

An original Modigliani, and a similarly long-necked lady of Beryl's own

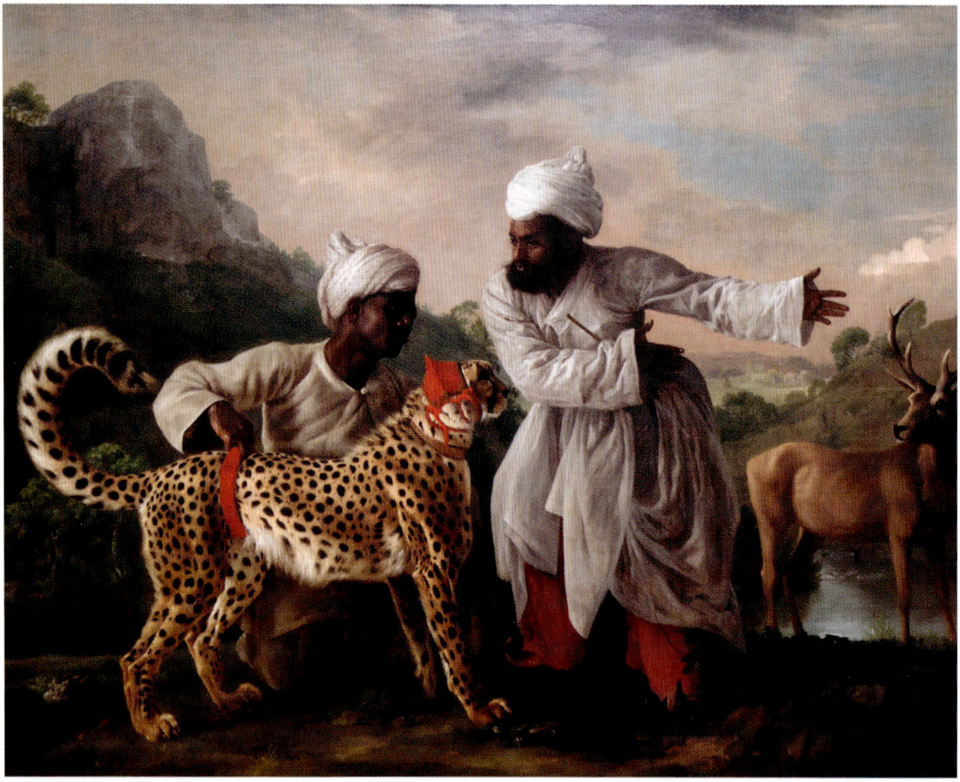

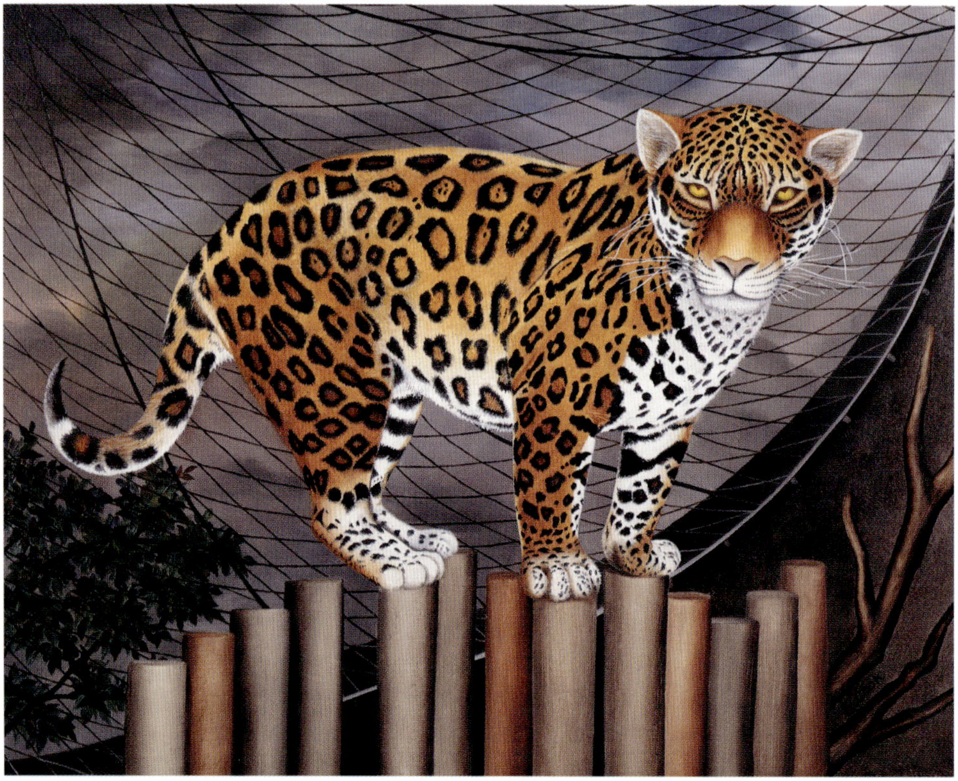

TOP
Beryl's favourite painting was *Cheetah and Stag with Two Indians* (c 1765) by George Stubbs, Manchester Art Gallery.

BOTTOM
The Jaguar
(1980s). A tour de force in fur

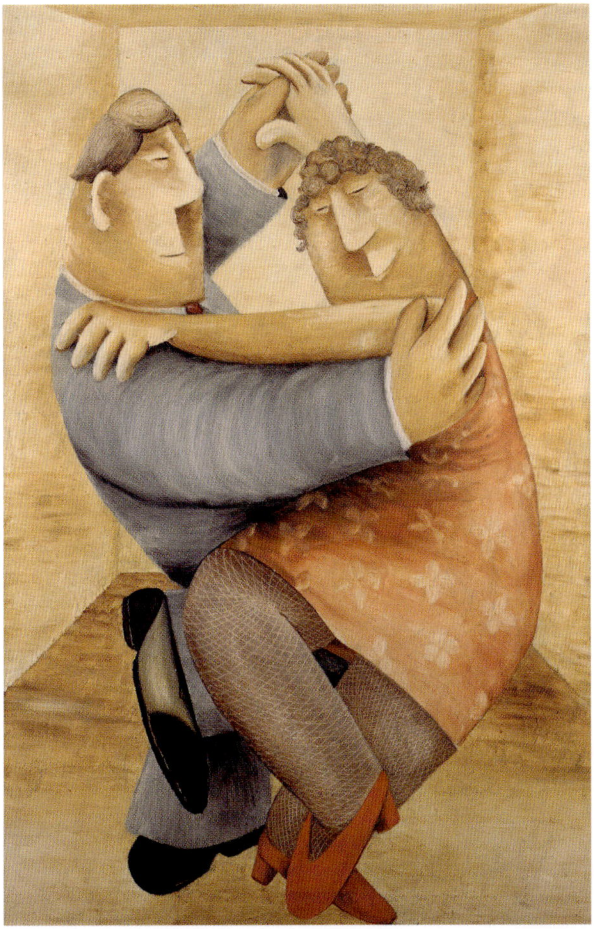

Couple Dancing
(1970), an experiment with Cubism

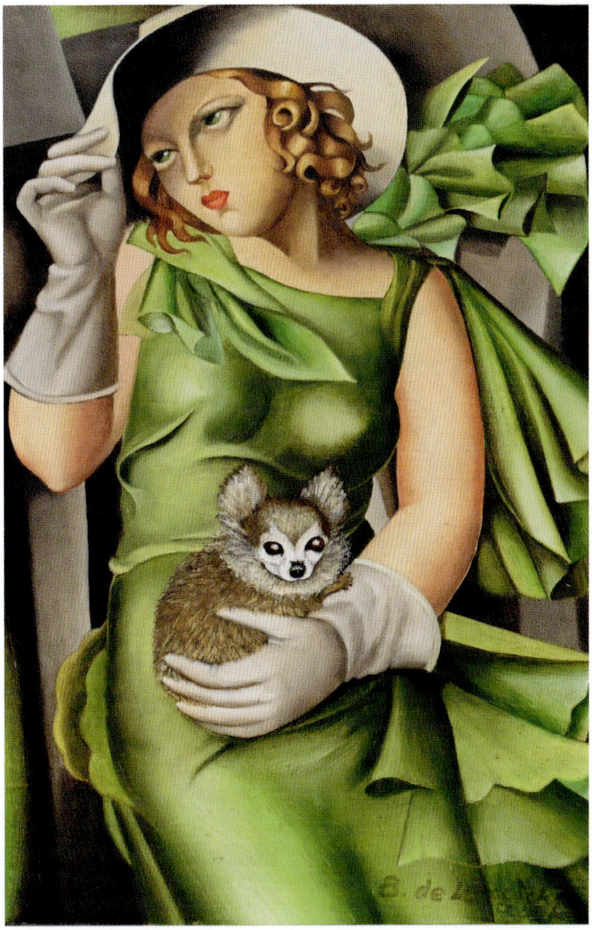

Beryl de Lempicka
(1990s), painted for Tony Martin

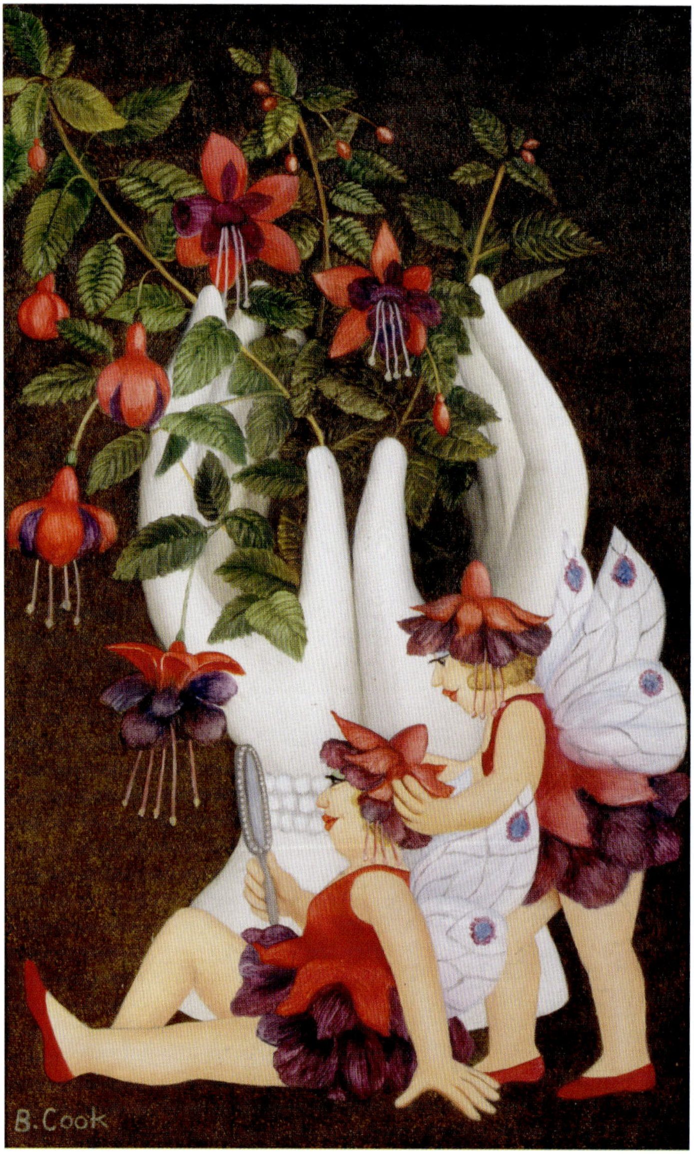

Fuchsia Fairies
(late 1980s), painted on a firescreen. Beryl painted this for her granddaughter Sophie, and was inspired by the Flower Fairies of Cicely Mary Barker (1895–1973).

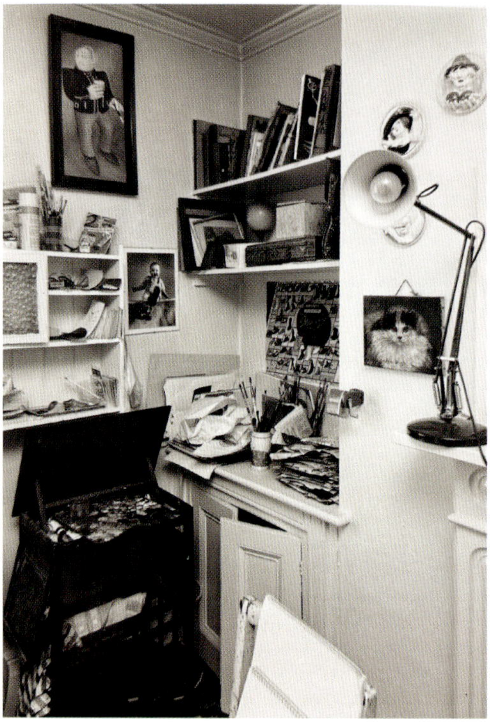

A corner of Beryl's studio, with the painting desk which had once belonged to Mabel Lucie Attwell. Beryl bought it from Tony Martin, whose shop was a short distance from where Attwell lived in Fowey, Cornwall.

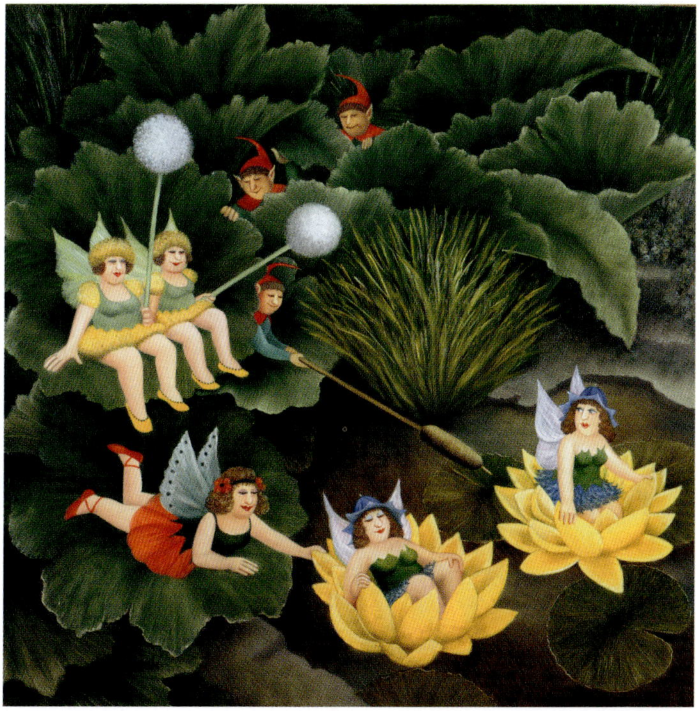

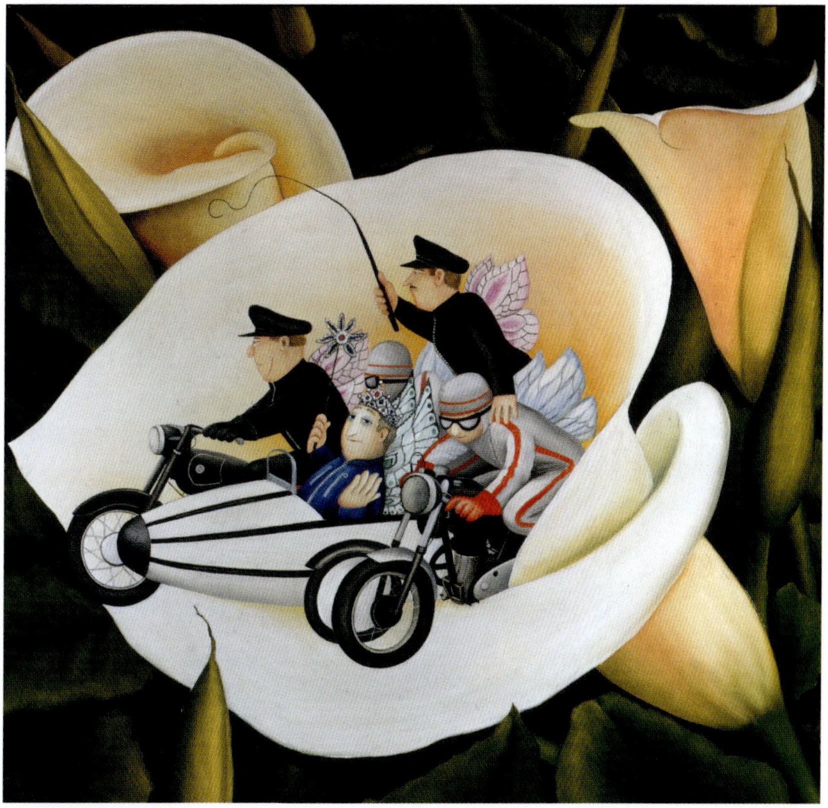

Fairies and Pixies
(1980s)

Queen of the Fairies
(1981). Beryl switched to modern, leather-clad fairies for this painting.

In 1984 Barbara wrote to Beryl, 'John tells me that you were wishing that you could paint like Rousseau (is that why you have bought an easel and are planning to do immense paintings?) . . . I always feel so sad when I think of him wheeling his paintings to the Salon in a wheelbarrow, then having to wheel them all back again after they had been rejected. Nothing like that has ever happened to you!'[9] Rousseau was, and still is sometimes, lumbered with the epithet 'Le Douanier Rousseau' because of his work as a customs officer. Rousseau started painting seriously in his early forties; by age 49, he retired from his job to work on his art full-time. Ridiculed during his lifetime by critics, he came to be recognized as a self-taught genius whose works are of high artistic quality. He is famous for his jungle pictures, although he never went to the jungle: like Beryl, he used children's books and visits to the botanical gardens as references.

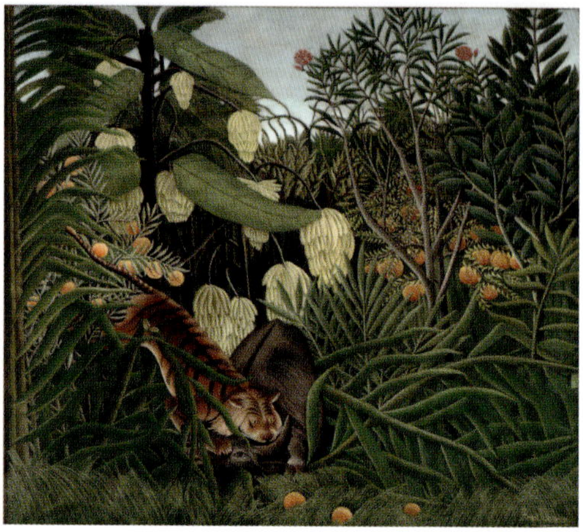

Exotic Landscape (1908), by Le Douanier Rousseau

Eventually, Rousseau was re-evaluated, though he is still often referred to as 'Le Douanier'. Major exhibitions of Rousseau's work 'countered the persona of the humble, oblivious naif by detailing his assured single-mindedness and tracking the extensive influence his work exerted on several generations of vanguard artists.'[10] It's time to do the same for Beryl Cook, I feel.

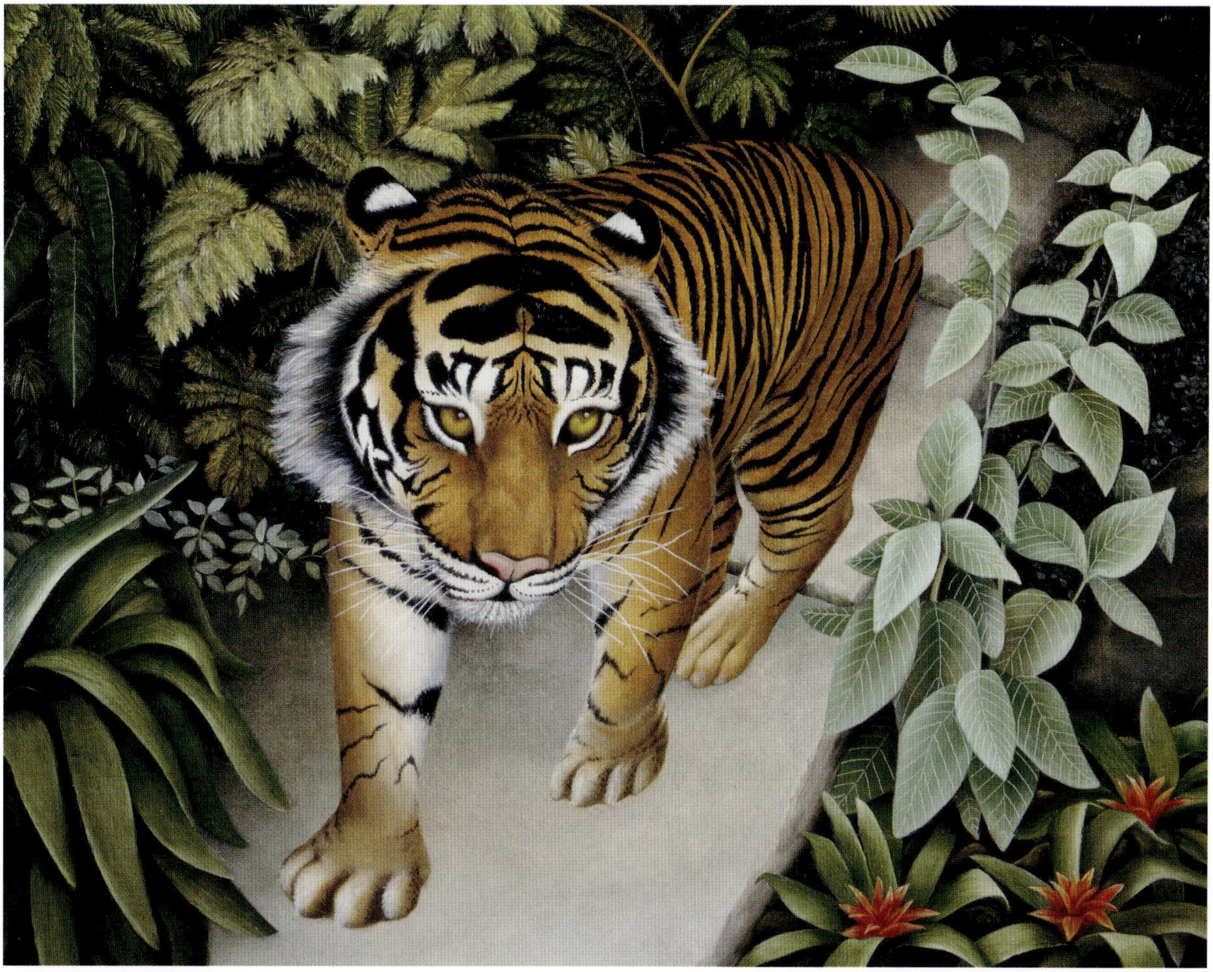

The Tiger
(1987), by the Seaside Landlady Beryl.
The foliage was inspired by a visit to Kew Gardens.

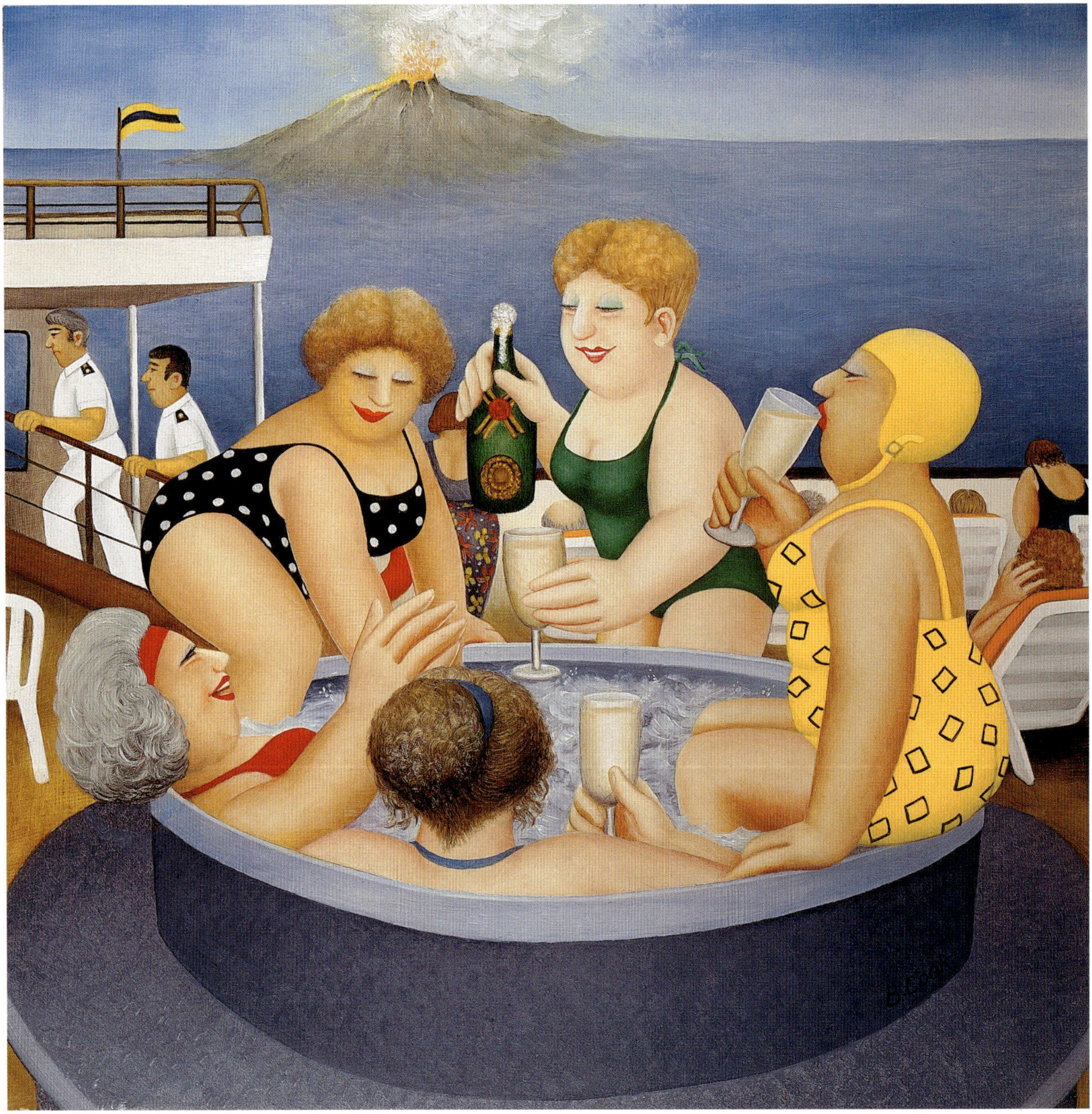

13

1976–1998: Plymouth & the World

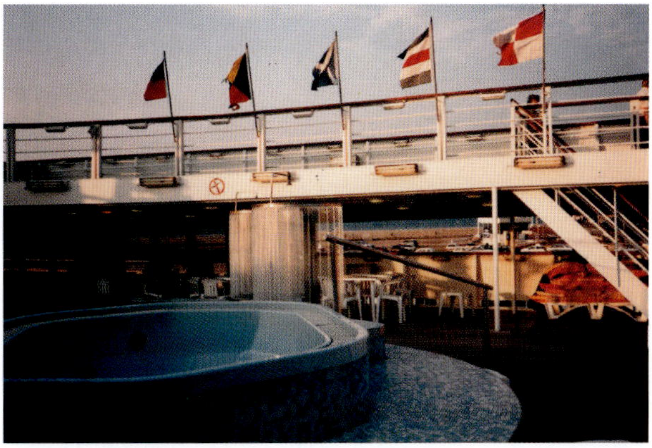

LEFT
Cruising 2
(c 2000), and its reference image above. This painting was inspired by Beryl's first cruise. She photographed the jacuzzi empty early one morning, and then painted in the figures back at home. She also added an erupting Mount Vesuvius in the background.

If *The Daily Mail* was right about the sudden increase in household income following Beryl's fame, you might have expected it to have gone to their heads. But Beryl was firmly of the view that she already had everything she wanted, and although she was confident enough to paint full time, there was no lottery-winner-type cash splash. Beryl continued to wear the same unshowy clothes, shop at Littlewoods, Woolworths and charity shops, and enjoy finding bargains to add to her collection. They remained at Athenaeum Street, though in due course they renovated the kitchen, installed central heating and double glazing, and built a sunroom, which the tortoises particularly enjoyed.

The Cooks were now able to travel in more comfort, and to stay at nice London hotels, but their holidays were mostly driven by Beryl's need to find inspiration for the next project. They were able to choose their own destinations, and to find inspiration in the things which Beryl had always enjoyed watching, if not joining in: food, music and dancing, seedy bars, gambling and enjoying the beach and pool, among others. The best were the destinations that included several of these, especially if there were shoes and prostitutes thrown in.

Of all the dances, the tango was tops. During their visit to New York in 1983 they visited the Roseland Ballroom in Manhattan, where Beryl watched a tango performed by a lady in a red dress whose partner kept very gingerly lowering her backwards, and it was touch and go whether he got her up again.

Beryl being Beryl, she worried that some of the hosts and hostesses (who charged $1 a dance) were more popular than others. But she loved a showcase of shoes just as she walked inside the Roseland. They also saw a rumba, and Beryl indulged her love of hands, a frequent motif in her work.

Barbara recommended the stage show *Tango Argentina,* saying it was the most wonderful thing she had ever seen, quite brilliant. On their next visit to London (in June 1991) John and Beryl went themselves, and Beryl wrote that it she too was now besotted by Carlos Borquez: 'the whole thing was quite staggering and the audience went mad'.[1] Beryl particularly liked the older performers and an old man playing jazz.

In 1994 the Cooks travelled to Buenos Aires especially to see, as Beryl described, 'this most exciting and seductive of dances'. They spent two weeks watching and listening to the tango every evening and sometimes during the afternoons.

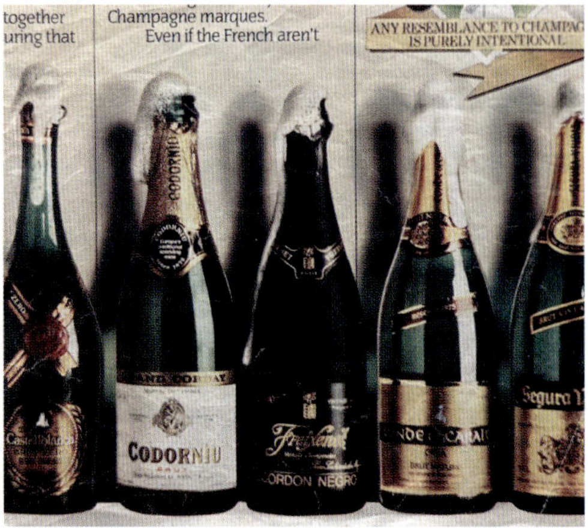

A magazine clipping, used for *Percy at the Fridge*. At the beginning of her painting career Beryl was a little embarrassed about using magazine clippings, until she found out other artists did the same.

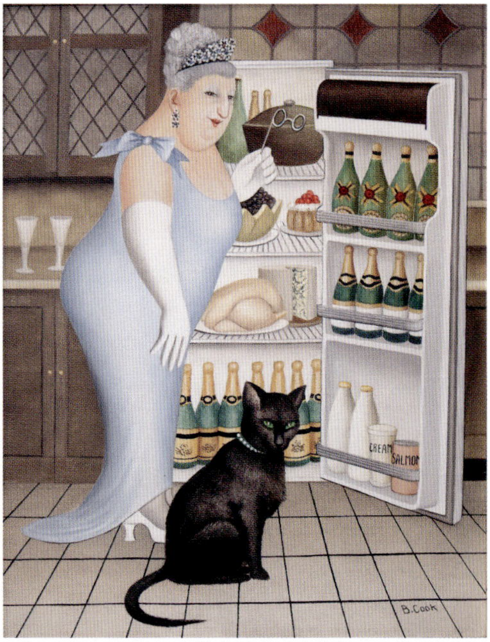

Percy at the Fridge
(1989), set in the new kitchen at Athenaem Street

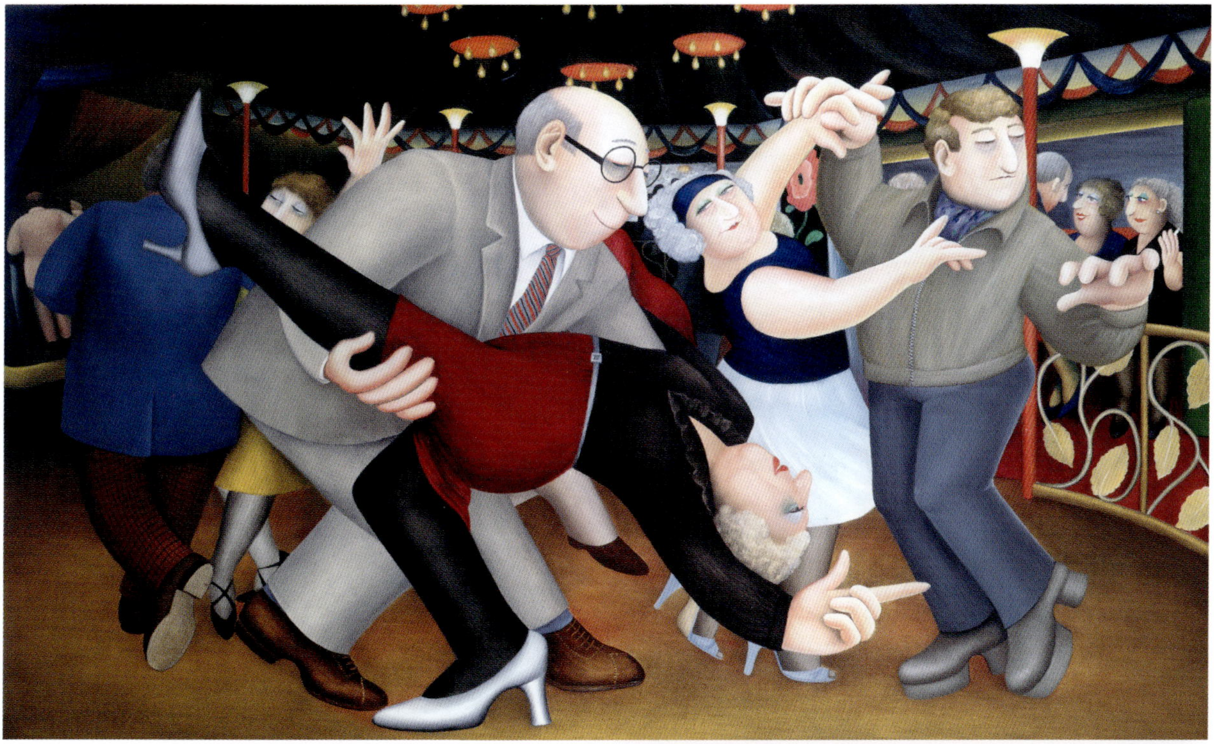

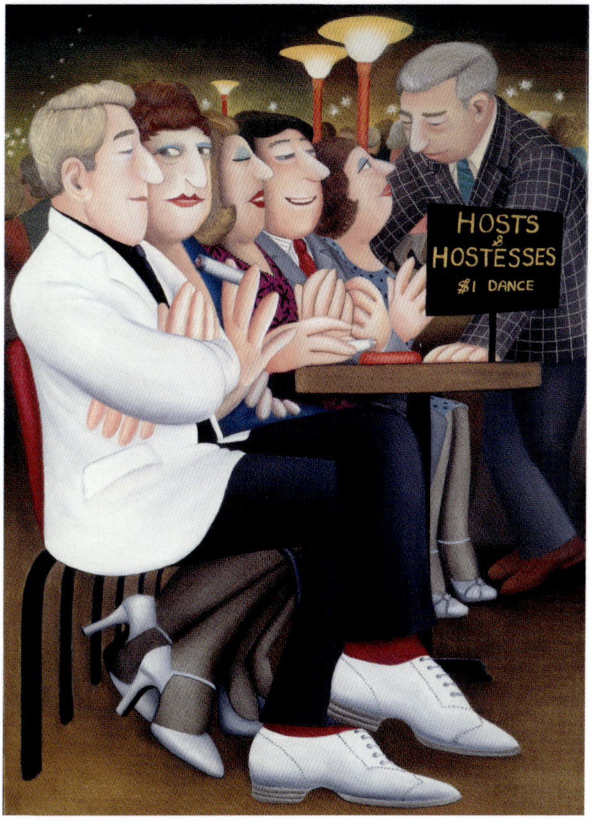

Tango
(1984–5). The man in the bomber jacket was in demand as a partner though he had difficulty with his platform shoes.

Hosts and Hostesses
(1984–5), in the Roseland Ballroom, waiting to be chosen

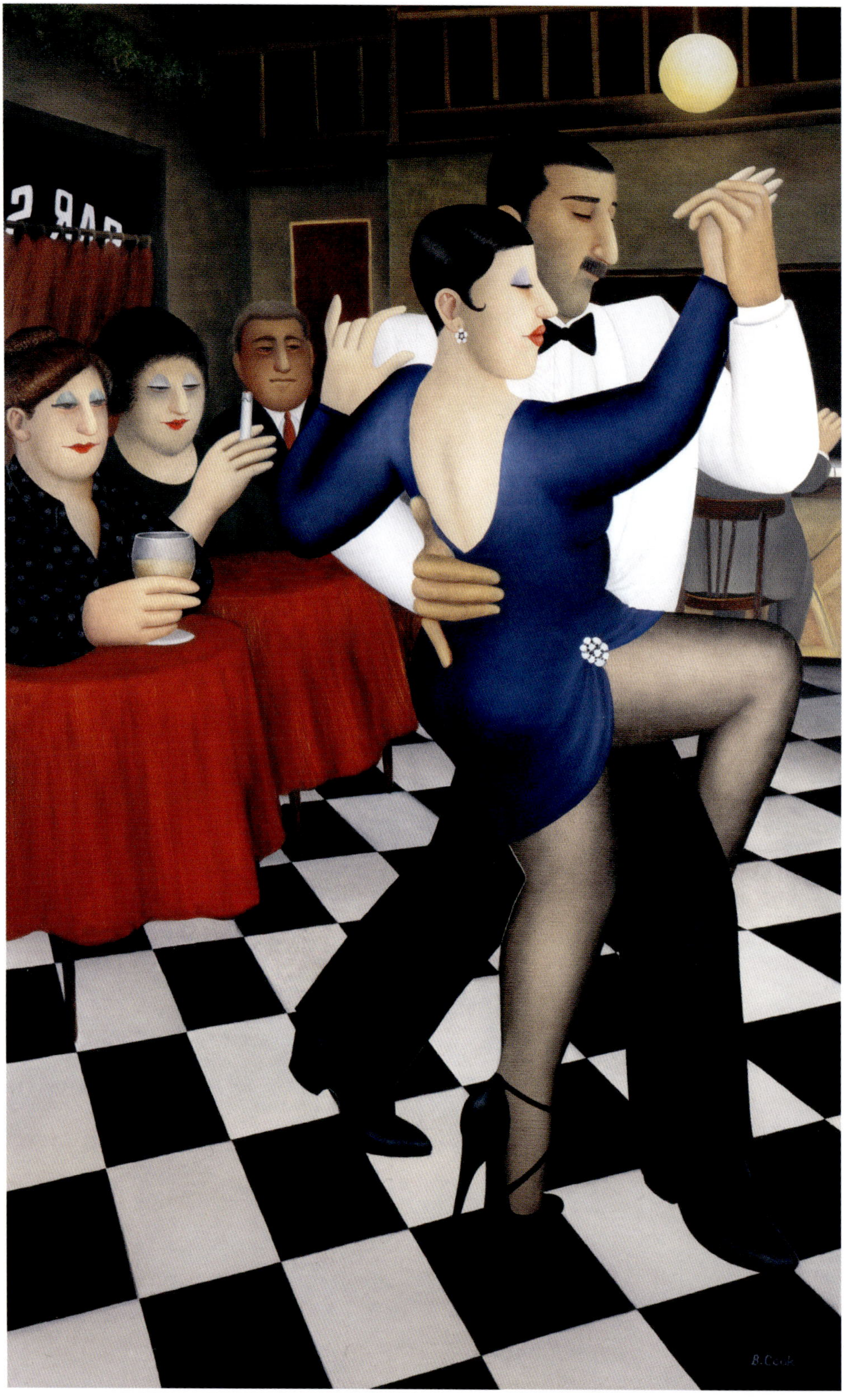

Tango in the Bar Sur, Buenos Aires
(c 1994), and Beryl's or John's photograph of it (opposite page)

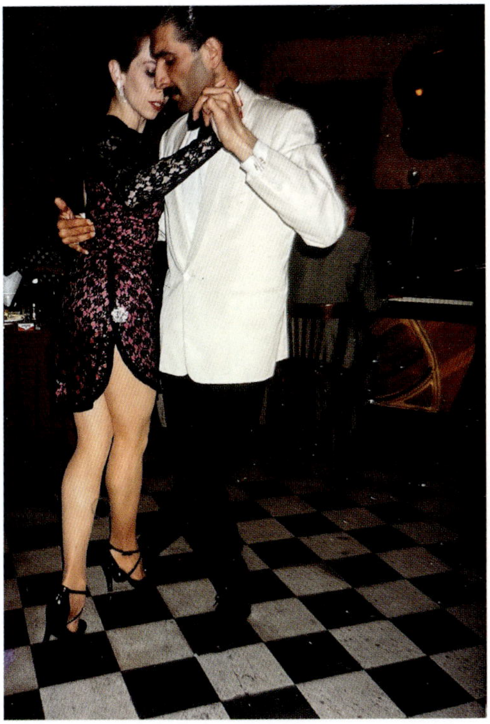

Beryl was sometimes a bit nervous of the food on holiday, and they often ate in their room, or in a simple diner-type establishment rather than a fancy hotel restaurant. However, she objected to the cost of room service when they stayed in New York, so they bought sausages, biscuits and gravy from Bojangles and took it back to their hotel room in the very fancy Algonquin Hotel. However, Beryl loved painting other people enjoying food – and Paris offered many opportunities (see page 183).

Beryl and John also travelled to Tenerife twice and found it offered a full house of sunbathing, food, dancing and music. Beryl was delighted to find it also well populated with twins, another obsession. Beryl wrote to Barbara:

> I am concocting yet another pic of Tenerife. And what a task I set myself with it – a pair of middle-aged twins having tea in a rather genteel café (in the better class side of the Island). As I had photographed the café through a large mirror I decided to paint the twins like this so I have not only two identical faces to paint but 4, and having to reverse everything in the mirrored side too [see page 184]. However, I seem to rather enjoy these battles (but they make me exhausted) and the pic is now ready to start painting tomorrow.[2]

She also wrote:

> I did enjoy it there, wonderful weather and riveting views of the tourist activities going on around me. The most amazing sight being the huge bulging bodies laying in several rows pointed sunwise on the sunbeds round the swimming pools. These they booked early with towels, taking possession after breakfast and staying all day, turning slowly and sizzling in the oil, just like purple walruses. I rarely saw anyone in the pool but in all fairness we weren't there most of the day . . . . What the Spanish thought of us all I can't imagine.[3]

There was also plenty going on in the evening, including dancing in the street, a particular pleasure for the Cooks. The bars had large open patios a few steps below pavement level and someone singing and playing the organ, or a little juke box.

The Cooks travelled to Cuba in 1999, possibly attracted by the combination of cigars and The Buena Vista Social Club, whose music was so popular at the time – this is speculation because there is relatively little correspondence about the holiday; sadly Beryl's great friend

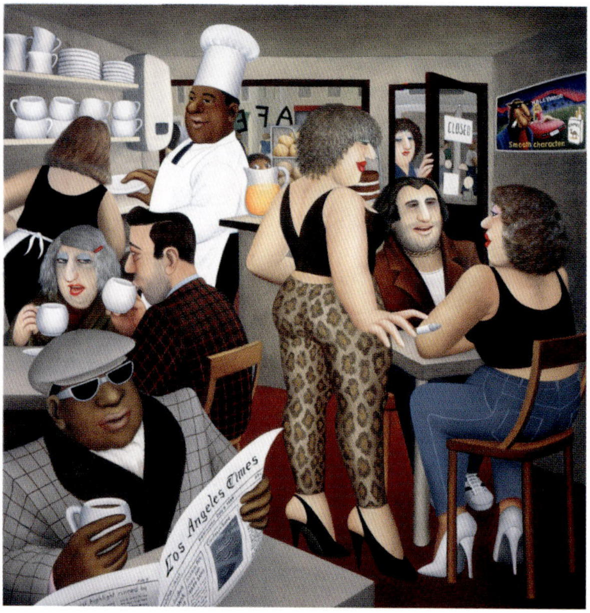

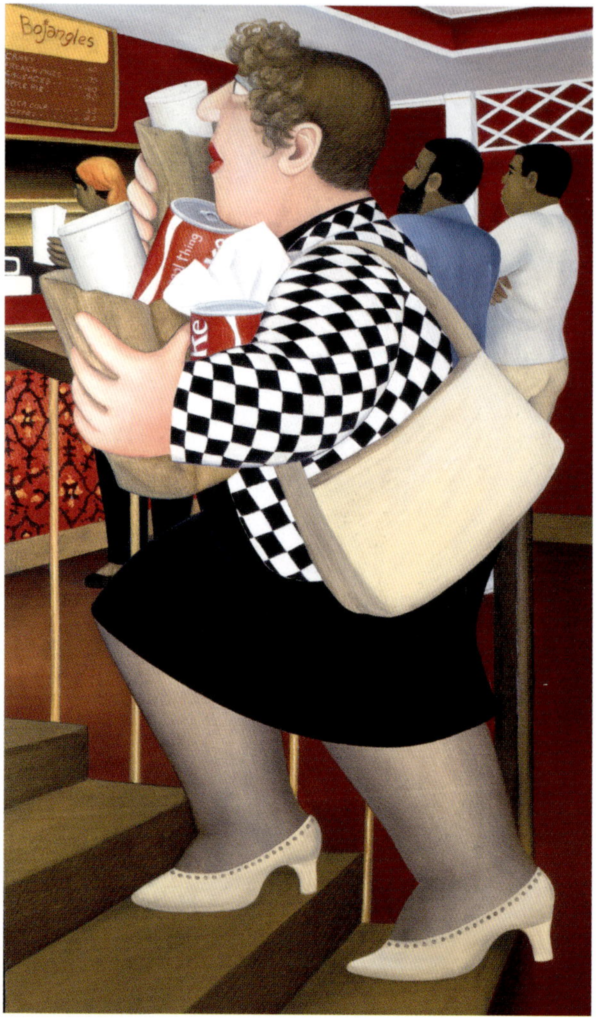

Hollywood Café
(1988). This was situated on Sunset Boulevard, and the Cooks visited after scouting out Forest Lawn for *The Loved One* (see page 154).

To Go
(late 1990s)

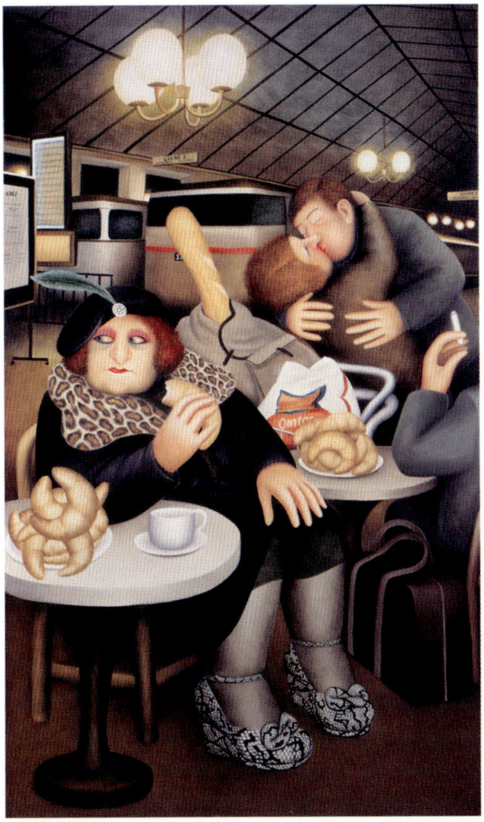

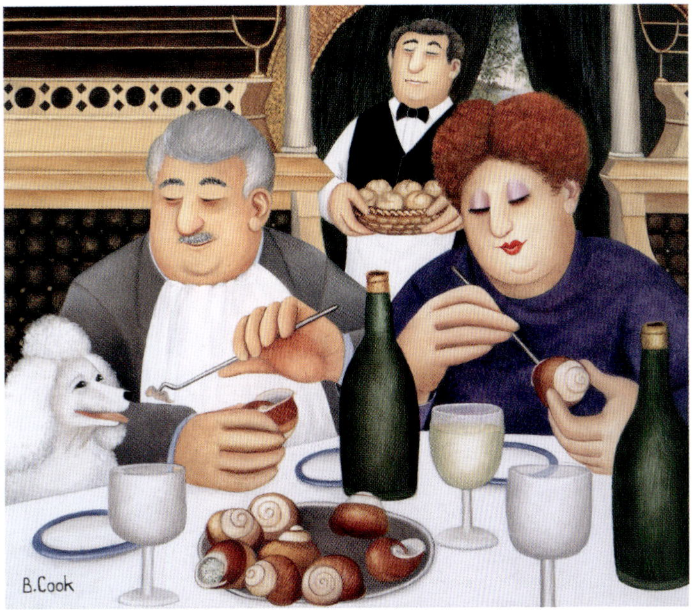

Gare du Nord
(1988). Joe Whitlock Blundell's favourite Beryl painting, also singled out for discussion by Mel Calman on *Kaleidoscope* on BBC Radio 4 June 1988 for the saucy French stick. The picture was actually all about the false snakeskin shoes, which Beryl kept until the last to paint, as a treat.

Escargots Pour Trois
(2000). Also known as *Dining in Paris,* this delighted Beryl at a time when dogs were not encouraged in British cafés and restaurants.

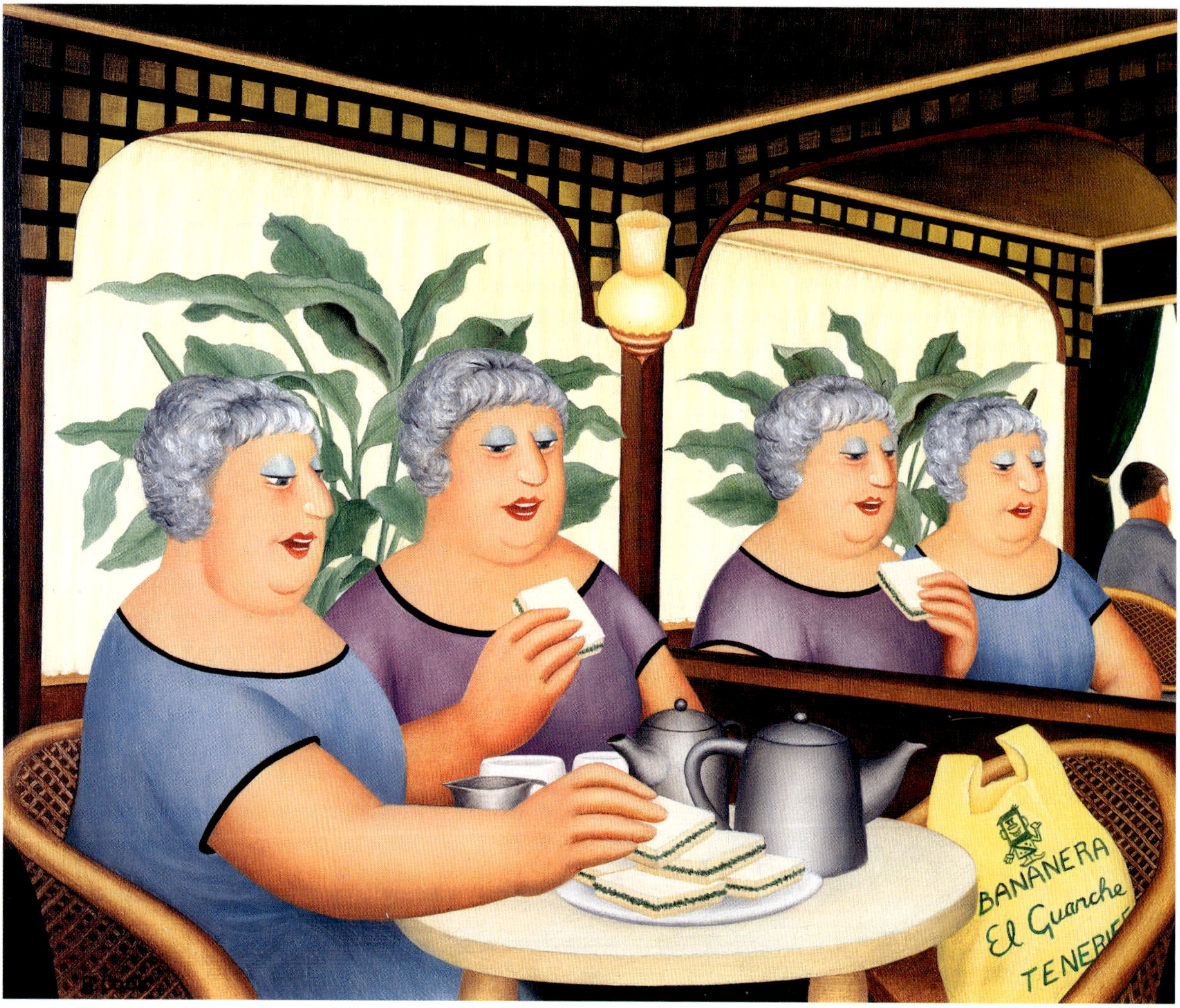

Reflections
(1993). Beryl was thrilled with the number of twins in Tenerife – but has made things even more difficult with the mirror.

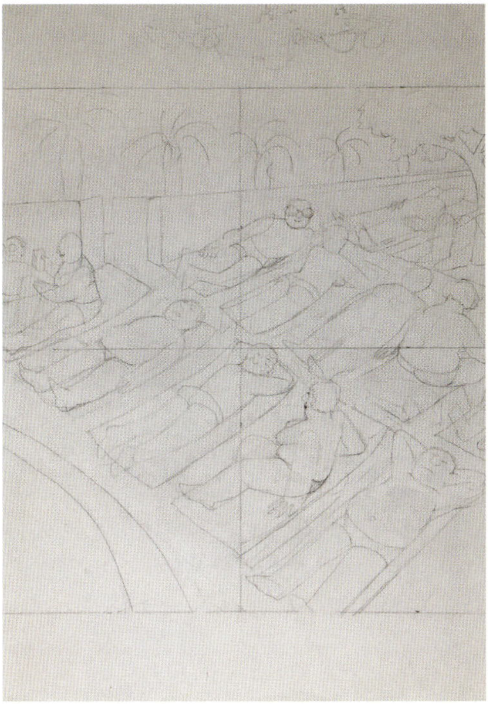

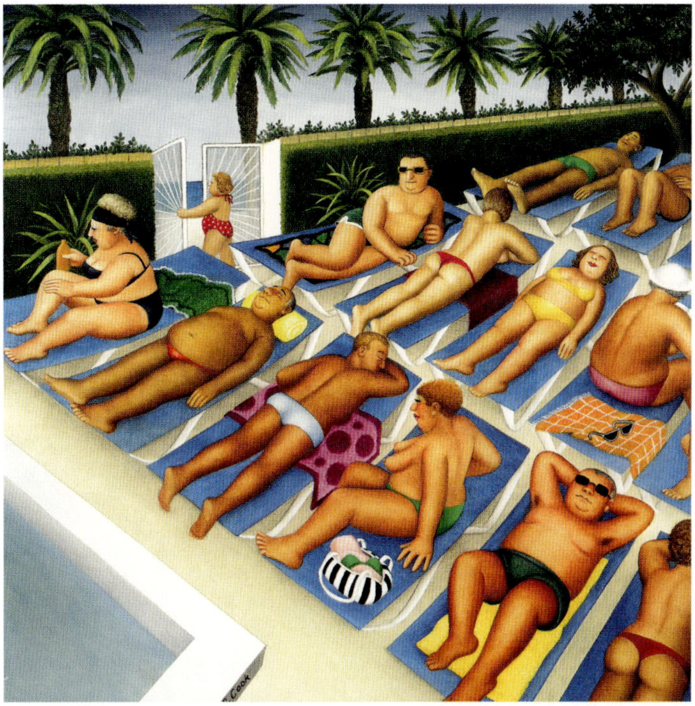

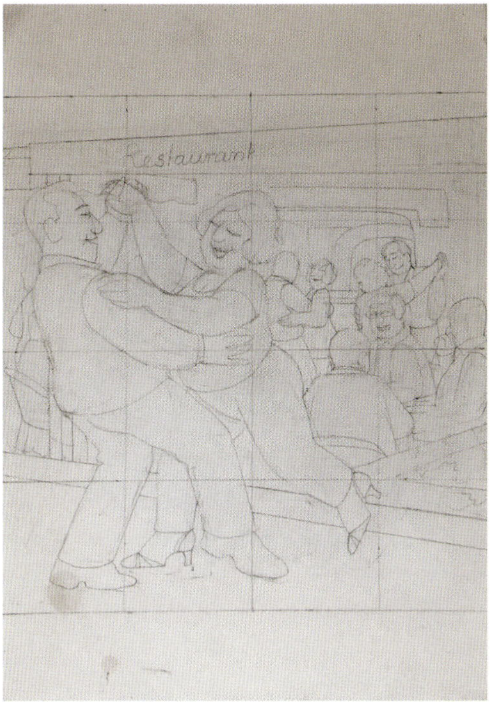

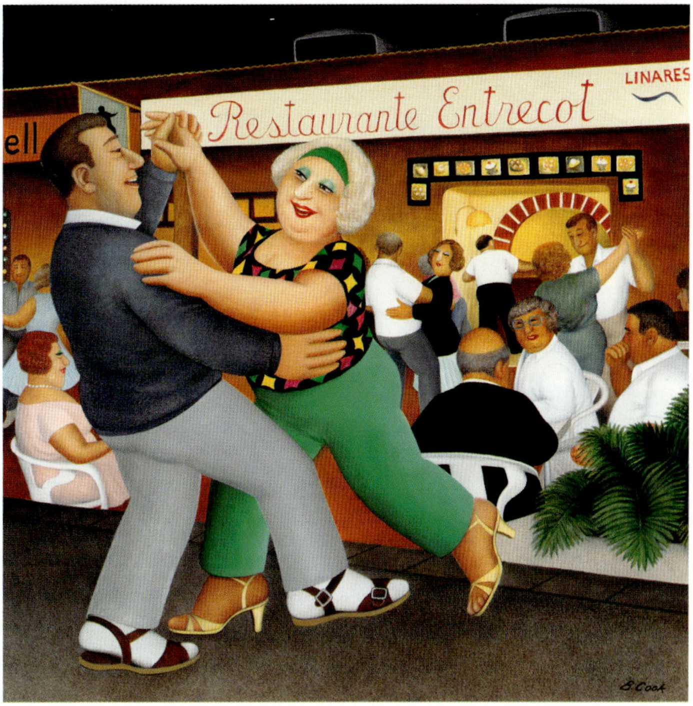

Tenerife Days and *Tenerife Nights*

(1993), along with their sketches. Beryl enjoyed painting pairs of pictures such as this. *Tenerife Days* has wonderful attention to detail and is a fine example of her mature style. It was chosen for the cover of *Happy Days* (Weidenfeld & Nicolson), which was published in 1995.

and correspondent Barbara Ker-Seymer had died in 1993. A sense of disappointment can be gleaned: after a single night their hotel was commandeered by Castro for a conference and the alternative was so awful that they came home early. The total result seems to have been one picture.

Cruising was published in 2000 when Beryl and John were 74, and less agile. A cruise offered an easier way of seeing a number of destinations (though Beryl found rather too much archaeology on one cruise), plus the attractions of watching all the activities on board.

Much as the Cooks enjoyed their travels, Beryl couldn't wait to start painting again on her return home: 'As soon as I get back from a trip I'm up those stairs like a gazelle'.[4] Memories had to be turned into paintings for the next book or exhibition. Nevertheless, Beryl tried to leave enough time between projects to paint scenes she saw in her beloved Plymouth, which she still found hugely inspiring. And, as always, she was inspired by family activities.

Family life was greatly altered in 1992 when the family bought Elvira's, a small café which John Junior and Teresa were to run. It still exists, in a wonderful location: Admiral's Hard, in Stonehouse, an area to the west of the Plymouth city centre. This is near where people queue to go across the Tamar to Mount Edgcumbe park in a foot-passenger ferry. It was rather run down, but the owner Elvira made a good living from it and worked alongside John and Teresa for a while to show them the ropes. Beryl and John Senior were delighted to find it full of marines chomping on sausage sandwiches and bacon and eggs. John Junior and Teresa are good cooks, and it was so successful that John (an ex-builder) renovated and enlarged it. John Senior apparently sat by the phone waiting to be called in to help – ferrying bread between shop and café and washing up.

Much of its trade then came from the nearby Marine Barracks. Marines would regularly pop in on their way back from a run, so that their daughter Sophie once told her teacher, 'My mother knows all the marines just by looking at their bottoms'.

The family also bought a plot of land on the Tamar estuary just over the border into Cornwall. Here they planted an orchard and grew fruit and vegetables. Several paintings show them at work – although Beryl always claimed to prefer watching.

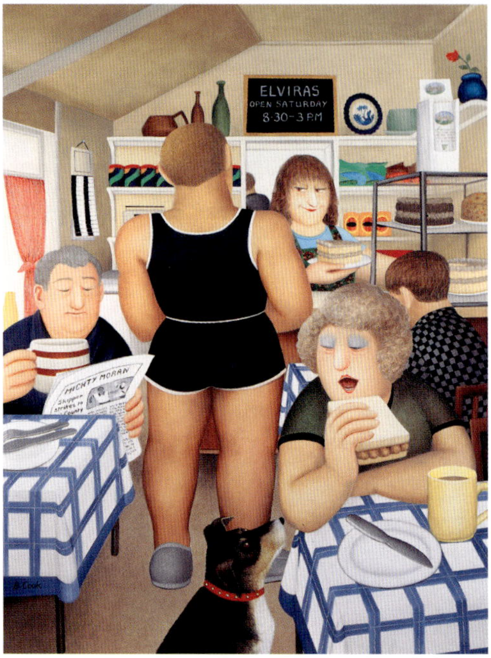

Elviras Café
(1997). Beryl has lovingly and accurately depicted the boiled fruit and coffee cakes, and the sausage sandwich that was offered to visiting dogs. She approved of dogs in pubs and cafés. This dog is Lizzie, 'a little energy packed bundle forever looking for trouble'.

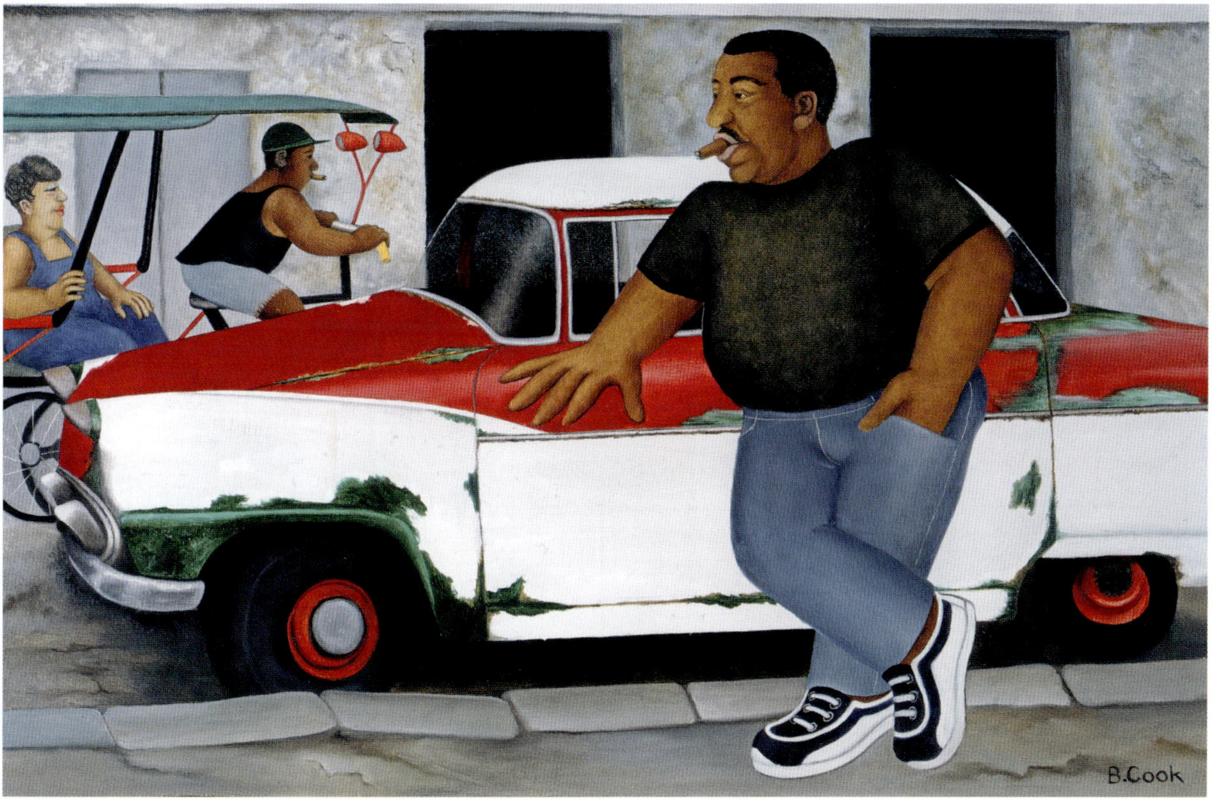

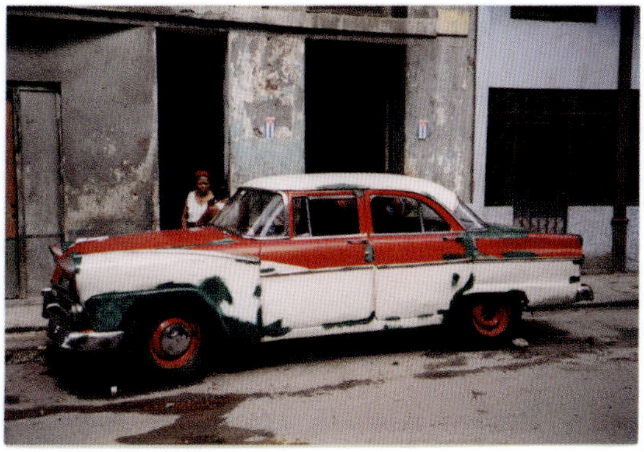

Havana

(2000). The lone picture resulting from the Cook's 1999 trip to Cuba.
Beryl has paid close attention to the photograph that either she or John took.

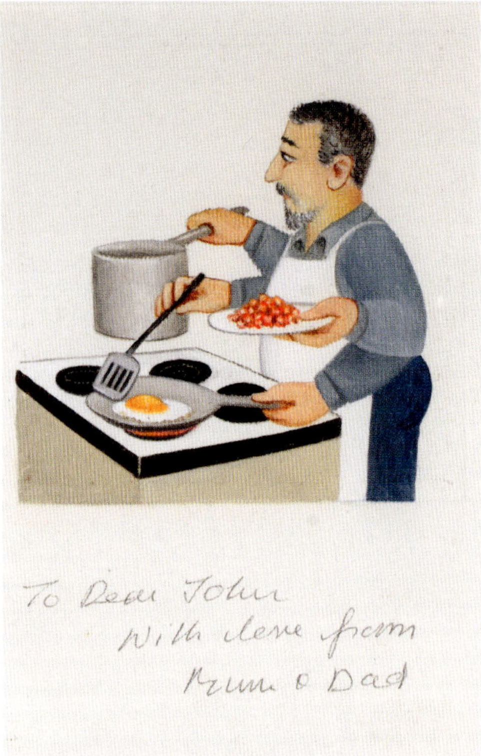

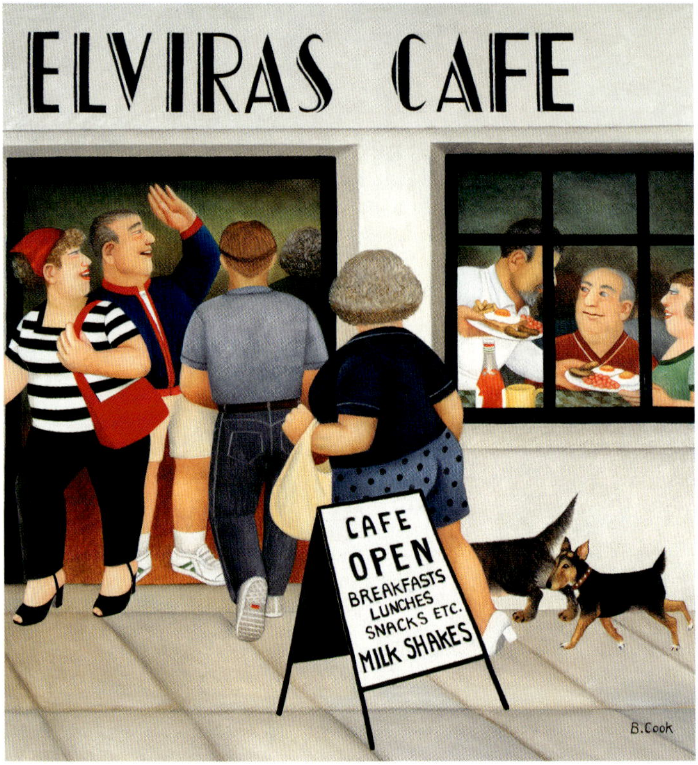

John Cooking
(mid-1990s)

Elviras Café
(2006). The family sold the café in 2002, but Beryl must have had very fond memories of it as she painted it again in 2006. John can be seen through the window serving a full English. Beryl has chosen to flip the actual position of the door, as can be seen in the photograph of John Senior outside it.

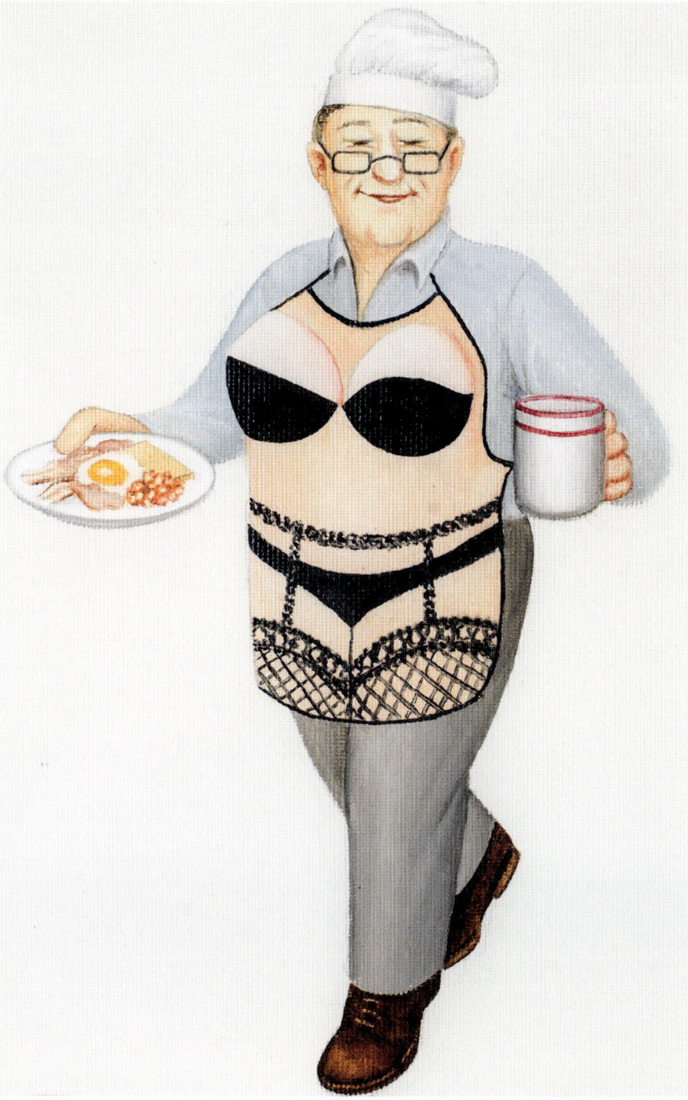

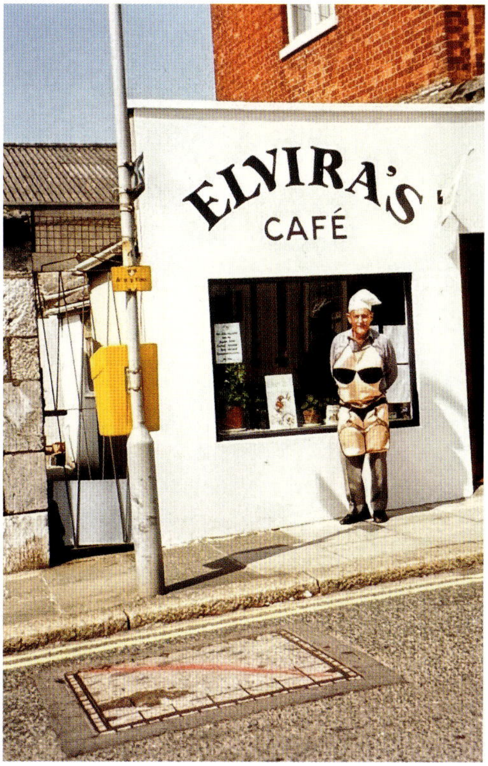

Untitled
(c 2000). Painting of John in the comedy apron,
and a photograph. The bosoms are inflated.

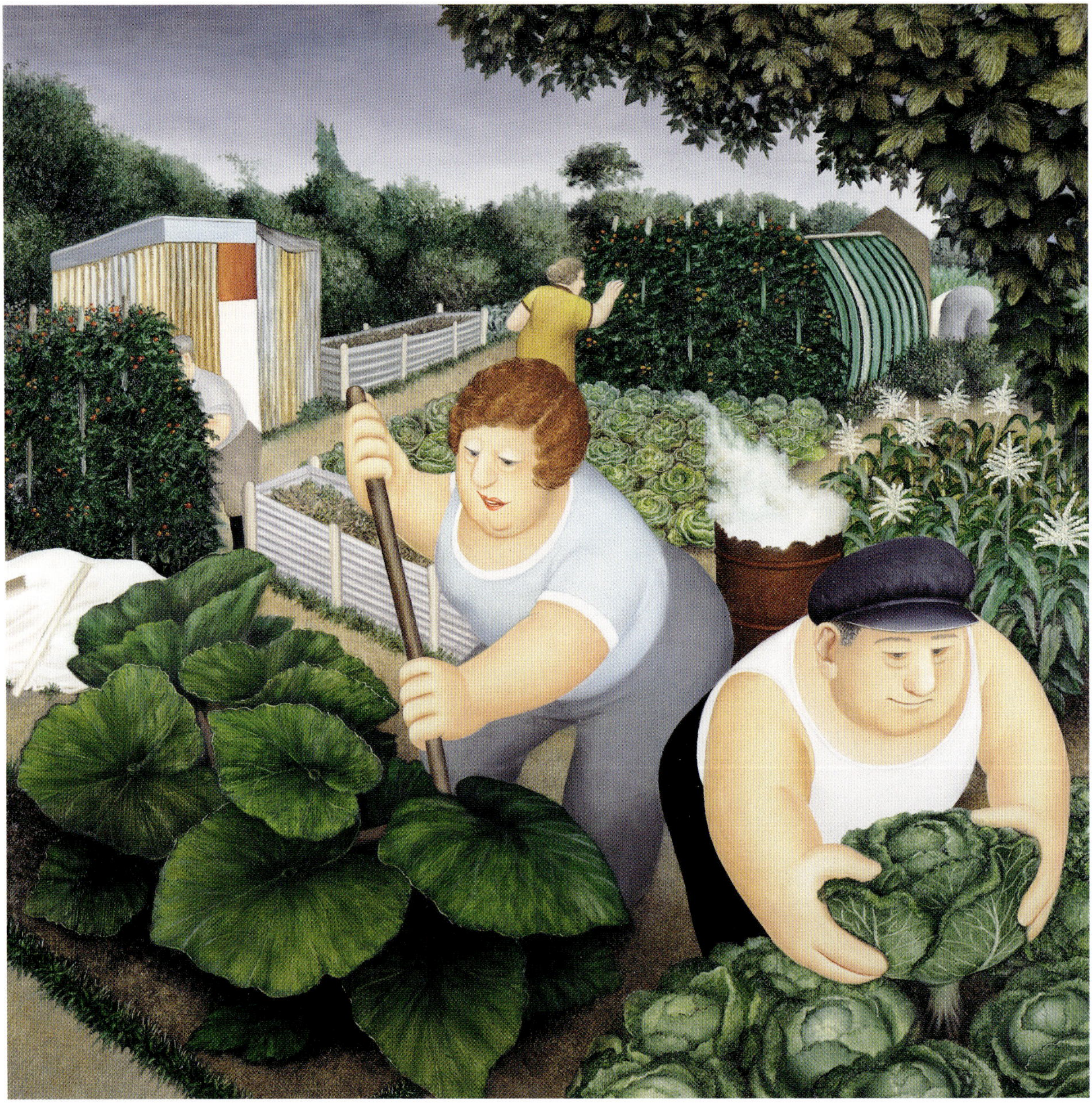

Rhubarb

(c 1984). These three paintings depict family activities on the land the Cooks acquired just over the Tamar into Cornwall. This is where they had the litigious neighbour (see page 105).

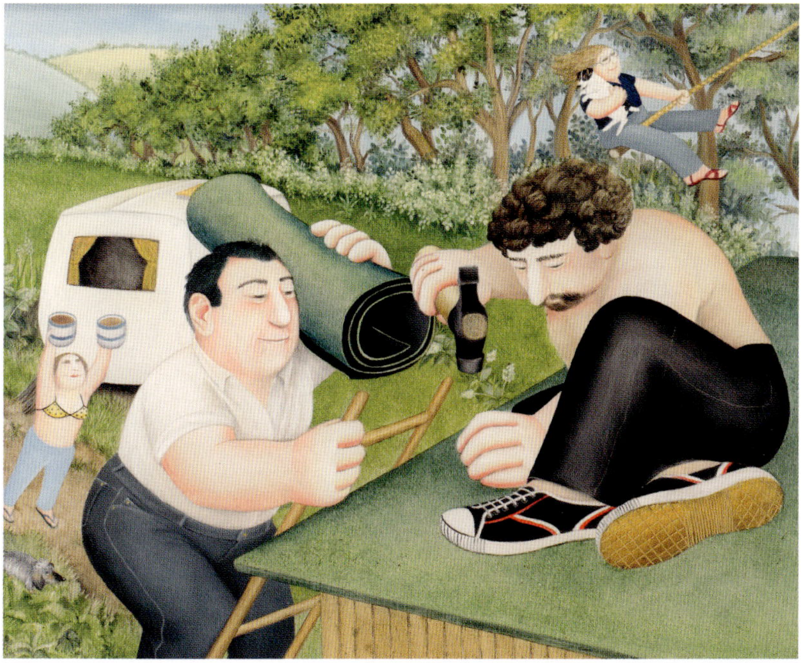

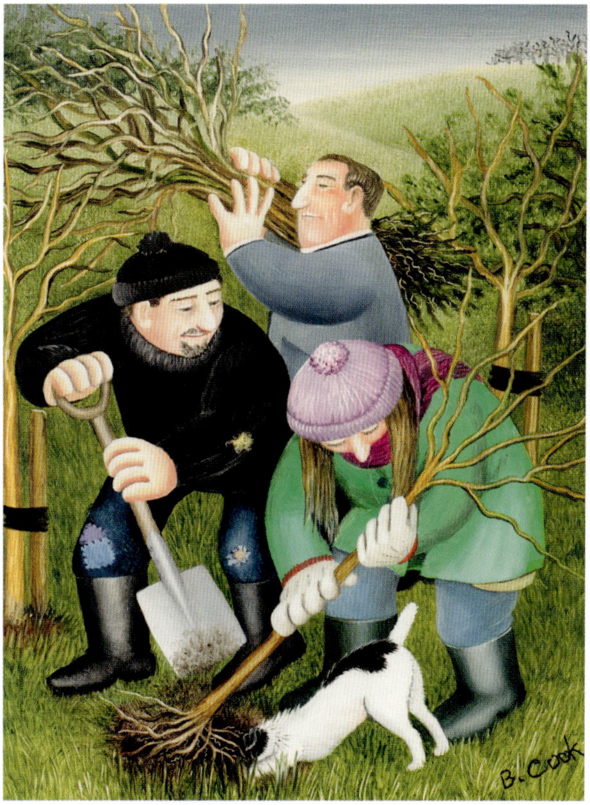

Felting the Roof
(1984)

Tree Planting
(c 1983)

The Cooks continued to enjoy the nightlife in Plymouth, especially The Dolphin and Union Street. Beryl wrote about The Dolphin to a student in 1994:

> I like pubs as you have gathered from the paintings but I like them when they have gone a little seedy and are well worn and used. My favourite here – and it is the most popular as well – is very old, has a concrete floor, furniture that is never changed, no videos and no food served. We bring in our own fish and chips if hungry, dogs are allowed and it is packed with local people and fishermen in their overalls. The laughter and talking is loud as the canned music coming from some of the other pubs – but how much more pleasant. There don't seem to be many of these sorts of pubs left down here.'[5]

In 1986 she reported to Barbara that the manager of a big pub we go to 'told me that he never gets any trouble there – I should think not either for he is six feet tall and wide, black suit and shirt with yellow tie and handkerchief, very snazzy, and surrounded by bouncers. In fact, he said, there's millions invested in the pubs and clubs round there and nothing else like it in the country.'[6]

Beryl describes how they usually sat in the doorway so they could get a good view of people arriving and see what the latest fashions were. In 1989 she wrote to Barbara:

> Last night we went to a beauty in Union Street. Girls dressed in hardly anything dancing all along the bar, boys clearing the tables in tiny white knickers and little weeny vests only covering their shoulders. We sat there with radiant faces watching it all, not able to say anything of course for the music was deafening. Shall hurry along there again as soon as poss.[7]

Plymouth was changing. Beryl observed, 'I don't really know why there's such a surge of building going on here, practically the whole of the city centre is going to be transformed as far as I can gather (huge shopping centres, fountains and so on). As all we've got at the moment is square concrete shops and carparks all going mouldy, and not beautiful Georgian houses to be destroyed, I'm all for it.'[8]

There was indeed a lot of building, including a northern ring road, pedestrianization of the city centre and huge new student accommodation blocks. International firms such as Plessey and Toshiba arrived in the new industrial areas, ship- and yacht-building flourished, and the hospital at Derriford also expanded. But it didn't last,

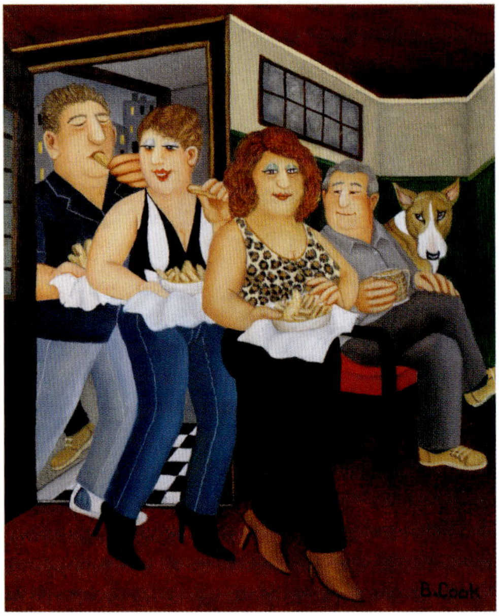

Hungry Trio

(1990s). The Dolphin customers bringing their fish and chips from the nearby Platters restaurant. Note the dog – Beryl wrote that she'd rather have more dog and less hygiene, as in France.[9]

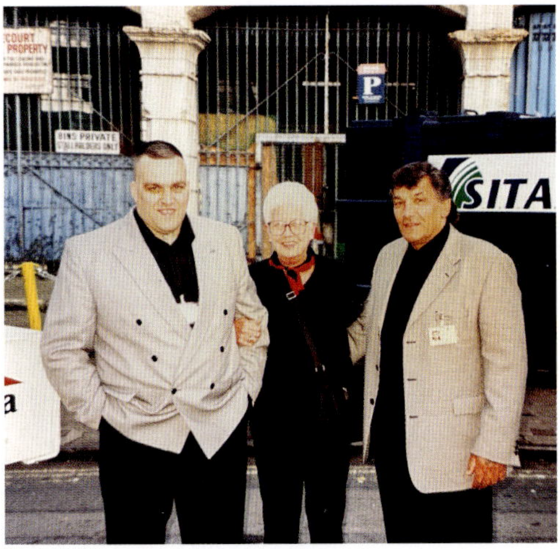

Beryl with bouncers

and in the 1990s the recession hit, some new buildings were abandoned and the Navy presence was greatly reduced. Plymouth, so dependent on the ups and downs of the Navy and the Dockyard, suffered particularly high unemployment.

Beryl wrote:

> I'm afraid the pub and nightclub scene in Union Street has gone for a burton now, the rising costs and diminishing number of sailors have more or less killed it off. It's dreadful to see the places so empty at nine o'clock at night, the volume so loud (the volume rises to compensate for the lack of custom I imagine) we are driven out. I'm told that for about two hours from eleven o'clock they are all packed and the fights start in the street afterwards. But I can't see how they can afford to keep these places open on two hours' business on Friday and Saturday nights. To remember how it used to be I shall have to look back at some of my old pictures, it's a good job I painted it all at the time. Another thing that worries me is the number of charity shops opening up in the main shopping centre here. I counted eight in just a small section the other day. As ordinary businesses close down because of the high rates they move in. I can see the time coming when the whole of the city centre is turned over to jumble and we shall have to travel by car to out of town superstores to buy any food![10]

Nowhere reflected the change so much as Union Street:

> We went into Union Street last night, for the last time I fear for it seems to be in its death throes. Hardly a soul about, big empty 'fun' palaces with blaring music, and not a customer in sight. And I keep remembering all the seedy little pubs, full of 'girls', that they tore down to make these places. Fortunately the Barbican, and The Dolphin in particular, is still very busy. Plenty of effing and blinding and loud laughter going on in there.[11]

And all of a sudden Beryl and John Senior fell out of love with Plymouth.

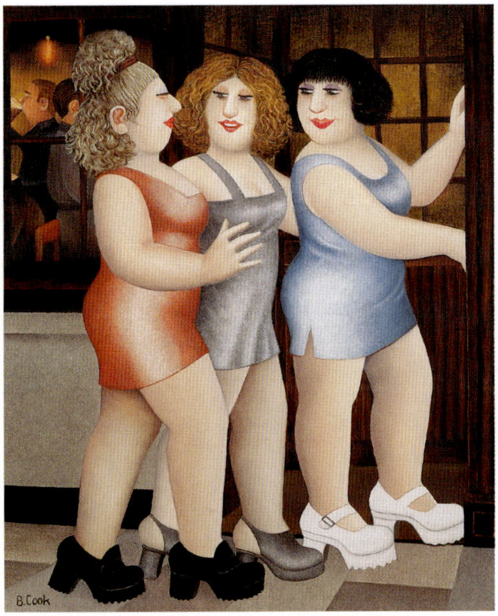

Satin Dresses
(1990s). Delicate satin dresses – and clumping shoes

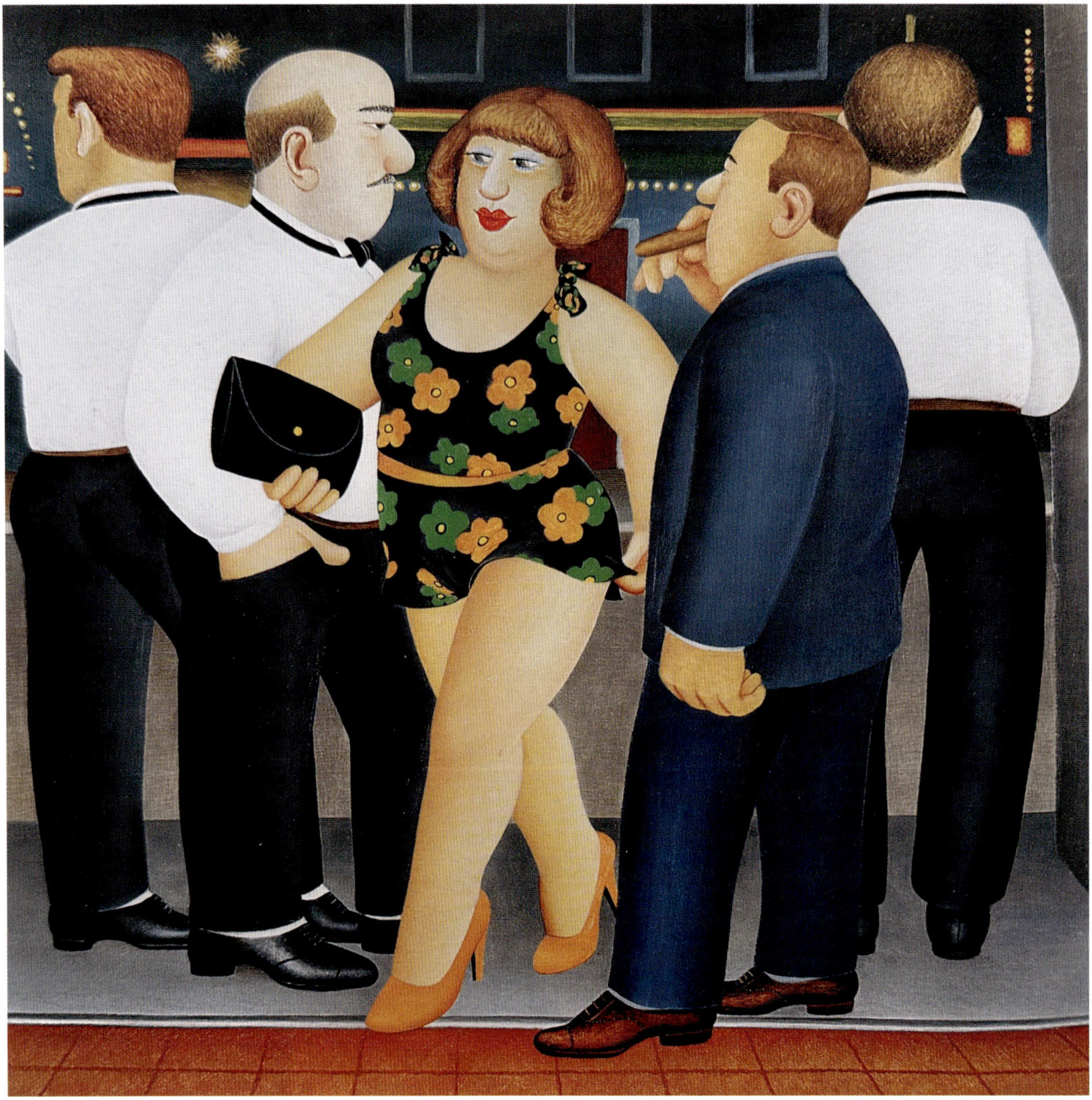

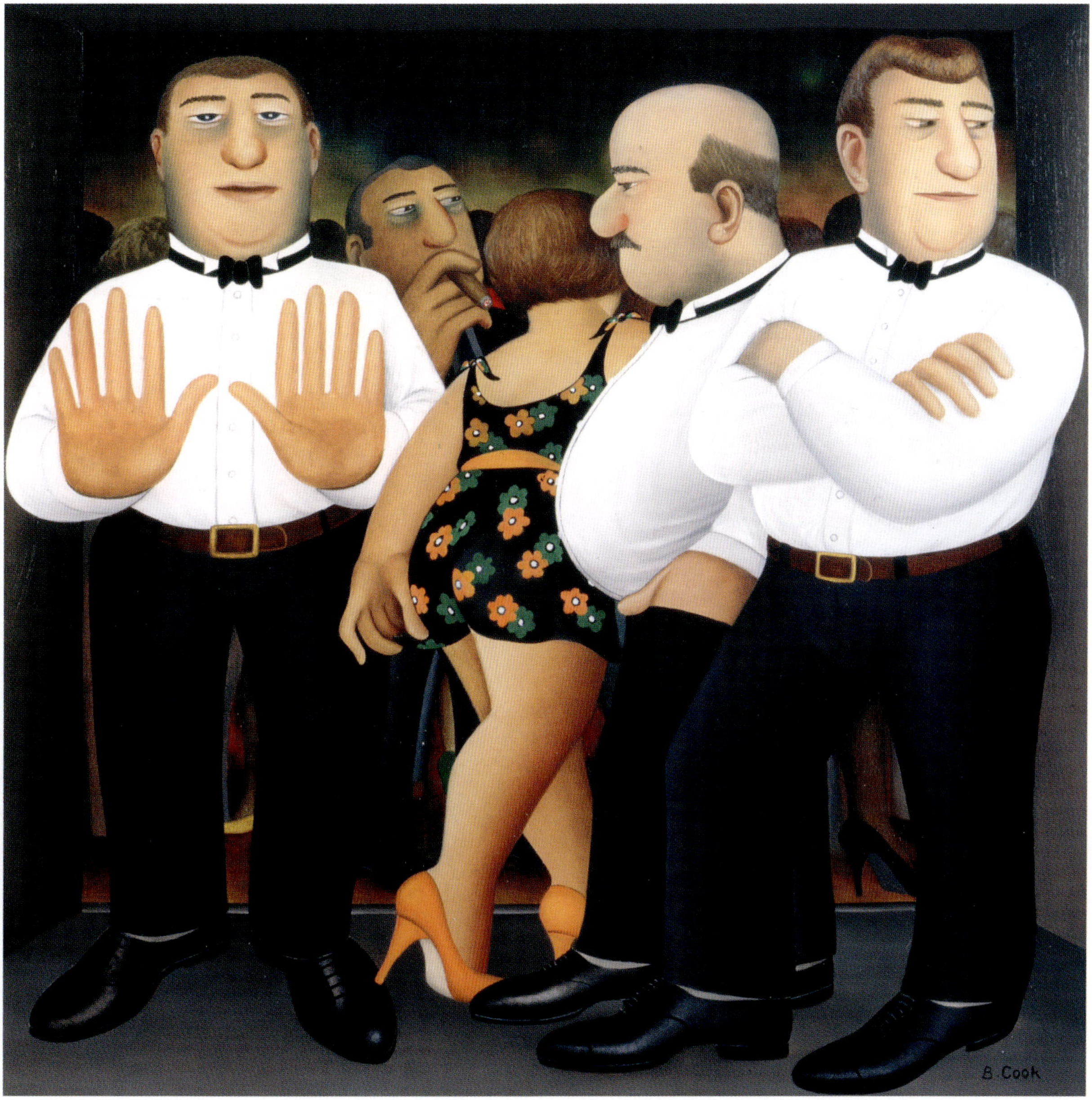

Bouncers and *Bouncers Back*

(1991). Beryl and John tended to turn up at nightclubs relatively early, while the bouncers were getting ready. She has used another favourite device – showing the same scene from the front and back – originally a suggestion from her editor, Joe.

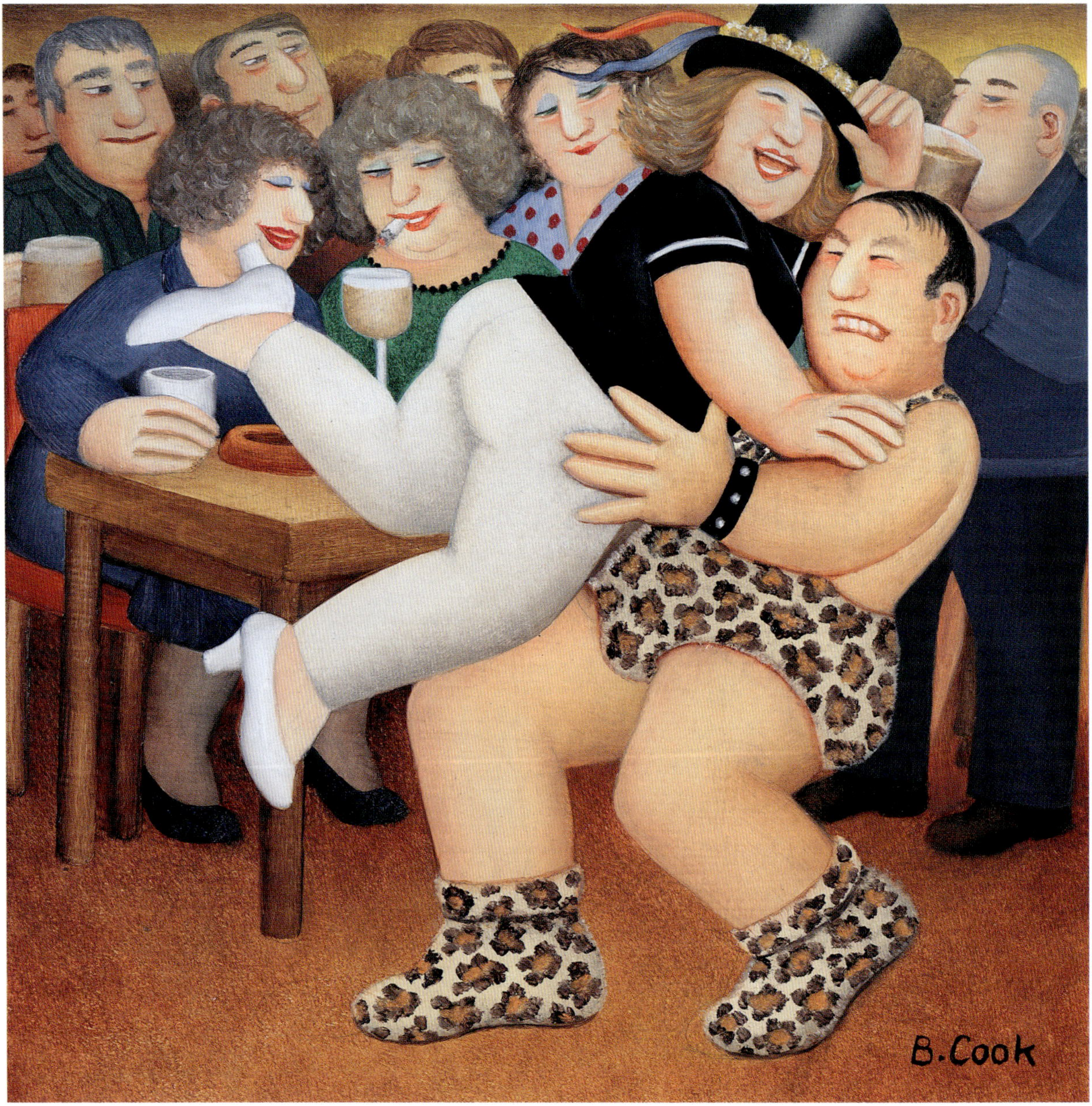

Tarzanogram 2
(mid-1990s). This depcits the hen party of Beryl's housekeeper Sue.
She was rather too heavy for Tarzan's attempted lift.
'I think poor Tarzan has probably retired with a hernia by now.'[12]

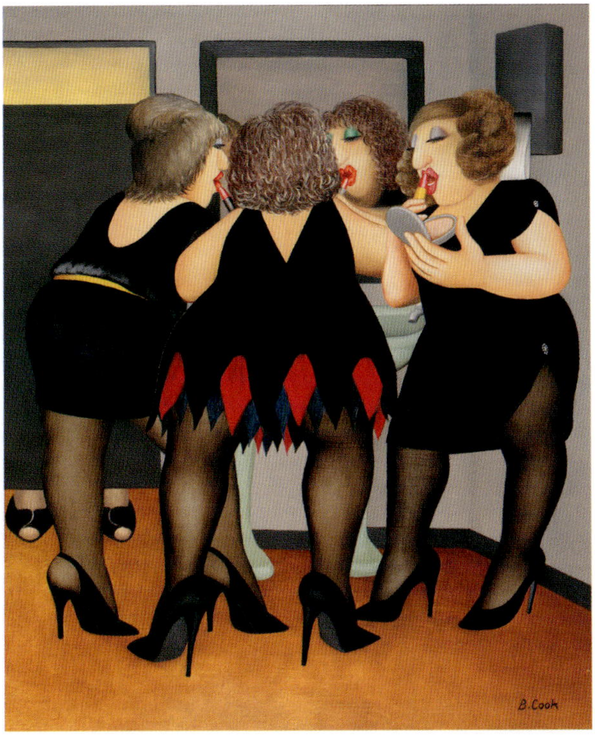

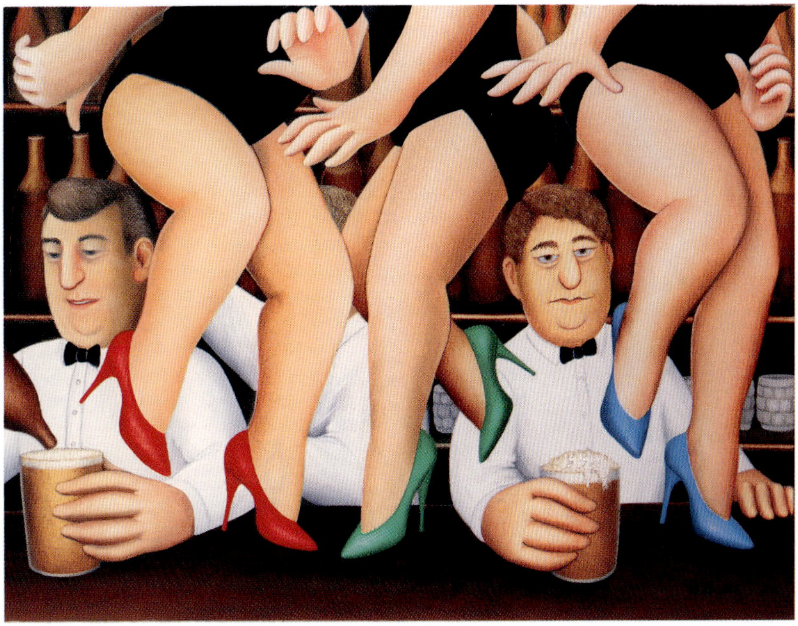

Getting Ready
(1980s). Note the shoes peeping out from under the toilet door, and the clever treatment of the girls' reflections as they touch up their lipstick.

Dancing on the Bar
(1989). Beryl was extremely taken by the whole idea of this and often told reporters that she would like to be the one dancing on the bar, but she was too shy.

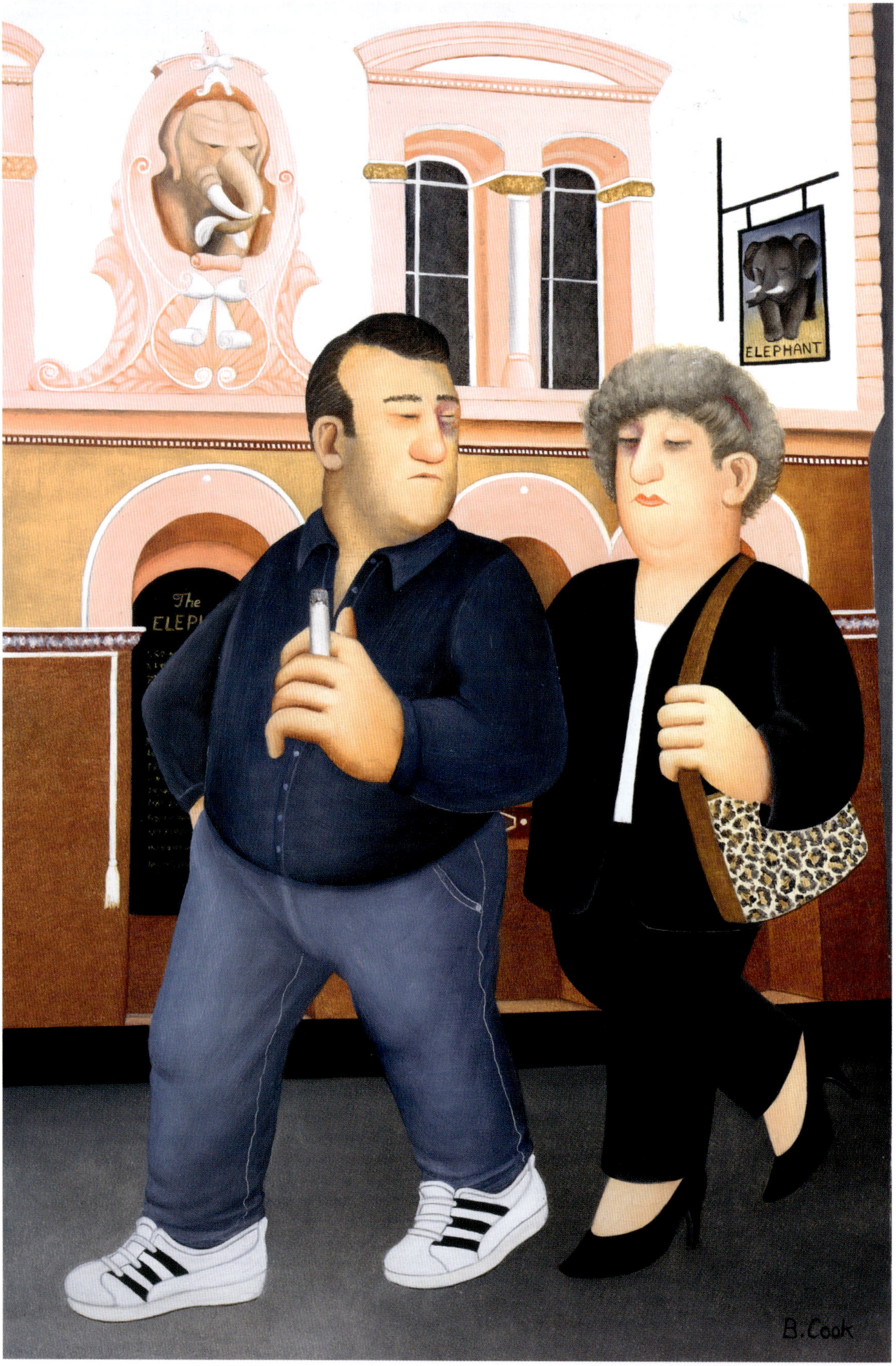
ELEPHANT
The
ELEPH
B. Cook

14

1998–2008: Bristol & Beyond

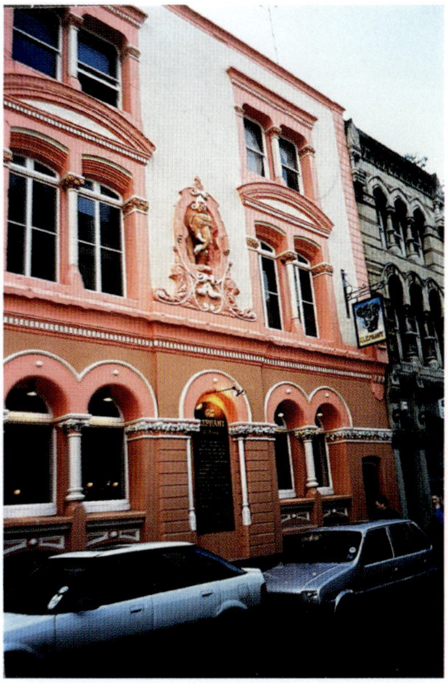

LEFT

The Elephant

(1998–2000), and Beryl's reference photograph above. The local paper ran a competition to try to find this couple, whom Beryl had spotted in a shopping centre. I'm not sure if they came forward, given they each had a black eye.

We are going to a modernised coach house, all fitted cupboards, only half the size (and twice the price) of this one. It is on the edge of Clifton Village and just across the bridge. Our granddaughter and family are there and more family a bit further up the motorway, but mostly I look forward to being much closer to London and Airports.

Letter from BC to Edward Lucie-Smith, undated but c 1998

Thus wrote Beryl to her friend Edward Lucie-Smith in 1998. Clifton is one of the oldest and most affluent parts of Bristol. Their new house was in Camp Road, so they proudly placed the Camp Corset man in the window. Inside, according to a reporter, were rag-rolled walls, stencilled borders and quiet buff carpets. The reporter felt that 'her eclectic mix of furniture – Art Deco sideboards, dining chairs with fake leopard skin cushions, floral sitting room suite – sits a little oddly with its new setting'.[1]

Beryl recreated her studio with exactly the same layout as at Athenaeum Street, even bringing with her a collection of fag ends and ashtrays. Although she had given smoking five years earlier, she missed it so much that she gave all her characters a cigarette if she could. Indeed, she painted *The Bridge Party* (see page 202) just because she missed cigarettes so much.

Aside from the changes to the Plymouth they had loved, there were other reasons for the Cooks' move. Beryl did not feel valued by Plymouth, and she had been very upset by infighting at the Plymouth Arts Centre which had

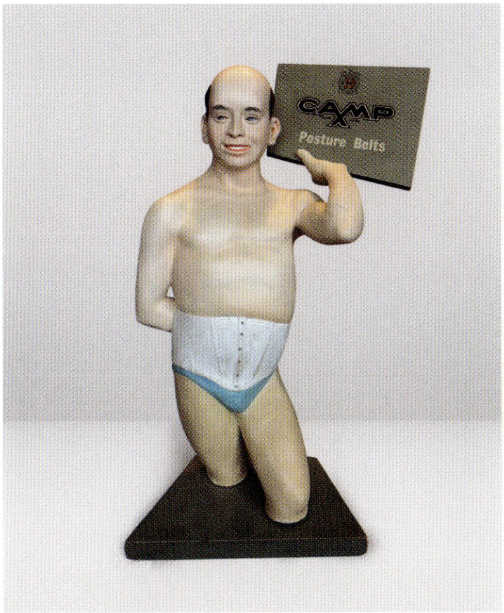

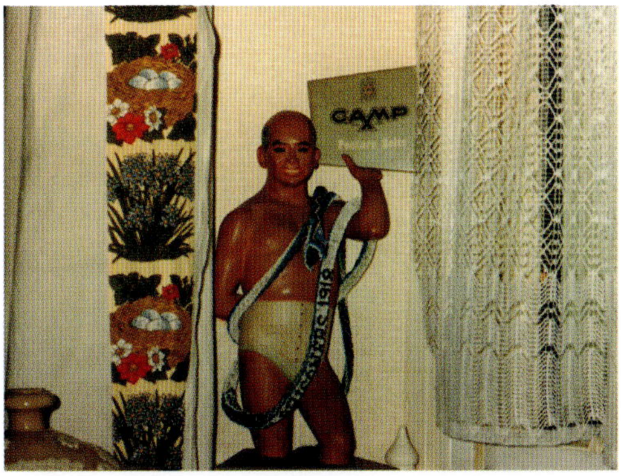

Camp Corset man, placed in the window of the Cook's house in Camp Road, Bristol. Also known as Hairless Harry, he appeared in many photographs and even on television as her favourite 'find'. He had been sold to her in New York as a 1940s advertising prop. She repainted him as she thought he looked a little peaky.[2] When J.J. Hayley sent her a picture of himself sculpting him in England in about 1958, she was sanguine: 'Henry has been much admired ... He smiles on, in his corset, hair gently receding, indifferent to all attention.'[3]

resulted in Bernard Samuels being ousted only a year before his retirement. The Centre's Board of Trustees had also sold all the prints and the large sign that she had painted for the Arts Centre.

Beryl wrote of another reason in her private letters. Beryl mistakenly thought that Plymouth City Museum and Art Gallery did not value her work. She had misunderstood a letter sent by a fan and thought that someone at the museum had said she wasn't held in high regard in Plymouth. In fact the letter (which is on file) says they were told this by an art shop, but that the fan had rung the museum who had been very nice about Beryl's work. They told the writer that they had four paintings, but they weren't on show at that particular time.

Also, The Alexander Gallery was in Bristol. Each year the Gallery produced two new Beryl Cook prints and she had to approve them and later sign the artists' proofs. Considering that this involved signing 750 at a time, and that she still wrote all her letters by hand twice (draft and final), as well as painting, it is not surprising that she now suffered from shoulder pain and arthritis. She and John Senior were, after all, now in their 70s.

Beryl admitted that she now worked more slowly, and that her memory was not quite as photographic as it had been. Now she would sit in the pub and do a little drawing or bring her camera and pretend that she was photographing John while actually photographing the other people there. Although the couple could be more anonymous in the larger city, there was quite a lot of press coverage, and the couple received a lot of invitations. John had to fend everybody off. 'He told one man that I was a recluse and that I couldn't go out. "Beryl's not very well", he'd say, or "Beryl's got a whitlow on her finger".'[4]

In some ways their lifestyle remained the same, with walking the dog on the Downs and visits to pubs at the weekend, popping by taxi to those in the centre of Bristol after a quick drink at the Quadrant in Clifton. Later Beryl wrote, 'we both loved Bristol, particularly the jazz, and I tried to get a TV company to film some of the musicians before it dies out, as a lot of them are a good age (as old as we are) and not a lot of youngsters take it up. We regard our stay there as a five-year holiday, and would be there now if ill health hadn't brought us back here to near to our family. The two pubs we used most were the Old Duke and the White Horse at Bedminster where the Dave Collet trio performed, but we visited many others – most of them painted by me.'[5]

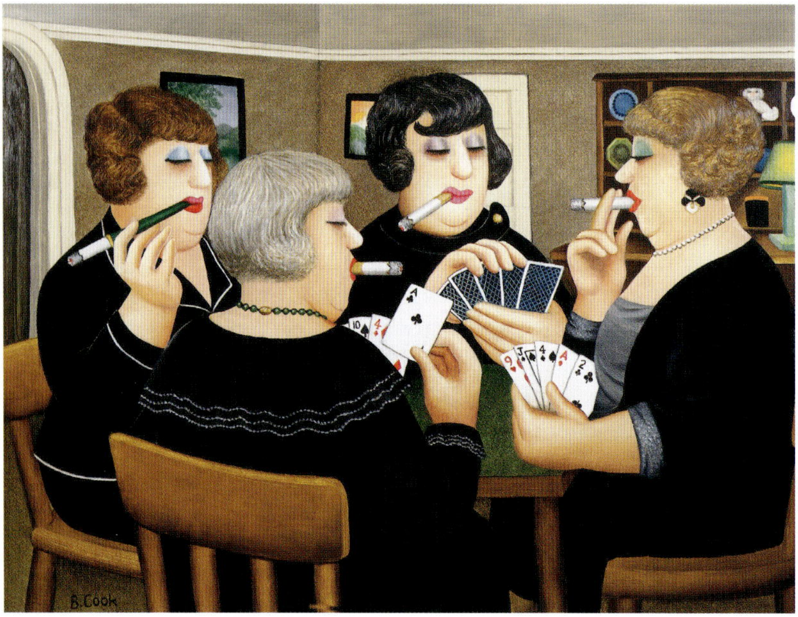

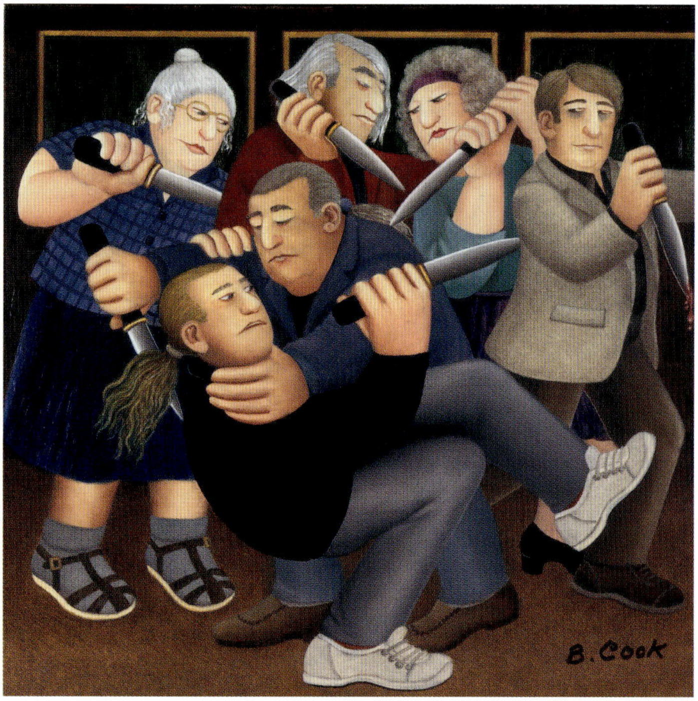

The Bridge Party
(1998). Beryl painted this just because she missed smoking so much when she gave it up.

Backstabbers
(1996). Beryl wrote on the back, 'This was painted soon after Bernard Samuels was ousted from his position as Head of Plymouth Arts Centre. This was done in the shabbiest manner possible . . . The large two-sided sign I had painted for Bernard and the Arts Centre together with various other things were swiftly sold off . . . '

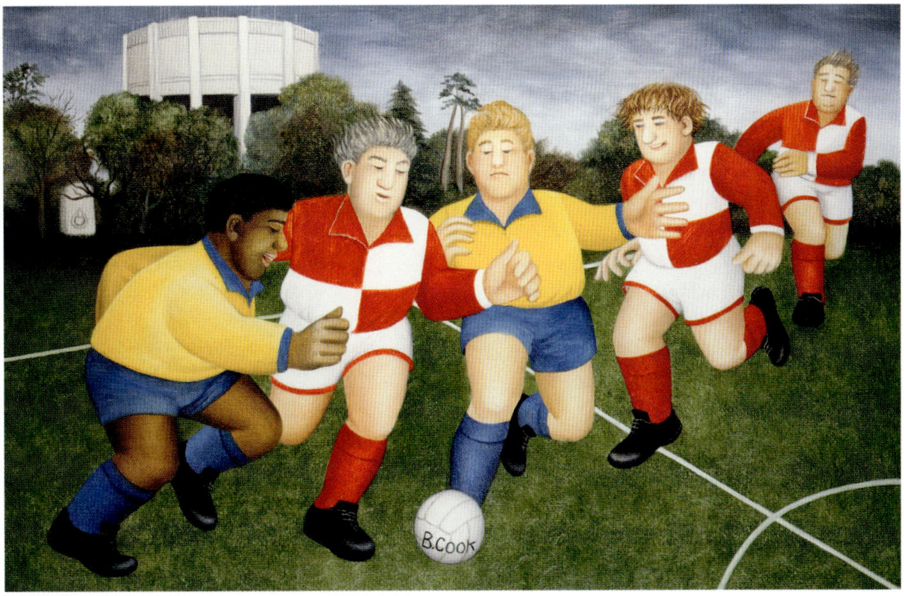

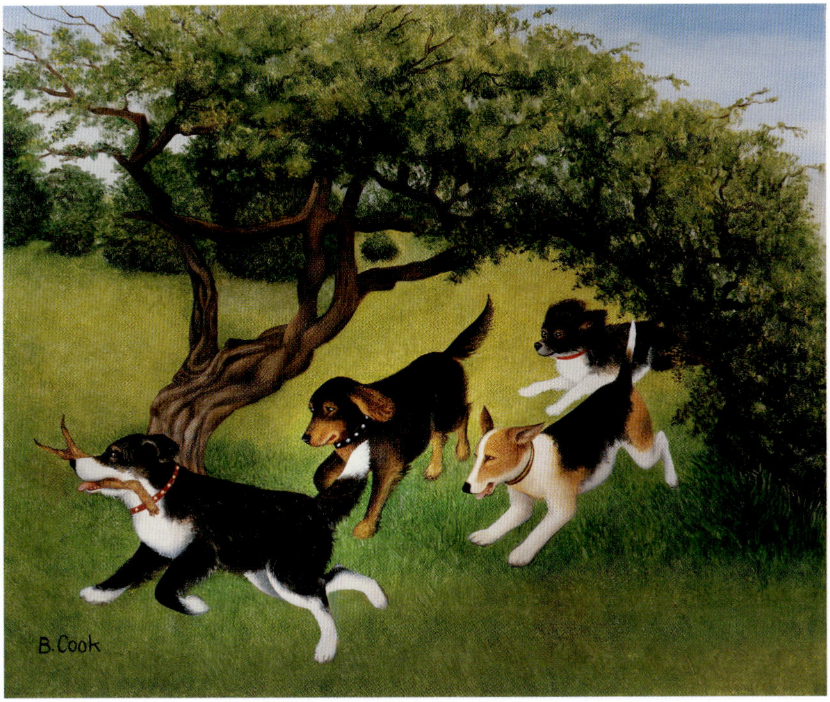

Pack of Dogs
(1998–2000). This is also set on the Downs.

Footballers
(1998–2000). In the background is the Durdham Down Water Tower, situated on Clifton Downs, where Beryl and John walked their dog Lizzie every afternoon.

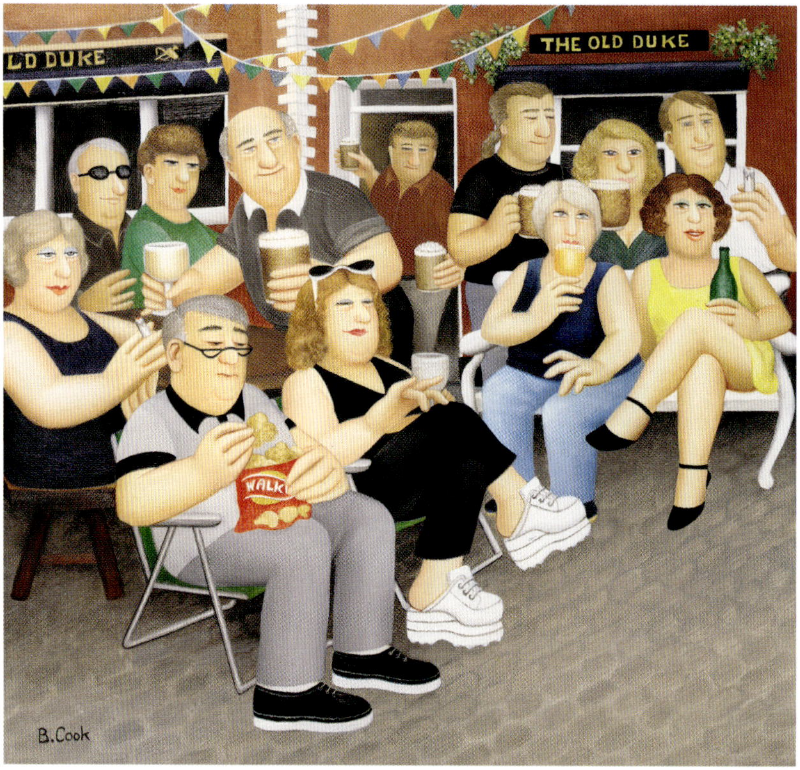

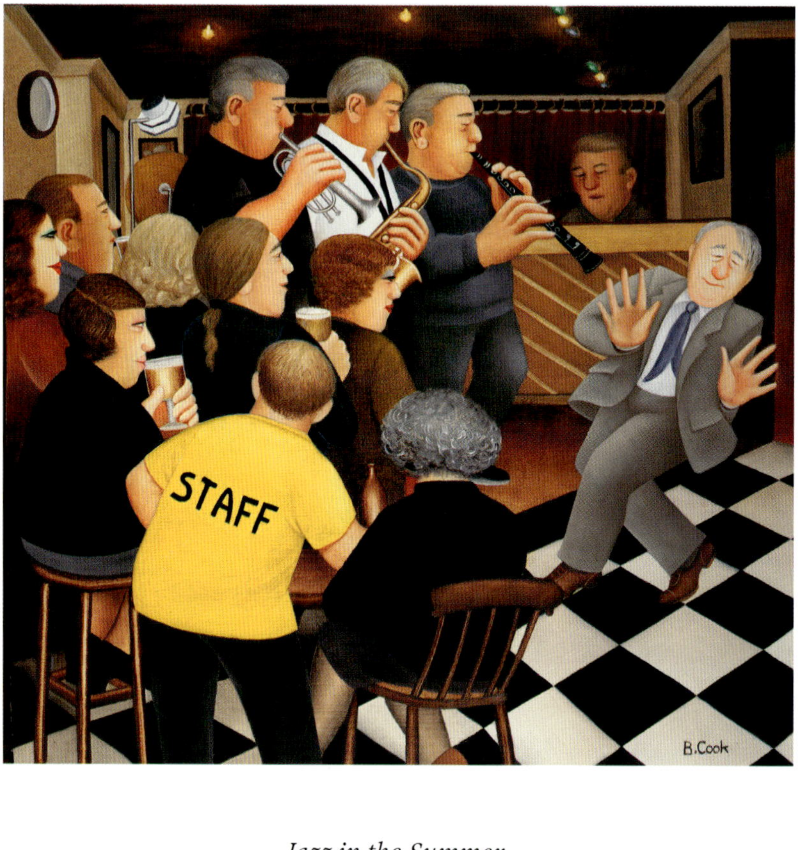

Jazz in the Summer
and *Jazz in the Winter*
(1998 and 1998–2000), both set in the Old Duke

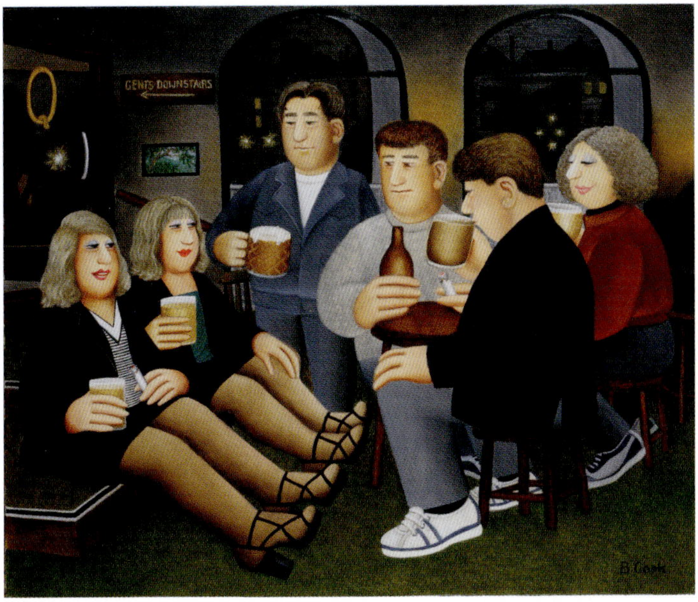

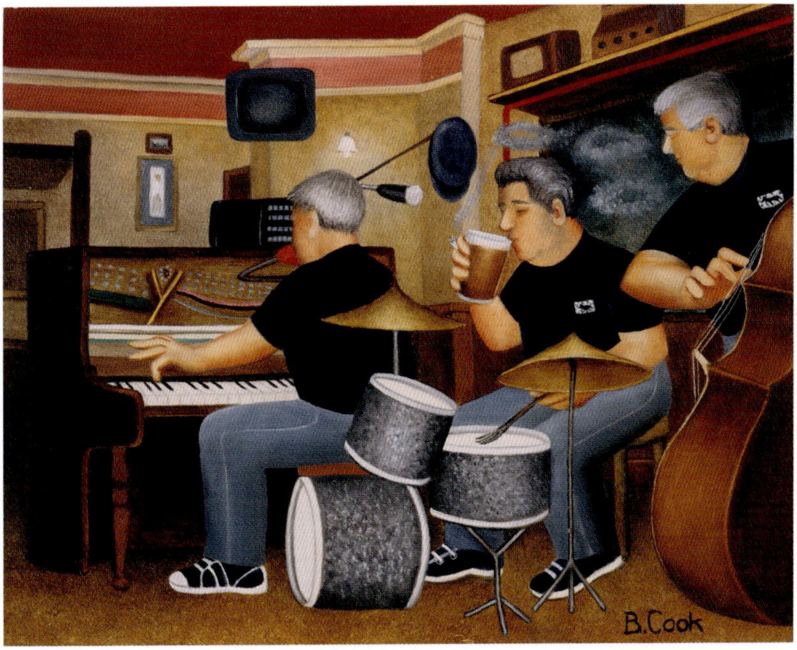

Strappy Shoes
(1998–2000). In the caption for this scene from The Quadrant in *Beryl Cook, Cruising* (Weidenfeld & Nicolson, 2000), Beryl mentions the shoes but also the popular men's haircuts of the era. The 'curtain' style makes the young man look particularly gormless.

The Dave Collet Trio at The White Horse
(1998). Beryl and John became friends with the Trio and the staff at The White Horse pub. The staff wrote a lovely note wishing them well when they returned to Plymouth. This painting was used for the Trio's CD cover, released in 2015, which was recorded at the pub.

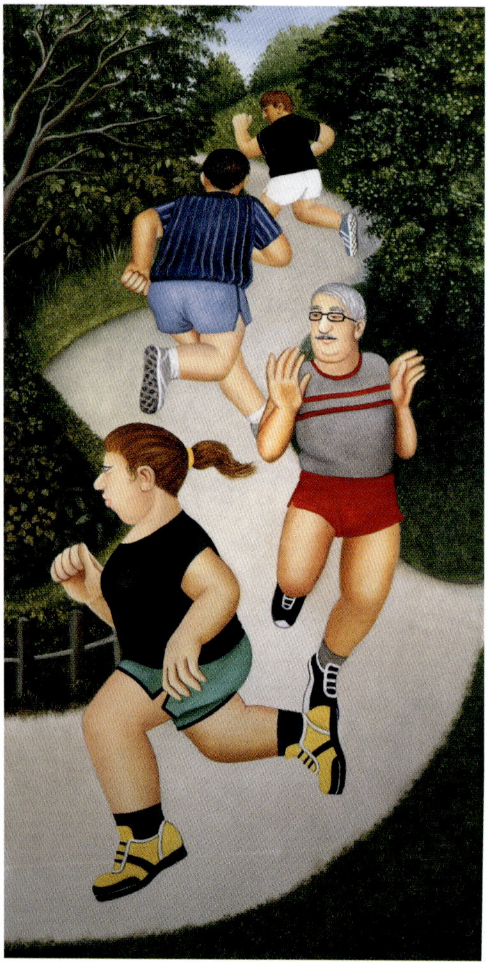

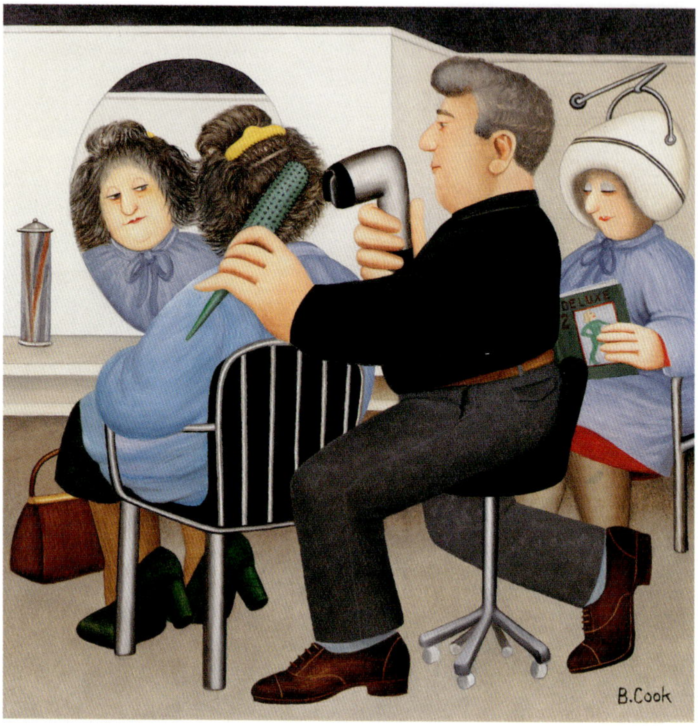

Morning Run
(1998–2000). A return to the sinuous composition which has allowed Beryl to crowd in more joggers than were actually present

Salon Philippe
(1998–2000). Hairdresser Philip Marsh, in Clifton Down, whizzing around the salon in his chair. Beryl explained in a letter that she had not actually seen this hairstyle in the salon. She was worried Philip would recognize himself but 'he was thrilled to bits in the end'.

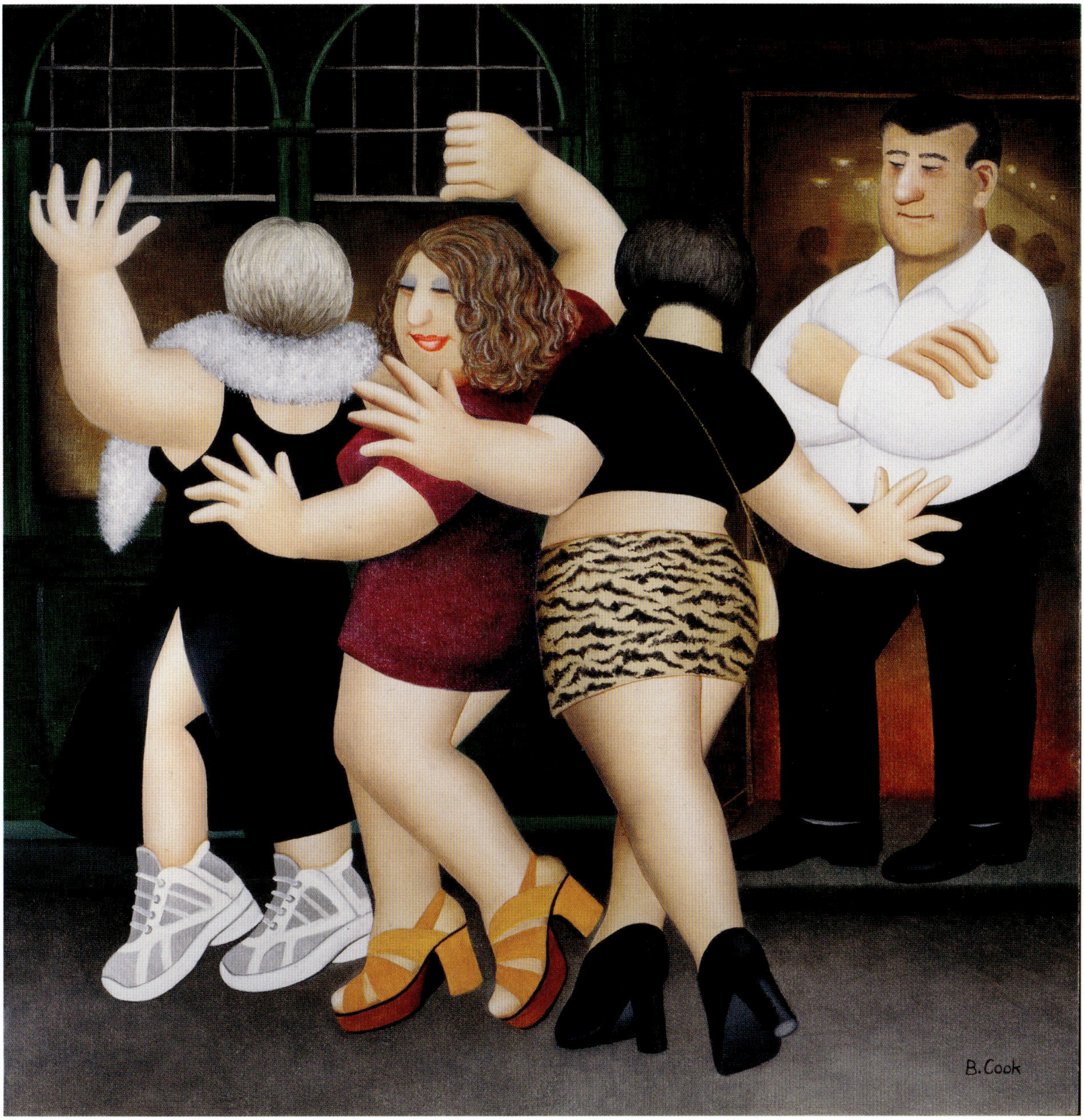

End of Term
(1998–2000). Revellers at The Porcupine in Bristol

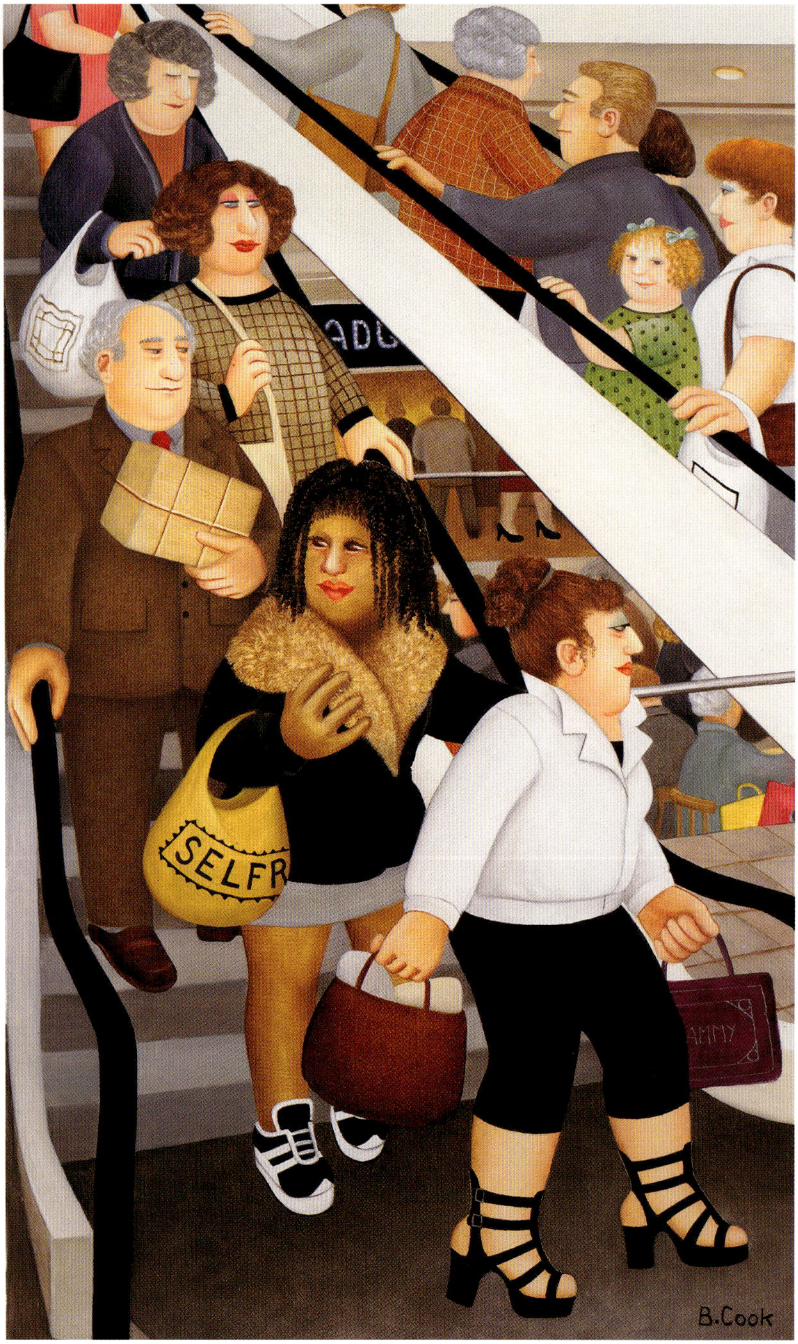

Shopping Mall

(1998–2000). A scene at Cribbs Causeway – Beryl had been correct in her prediction of out-of-town shopping malls. This one includes an ice rink, a cinema, a bowling alley and a gym alongside the shopping mall and a retail park. Beryl preferred Broadmead (a shopping centre in a historic part of Bristol), apart from the escalators.

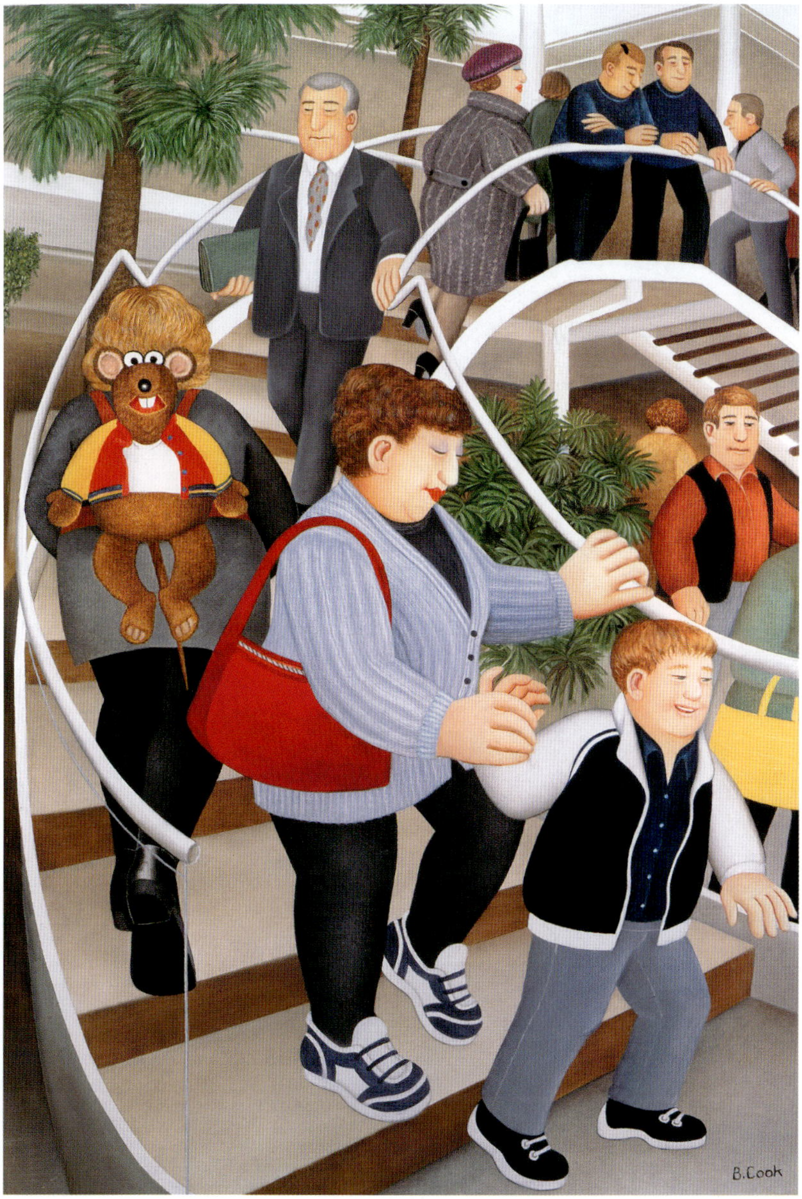

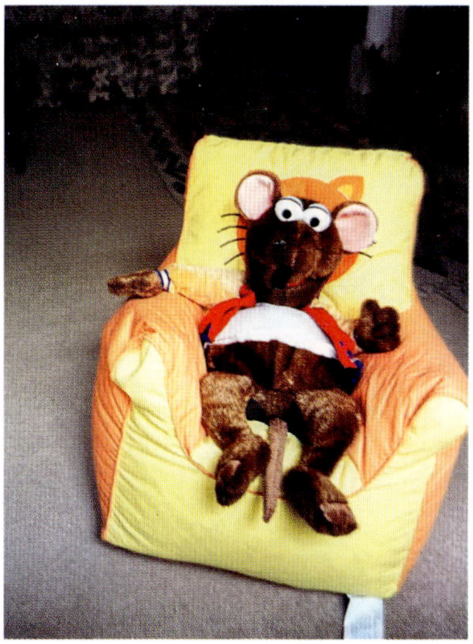

Shopping with Robin
(2000) and Beryl's photograph of the backpack. 'Here's Robin on a shopping spree. Normally he sits on a small armchair in our sitting room, but when I needed a backpack for the girl going up the stairs, he had to make himself useful.'[6] Robin is Rizzo the Rat from the Muppets.

By 2002, Beryl's health was declining. I asked Beryl's son, John about his mother's later years, and he wrote:

> Her posture in front of her easel was not the best, she most often would have her legs crossed and be leaning forwards with her back bent. Hours, days and years spent in this posture took their toll and by this time she was beginning to suffer from back strain and her joints were complaining. Unbeknownst to all of us she also must have felt unwell from a developing cancer, as she organised a return from Bristol to Plymouth quite rapidly, telling us that they needed to be closer to us for health reasons in their old age.

In Plymouth they chose a smaller house just round the corner from Athenaeum Street, in Alfred Street. John Junior continued: 'My parents had a housekeeper called Sue, a very round and jolly lady who they were very fond of, who had been with them for many years before they moved to Bristol, and she came back to look after them on their return to Plymouth. With Sue's help my father was able to still take care of all the day-to-day chores of housework and catering and to chauffeur my mother on shopping and library expeditions.'

The painting studio was set up just the same again, and the couple returned to The Dolphin once or twice a week, now armed with a digital camera. The Dolphin was mercifully unchanged, apart from a lavatory refurbishment. There had been an enormous hole in the ceiling. Someone had fallen through and landed on a man who was using the lavatory underneath.

In 2004 BBC 1 showed an animated two-part film, *Bosom Pals*, based on Beryl's paintings and set in The Dolphin. It was written by Dawn French, who wrote:

> I love Beryl Cook's work for lots of reasons. I feel nostalgic about the connections with Plymouth, where I grew up . . . Like me, Beryl loves the place and the people, and she illustrates the jolly alongside the tough. I always feel that I would like to meet the people she paints. I love the detail in her work – you always find more when you look closer. Most importantly, her paintings never fail to cheer me up.[7]

The animation involved a quarter of a million pictures and starred Dawn French, Alison Steadman, Timothy Spall, Sophie Thompson, Jessica Stevenson, Geraldine McNulty, Rosemary Leach and Robert Pugh. Timothy Spall played

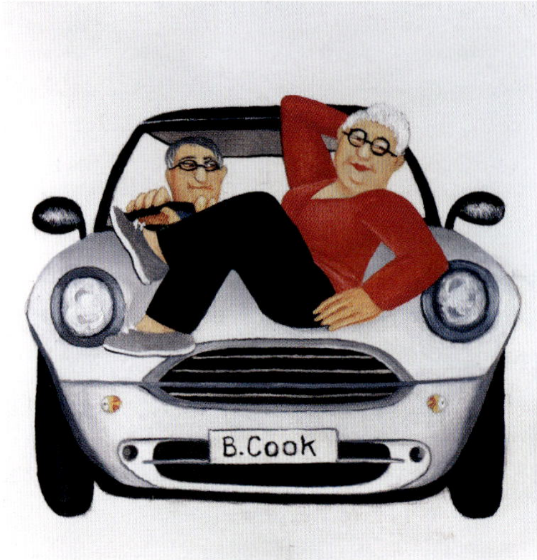

Untitled
(c 2002). As they did not have a garage, John Senior bought a mini, but it proved rather difficult to get in and out of. The painting is a joke based on the sort of adverts that car companies used in the 1970s.

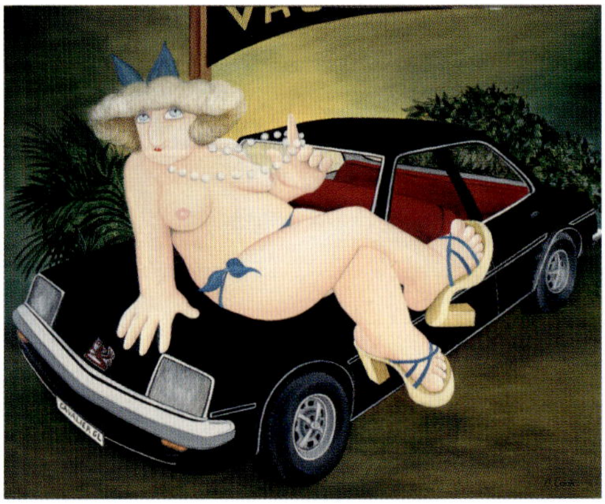

Motor Show
(1970s). This was also based on the car adverts of the 1970s. Beryl painted it as a present for John, who was of course in the motor trade at the time.

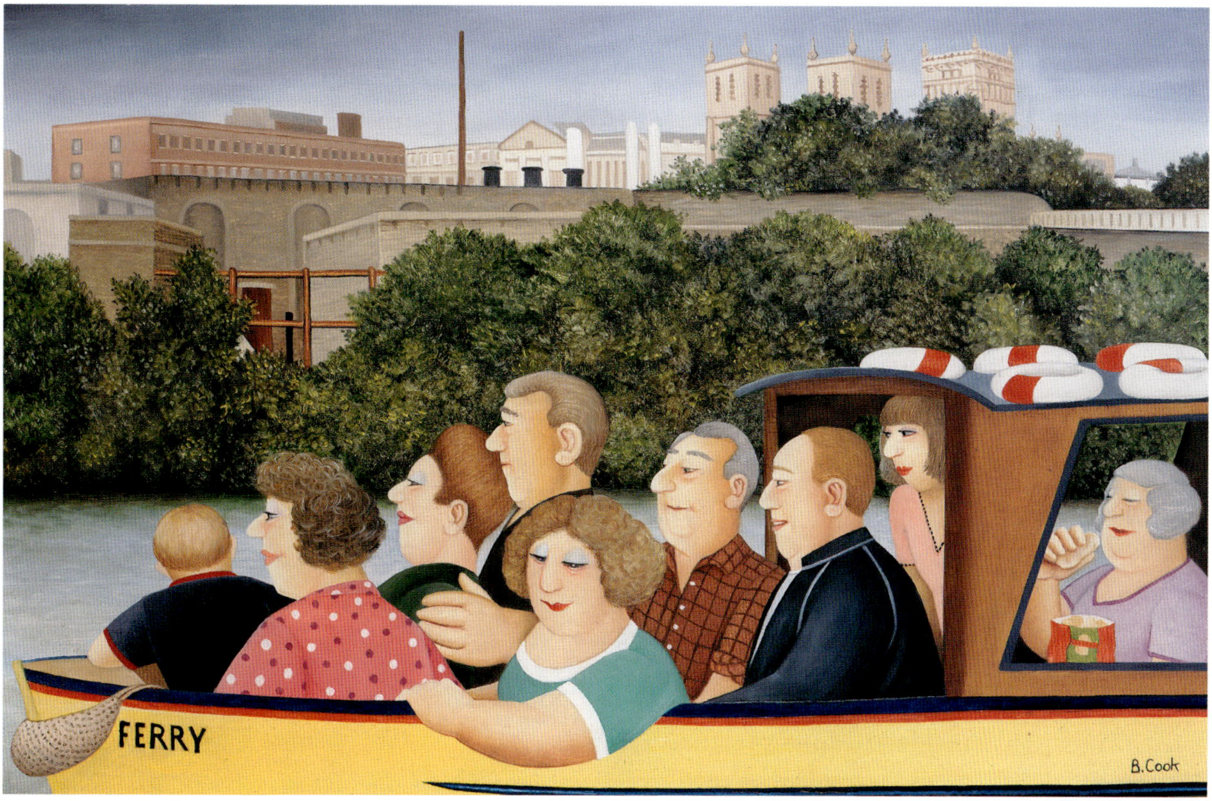

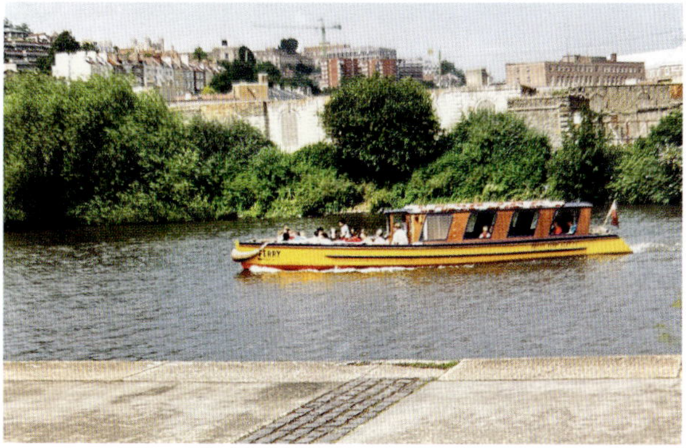

The Ferryboat

(2001) and Beryl's reference photograph. Beryl donated *The Ferryboat* and *Jazz in the Winter* (see page 204) to Bristol Museum and Art Gallery in 2002. She wrote, 'The painting of *The Ferryboat* came about because of my fondness of the waterfront here. Whenever we have visitors to stay John always takes them to see the SS *Great Britain* and while they are busy with this the dog (Lizzie) and I sit watching the traffic on the river. This painting is my second attempt, and as I have several more drawings there may be another, hopefully with bridges as well.'[8]

Billy the landlord, the only character based on a real person (see page 39).

In 2006 Beryl turned 80 and the Portal mounted an exhibition to mark the occasion. For once, Beryl did attend the opening – as a tribute to the long relationship she had with the Portal Gallery and its owner, Jess Wilder.

John Junior finishes Beryl's story:

> By Beryl's 80th birthday it was obvious to us all that her health was in serious decline. She was spending less and less time in her studio as her back was giving her more trouble, and she couldn't stay long in front of her easel. By Christmas of 2007 her cancer had returned and sadly, in the New Year more health complications set in.
>
> Around this time, during one of our conversations I asked her about some of the negative comments that had been made about her paintings by a few members of the 'art establishment' over the course of her artistic career, did they bother her?
>
> I shall never forget her reply: 'Quite frankly John, I don't give a f***!' Then she grinned and said, 'Look, earlier in my life as an artist I would have appreciated some support from them. Now, when you get all the wonderful fan mail that I have received over the years, who needs anyone else's approval?'

She managed to finish her last ever painting around the end of February 2008, *Crutch Dancing*, which was a rework of *Back Bar of the Lockyer Street Tavern* (see page 45). After she put her paintbrushes aside for the last time her health went straight downhill, the cancer took hold and she died on the 28 May 2008.

John finished by saying:

> Not to leave this on a sad note, I would like to tell you about a short conversation Ma had with my father very near the end. In the evening she had been lying still for some time looking intently towards the ceiling across from the foot of the bed. My father asked her what she was looking at.
>
> 'Can't you see it John?' she replied. He couldn't see anything other than the ceiling.
>
> 'The light, can't you see the light? ... I'm not afraid, John, because I know that's where I'm going.'

John Senior died on 3 June 2014.

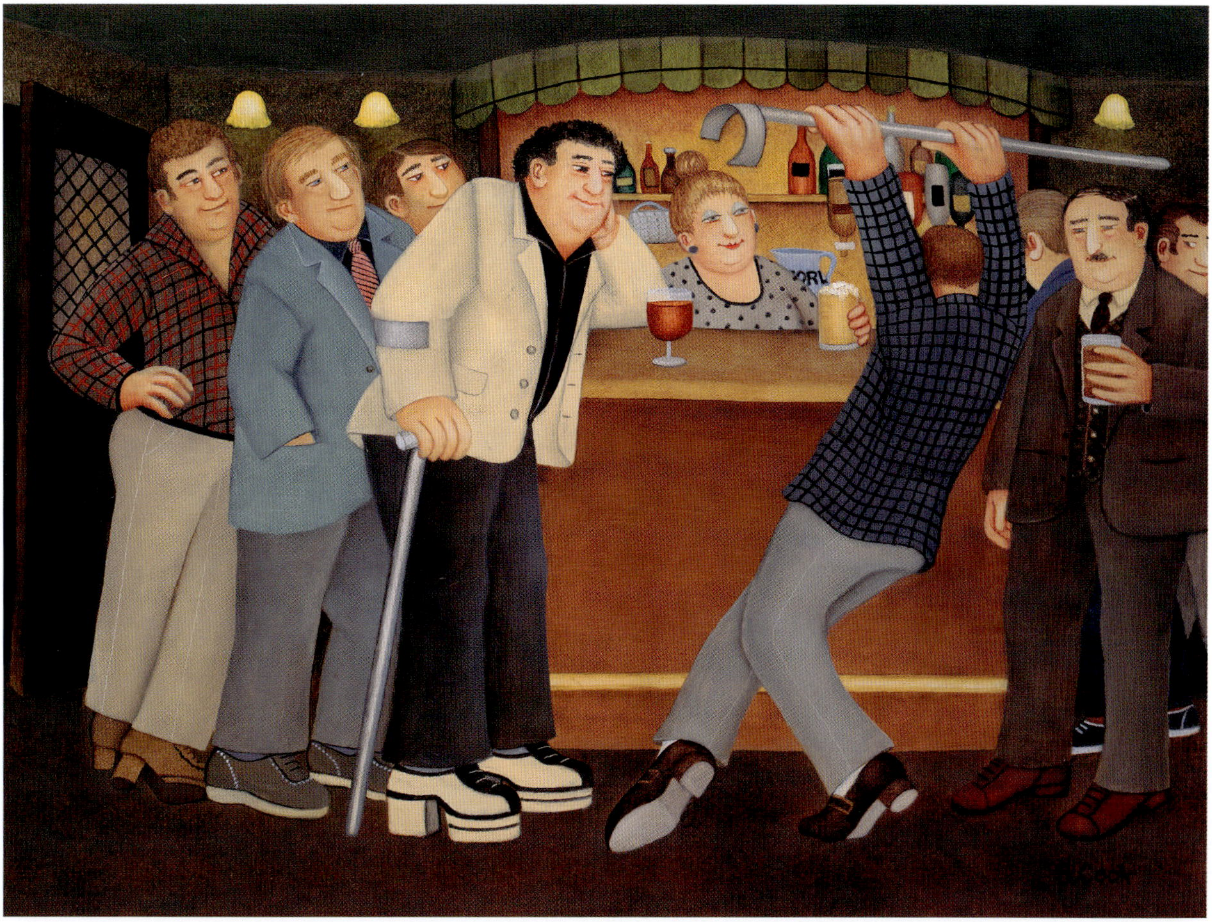

Crutch Dancing

(2008), Beryl's last painting. This is really a variation of Beryl's earlier paintings of the same subject (see page 45). It's not a direct copy, and it was painted from memory.

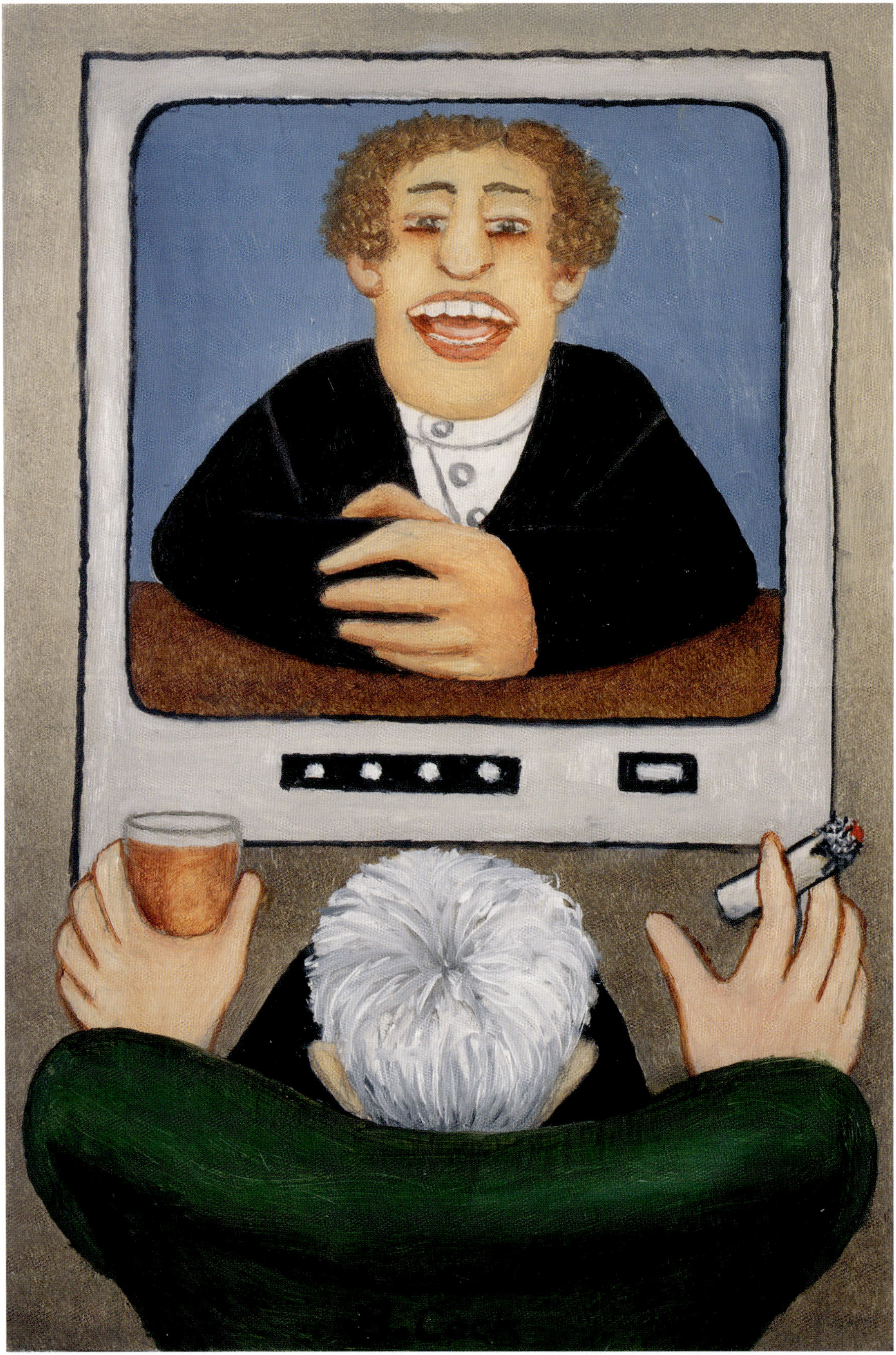

15

Re-evaluation

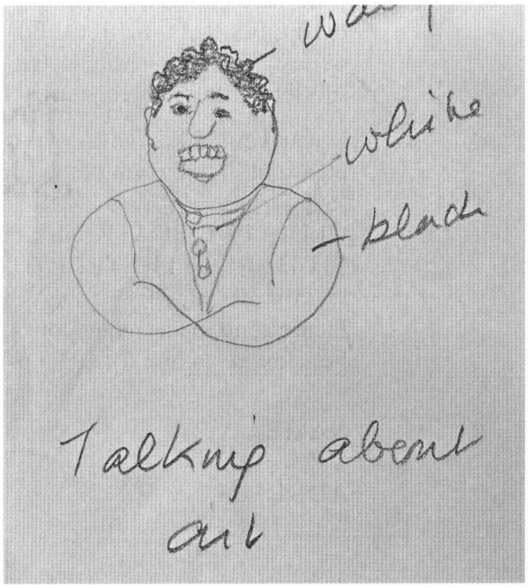

LEFT
Talking about Art
(2006), and its pencil sketch. Beryl hated art speak and insisted that her paintings have no message.

Even the least arty among us can immediately identify the work of two living British artists. Dead cow in a tank – Damien Hirst. Fat women living it up – Beryl Cook. Let's hope the two never collaborate.

'More Sauce from the Master Cook',
Yorkshire Evening Press 4 April 2000

Beryl hated pretentious art talk and once crawled out of the front room on her stomach to avoid being seen through the window by a persistent artist who insisted on inviting himself in.

A reviewer wrote, 'Beryl Cook's London exists largely in the imagination . . . while her totemic portrait of London as a middle-aged housewife is affectionate and topical, it is also very narrow. There are no colours on her palette for the homeless brain-surgeon of Carrington House, the inmate of a mental ward in Tooting Bec or the terrified grandmother of a Stepney high-rise.'[1]

But it's Beryl Cook's London, not his. It wasn't that she didn't notice things, she said, she just didn't want to dwell on them. Because there isn't enough suffering or anxiety in her art may be one reason that she was not 'accepted' by the art establishment. This seems an attitude that is reserved for art – we don't complain if a novel, film or ballet is overly happy or even funny. However, in recent years there has been a better understanding of the wellbeing outcomes of looking at, or being involved in, art. The term 'naïve artist' has also largely been abandoned, but 'outsider art', which sometimes replaces it, doesn't really work either (both are defined on Tate's website).[2] But whatever it is called, such art is becoming more accepted by the art world.

There can be no doubt about the joy that Beryl's art still brings to her fans, and during her lifetime many people wrote to tell her so. Dawn French called her 'visual Prozac'.[3] Her work lifts the spirits, as seen in fan letters:

> You say you have no message. You are wrong. Your message is 'Cheers' as no-one can look at your paintings and remain downhearted. (SP, England, 1986)

> There's not a day goes by that I don't stop at one of the pictures to admire it and smile. It gives me great joy to have your art in my home. (JB, New York, 2001)

> You don't need any art school, but there's a heap of art schools who need you . . . life is a joke, but some folks always tell it badly. You "tell it like it is" with honesty and kindness as well as rollicking gusto, and such integrity as far as I am concerned would invest even *mud* with life. (N, South Africa, 1980)

One woman felt *Bryant Park* (see page 218) spoke to her, saying it conveyed: 'I don't care if my stockings are showing, that my dress is too tight, that I'm a bit chubby or that I smoke cigarettes. Let the world think what they may, I'm happy. But of course, I must still wear lipstick.' The woman continued: 'Although I *do* care how I look, I would love to be that lady lying on the park bench and maybe someday I will. And so the image was imprinted on my brain.' In 1996, as she told Beryl in a letter, she moved to Bryant Park.

The paintings also brought comfort. One woman was in hospital over Christmas and felt especially bereft when her visitors left. But her brother gifted her *The Works*. She laughed until her stitches ached. 'The expression of the first pig of *Come Dancing* [see page 218] brought tears to my eyes, but the cover painting [*Sabotage*, see page 69] is still my favourite.'

Another woman was full of grief. She wrote what a lift she got from looking at the pictures and reading the books and cards; 'their buoyancy is so uplifting and even in my darkest moments I can feel some joie de vivre'.[4] Beryl replied with a signed card and a copy of her new book.

In 2002 a woman thanked her for 'the gift of joy that you gave my father at the end of his days'. He was confused and agitated. 'Your books saved the day. Your books were the last presents that he really appreciated . . . I shall never forget my Father's smiling face and his chuckles as he viewed your work.'[5]

Beryl's work always had a gay following. The 1976 *Sunday Times Magazine* had Plymouth's Lockyer Tavern on the front, and her first book, *The Works*, opens with the same painting, followed by *Brian Entertains* (see page 48), *Angela Singing* (see page 219) and *Sylvia* (see page 51).

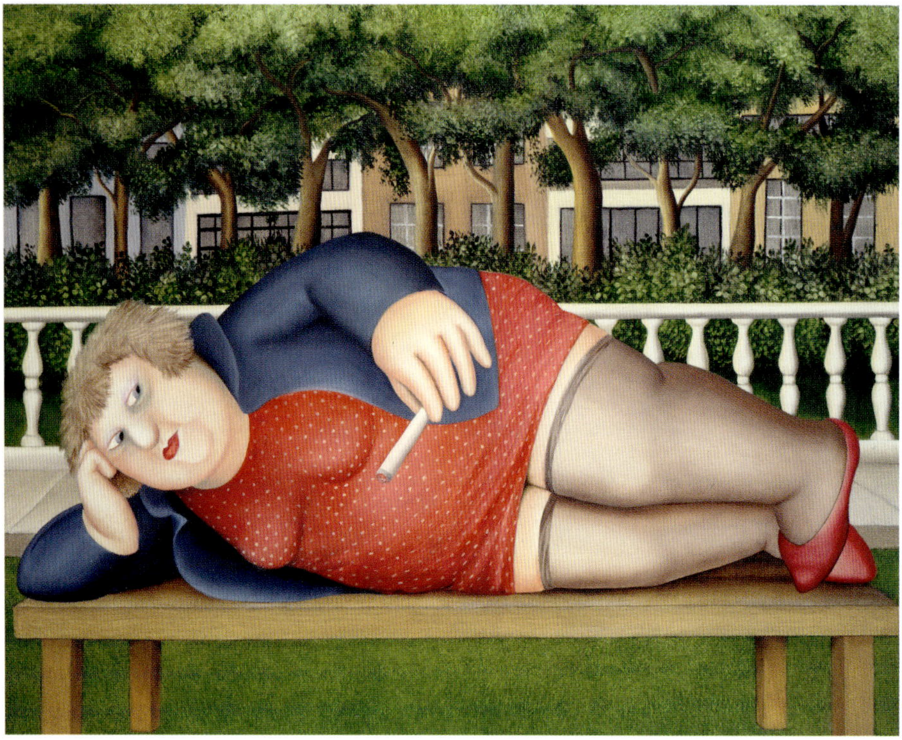

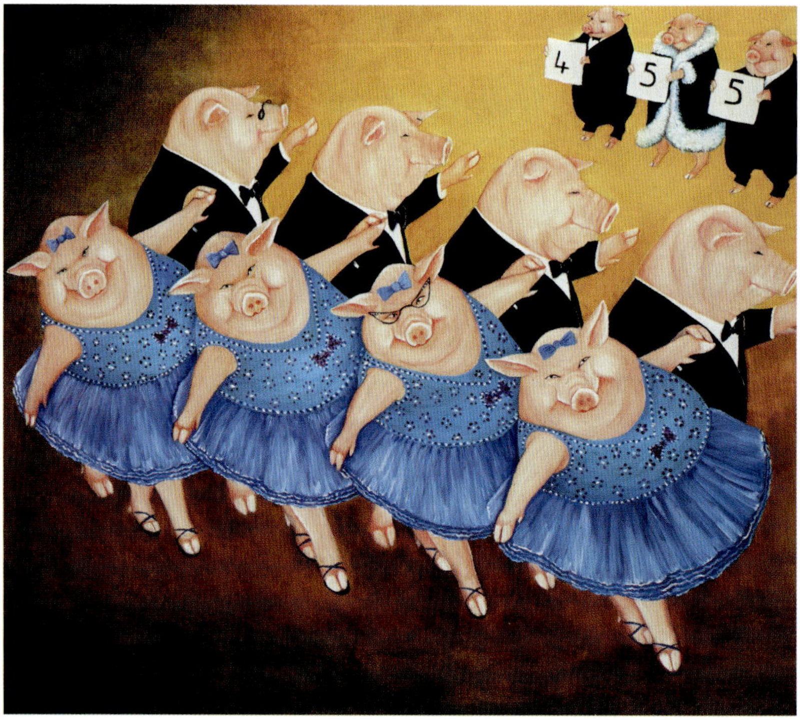

Bryant Park
(1985)

Come Dancing
(1975–8). *Come Dancing* was one of Beryl's favourite television programmes. It was much more formal than its recent reincarnation, *Strictly Come Dancing*. I too found it unintentionally funny.

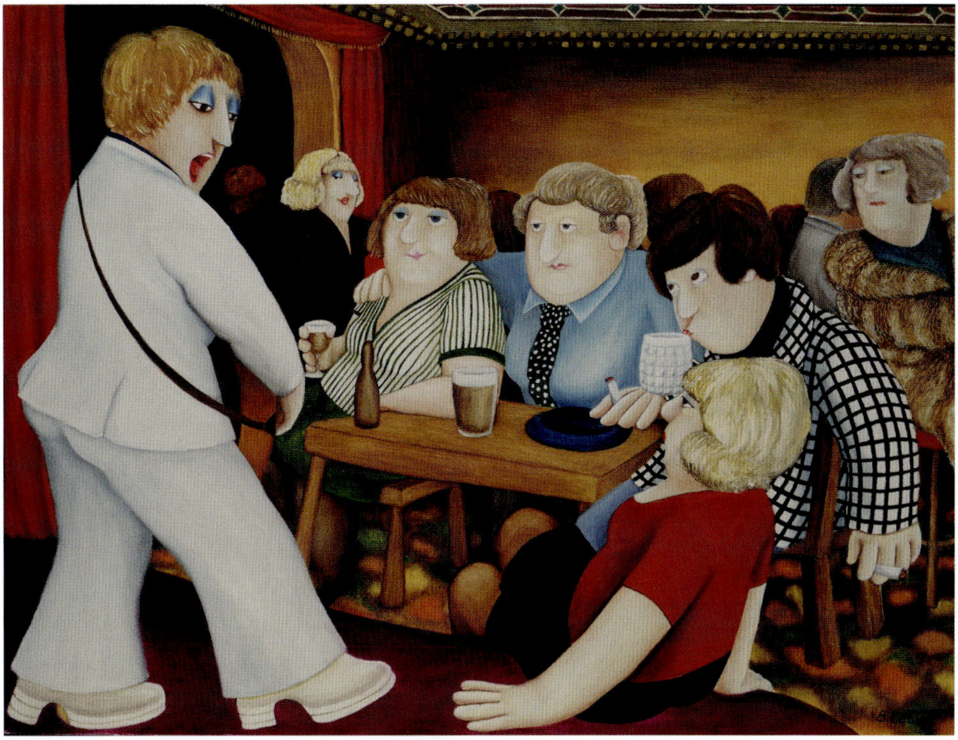

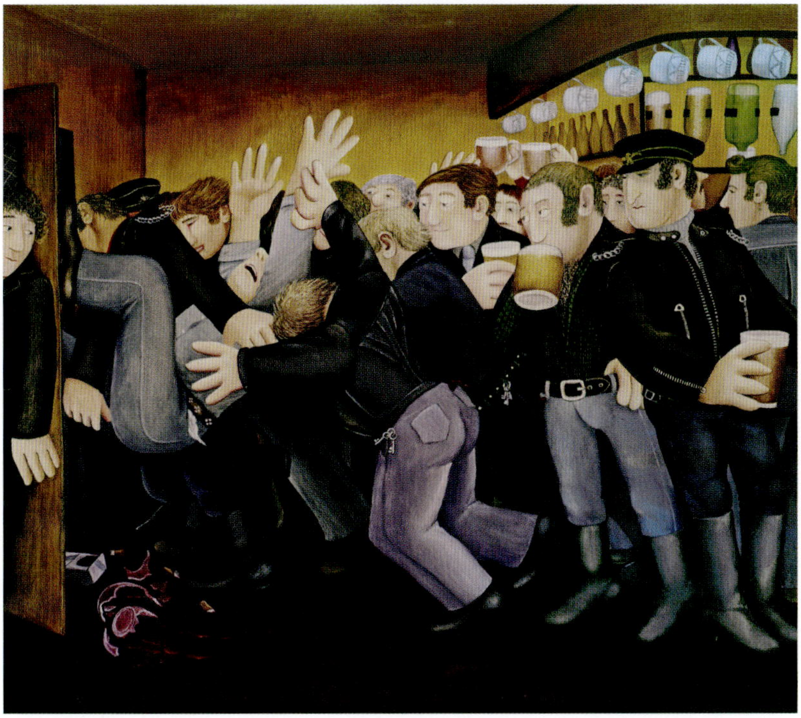

Leather Bar

(c 1980). Probably the Coleherne pub, Earl's Court, which Beryl visited with Edward Lucie-Smith. Note the handkerchiefs and keys, used to signal sexual preferences. The Coleherne became a notorious leather bar in the 1970s with blacked out windows, when it was nicknamed the 'Cloneherne'. Its customers suffered from police harassment and the attention of three serial killers. It is no longer a gay pub.

Angela Singing

(c 1977). The front bar of The Lockyer

Many of us think that male homosexuality was decriminalized in England and Wales in 1967, but until 2000, this only applied to a maximum of two men, both over 21 and only in private. In that same year the government lifted the ban on homosexuals serving in the armed forces. That's right, 2000. The actual law was not repealed until 2016. Despite the partial-decriminalization in 1967, police harassment of the LGBTQ+ community and raids on pub and clubs continued. For a very long time, members of the LGBTQ+ community mistrusted the police as a response to decades of anti-gay culture and policing, and a view that the police force took less interest in marginalized victims of crime, such as gay people and prostitutes. Understandably, many gay people did not feel able to come out to their work colleagues or even their families.

In 1979 DA wrote to Beryl:

> I find your pictures observant, witty and usually hilarious, but most of all, I appreciate your happy approach to life, especially your acceptance of the 'gay' world – portrayed in your pictures of the old Lockyer, and your comments about them, – an attitude which I find refreshing and extremely rare in Plymouth. Perhaps I never met the right people, or maybe things have changed over the eighteen years since I lived there. ...meanwhile thank you for the pleasure and fun your paintings and book give to so many people and for putting the modern Plymouth firmly on the Art World's map.

In 1982, PL wrote that he was:

> pleased to discover most of your stuff has been done in and around Plymouth as I spent 4 very pleasant years there from '75 –'79 while serving in_in Plymouth, the town most sailors prefer, the daft ones anyway . . . I was further surprised to see so many of your paintings being about the Lockyer Tavern, as I first found out about it while living in a bedsit in Lockyer Road in 1978 and with the Lockyer, Gypsy Moth and Mr Harry's had a very gay time indeed while living in Plymouth, until that is the Navy found out about 'me dirty deeds' and chucked me out from Drake Barracks . . . not that I blame the fun people of Guzz in anyway after all it's hardly their fault the Navy is so pathetically stupid in its attitude to gay people . . . also the pictures of sailors are so funny, especially the camp ones which you usually seem to slip in. Perhaps you are aware of something the bloody navy isn't?

Beryl was indeed very clever at signposting her LGBTQ+ paintings discretely, particularly in the earlier works.

RIGHT, TOP
Top Dogs
(c 1982). This was originally known as *Gay Dogs* (note the gentlemen's toilets in the background).

RIGHT, BOTTOM
Ruby's Wheels
(c 1982). This is *Top Dogs'* pair. I have not found any hidden meaning in this one. Ruby has been given responsibility for driving due to her big paws.

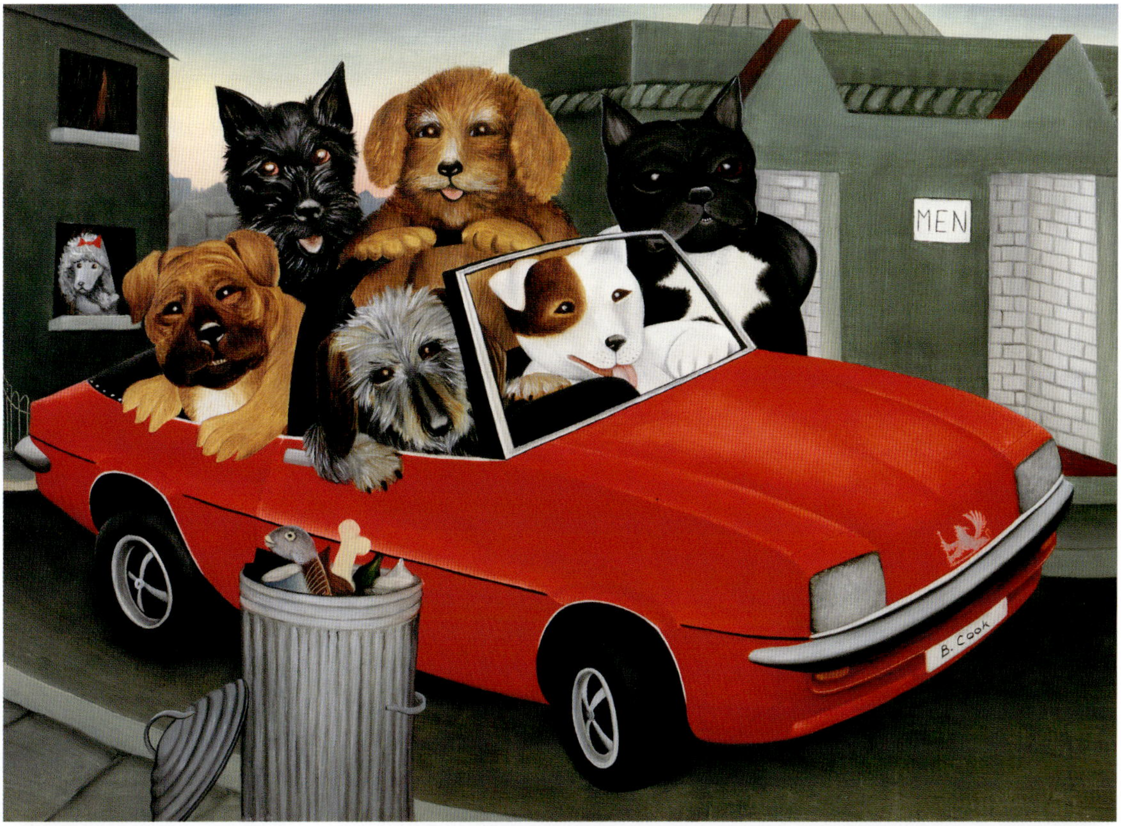
MEN
B. Cook

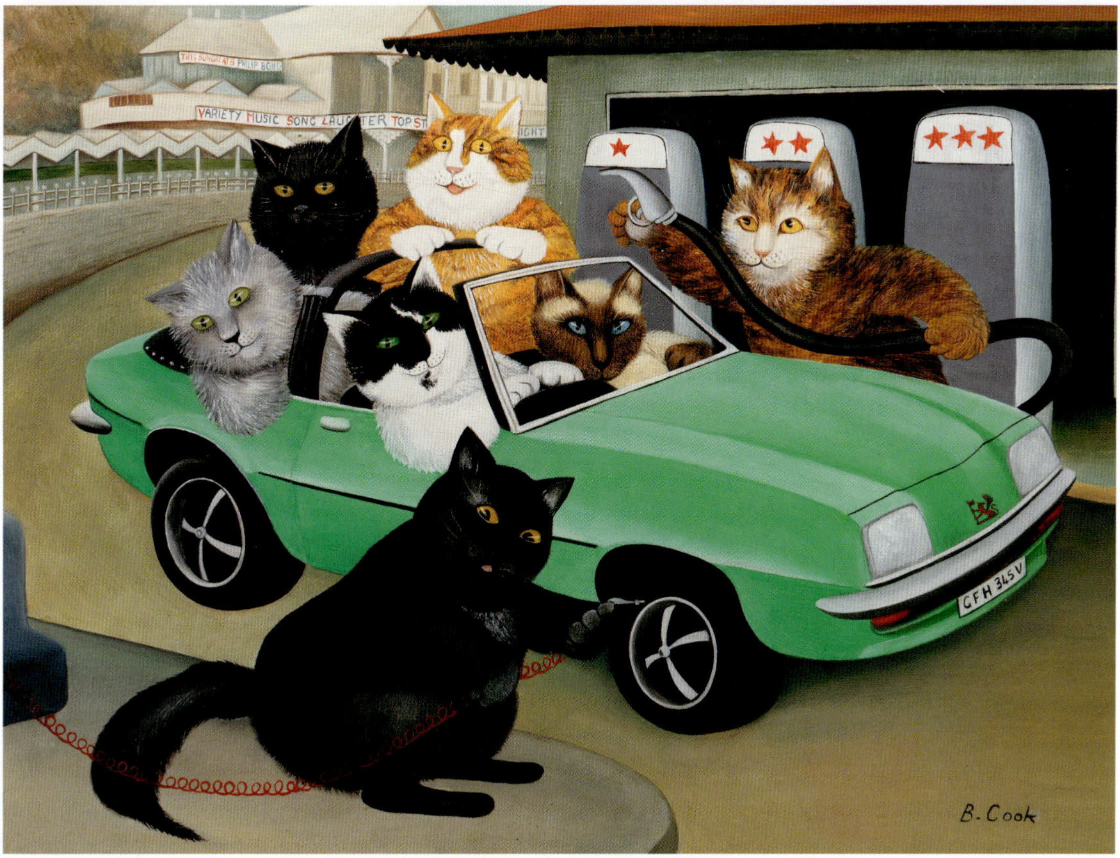
VARIETY MUSIC SONG
GFH 345V
B. Cook

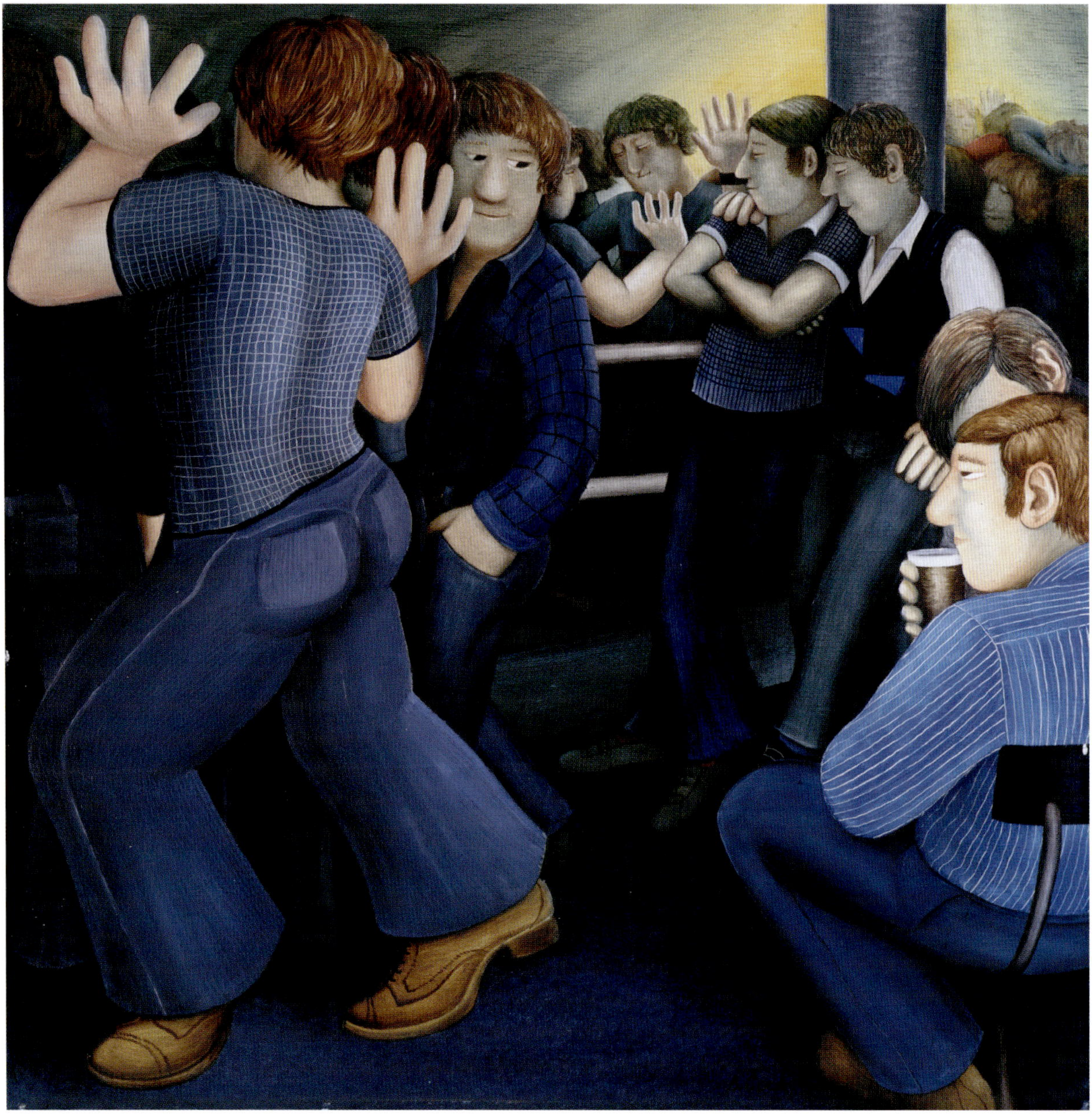

Bangs Disco

(c 1977). The gay disco known colloquially as Bangs started in 1976 in the basement of the London Astoria, and became Funboat in 1985 and later G-A-Y.[6]

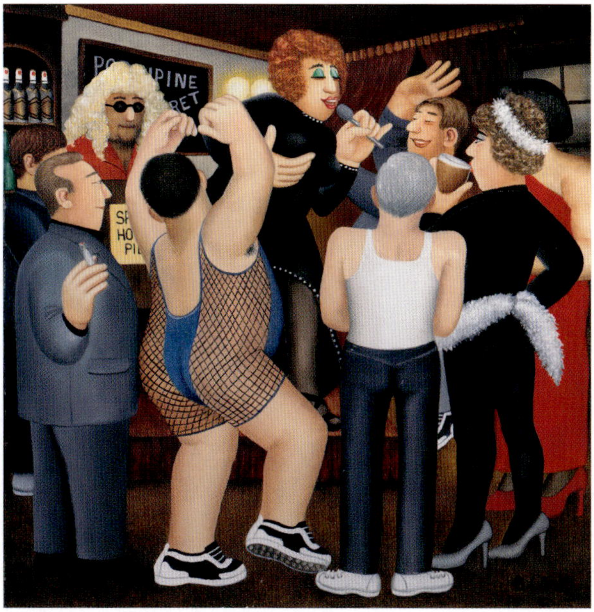

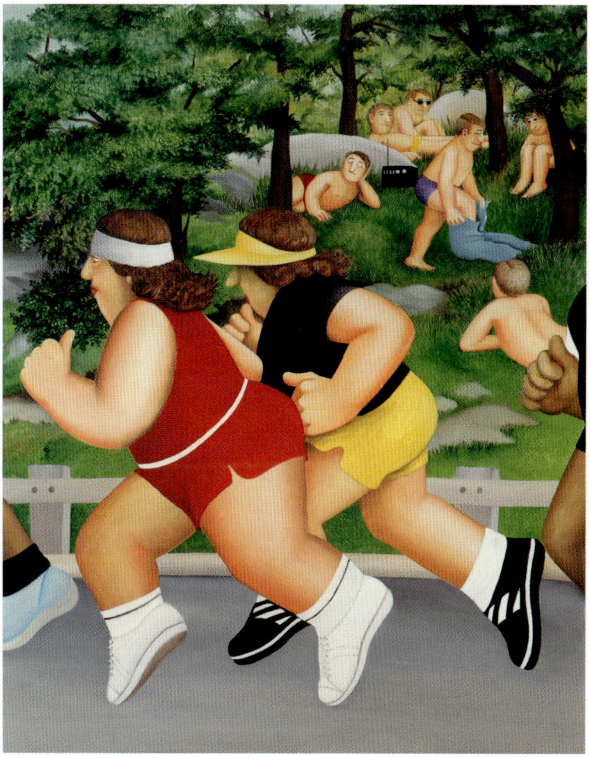

Party Boys
(1980s). The person in the white feather boa is drag queen Sheila Blige, who described herself in a letter to Beryl in 2002 as the 'Bitch with an Itch, and drag in a bag'.

Six Thousand Women Running
(c 1985), shown in Central Park in New York, against a background Beryl had seen on a previous visit of 'a little green dell with men sunbathing'.

Beryl did not need to be validated by the Art Establishment – she had her fans. But as a sensitive person, she did have wobbles. Good friends, whose opinions she respected, did their best to reassure her. Barbara Ker-Seymer wrote to her in October 1988:

> All artists who are any good, have doubts about their merit. It seems to me that you have succeeded very well in what you want to do, which is to give people pleasure, it has to be very satisfying to give pleasure . . . you should have NO doubts AT ALL EVER about your paintings. You are not really to be compared with other painters as you paint entirely your own way, the way you want to, you have the most wonderful pure colour, and what never fails to amaze me is your natural sense of composition. The serious critics all agree.

Even so, these feelings seem to have persisted. Anyone with self-doubt knows how criticism can rankle. It's worth just reiterating how extraordinary Beryl's achievements were. Her paintings were acquired by an extraordinary spectrum of people, literally from peers of the realm downwards. She had numerous painting commissions, and met and made friends with a number of the people she painted, including Scottish actor Gregory Fisher, ballet dancer Wayne Sleep (see page 154), and as already mentioned, Rodney Bewes, Christopher Logue, Dawn French and George Melly.

The Royal Commission on the Historic Monuments of England photographed her studio for posterity. She had entries in Debrett's and Who's Who, which listed her books and exhibitions, and was even elected to a London Club. She may not have made it to the Tate Gallery, but Beryl's works were in several public collections during her lifetime.

Three paintings were specially commissioned in 1992 by Julian Spalding, then Director of Glasgow Museums, for their new Gallery of Modern Art. His reasons are interesting. He didn't want his acquisitions budget swallowed up by the art market, which he said, 'values art more for its investment potential than its aesthetic content.'[7] Buying from living artists would also allow the curators to record why the painters do what they do, which he felt was vital for a broad audience. He said that Glaswegians are naturally cultured people – it would never occur to them that art was elitist.

Beryl had at least 32 exhibitions devoted solely to her work and lent to many others. Beryl Cook exhibitions break visitor records – the one at Durham Art Gallery in 1997 was the most popular in the 30 years since the gallery opened.

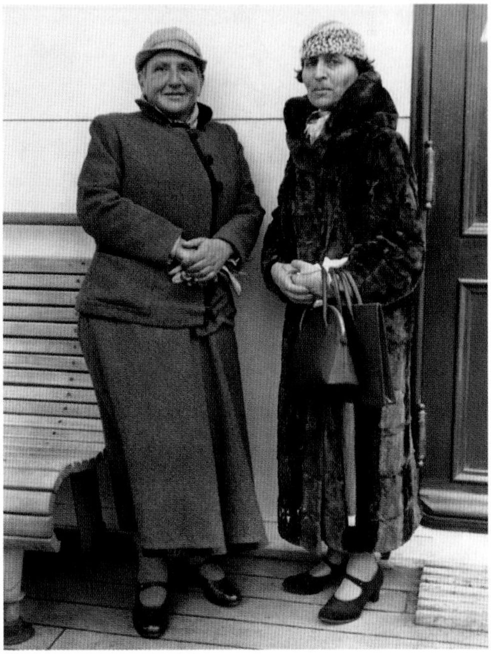

Gertrude Stein (1874–1946), novelist, poet, playwright and art collector, and her life partner, Alice B. Toklas (1877–1967)

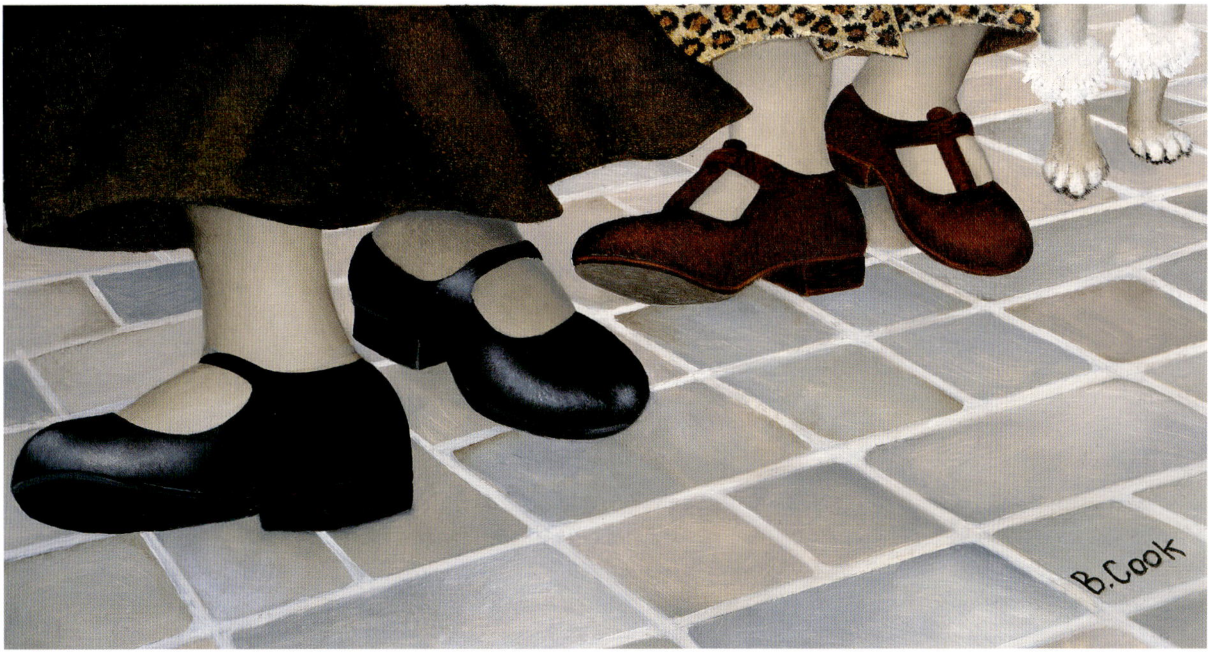

Gertrude's Shoes
(2006). Gertrude Stein and Alice B. Toklas' feet with the forepaws of their poodle, Basket, or possibly Basket II. The feet are rather jauntier than in the original Bettman photograph of 1934 (see page 224).

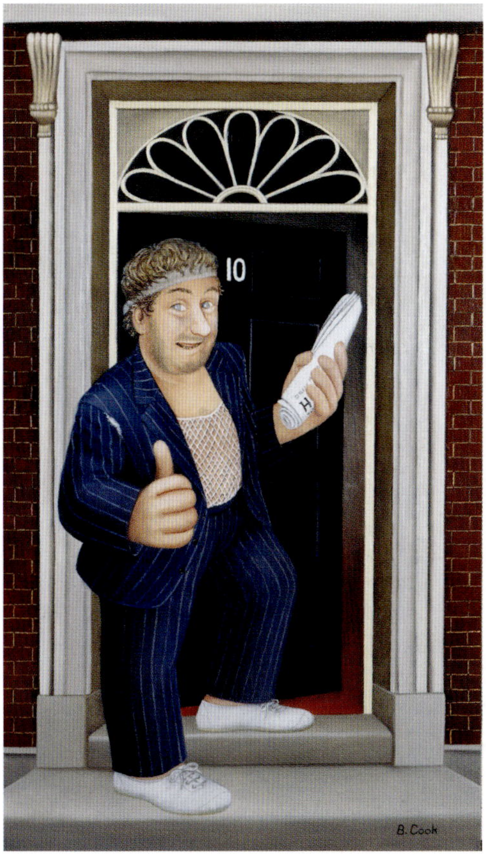

Rab C. Nesbitt
(1992). Gregory Fisher as the titular character in the sitcom *Rab C. Nesbitt* outside 10 Downing Street. This painting was commissioned by his wife.

Plymouth City Museum had acquired two of her pictures at her very first show (something almost unheard of) and Beryl shortly afterwards gave them *Back Bar of the Lockyer Street Tavern* (see page 45). It has continued to acquire works by her, including a bequest from Bernard Samuels and purchases from the estate of Tony Martin. At the time of writing, The Box has ten works by Beryl.

The South London gallery Studio Voltaire exhibited her work alongside of the homoerotic work of Tom of Finland (1920–1991) in 2024. Reviewing the show, Susie Goldberg wrote in *The Times,* 'Cook's work is reaching new audiences, including twentysomethings like me who approach her without preconception. We're seduced.'[8]

The Government Art Collection must have agreed, because it purchased *Window-Dresser 2* (see page 229) from Studio Voltaire in 2025. This will be made available to British government buildings in the UK and across the world, and is having its public debut at The Box in Plymouth. Another national collection gained a Beryl Cook in 2025, when Edward Lucie-Smith donated his charming picture *Edward Lucie-Smith as a Bard* (see page 228) to the National Portrait Gallery.

Beryl was awarded the OBE in 1995 for services to art. She turned down Desert Island Discs four times. And all this was achieved while she was actively avoiding publicity and adulation.

Beryl has repeatedly been called Britain's favourite painter, and her work is instantly recognizable as a 'Beryl Cook'. So are the sorts of people she painted. Her work is known across the world, and its popularity has not diminished since her death. Indeed, there are pleasing signs that she is being re-evaluated, and once any residual snobbery has been surgically removed from art historians, she will be recognized for what she was – a consummate artist whose work has depth and lasting meaning – even if she said repeatedly 'I have no message'.

Beryl always worried that her fame was transitory. Jess Wilder of the Portal Gallery wrote to reassure her:

> Your pictures are absolutely unique in reflecting life in late twentieth century Britain, what people wear, how they enjoy themselves, you are an important social historian. Your paintings speak for themselves, and give a huge number of people through your books and cards a very great deal of pleasure. As I'm sure you know, the only reasons others of this world feel it necessary to become personalities (apart from being terrible show-offs) is to hide a distinct lack of talent. You will be remembered long after they have been forgotten. Please believe me!'[9]

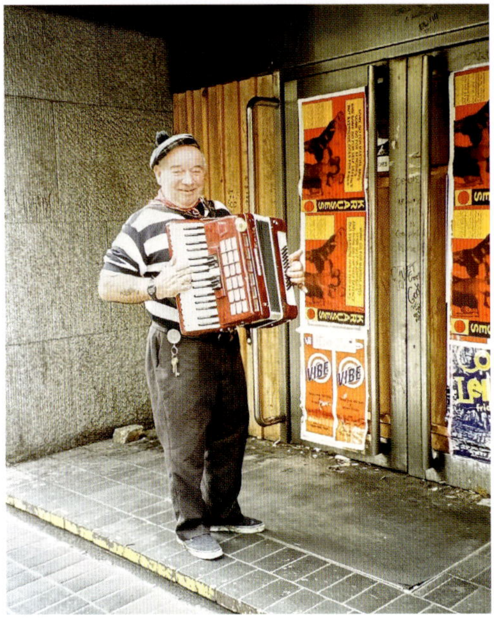

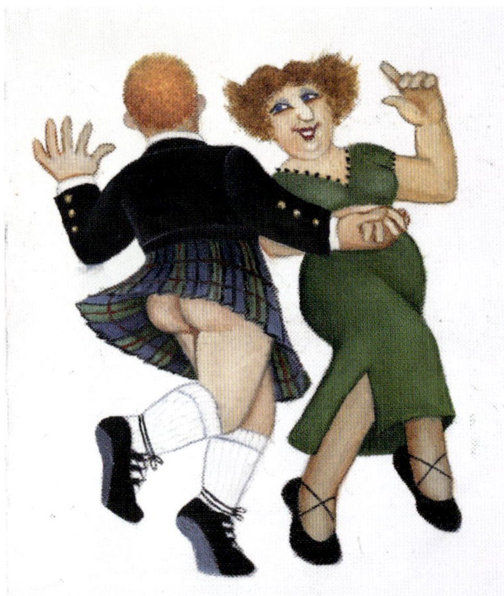

Birthday card painted by Beryl for Julian Spalding (2007). Spalding used this on the cover of his book *Art Exposed,*[10] in which he devotes a chapter to Beryl. He denies he has red hair.

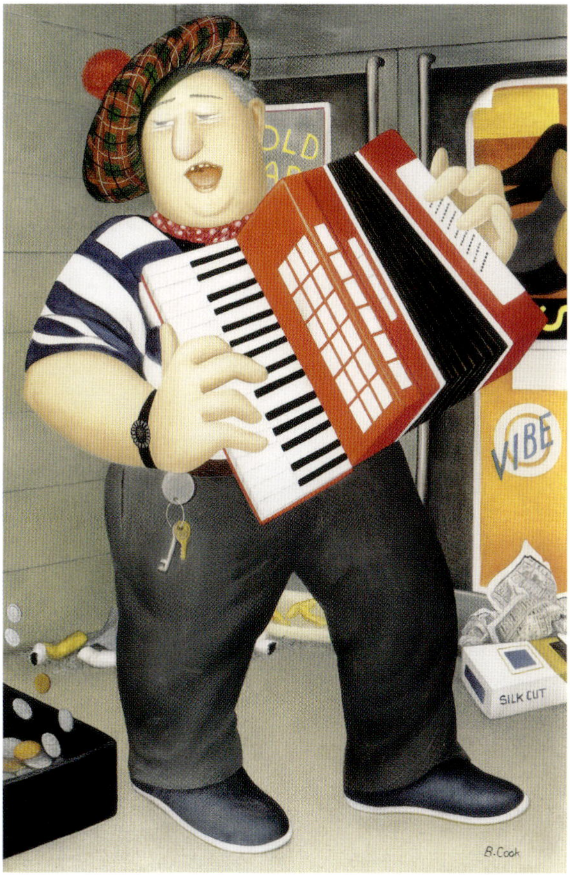

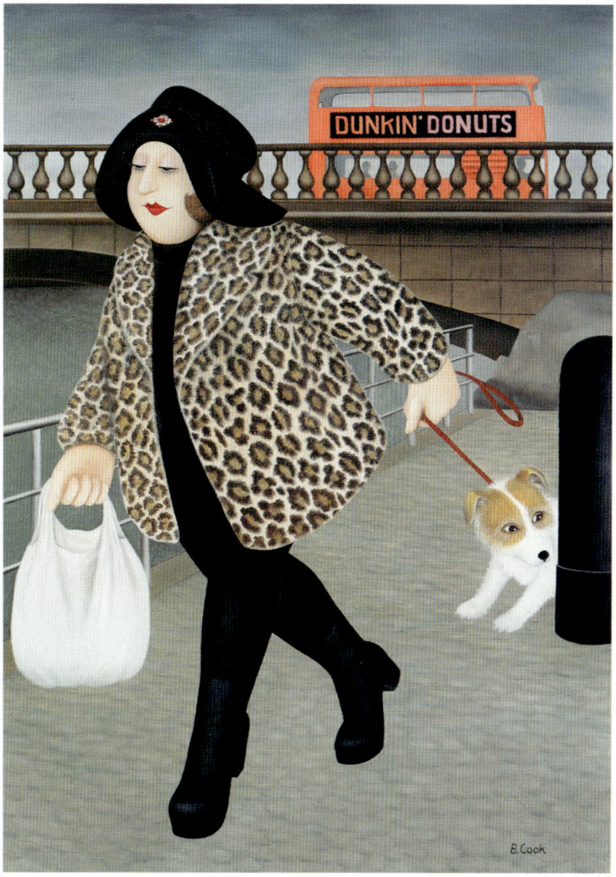

Accordion Player
(1992) and Beryl's reference photograph. Beryl was disappointed by the lack of tartan actually being worn around the streets of Glasgow, but spotted this busker's plaid bonnet. She was compelled to make it larger.

By the Clyde
(1992), also known as *Dunkin Donuts*. Typical dog, pulling on the leash to smell the bollard!

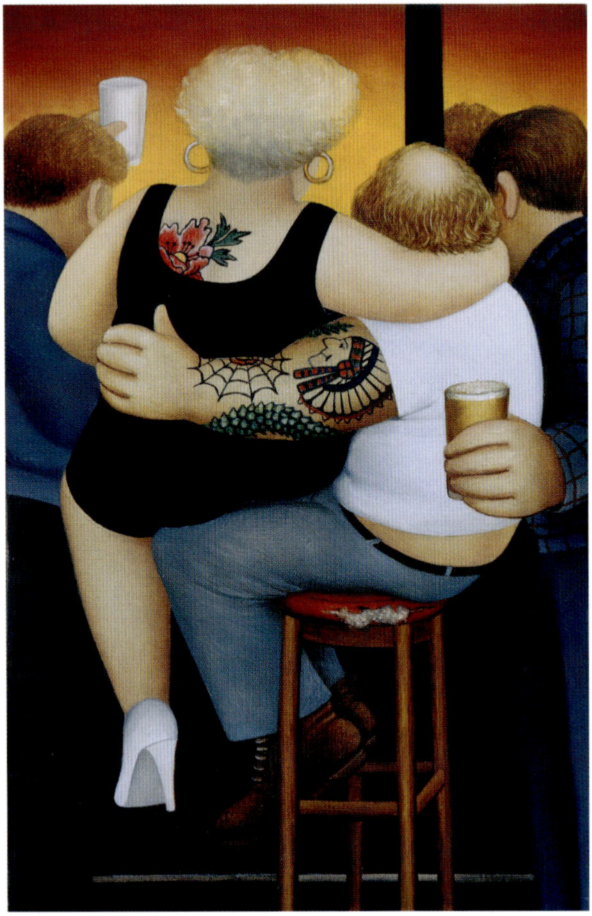

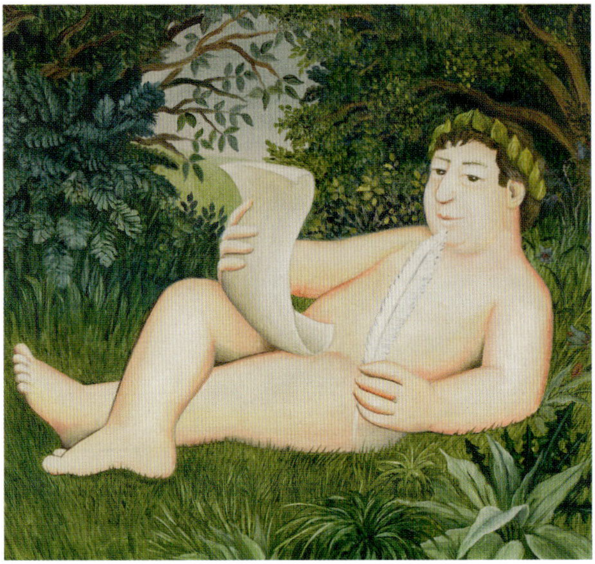

Two on a Stool
(1991). Beryl donated this painting to Durham City Museum in 2004.

Edward Lucie-Smith as a Bard
(1983). Painted as a gift for Ted and gleefully donated by him to The National Portrait Gallery in 2025. In a letter to Beryl dated 25 March 1983, Ted said it was 'just how I've always wanted to look'.

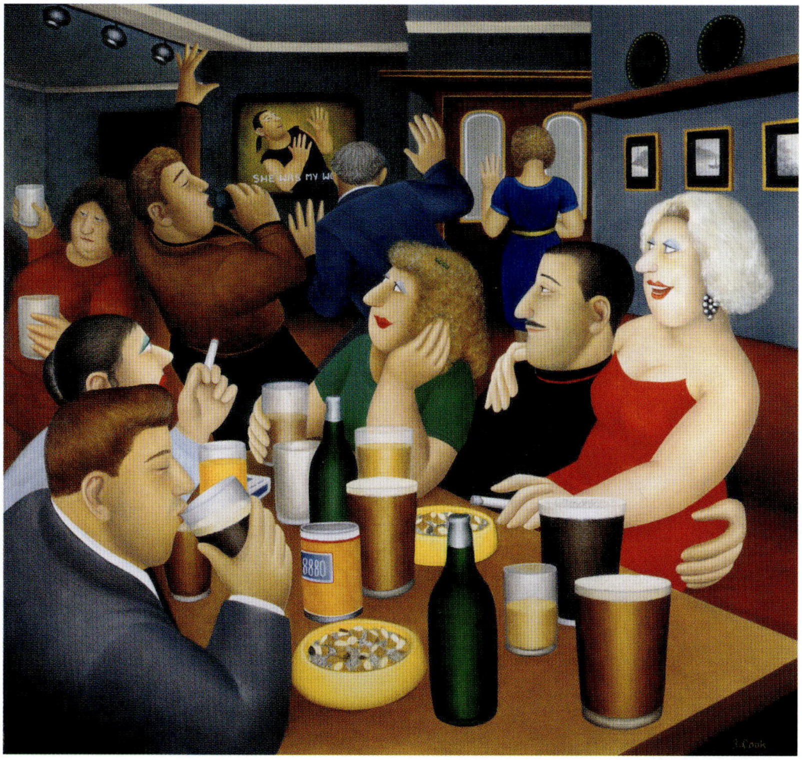

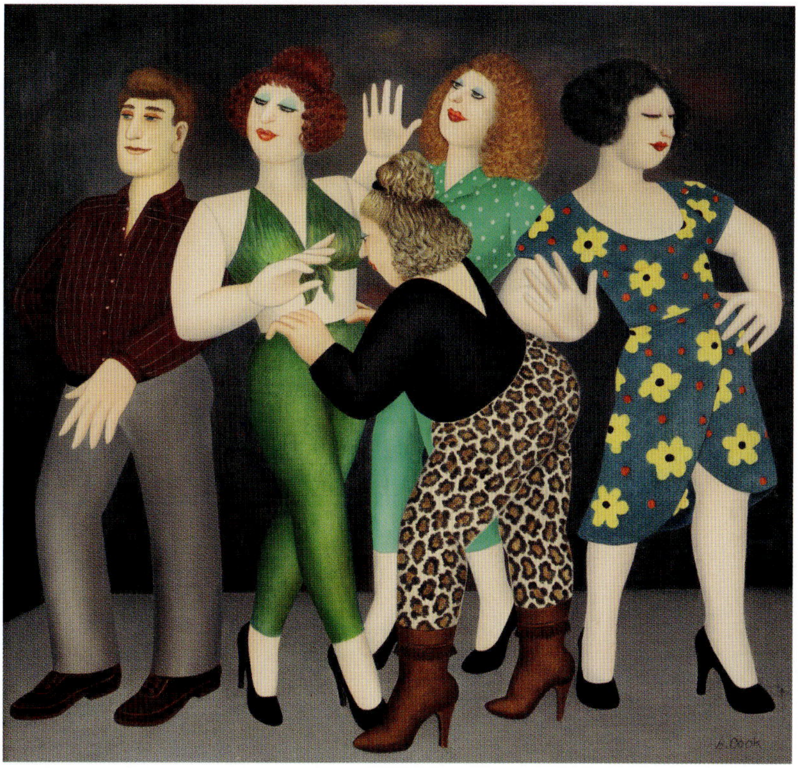

Karaoke
(1992). This was Beryl's first experience of karaoke
but of course nobody could persuade her to take to the stage.

Window-Dresser 2
(1994)

In my bullish introduction, I stated that it was time that Beryl's art was reassessed. A year later, in early 2026, the reassessment is well under way.

The exhibition *Pride and Joy* at the Box has received outstanding reviews, including a five-star rating from *The Guardian* and huge enthusiasm from the more establishment *The Art Newspaper*. The latter wrote:

> A new show at Plymouth's The Box gallery, *Beryl Cook: Pride and Joy*, until 31 May, places the late artist in the established Western art canon, tracing her links to figures such as Rubens and Amedeo Modigliani . . . "We're not just telling Beryl Cook's personal story but approach her work as art historians [would]. That just hasn't really been done before—that kind of deeper contextualisation of her work and her career," Terah Walkup, the exhibition curator, tells *The Art Newspaper*. The exhibition takes Cook's themes and influences seriously, after decades of critical neglect.[11]

Such an approach would have been anathema to Beryl, who hated art speak and deliberately called herself a painter, not an artist. But she would have been astonished – indeed, proud and joyful – to know that her work was on display alongside original paintings by Rubens, Brueghel the Younger, Stanley Spencer and Edward Burra.

Beryl repeatedly said that her work had no message. Like her fans, I disagree. She encourages us to see the everyday through a different, non-judgemental eye, and to enjoy the positive in life. As a critic for *The Guardian* wrote, 'ordinary' people are in fact extraordinary, and life 'is precious and fantastical, and we should spend every possible second celebrating it.'[12]

For anyone who may have lost sight of this, I prescribe a dose of Beryl Cook. You cannot fail to feel joyful, and you may break out in leopard print and dance the tango.

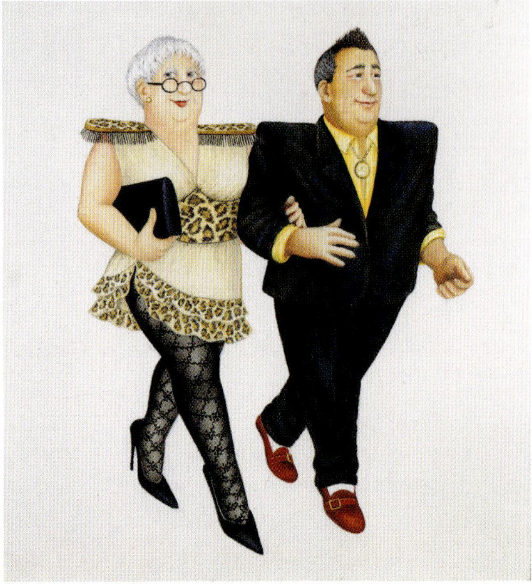

ABOVE
Trace + Kev
(1987). Beryl's paintings provide a 40-year commentary on fashion. Here, Beryl and John's alter-egos are in peak shoulder pads. Often interpreted as 'power dressing' for women in the workplace, these were made fashionable by *Dynasty*, the number one soap on American television in the mid-1980s. Joan Collins, who was on the show, became an avid collector of Beryl's work.

RIGHT, TOP LEFT
Telephone
(early 1980s). The iconic red telephone kiosk has been on Britain's streets for over 100 years, a reminder of the time before widespread landlines and mobiles. A woman is braving the pungent aroma in order to chat to a friend. She is ignoring the cards that advertize 'personal services'. Beryl had a loyal fan who collected these cards for her.

RIGHT, TOP RIGHT
Car Boot Sale
(1980s). In the 1980s car boots sales exploded in popularity, reflecting the growth in consumerism and the realization that some of us had far too much stuff. They became a key part of many people's weekends, often with food, antiques, plants and knock-off goods available. This one is particularly crammed as Beryl 'arranged five car boots into a fairly small space'.

RIGHT, BOTTOM
Party Girls
(c 1985). When Jacqueline Gold joined her father's firm Ann Summers in 1981, she reinvented Tupperware parties so that women could buy lingerie and sex aids at events in their own homes. Beryl shows women of a certain age – and size – enjoying their sexuality.

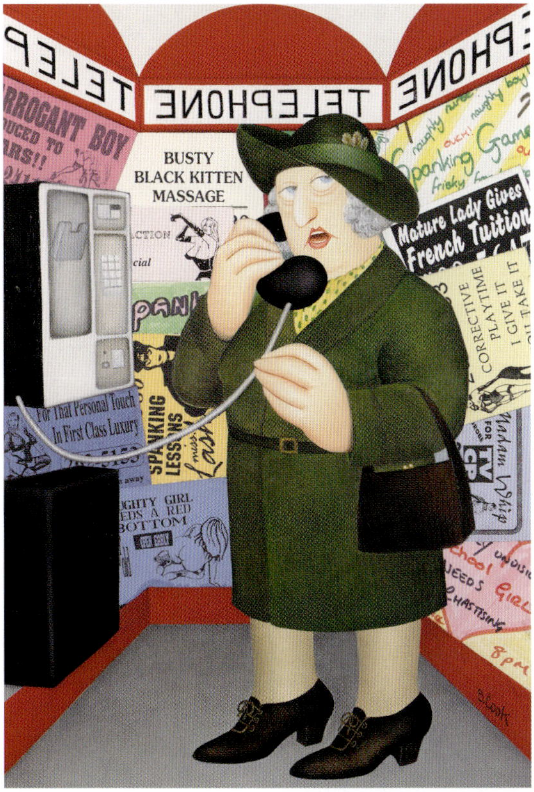
TELEPHONE
RROGANT BOY
BUSTY
BLACK KITTEN
MASSAGE
Spanking Games
Mature Lady Gives
French Tuition
CORRECTIVE
PLAYTIME
I GIVE IT
For That Personal Touch
In First Class Luxury
SPANKING
LESSONS
UGHTY GIRL
EDS A RED
BOTTOM
B.Cook

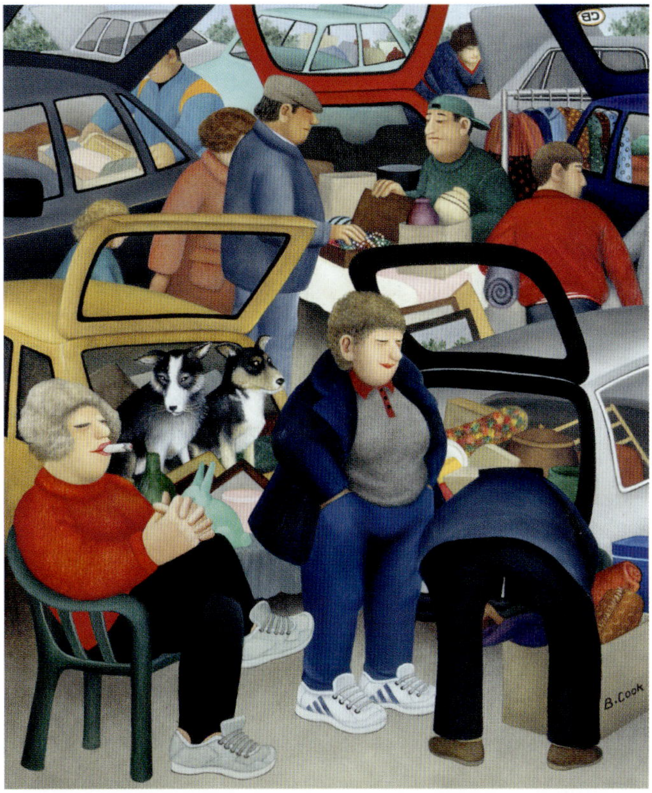
B.Cook

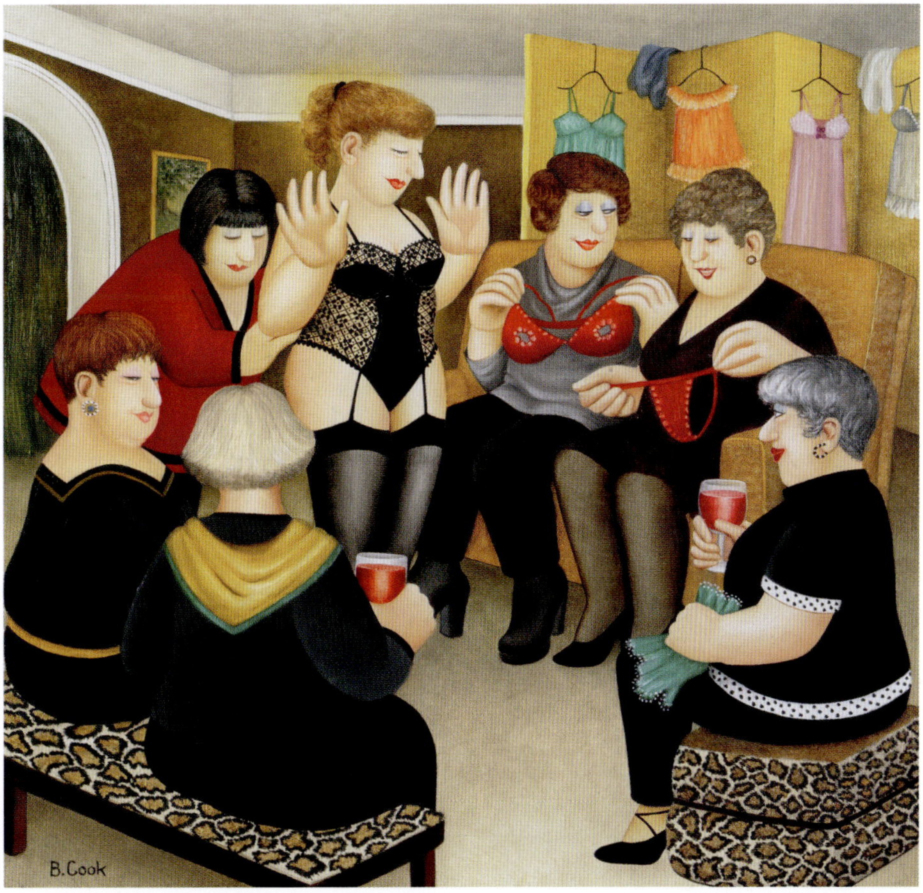
B.Cook

References

Chapter 1

1. Tisi Benvenuto called Garofalo, *Madonna and Child with a Little Bird*, 1517
2. 1921 census and war record on Ancestry.com
3. ourberylcook.com/pages/history
4. Letter from BC to Barbara Ker-Seymer postmarked 24 October 1988
5. Undated letter from BC to Kendrick School c. March 2002
6. Ruth Wishart, 'Fun is Back in the Frame', *The Herald* (Glasgow), 26 March 1995
7. Frances Hardy, 'Perils of Beryl', *The Daily Mail*, 28 March 1998
8. Ourberylcook.com/pages/history
9. Maureen Cleave, 'Cook's Tour', *Observer Magazine*, 2 October 1983
10. What was it like to be in Rhodesia as a white? Quora, 2018

Chapter 2

1. *Looe Official Guide*, The Looe Urban District Council, 1963
2. See *Sabotage*, page 69.
3. Ruth Martin, 'That's Life Beryl Cook Style', *My Weekly*, 21 April 1979

Chapter 3

1. *Beryl Cook, the Bumper Edition*, Victor Gollancz, 2000
2. Susan de Muth, 'Dragged up the Stairway to Paradise: Susan de Muth in bed with Ruby Venezuela', *The Independent*, 8 August 1993
3. Nigel Robinson, Gay Star News, 2018, requoted at www.gageohrn.com/ruby-venezuela
4. Quoted in Chris Robinson, *Union Street*, Pen and Ink publishing, 2000
5. Quoted on Plymouth Live, 21 July 2021
6. Letter from BC to Edward Lucie-Smith, 19 January 1980

Chapter 4

1. 'Beryl Cook – A Personal Memoir' in Beryl Cook, *The Bumper Edition*, Victor Gollancz, 2000
2. Gay Search, 'The Comic Genius of Beryl Cook', *Woman*, September 1979
3. 'The Private Views of a seaside landlady', *Woman*, July 1976
4. 'Beryl Cook – A Personal Memoir' in Beryl Cook, *The Bumper Edition*, Victor Gollancz, 2000
5. Ruth Wishart, 'Fun is back in the frame', *The Herald* (Glasgow), 26 March 1996
6. This account is taken from Bernard Samuels, 'Debut' in *Beryl Cook on the Town*, Devon Books, 1988 and his speech at the opening of the 2017 exhibition in the Civic Centre, Plymouth
7. Ibid
8. Frank Wintle, 'Artist who sees a vulgar beauty', *Western Morning News*, 21 November 1975
9. Ibid 6

Chapter 5

1. Figure for 1976 from figures compiled by the Audit Bureau of Circulations via Wikipedia
2. Recounted on *The South Bank Show*, ITV, 1979
3. 'Setting the Scene', Bernard Samuels, in exhibition catalogue for Beryl Cook 1926–2008 by Jess Wilder and Sarah Chapman, University of Plymouth Press, 2008
4. Faith Stewart-Gordon, *The Russian Tea Room*, Simon and Schuster, Inc, 1999

Chapter 6

1. Yvonne Thomas, 'She's naughty ... but nice!', *Daily Mail*, 21 February 1979
2. 'When naivety is good for business', *Financial Weekly*, 2 March 1979
3. Diana Winsor, *The Telegraph Sunday Magazine*, 21 September 1980
4. Yvonne Thomas in *The Daily Mail*, 21 February 1979
5. Beryl Cook, *The Bumper Edition*, Victor Gollancz 2000

Chapter 7

1. Kaleidoscope, BBC Radio 4, 31 May 1977. Transcription in the Cook archive.
2. Adrian Searle, 'Call this a national treasure?', *The Guardian*, 24 July 2007, downloaded 2025
3. Allen Saddler, 'Ladies of a certain size', *The Independent*, 12 December 1995. Independent Digital News & Media Ltd.

Chapter 8

1. Alex Hamilton, *Company*, January 1981
2. Gay Search, 'Ivor Way with the Ladies', *Woman*, 17 March 1980
3. Letter from Dan Farson to BC, September 1982
4. Daniel Farson, 'Cook's Tour,' *Sunday Today*, 22 March 1987
5. Letter from BC to Barbara Ker-Seymer, 13 December 1987
6. Letter from Barbara Ker-Seymer to BC, 19 December 1990
7. 'Funny Talk', review by David Wade of Judith Bumpus' series *Conversations with Artists*, newspaper unknown, c 1980 – 1982 (when the series was broadcast)
8. BC to Barbara Key-Seymer, 19 December 1990
9. Alex Alexander, 'Warning posters stir up a sex storm', *Western Morning News*, 5 September 1992
10. Anonymous, *The Daily Mail*, 25 March 1995

Chapter 9

1. Information from Arlene Sobel, 'One Woman's World: Beryl Cook Painter', *Woman's World*, July 1981, and from an interview with John Cook Junior, August 2025
2. Zoe Uglow, 'Ladies' hairdresser Giovanni honoured by his Italian home town', *Tavistock Times Gazette*, 25 October 2015
3. Beryl Cook, *The Bumper Edition*, Victor Gollancz, 2000
4. Madam Arcati, tony-dingle.blogspot.com/search/label/gay%20pubs, 28 March 2012

Chapter 10

1. Judith Bumpus, 'The Artist at Work: Beryl Cook', *Art and Artists*, September 1982
2. Diana Winsor, *The Telegraph Sunday Magazine*, 21 September 1980
3. Gay Search, 'The Comic Genius of Beryl Cook', *Woman's Journal*, September 1979
4. Maureen Cleave, 'Cook's Tour', *Observer Magazine*, 2 October 1983
5. Judith Bumpus, 'The Artist at Work', *Art & Artists*, September 1982
6. Ibid 4

Chapter 11

1. Letter from BC to Barbara Ker-Seymer, 12 June 1989
2. Letter from BC to John George, 4 September 1980
3. Judith Bumpus, 'The Artist at Work: Beryl Cook', *Art and Artists*, September 1982
4. Letter from Barbara Ker-Seymer to BC, 2 June 1985
5. Letter from BC to Barbara Ker-Seymer, 20 January 1991
6. Letter from BC to Barbara Ker-Seymer, 19 February 1989
7. Letter from Barbara Ker-Seymer to BC, 8 February 1990
8. Letter from BC to Barbara Ker-Seymer, 19 May 1992
9. Letter from BC to Barbara Ker-Seymer, November 1988

Chapter 12

1. www.tate.org.uk/art/art-terms/naive-art
2. Judith Bumpus, 'The Artist at Work: Beryl Cook', *Art and Artists*, September 1982
3. Letter from Barbara Ker-Seymer to BC, 1 July 1985
4. Letter from Barbara Ker-Seymer to BC, 21 October 1984
5. Undated card from Barbara Roett to BC sent from Barbara Ker-Seymer's bedside just before she died
6. Letter from BC to Barbara Ker-Seymer, 12 October 1981
7. Letter from BC to Barbara Ker-Seymer, 6 May 1990
8. barcelonasecreta.com/en/death-monica-del-raval/
9. Letter from Barbara Ker-Seymer to BC, 18 December 1984
10. Critic Roberta Smith, quoted on Wikipedia

Chapter 13

1. Letter from BC to Barbara Ker-Seymer, 7 June 1991
2. Letter from BC to Barbara Ker-Seymer, 18 April 1993
3. Letter from BC to Barbara Ker-Seymer, 28 February 1993
4. Quoted in Val Hennessy, 'Saucy Beryl', *More!*, 1988
5. Letter to SW 1 May 1994
6. Letter from BC to Barbara Ker-Seymer, 27 April 1986
7. Letter from BC to Barbara Ker-Seymer, 21 May 1989
8. Letter from BC to Barbara Ker-Seymer, 30 October 1988
9. Caption to *Dog in the Dolphin*, *Beryl Cook, the Bumper Edition*, Victor Gollancz, 2000
10. Letter from BC to Barbara Ker-Seymer, 17 May 1992
11. Letter from BC to Barbara Ker-Seymer, 21 June 1992
12. *Beryl Cook, The Bumper Edition*, Victor Gollancz, 2000

Chapter 14

1. Frances Hardy, 'The Perils of Beryl', *Daily Mail*, 28 March 1998
2. Isabel Albiston, 'The world of Beryl Cook, artist', *Telegraph Magazine*, 14 July 2007
3. Letter to BC from J.J. Hayley of Marler Hayley, 17 October 1983, and reply from BC, 27 October 1983
4. 'I'm really just a voyeur', *The Daily Telegraph*, 4 December 2000
5. Steve Wright, 'Beryl Cook Iconic Artist', *Venue* (Bristol & Bath) (c 2002)
6. Fax from BC to the Portal, 30 March 2000
7. Dawn French, 'Bosom Buddies', *Night and Day*, 25 January 2004
8. Letter from BC to Sheena Stoddart, Curator of Fine Art at Bristol Museum and Art Gallery, 21 April 2002

Chapter 15

1. Nicholas Shakespeare, 'Off the goatpath', *Daily Telegraph*, 23 July 1988
2. https://www.tate.org.uk/art/art-terms/o/outsider-art
3. Dawn French, foreword to *Beryl Cook, Cruising*, Victor Gollancz, 2000
4. Mrs H, November 1986
5. HG, England, 2000
6. LGBT archive www.lgbtarchive.uk (retrieved September 2025)
7. Julian Spalding, *Gallery of Modern Art Glasgow, The First Years*, Scala Books, 1996
8. Susie Goldsbrough, 'The Raucous magic of "Rubens with jokes"', *The Times*, 11 May 2024
9. Letter from Jess Wilder to BC, (undated but c 2000)
10. Julian Spalding, *Art Exposed*, Pallas Athene, 2023
11. Gareth Harris, '"Rubens with jokes": UK exhibitions place Beryl Cook in the arthistorical canon', *The Art Newspaper*, 23 January 2026
12. Eddy Frankel, 'Beryl Cook: Pride and Joy review – a saucy parade of bouncing bosoms, smirky smokers and a spot of BDSM', *The Guardian*, 22 Jan 2026. Courtesy of Guardian News & Media Ltd.

Picture Credits

20 National Gallery of Modern Art, New Delhi; **39, top** Plymouth Live; **61, top** SWiB (the South West Image Bank); **141, left** Smith Archive/Alamy; **161** Gift of Edgar William and Bernice Chrysler Garbisch, Courtesy National Gallery of Art, Washington; **162, top** Allstar Picture Library Ltd/Alamy; **163, top** © Estate of Stanley Spencer. All Rights Reserved 2020 / Bridgeman Images, Photo: Tate; **164** Copyright: Estate of the Artist, c/o Lefevre Fine Art Ltd, London. Image credit: Bridgeman Images; **169, top** DEA PICTURE LIBRARY/Getty; **170, top** Peter Barritt/Alamy; **174** Gift of the Hanna Fund 1949.186, The Cleveland Museum of Art; **224** Bettmann/Getty

About the Author

Hilary Bracegirdle has enjoyed a career as a curator and director in a variety of museums, starting with the V&A and including The National Horseracing Museum in Newmarket and the Royal Cornwall Museum in Truro. She also held several roles at Plymouth City Museum and Art Gallery (now known as The Box). She has looked after an extraordinary collection for Devon and Cornwall Police, worked as a heritage consultant and in 2015, completed the maximum six-year term as Committee Member, SW Committee for the Heritage Lottery Fund.

In the course of her work, Hilary has curated numerous exhibitions in the UK, Germany, the US and Japan. None of them made people quite so joyful as the Beryl Cook exhibition that she developed for Plymouth City Council in 2017. She continues to be in demand for her lively talks about Beryl.

Hilary has written numerous reports, options appraisals, strategies and business cases, and has published and edited catalogues, but none of them have been especially amusing. *Beryl Cook* is her first book.

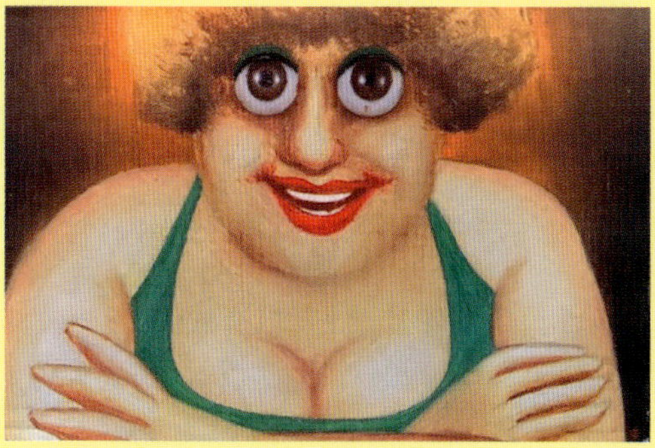

Like Beryl Cook, Hilary is rather shy, so she uses this Beryl Cook painting on her business card. It has led to some misunderstandings.

Acknowledgements

I feel privileged to have been asked by Beryl Cook's family to write this book and so my principal thanks must go to them – John Junior, Teresa, Sophie and her husband Olly, and Alexa. It has been an enormous pleasure from beginning to end and very much a joint enterprise. The family allowed me free access to their archive of letters, private Beryl Cook paintings and craftworks, and their own memories. As a result, a picture of the real Beryl Cook – the Beryl Cook who guarded her privacy so closely – emerged. Thank goodness, or it would have been a very short book indeed.

Beryl's extensive correspondence shows how important family and friends were to her. She took care to tell people what they meant to her, especially if they were feeling low. I'd like to do the same, and acknowledge the importance of my own family and friends: my daughter Mary and grandchildren Summer, Polly and Lowenna (Polly has already mastered the Beryl Cook side-eye), and my parents Pat and David; all my friends, but especially Glenn Benson, Karen Jones, Julie Stanley, Jenny Mercer and Cathryn Goodchild. Another dear friend, Christina Dixon, kindly read my draft and helped me reorder my text, and Terah Walkup also read the draft and and joined me in exploring the archive.

Another Beryl lesson is that of loyalty, not only to friends but also to business partners. Naturally, the two categories merged, and most of those with whom she worked became friends. Their dealings are marked by courtesy and consideration, and although she had plenty of offers, she stayed with them. When by mutual agreement she did change publisher, she wrote to say how much she had appreciated their professionalism and working relationship. No wonder Joe Whitlock Blundell (John Murray), Jess Wilder (Portal Gallery), Edward Lucie-Smith, the late Tony Martin and the late Bernard Samuels spoke so warmly of Beryl. Thank you to them for allowing me to interview them, for permission to quote them and for sharing the private paintings that Beryl created for them. I was too shy to approach Dawn French for an interview, but I am grateful for her permission to quote her as well. I have listed all the permissions given and apologize for any inadvertent oversights or failures to track people down.

I must make a special mention of Max Ker-Seymer and his late mother, Barbara Ker-Seymer. Between their first letters in 1979 and Barbara's death in 1993, she and Beryl

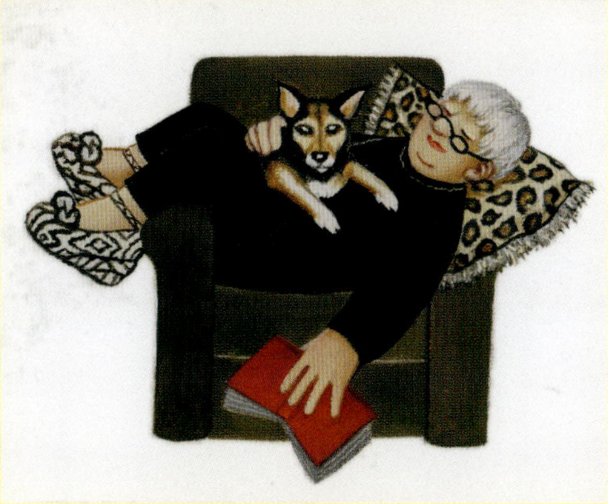

Untitled
(1990s), featuring Beryl and Lizzie. Beryl has fallen asleep while reading – a frequent occurrence. Note her favourite shoes.

corresponded weekly, and without this archive we would know so much less about both of their lives (Barbara is at last being recognized as a great photographer in her own right, just as Beryl is becoming properly appreciated within art history). Max responded so kindly and warmly when I asked him for permission to quote from his mother's letters and provided images of delightful – and previously unknown – paintings inherited from his mother.

I first became involved with Beryl Cook when I was working at Plymouth City Museum and Art Gallery (now The Box). The family approached me and asked if we were interested in hosting an exhibition drawing on their family collection. I bit all their hands off. I'd never before been involved in an exhibition which brought such joy to those who visited – and to me. I would like to acknowledge Plymouth City Council and the staff of the Museum and Art Gallery – then and now – for mounting the exhibition and for placing Beryl where she belongs: at the centre of the art displays in The Box. Their major exhibition in 2026, the centenary of Beryl's birth, is spearheading a serious reassessment of Beryl Cook's work, and I have hugely enjoyed collaborating with Curator of Art Terah Walkup and Box volunteer Kit Barton. Plymouth City Council has made a remarkable investment in its museums and cultural services and has a laudable commitment to increasing the number and types of people who engage with them.

Thank you too to my publishers, Frances Lincoln, especially Philip Cooper and Katerina Menhennet, and to Sarah Lawrence of This is Iris for brokering the deal. It's not easy getting a publisher these days.

Even though this book is based on original research, interviews and primary documents, I have had frequent recourse to Wikipedia. Wikipedia is a charity and 2026 will be its 25th anniversary. I have given a donation in recognition of this wonderful resource.

Beryl was worried about her letters being published in case she had been unkind or libellous, but I found nothing of concern – unless, and in very few instances, she had been crossed or misused in some way. She never forgave. To my backstabbers – you know who you are.

Index

Page numbers in *italics* refer to illustrations

A

Accordion Player *226*, *227*
Aids Crisis Trust 119, *123*
Albemarle Street *85*
The Alexander Gallery 84, 201
Alliance Freezing Works of New Zealand 147, *151*
Angela Singing 217, *219*
Anyone for a Whipping? *60*, 119
Art and Artists 95, *95*, 127, *146*, 147, *147*, 169
Art Class *71*
The Art Newspaper 230
The Artist *89*
At the Cinema 146–7, *148*
At Ease *9*
Attwell, Mabel Lucie *122*, 169

B

Back Bar of the Lockyer Street Tavern *45*, 226
Backstabbers *202*
Baltic Centre for Contemporary Art 162
Baltic Gallery Gateshead 96
Bangs Disco *222*
Bar & Barbara *64*, *65*
Barker, Cicely Mary 169, *172*
Basil the Warthog *121*
Beach at Looe *24*, 34
Bed Show in Soho *102*, 104
'Bendy Footballers' *28*, 29
Benn, Tony *148*
Bertie and the Big Red Ball 87
Bertie in the Pub *86*
Beryl Asleep *27*
Beryl Cook, The Bumper Edition 88
Beryl Cook, Cruising *205*
Beryl Cook: Pride and Joy 230
Beryl Cook's London 87, *88*, 104, *138*
Beryl Cook's New York (book) 87, *88*
Beryl Cook's New York (1985 exhibition) 103
Beryl de Lempicka *171*
Bewes, Rodney 29, 79, 132, *132*, 224
Big Julie as Nell Gwyn *50*
A Bird in the Hand *82*
Birds in St James's Park 132, *138*
Blake, Peter 95, 166
Blundell, Joe Whitlock 55, 84, 87, 154, 162, *162*, *183*, *195*
Bosom Belles 27, *27*
Bosom Pals (BBC 1) 210, 212
Botero, Fernando 169
Bouncers 87, *194*
Bouncers Back *195*
Bowlers of the Hoe *39*
The Box 226, 230
Breakfast Time *129*
Brian Entertains *48*, 136, 217
The Bridge Party 200, *202*
Bright Young Things 74, 164
British Film Institute (BFI) 146–7, *148*
British Rail 147
Bryant Park 217, *218*
Bumper Cars *139*
The Bumper Edition 103
Burra, Edward 72, 74, 95, 113, 132, 164, 166, *167*, *168*, 169, 230
  Three Sailors at the Bar *164*, *165*
The Butchers *42*
By the Clyde *227*

C

Camel Hair Coat *5*
A Cartwheel for Billy *116*
Chatterbox *98*
Checking Up *87*
Checkout Girl *111*
Children's Book of Bible Stories *120*
Chive pot *61*
Christie, George 97, 152, 154
Coleherne *219*
The Collected Works of Beryl Cook (1975), Plymouth Arts Centre 60–3, 66, 71
The Collected Works of Beryl Cook (1976), Whitechapel Gallery 71
Come Dancing 95, 217, *218*
Coming Down the Stairs *108*
Company 100
Conversations with Artists (BBC Radio 3) 104
Cook, Alexa *52*, *53*, 54
Cook, John *18*, *19*, 54, *59*, *68*, *77*, 112, *158*, *189*
  as Beryl's manager *77*, 78–9, 88, 105, 118, 119, 146
  Beryl's paintings 60, *60*, 126, 127, *128*, *129*, 132
  death 212
  marriage to Beryl 18
  travels with Beryl 87–8, 95, 166, 169, 178–81
  work 26, 38, 71, 110, *210*
Cook, John Junior 16, 18–20, 23, 29, 34, 54, 71, 186, 210, 212
Cook, Sophie *172*, 186
Cook, Teresa 34, 38, 52, 53, 54, *142*, 186
The Cornish Times 63
Couple Dancing *171*
Cruising 87, 186
Cruising 2 *176*
Crutch Dancing *213*
Cushion *56*

D

The Daily Mail 78, 178
Dancing on the Bar *197*
The Dave Collet Trio at The White Horse 201, *205*
Devon County Ladies' Bowling Association 96, *96*
Diamond Lil's 48, 84
Dining Out *90*
The Dolphin Hotel 39, *39*, *44*, *46*, 84, 100, 112, *116*, *117*, 192, 210, 212
Don't be a lout, Andrew *17*
Dustbin Men *130*

E

Eating Chips in a Municipal Shelter 66, *67*, 71
Edward Lucie-Smith as a Bard 226, *228*
The Elephant 198, 199
Elvira's Café 186, *188*
Elviras Café (1997) *186*
Elviras Café (2006) *188*
End of Term 207
Escargots Pour Trois 183

F

Fairies and Pixies 169, *173*
Farrell-Vinhay, Peter 23
Farson, Daniel 87, 103–4, *103*
Feeding the Tortoises 2
Felting the Roof 191
The Ferryboat 211
Financial Weekly 78
Fisher, Gregory 224, *225*
The Flintstones 162, *162*
Folio Society *17*, 18, 154, *157*, 158
Footballers 203
Footballers on Looe Beach 29, *32*
Forest Lawn Memorial Park 154, 158, *158*, *182*
Four Hungry Cats 68, 71, 84
French, Dawn 210, 216, 224
Fuchsia Fairies 172

G

Gallery Five 78, 79, 106, 113
Garden Centre 132, 136, *137*
Gare du Nord 183
George, John 95, *146*, 147, 169
Gertrude's Shoes 225
Getting Ready 197
Girls on the Town 159
Glanville House 38, *52*, 54–60, 71, 110, 126, 178
Glyndebourne 152, 154, *155*
Going Towards Art 70
Goldberg, Susie 226
Gollancz 87, 88
Government Art Collection 226
The Guardian 63, 94, 96, 230
Gwyn, Nell *50*
Gypsy Moth IV 100, 113, 220

H

Hairdressing Salon 113
Hamilton, Alex 100
Hangover 21, 27, 66
Happiness is Egg-shaped 60
Happy Days 87, 185
Havana 187
Heineken 147, *150*
Hello Sailor 165
Hen Party 1 46
Hen Party 2 115
Henry, Norman 87, 169
Hicks, Edward, *Peaceable Kingdom 161*, 169
Hoffman, Dustin *70*, 166
Holiday Trio 35
Hollywood Café 182
Holmes, Billy 39, *39*
Hosts and Hostesses 179
Hungry Trio 192

I

Isherwood, Christopher, *Mr Norris Changes Trains* 154, *156*

J

The Jaguar 170
Jaws Mania 46
Jazz in the Summer 204
Jazz in the Winter 204, 211
Jess the Portal Bunny 80
Joe's Shoes 84
John and Cats at Athenaeum Street 59
John Cooking 188
John Murray 78, 84, 85, 87, 103
Jonah and the Whale 120
Juggling with Beer Bottles (Bottle Throwers) 29, *31*

K

Kaleidoscope (BBC Radio 4) 94–5, *95*, *183*
Karaoke 229
Kendrick School 16, 18, 158
Ker-Seymer, Barbara *64*, *65*, 72–4, *75*, 87, 95, 103, 104, 105, 113, 132, 136, 146, 147, 152, *156*, 162, 164, 166, 169, 174, 178, 181, 192–3, 224
Kinnock, Neil *148*

L

La Paloma Dancehall 133
Ladies Bowling 95
Ladies Night (Ivor Dickie) 100, *101*
Lady of Marseille 168
Langan's Restaurant *90*
Lansley, Adrian Stephen Barton 16
Lansley, Cynthia 16, *19*
Lansley, Ella (née Francis) *15*, 16, 18
Lansley, Freda 16, 18, 19
Lansley, Mary 16, *19*, 20
Lansley, Stephen 16
Leather Bar 219
Lefevre Gallery 166, *167*
Lempicka, Tamara de 169

Levy, Lionel 78–9, *80*
The Likely Lads (TV sitcom) 29, 96, 132
Lockyer Tavern 39, *44*, *45*, *48*, 66, 113, 212, 217, *219*, 220, 226
The Lockyer Tavern 44
Log box 29, *32*
Logue, Christopher 152, *153*, 224
London Lighthouse Hospice 119
London Zoo 119, *160*
Looe Official Guide 26, 34
Lucie-Smith, Edward 84, 87, 94–5, *95*, 104, 169, 200, *219*, 226, *228*
Lunchtime Refreshment 105, *106*

M

McGill, Donald 146, 162
Madame JoJo's 123
Madame JoJo's *102*, 103, 119, *123*
Magical Evening at Glyndebourne 155
The Mail on Sunday 103
Man at Door with Child 60
Man with Blue Eyes 136, *140*
Marsh, Philip *206*
Martin, Tony 29, 34, *34*, 48, 55, 60, 71, 95, *122*, *142*, 226
Beryl de Lempicka 171
Melly, George 103, *103*, 104, 119, 224
Modigliani, Amedeo 29, 169, *169*
Mop Heads 140
Morning Run 206
Motor Show 210
Murray, Jock 84
Musicians 71

N

National Portrait Gallery 226, *228*
No Man is a Stranger to His Valet 83
Noah's Ark 81
Nude on Leopardskin 152

O

Observer Magazine 147, *150*
Old Duke 201, *204*
The Oldie 147, *145*
One Bowling Lady Giving Another Bowling Lady a Surprise see *Sabotage*

P

Pack of Dogs 203
Packing the Car 74
Paddington Station 91
The Pannier Market 42 (1980s), *58* (c 1975)
Party Boys 223
The Peaceable Kingdom 160
Pearce, Brian 39, 43, *45*, *47*, *48*
Pegleg 27, *30*
Percy at the Fridge 152, *178*
Personal Services (film) 147
Personal Services 1 149
Personal Services 2 149
Piano and Percussion 27, *28*, 29
Pick n Mix 43
Picnic 73
Plymouth Arts Centre 60–3, 66, 71, *71*, 79, 84, *92*, 97, 200–1, *202*
Plymouth City Museum and Art Gallery *45*, 61, 226
Plymouth Library 112–13
Poetry Reading 152, *153*
Pop Artists 166
Portal Gallery 72, 78–9, 80, 84, *85*, *90*, 94, 95, 96, 97, 103, *143*, 146, 212, 226
Potter, Ronnie 48
Private Eye 147, *148*
Private View 76, 84, *167*
Public Library 114

Q

Queen Dancing 136, *141*
Queen of the Fairies 173

R

Rab C. Nesbitt 225
Raval, Monica del *168*
Reading the Sunday Papers 66
Reclining Nude 29, *33*
Red-light District 58
The Red Umbrella 168
Reflections 184
Rhubarb 190
The Rialto Bridge 134, *135*
RIP to Art and Artists 146
Robinson, Nigel 43
Roett, Bar 64, 74, *74*
Roseland Ballroom 178, *179*
Rousseau, Henri 169, 174
Exotic Landscape 174
Rowing Eight 132, *132*
Roy, Jamini, *Bride and Two Companions 20*, 23
Roy Rogers *128*, *129*
Ruby and Minnie 123
Ruby, Minnie and Lottie 130
Ruby Venezuela 102
Ruby's Wheels 221
The Russian Tea Room 70

S

Sabotage 60, *69*, 71, 79, 127, 217
Saddler, Allen 63, 66, *92*, 94, 97
Sailors in The Dolphin 44
Sailors and Virgins 36

St Francis and the Birds 163
Salon Philippe 206
The Salvation Army 122
Samuels, Bernard 60, 61, 63, *70*, 71, 78, 201, *202*, 226
Sandy Sat with the Painter and His Model 157
Satin Dresses 193
Scargill, Arthur *148*
Search, Gay 100, *101*, 103
Searle, Adrian 96
Self-portrait 88
Self-portrait in Science Lesson at Kendrick School 16, *17*
Self-portrait with Flag 88
Senior Citizen Railpass 144, 147
Serota, Nicholas 71
Shopping Mall 208
Shopping with Robin 209
A Short Pause 40
Sisters Fighting 16, *16*
Six Thousand Women Running 223
Sleep, Wayne 154, *154*, 224
Smithfield Market 147, *151*, 152
The South Bank Show (ITV) 71, 72
Spalding, Julian 224, *226*
Spall, Timothy 210, 212
Spark, Muriel, *The Prime of Miss Jean Brodie 17*, 18, 157, 158
Spencer, Stanley 26, 162, 164, 169, 230
  St Francis and the Birds 163
Sponziello, Giovanni 112, *113*
The Staircase 105
Stein, Gertrude *224, 225*
Stewart-Gordon, Faith *70*, 71, 87, 169
Still Life with Husband 79
Strappy Shoes 205
Strawberry Pickers 131
Strippergram 117
Stubbs, George 169
  Cheetah and Stag with Two Indians 170
Studio Voltaire 226
Sunbathing 52, 127
The Sunday Times 62, 63, 66, 94, 113, 217
Sylvia 51, 217

T

Talking about Art 214
Tango 179
Tango in the Bar Sur, Buenos Aires 180, 181
Tarzanogram 2 196
Tate Gallery 162, 224
Tea in the Garden 105, *107*
Ted and Heinrich 94
Tenerife Days 185
Tenerife Nights 185
Tennis 142
Teresa in a Fox Fur 152
Tesco 74, *75*
Thatcher, Margaret *148*
Thoughtful Schoolgirls 60
Three Dancing Ladies 61
Three Green Bottles 26, 27
Three for a Quango 143
The Tie 89
The Tiger 132, 136, *175*
The Times 226
To Go 182
Togetherness 104
Toilet seats 55, *57*
Toklas, Alice B. *224, 225*
Tom Dancing 47
Tonging the Curls 29, *33*, 34
Top Dogs 220, *221*
Tope, Joanna 55, 60, 71
Tree Planting 191
Two Greek Gods 80
Two on a Stool 228
Two with Shrimps, Parrot and Potty 60

U

Union Street 49

V

Venezuela, Ruby 39, 43, *48*, *102*, 103
Virgin & Child 14
Vultures 22

W

Walkies 41
Walking in File 157
Walkup, Terah 66, 230
Wallis, Alfred 162, *162*
Walser, David 79
Watching Television 59
Waugh, Evelyn 74
  The Loved One 154, *156*, *158*, *182*
Wedding Photograph 67, 127
Welcome 38
Western Morning News 61, 63, 105
White, Pat 158
The White Horse 201, *205*
Whitechapel Gallery 71
Whittle, Frank 63
Wilde, Tom *45*, *47*
Wilder, Jess 79, *80*, 96, 212, 226
Williams, Tammy 48
Window-Dresser 2 226, *229*
Woman 100, *101*
Woman's Journal 100
The Works 78, 84, *89*, 95–6, 217
The World of Beryl Cook (2007) 96

Z

Zoladex *159*

Back cover image: *Meadow Suite* (1983)

Quarto

First published in 2026 by Frances Lincoln,
an imprint of The Quarto Group.
One Triptych Place, London, SE1 9SH,
United Kingdom
T (0)20 7700 9000
www.Quarto.com

EEA Representation, WTS Tax d.o.o.,
Žanova ulica 3, 4000 Kranj, Slovenia
www.wts-tax.si

A catalogue record for this book is available from the British Library.

ISBN 978-1-8057-0262-7
Ebook ISBN 978-1-8057-0263-4
10 9 8 7 6 5 4 3 2 1

Printed in Guangdong,
China TT062026

FSC
www.fsc.org
MIX
Paper | Supporting responsible forestry
FSC® C016973

Design by
Mathilde Lambert

Publisher
Philip Cooper

Managing Editor
Laura Bulbeck

Editor
Katerina Menhennet

Senior Designer
Isabel Eeles

Senior Production Controller
Rohana Yusof